THE HOLY SPIRIT AND CHF

Simeon Zahl is Professor of Christian Theology at the University of Cambridge and a Fellow of Jesus College.

'It is not an easy thing to meet all the expectations placed on a systematic theologian, and [*The Holy Spirit and Christian Experience*] shows what emerges when someone actually does manage to meet all these expectations. This is what it looks like, one might say, when a theologian genuinely works in a way that is biblically rooted, historically rich, and engaged in contemporary debates, while also combining commitment to a particular tradition with ecumenical generosity and interdisciplinary expansiveness, bringing together careful conceptual analysis with practical and pastoral relevance, and when all this is done with proper attention to the scholarly literature in each of the areas touched upon, and with a self-reflexive clarity.'

Karen Kilby, *Syndicate*

'A fresh and inventive book . . . It is a rare occasion when a book reminds one of why one loves theology (and here the choice of words is deliberate). Simeon Zahl's *The Holy Spirit and Christian Experience* is that kind of book.'

Fellipe do Vale, *Journal of Reformed Theology*

'In this much-needed corrective, Zahl challenges the silence in mainstream Protestant theology surrounding "experience," both as method and as data.'

Sarah Hinlicky Wilson, *Lutheran Quarterly*

'A well-argued book, wide in its engagements, generous in its challenges and savvy in its constructive efforts.'

Calvin Lane, *Scottish Journal of Theology*

'What Zahl has accomplished in this book is to swim upstream against many dominant trends in mainstream theology in order to regain a place for experience in theology . . . [T]his book will prove to be a milestone . . . It is a book that deserves to be read by all Protestant theologians, including all Pentecostals.'

Stephen Edward Harris, *Pneuma*

The Holy Spirit
and
Christian Experience

SIMEON ZAHL

OXFORD
UNIVERSITY PRESS

OXFORD
UNIVERSITY PRESS

Great Clarendon Street, Oxford, OX2 6DP,
United Kingdom

Oxford University Press is a department of the University of Oxford.
It furthers the University's objective of excellence in research, scholarship,
and education by publishing worldwide. Oxford is a registered trade mark of
Oxford University Press in the UK and in certain other countries

First published 2020
First published in paperback 2022

Published in the United States of America by Oxford University Press
198 Madison Avenue, New York, NY 10016, United States of America

British Library Cataloguing in Publication Data
Data available

Library of Congress Cataloging in Publication Data
Data available

ISBN 978-0-19-882778-8 (Hbk.)
ISBN 978-0-19-288238-7 (Pbk.)

Table of Contents

Acknowledgments

In the six years I have worked on this book, I have been fortunate to have received help and support from a great many sources. The project has travelled with me through three universities: from St. John's College at the University of Oxford, to the Theology and Religious Studies Department at the University of Nottingham, to the Faculty of Divinity at the University of Cambridge. Each institution has provided invaluable support and encouragement. At St. John's, my particular thanks go the College for providing an ideal research environment as a Junior Research Fellow, and to my colleagues and friends in the SCR, especially Graham Barrett, Maria Bruna, Antonia Fitzpatrick, Peter Fifield, Matthew Walker, Hannah Williams, and Judith Wolfe. At Nottingham, I am grateful to all of my TRS colleagues, with a particular debt of gratitude to Frances Knight, the finest department head I could have hoped for. At Cambridge I am especially grateful to Ian McFarland for smoothing my transition, encouraging my research, and helping to create the space I needed to complete the project.

This book has been improved immensely as a result of feedback received while presenting versions of the material at many universities in the UK and in the USA, including Oxford, Cambridge, St. Andrews, Edinburgh, Exeter, Nottingham, Aberdeen, King's College London, Durham, Harvard Divinity School, Notre Dame, and the University of Pennsylvania, as well as at the Society for the Study of Theology and the Christian Systematic Theology Group at the American Academy of Religion. I have benefited greatly from questions, responses, and insights received in these contexts, and am extremely grateful for these invitations and opportunities.

Many colleagues have been generous with their time and expertise, extending and improving my thinking on the project in many directions. Here I am especially grateful for ongoing conversations with Donovan Schaefer, Susannah Ticciati, Bill Wood, Joel Rasmussen, Tarah van de Wiele, Jonathan Linebaugh, Graham Ward, and Natalie Carnes. Matthew Fell has been invaluable as a research assistant, reader, and interlocutor in the final stages of the project.

A special debt of gratitude is owed to five people who have provided crucial support throughout the writing process. Karen Kilby has been a mentor, theological kindred spirit, and asker of enormously shrewd questions for many years. Without her advice at a key point, this book would have taken years longer, and would have been much less interesting. Mike Higton has helped reassure me of the value of the project from its inception, has been an incisive reader of the manuscript, and has been an ideal dialogue partner at every point. David Ford first turned my academic attention to the Holy Spirit many years ago, and has been a source of wise judgment and encouragement from the beginning of the project through to its completion. Paul Nimmo's outstanding theological judgment, expert editorial eye, and ability to see both the forest and the trees have been invaluable, especially in the final months of this project, and are deeply appreciated. My wife, Bonnie Poon Zahl, has contributed to the project at every stage, intellectually as well as personally. As a psychologist of religion and lifelong student of religious experience, she has been a central inspiration and my primary dialogue partner over many years, even as she has also provided unflagging support, encouragement, and humor at home. My gratitude to her is beyond words.

The friendship of Jamin Warren and Colton Houston is a gift that seems only to grow as the years go on. They have been with me through thick and thin. I have also been sustained over the course of the project by the ministry of St. Aldates Church, with particular gratitude for the wisdom and support of Charlie Cleverly. My brothers John Zahl and David Zahl, and my mother Mary Zahl, have helped make sure the book, and hopefully also its author, never got lost in the clouds. Their steadfast encouragement has meant more than they know. I am also deeply grateful to my parents-in-law, K.T. Poon and Vivianne Au, for their faith and support through the ups and downs of academic careers, and for always being there when we have needed them.

My children, Thomas, Jane, and Arthur, have lived more than half their lives with 'Baba's book' in the background. They have been the source of my deepest joys while working on this project, and have taught me more about the connection between love and delight than Augustine ever could.

This book is dedicated with deepest affection to my father, Paul Zahl. First and greatest teacher, he taught me that for theology to be worth anything, it must traffic in real life, and that real life begins in the heart.

Abbreviations

Augustine abbreviations:

Civ.	*The City of God*
Conf.	*Confessions*
Doctr. chr.	*On Christian Teaching*
Ep. Io. tr.	*Homilies on the First Epistle of John*
Gr. et pecc. or.	*On the Grace of Christ and Original Sin*
Io. eu. tr.	*Homilies on St. John's Gospel*
Nat. et gr.	*On Nature and Grace*
Serm.	*Sermons*
Simpl.	*To Simplicianus*
Spir. et litt.	*On the Spirit and the Letter*
WSA	*The Works of Saint Augustine: A Translation for the 21st Century*, New City Press, 1990–

Other abbreviations:

Ap	*The Apology of the Augsburg Confession*
AC	*The Augsburg Confession*
BC	*The Book of Concord: The Confessions of the Evangelical Lutheran Church*, edited by Robert Kolb and Timothy Wengert Fortress Press, 2000
BSLK	*Die Bekenntnisschriften der Evangelisch-Lutheranische Kirche*, 6th ed., Göttingen, 1967
CR	*Corpus Reformatorum*
LW	*Luther's Works*, Concordia Publishing House, 1955–
MW	*Melanchthon's Werke in Auswahl*, C. Bertelsmann Verlag, 1951–
PL	*Patrologia Latina*
WA	*D. Martin Luther's Werke. Kritische Gesamtausgabe*, Weimar, 1883–1993
WA Deutsche Bibel	*D. Martin Luther's Werke. Kritische Gesamtausgabe. Deutsche Bibel*. Weimar, 1906–1961
WA Tischreden	*D. Martin Luther's Werke. Kritische Gesamtausgabe. Tischreden*. Weimar, 1912–1921

In premodern and early modern works, references to text locations other than page numbers are rendered in Arabic rather than Roman numerals. Thus the fifth paragraph of the twelfth article of the *Apology of the Ausgburg Confession* is rendered *Ap* 12.5, and the third paragraph of Chapter 6 of Book 4 of the *Confessions* is *conf.* 4.6.3. Abbreviations for Augustine's works follow those used in the *Augustinus Lexicon*. For citations of texts from Melanchthon, Luther, and Augustine, traditional location is followed where possible by the page reference in the original language version followed by the page reference in the English translation being used. Translations of such works have been taken where possible from authoritative English versions, with occasional modifications. Where the translator is not otherwise indicated, translations are my own. Where the original language helps clarify a point, I have at times included key terms and phrases in the original in square brackets after the English. This has been especially important for terms related to affect and desire, where technical precision in other languages is often lost in translation.

Sections of Chapter 1 and Chapter 3 have appeared previously in Simeon Zahl, 'On the Affective Salience of Doctrines,' *Modern Theology* 31, no. 3 (2015).

Introduction

Ideas are often poor ghosts; our sun-filled eyes cannot discern them; they pass athwart us in thin vapour, and cannot make themselves felt. But sometimes they are made flesh; they breathe upon us with warm breath, they touch us with soft responsive hands, they look at us with sad sincere eyes, and speak to us in appealing tones; they are clothed in a living human soul, with all its conflicts, its faith, and its love. Then their presence is a power, then they shake us like a passion, and we are drawn after them with gentle compulsion, as flame is drawn to flame.

—George Eliot, *Janet's Repentance*[1]

In this striking passage, George Eliot meditates on the uneasy relationship between religious ideas and their practical and emotional impact on human lives. It is no easy thing, Eliot observes, for ideas to "make themselves felt."

The context of the passage is a scene in one of Eliot's early novellas in which a young clergyman, Mr. Tryan, successfully conveys religious consolation to Janet Dempster, a woman suffering acutely from feelings of guilt and despair. Eliot's main interest in the passage is in the dynamics of Tryan's pastoral effectiveness in light of his theological views. How exactly is it that he succeeds in transmuting his doctrinal convictions, in this case certain theological ideas about atonement and forgiveness,[2] into meaningful help for Janet in her distress? Abstract doctrines on their own, Eliot believes, will make little headway in a case of real human suffering like Janet's. In her view, if a doctrinal concept is to be experienced with compelling power it must first be "made flesh," and here this means being lensed through a sincere compassion grounded in the minister's own painful personal history. As a result of Tryan's experientially integrated approach, the "poor ghosts" of his courtroom

---

[1] George Eliot, *Janet's Repentance*, in *Scenes from Clerical Life*. ii (Edinburgh: William Blackwood and Sons, 1878), p. 236.

[2] I.e., 'phrases about the blood of cleansing, imputed righteousness, and justification by faith alone' (Eliot, *Janet's Repentance*, p. 162).

The Holy Spirit and Christian Experience. Simeon Zahl, Oxford University Press (2020). © Simeon Zahl.
DOI: 10.1093/oso/9780198827788.001.0001

atonement theories, which might easily have "passed athwart" Janet in her plight, instead find deep purchase. By the end of the scene, "their presence is a power," Janet's life is transformed, and an elegant argument has been made about the relationship between religious ideas and their human effects.

Eliot's narrative draws attention to a question of foundational significance for Christian theology: how is it that meaningful and effectual connections come to obtain between theological doctrines and the practical experiences of Christians? As Eliot is well aware, it is one thing to assent intellectually to a doctrine, and it is quite another to be moved and transformed by it.

This question can be viewed from the other direction as well. In what ways, we might ask, are theological doctrines themselves developed from and sourced by the living concerns and experiences of Christians, and of human beings more broadly? Doctrines do not develop in a vacuum or fall from the sky fully formed. Human reasonings, including theological reasonings, are never fully extricable in a given moment from our feelings, our moods, our predispositions, and the personal histories we carry with us. Furthermore, as we shall see, doctrines have often come to expression in the history of Christianity not least through an ongoing engagement with what have been understood to be concrete experiences of God's Spirit in history.

These questions bring us to two claims that lie at the heart of this book. The first, preliminary claim is that, despite arguments to the contrary, "experience" cannot really be excluded in theological inquiry, at least not if doctrines are to be anything more than Eliot's "poor ghosts." Experiential dimensions are often foundational in theological reflection, both in terms of how doctrines develop and in how they come to have practical effects in the world, but they are rarely adequately examined or acknowledged. Experiential factors tend either to hum along beneath the surface like background programs, unstated and under-recognized, or to be made use of at an early stage in a doctrine's development only to be discarded and forgotten once the doctrine has reached a more mature state. And in modern Christian theology, "experience" has often been explicitly excluded and suppressed as a legitimate dimension of theological reflection.

This argument about the inescapability of "experience" in theology is made most directly in Chapter 1, but really it animates the entire project. Over the course of the book, I make an extended case for the importance of attending to "experience" in Christian theology. I seek to explain why experience has often been thought to be a problematic category in modern Christian thought, and I develop a set of methodological resources for attending to the role of experience and related domains of subjectivity in theology while avoiding common pitfalls. I then put these tools into practice, demonstrating their critical and constructive power for thinking about salvation and sanctification. At every stage, the argument is shaped by an abiding interest in the affective and experiential dimensions of Christian theological reflection, both in how doctrines develop and in the impact they come to have on human beings in the world.

The second major claim being made in this book is that in speaking about "experience" in Christian theology we are speaking at the same time about the doctrine of the Holy Spirit. To enter into the topic of "experience" from the perspective of Christian theology is to enter into a discourse that is more specific than the one that exists around the general theme of "religious experience." For all its variety and complexity, Christian experience of God has particular contours and features, a particular vocabulary, and particular forms that are internal to a particular set of historical, biblical, and dogmatic traditions. Above all, the theological topic of Christian "experience" is deeply and necessarily intertwined with the theology of the Holy Spirit, such that it is not really possible to speak persuasively or rigorously about the place and function of "experience" in Christian theology apart from the theological framework of pneumatology. The doctrine of the Holy Spirit thus provides compelling justification for attending to lived experience in Christian theology, and supplies a powerful theological language for engaging in such attention.

An important implication of the relationship between pneumatology and experience is the way it focuses theological attention on the theme of *affect and emotion*. For the purposes of this book, I take affect to be a mode of experience that is tethered to physical bodies and that encompasses emotion, feeling, and desire. As we will see, a fundamental feature of the pneumatological "grammar" of Christian experience is a thick connection between the work of the Holy Spirit and experiences of feeling and desiring. The result is that consideration of affect from a pneumatological perspective opens up a very rich seam in Scripture and in later theological tradition, and allows for the large and complex topic of "experience" to be engaged in a more precise and conceptually rigorous way.

The second claim, about the connectedness of theologies of experience to theologies of the Holy Spirit and the implications of this connection, is the primary topic of Chapter 2. The remaining chapters then put these methodological arguments into action to resource a new experiential account of two fundamental topics in pneumatology: the work of the Spirit in salvation and the work of the Spirit in sanctification. Biblically as well as traditionally, these constitute two of the most fundamental arenas of activity associated with the Holy Spirit, and together they provide an excellent test case for the methodological approach to experience proposed here. What is new in my explorations of the pneumatology of salvation and sanctification—and, potentially, more controversial—will be a deliberate and sustained attention to the concrete practical and affective effects of the doctrinal claims made under the auspices of these themes (broadly, what I have elsewhere called "the affective salience of doctrines"[3]), as well as to ways that doctrinal claims about the Holy Spirit are resourced by experiential factors.

I have become convinced of the importance for contemporary theology of reflection on questions of "experience" for three main reasons. The first is that this topic goes to the core of a set of questions about the intellectual and spiritual plausibility of Christianity in late-modern cultural settings where such plausibility can no longer be taken for granted. In this context, I am persuaded that theology today needs to develop a much better account of the gap that so often exists between theological concepts and the experiences of Christians than is usually the case. Why are some theological ideas life-changing for certain people, but dry as dust for others? Why are theologians so prone to developing systems of great intellectual coherence and elegance, but which bear only passing resemblance to the lives Christians actually seem to lead? Such questions are particularly salient in Western, developed-world contexts where it can no longer be taken for granted that people will find themselves animated and compelled by Christian ideas.

A second spur to engage anew with the theological question of experience has arisen out of my interest in the theology of the early sixteenth century, especially the theologies of Martin Luther and Philip Melanchthon. Recent years have witnessed widespread acceptance in academic theology of what, I have become convinced, are significant misreadings and misunderstandings of the theological legacy of early Protestantism. A good example of the sort of misreading I have in mind is the argument, expressed by John Milbank amongst others, that the doctrine of justification by faith alone can be dismissed as an inherently cold and rationalistic doctrine—a "legal fiction." Another is the argument, made most influentially by Jennifer Herdt and Reinhard Hütter, that Luther's critique of Aristotelian and Thomist conceptions of virtue in theology is successfully refuted once we recognize that divine and human agency are not part of a zero-sum game, but operate "non-competitively." A third is the argument, associated most famously with Krister Stendahl's work on the theology of the apostle Paul, that traditional Protestant theologies of salvation have become increasingly obsolete due to their dependence on an experience—the possession of a "troubled conscience"—to which modern people can no longer relate. Each of these arguments has been widely accepted as persuasive in contemporary theology, including by many Protestants, and they have exerted substantial influence within the field. And yet, for a number reasons, some of which I will demonstrate in detail in Chapter 3 and Chapter 4 of this book, all of these

---

[3] Simeon Zahl, 'On the Affective Salience of Doctrines,' *Modern Theology* 31, no. 3 (2015).

arguments require very substantial qualification when subjected to serious theological and historical scrutiny.[4]

Why have so many contemporary theologians found flawed arguments about major Protestant distinctives to be compelling, and why have these theological narratives encountered so little resistance? The present study has arisen to a substantial degree out of reflection on these questions. I have become convinced that the underlying issue in each case is less about the particular readings of the Reformers involved than it is about deeper theological assumptions and methodological commitments that have created conditions under which misreadings such as these can flourish. As I will show, attention to what has gone wrong in these cases throws into relief a series of ways that modern Christian thought has built subtle but powerful walls between theology and lived experience. In the process of diagnosing these problems, findings have emerged that have implications that go well beyond the questions about early Protestant theology that initially gave rise to them, opening up broad questions about subjectivity, emotion, and embodiment in theological discourse.

At the same time, I have also come to believe that there are powerful but untapped resources in these same early sixteenth-century theologies for reflecting on the problem of how Christian beliefs and practices can and do become compelling to modern people, and for reflecting on the theology of salvation in particular. It seems to me that these resources are overdue for renewed exploration, rigorous analysis, and constructive retrieval. Indeed, it may be that the legacy of the Protestant Reformation can best serve contemporary theology not by giving up or watering down its distinctive vision, but by recovering its best insights, repairing them where they have gone wrong, and translating them in compelling new ways for the contemporary world. In the final three chapters I seek to do just this, retrieving key insights from Martin Luther and Philip Melanchthon, as well as Augustine, to resource a pneumatological and experiential soteriology for the present day.

A third significant influence on the approach to "experience" in this book has been personal as well as intellectual contact with the dynamism, creativity, and experiential power of the worldwide Pentecostal and charismatic movements. In my view these movements possess vital untapped theological and especially pneumatological resources, including for theologians who are neither Pentecostal nor charismatic. Although a great deal of thought and energy

---

[4] The "legal fiction" argument will receive sustained attention in Chapter 3, in an expansion of arguments I make in Zahl, "Affective Salience." The second argument, about contemporary criticisms of Luther as ostensibly failing to understand the "noncompetitive" character of divine and human agency, and its implications for virtue ethics, is one I have made at length elsewhere and will not rehearse here. See Simeon Zahl, 'Non-Competitive Agency and Luther's Experiential Argument against Virtue,' *Modern Theology* 35, no. 2 (2019). The third argument, about 'the troubled conscience', will receive extended treatment in Chapter 4.

has gone into investigating the relationship between theology and modernity in recent years, Pentecostalism continues to have significant insights to offer to academic theology as the discipline reflects on the place of Christianity in the modern world. Although my interest in Pentecostal and charismatic theologies is not always on the surface in the chapters that follow, it does lie behind the book and helps inform its aims.[5] In seeking to reintegrate meaningful attention to experience and emotion into contemporary theology through the doctrine of the Holy Spirit, one significant aim of this book is to help establish conditions for a more fruitful engagement between Pentecostal and charismatic theologies and mainstream academic theology than currently tends to be elicited.

Weaving together these threads, *The Holy Spirit and Christian Experience* makes the case that contemporary theology needs to recover the resources and insights of Christian experience of God and world, and that one way to do this wisely and well is through sustained attention to the doctrine of the Holy Spirit. It then puts these arguments into practice by describing the core features of a new pneumatological soteriology that is integrated with a thick account of embodied Christian experience.

Structurally, the book is divided into two main parts. The first part, comprising the first two chapters, is historical and methodological, focusing on the importance as well as the irreducibility of experiential dynamics in theology. The second part, comprising the remaining three chapters, is reparative and constructive, articulating a new approach to salvation and sanctification from the perspective of experience of the Holy Spirit.

Over the course of these chapters, the argument intervenes in a number of contemporary theological discussions in addition to those already mentioned. In part, the book can be seen as a contribution to the turn in recent years towards new constructive reckonings with embodiment and subjectivity in theology. Through a focus on affect and emotion, I provide fresh arguments for why issues of embodiment and subjectivity are matters of core rather than peripheral significance for Christian theology, which complement other arguments that have been made. Here this study has particular affinities with the recent movement towards emphasizing the significance of spirituality for theology.

At the same time, the approach to "experience" being proposed here is also shaped by a specifically Protestant trajectory of theological history. In the shadow first of Martin Luther and then of Karl Barth, Protestant theology has tended to view "experience" and "subjectivity" as at best ambivalent and at worst catastrophic categories for theology. In this connection, the book seeks

---

[5] For more sustained and explicit engagement, see Chapter 7 in Simeon Zahl, *Pneumatology and Theology of the Cross in the Preaching of Christoph Friedrich Blumhardt: The Holy Spirit Between Wittenberg and Azusa Street* (London: T&T Clark/Continuum, 2010).

to provide a direct challenge to Protestant perspectives that express skepticism of appeals to embodiment and subjectivity in theological discourse.

A particularly important feature of the book is its deployment of the theoretical framework known as "affect theory." This framework, which emerged out of critical theory and queer theory in the 1990s, has helped point the way beyond reductive binaries between social constructionism and essentialism in recent critical discourse. In Chapter 4, I demonstrate the power of affect theory as a resource for contemporary theology. In particular, I argue that it can help take us beyond the problematic assumption, taken for granted in much Christian theology in recent decades, that Christian life is shaped primarily if not exclusively through the instruments of language and discursive practices. Insights from affect theory can help lead theology toward a more persuasive account of the relationship between cultural influence, religious practice, and the experiences of the feeling body.

Ultimately, however, the methodological dimensions of the book are in service of a constructive theological proposal. At the heart of the book is a description of a new approach to the theology of grace in a pneumatological key. Central to this constructive vision is a retrieval of a soteriological tradition that I will describe in the final chapter as "affective Augustinianism." This tradition can be found in different forms in three related figures: Philip Melanchthon, Martin Luther, and Augustine of Hippo. Resourced by this retrieval, the aim of the constructive chapters is to develop a pneumatological theology of salvation and sanctification that is compassionate, dynamic, and diagnostically powerful, while also being closely attentive to embodiment and to other forms of material embeddedness.

Against this background, *The Holy Spirit and Christian Experience* follows a particular trajectory of argument. Chapter 1 provides initial clarification of how the term "experience" will be used in the book. It then examines the history of ambivalence about "experience" in Protestant theology from Martin Luther through to the present, which has shaped contemporary theology's anxieties about subjectivity and experience, including for those who are not Protestants. Finally, it provides a series of arguments for the importance as well as irreducibility of "experience" in theology, both historically and today.

Chapter 2 argues that a constructive recovery of the category of "experience" in theology is best accomplished through the lens of pneumatology. Thinking about experience in terms of the work of the Holy Spirit helps specify what we mean when we talk about Christian "experience," while also avoiding the problems that arise in appeals to more general concepts of "religious experience." The chapter shows how a pneumatologically informed theology of experience draws attention to a problematic tendency towards abstraction in much modern systematic theology. It then argues that the work of the Spirit is likely to take forms that are "practically recognizable" in the lives of Christians in the world, exhibiting both temporal specificity and affective impact.

The third and fourth chapters then apply this pneumatological and affective account of "experience" to examine the work of the Spirit in salvation. Chapter 3 focuses on the movement in contemporary soteriology away from theologies of justification by faith and towards theologies of participation and *theosis*. It analyzes a series of recent accounts of participation to demonstrate that such soteriologies either have significant difficulties in articulating how the saving work of the Spirit is experienced in bodies (Torrance and Tanner), or else end up with a problematically optimistic account of the Spirit's transformative work in Christians (contemporary neo-Thomists). It then argues that Philip Melanchthon's sixteenth-century account of justification by faith is substantially more successful on both counts. This is due to Melanchthon's extensive use of affective categories to make sense of how salvation in the Spirit comes to be experienced in ways that are legible in embodied human experience. The chapter concludes by drawing on patristic accounts of soteriological participation to argue that affective transformation of the kind described by Melanchthon can be construed as a form of soteriological participation.

Chapter 4 gives an account of saving encounter with divine grace, through the Spirit, in the context of embodied experience. The chapter draws on the insights of affect theory to argue for the ongoing experiential plausibility of the doctrine of sin in the contemporary world, and to show that theologians in recent decades have tended to make assumptions about the plasticity of human experience through the instruments of language and discursive practice that require substantial qualification. The remainder of the chapter builds on these insights together with the theology of Martin Luther to describe Christian experience of grace in terms of an affective pedagogy effected by the Spirit through the instruments of the law and the gospel.

Chapter 5 then turns to the work of the Spirit in the transformation and sanctification of Christians. It argues that accounts of sanctification that build upon the idea of an instantaneous implantation of new moral powers in the Christian upon receipt of the Spirit have significant problems. It then turns to Augustine's theology of delight and desire to provide an experientially and affectively persuasive alternative account. The second half of the chapter shows that this "affective Augustinian" approach has a number of further advantages: it can account for the fact that sanctifying experience of the Spirit exhibits variability and that human beings are often a mystery to themselves; it can affirm a qualified role for practice and habituation in Christian sanctification; and it directs attention to the social as well as materially and culturally embedded dimensions of sanctification. The chapter concludes by arguing that an "affective Augustinian" vision of Christian transformation can account effectively and compassionately for the persistence of sin in Christians.

Finally, the Conclusion reflects on the wider implications of the book's focus on the connections between doctrines, affects, and experiences, indicating a number of directions for future work that make use of the methodological toolkit described and deployed in earlier chapters. It then sites the pneumatological and affective soteriology proposed here as charting a new path forward within a contemporary Protestant theological landscape hitherto dominated by the vision of Karl Barth, on the one hand, and "Protestant Thomism," on the other.[6]

---

[6] John Bowlin, 'Contemporary Protestant Thomism,' in *Aquinas as Authority*, eds. Paul Van Geest, Harm Goris, and Carlo Leget (Leuven: Peeters, 2002).

1

Recovering Experience in Christian Theology

Did you experience so much for nothing?
—Galatians 3:4

Few themes are more important in Christian life, and few are more fraught in Christian theology, than "experience." The New Testament indicates that this perennial tension seems to have surfaced in the earliest days of the Christian church. We see debates about the nature and authority of "experience" already emerging as the Johannine author finds himself needing to establish criteria for helping Christians to discern between true and false spirits (1 John 4:1–3), and in the apostle Paul's efforts to frame charismatic experiences in the church at Corinth within a larger theological picture, tempering their excesses without denying their validity or importance (1 Cor. 12–14).

Attention to Christian experience raises fundamental theological as well as practical questions. Can Christians trust their own experiences of God, their experiences of the world, and their experiences of themselves? Can such experiences ever lead to conclusions or insights that have normative implications for others, or for the church more broadly, or is their significance and impact always restricted to the one doing the experiencing? Are certain kinds of experiences a reliable mark of having become a Christian? And what of the doctrine of sin, so integral to Christian soteriology, which seems to suggest that human beings will be prone to misunderstanding and misusing their own experiences, including perfectly authentic experiences of God?

These questions arise across Christian confessions, but they have proven to be most acute for Christians in Protestant traditions. Martin Luther developed his theology of justification by faith through a process of reciprocal interpretation between exegesis and experience,[1] and argued that "experience alone makes the theologian."[2] But, following encounter with theological appeals to

---

[1] See Zahl, "Non-Competitive Agency," pp. 211–16, as well as *WA* 3:44; *LW* 10:49.
[2] *Sola experientia facit theologum. WA Tischreden* 1:16; *LW* 54:7.

The Holy Spirit and Christian Experience. Simeon Zahl, Oxford University Press (2020). © Simeon Zahl.
DOI: 10.1093/oso/9780198827788.001.0001

subjective experience in the arguments of radical reformers like Andreas Karlstadt in the 1520s, Luther altered course. He began to qualify the role of experience substantially, arguing that in matters of salvation "you must judge solely by the Word, regardless of what you feel or see."[3] Four hundred years later, Karl Barth expressed an even more powerful skepticism of appeals to subjectivity and experience in Christian theology: "No, thy impress of revelation, thy emotion, thy experience and enthusiasm, are of this world, are flesh."[4]

At the same time, many Protestants over the past 500 years, especially pietists, evangelicals, and charismatic Protestants of various kinds, have viewed these sorts of moves as problematic overcorrections. The eighteenth-century revivalist George Whitefield, for example, had little time for the kind of experiential skepticism that can be found in Luther and Barth, despite being a convinced Protestant who held to the traditional Protestant position on justification by faith. For Whitefield, saving encounter with the Spirit of God always involves some kind of affective experience. "To Talk of . . . having the Spirit of God without feeling it," he argued, "is really to deny the Thing."[5] And here Whitefield would seem to be in good company. Seeking to persuade the church in Galatia that saving receipt of the Spirit comes not "through the law" but simply by "believing" the message preached to them, Paul himself asks in exasperation: "Did you experience so much for nothing?" [*tosauta epathete eike*] (Gal. 3:2, 4). Here Paul seems to be taking for granted that the Galatians' initiation into Christian faith involved some kind of powerful communal experience of the Holy Spirit and indicates that he is perfectly happy to refer to this experience as a source of significant theological information. In other words, he seems to be making just the sort of theological move that Luther and Barth seem to be worried about: drawing on shared experience of a specific, religiously powerful communal encounter with God's Spirit to help make his case about the nature of salvation.

A key aim in the present chapter is to illuminate what is really at work in these disagreements that have cropped up continually in the history of the church, and especially in the Protestant churches. In the Introduction, I described "experience" as a topic of fundamental theological importance that has come to be occluded and ignored in much modern Christian thought. In this first chapter, I seek to explain why "experience" has become such a fraught concept in modern theology, particularly in the context of these long-standing Protestant debates. I will then make the case that engagement with "experience" is in fact inescapable for the theologian, including in cases where

---

[3] *WA* 36:494; *LW* 28:70.

[4] Karl Barth, *The Epistle to the Romans*, 2nd ed., trans. Edwyn C. Hoskyns (Oxford: Oxford University Press, 1968), p. 72.

[5] George Whitefield, "Is It a Crime for a Believer to Speak of His Having Communications Directly from the Spirit of God?," in *Religious Enthusiasm and the Great Awakening*, ed. David S. Lovejoy (Englewood Cliffs, NJ: Prentice-Hall, 1969), p. 106.

it is formally excluded in theological method. First, however, a few preliminary observations are needed about the term "experience" and how it will be used in this book.

THEOLOGY AND EXPERIENCE

The term "experience" is notoriously complex, and can have a very wide range of meanings depending on how it is used.[6] As a category, it also serves as something of a lightning rod in theology, often provoking strong views "for" and "against." Between failure to recognize the multiplicity of the term's possible meanings, on the one hand, and strong preconceived notions about what "experience" is, on the other, it is a topic where there are more obstacles than usual to rigorous and worthwhile constructive discourse.

The concept of "experience" at work in this book will ultimately be quite specific, but in order to avoid misunderstanding it will be necessary to proceed carefully and deliberately in articulating it. It is only after I have examined the troubled history of "experience" in modern theology, engaged with work on "religious experience" from the disciplinary perspective of religious studies, made a careful case for the theological value of reading the term in close connection with the peculiar contours and characteristics of biblical pneumatology, and finally articulated and justified a criterion of what I will call "practical recognizability" in relation to experiences of the Holy Spirit, that a more complete picture will be given at the end of Chapter 2.

Nevertheless, to avoid misreading it is necessary to make two basic conceptual clarifications about "experience" at the outset.

The initial clarification is to observe that there are two fundamentally distinct ways of understanding the relationship between "experience" and the practice of theological reasoning. The first way that the function of experience in theology can be theorized is as one of the major "sources" on which theology can explicitly draw and on the basis of which it can make its claims. It is this approach that is often in view in introductions to theological method, where experience is arrayed alongside other theological "sources" like Scripture, reason, and tradition.[7] The idea here is that a useful way of differentiating between methodological approaches is to assess the relative weight

---

[6] For analysis of a range of such uses in nineteenth century theology, see Simeon Zahl, "Experience," in *The Oxford Handbook of Nineteenth Century Christian Thought*, eds. Joel Rasmussen, Judith Wolfe, and Johannes Zachhuber (Oxford: Oxford University Press, 2017).

[7] For a classic exposition of this typology, see the chapter "The Sources of Theology" in Alister E. McGrath, *Christian Theology: An Introduction*, 3rd ed. (Oxford: Blackwell Publishing, 2001).

that a given theologian or tradition gives to each "source." Thus when we read Luther arguing that on the matter of indulgences "The Scriptures . . . are to be preferred to the bull in every case," it is assumed that, roughly speaking, Luther is putting to use a methodology in which the Bible has greater theological authority as a "source" than church tradition.[8] Likewise, when we read Schleiermacher's claim that "Christian doctrines are accounts of the Christian religious affections set forth in speech,"[9] we assume that Schleiermacher is therefore a theologian who prioritizes experience—in this case "the Christian religious affections"—over other possible sources.

But theological "sources" can also be used in a more ad hoc and less hierarchical way, and this is often the case when theologians appeal to experience. When in Galatians 3:2–4 Paul appeals to the Galatians' early experiences of the Spirit to support his argument that justification does not come "through the law" (Gal. 2:21) ("Did you receive the Spirit by doing the works of the law or by believing what you heard? . . . Did you experience so much for nothing?"), he is making explicit use of experience as a theological "source." Philip Melanchthon makes a similar move when in the 1521 *Loci communes* he supports his argument about the bondage of the will with the observation that "experience teaches that there is no freedom in the affections."[10] New Testament scholar James Dunn makes the same sort of argument when he concludes his analysis of the "divided I" in Romans 7 by asserting that his own interpretation is more "in tune with personal and social reality" than that of his opponents.[11] In each of these cases, "experience" is explicitly appealed to in support of a broader theological argument, though not in such a way that its status within a hierarchy of sources is immediately obvious.

Regardless of whether the argument involves a direct appeal to a hierarchy of sources or a more ad hoc appeal to experience to supplement other arguments, explicit appeals to experience as an authoritative theological "source" have long been viewed as controversial and problematic in theology, as we shall see. For now, it is enough to recognize that one major way that theologians think about the relationship between theology and "experience" is in terms of appealing to experience formally and explicitly as a more or less authoritative "source" of theological information. Sometimes, this involves appeal to "religious experiences" in particular—i.e., experiences that have God as their explicit agent or object—but it often does not. For example, one could

---

[8] *WA* 2:8; *LW* 31:262. In this case, Pauline descriptions of justification are taken to have greater authority on the soteriological issue of indulgences than the papal bull *Unigenitus*.

[9] Friedrich Schleiermacher, *The Christian Faith* (Edinburgh: T&T Clark, 1999), p. 76 (§15).

[10] *MW* 2.1:40; Philip Melanchthon, *Commonplaces: Loci communes 1521*, trans. Christian Preus (Saint Louis: Concordia Publishing House, 2014), p. 59.

[11] James D.G. Dunn, *The Theology of Paul the Apostle* (London: T&T Clark, 1998), p. 476.

also appeal to certain dimensions of experience in the world to inform theological anthropology, as in the Melanchthon example above.

But there is another way of understanding the function of "experience" in theological discourse. "Experience" can also refer not to the formal and explicit sources we appeal to but to *the complex effects of the theologian's subjectivity on the processes by which they arrive at and are persuaded of theological conclusions.* These effects are often unconscious or otherwise non-explicit, and they tend to be underexplored and underestimated in discussions of theological method. But they can also be very powerful.

What do I mean by effects of the theologian's "subjectivity" on the process of arriving at doctrinal conclusions? "Subjectivity" here is a catch-all for a variety of complex dynamics: for example, the way that our personal history with a denomination or confession will often implant biases for or against particular theological positions; or the ways that cultural histories and the norms of communities in which we are embedded shape which topics, texts, and figures we find compelling or off-putting; or the way that an idea communicated through a hymn might be more compelling than the same idea communicated in an academic paper or lecture; or the way that the persuasiveness of a theological idea in a given instance can be powerfully affected by whether or not we like and respect the person teaching it to us; or how the likelihood of our minds being changed by constructive criticism is influenced by the affective and tonal framing of the critique (e.g., whether the overall tone is appreciative vs. aggressive); or the fact that, according to an extensive body of cognitive scientific evidence, psychological factors like mood states, anxiety, and depression appear to play a consistent and non-trivial role in how we process of information, including theological information.

For these reasons and many more, there are grounds to think that the way we receive and process ideas and whether we find them compelling is significantly affected by the affective texture and atmosphere in which we encounter them, by our personal history and temperament, by our social context, even by our mood. In a given concrete instance, the event of being persuaded of a theological idea or position is rarely, if ever, a pristine "rational" process. Rather, it is an "experience," in that it proves under scrutiny to be operating in a complex affective, psychological, and social atmosphere that has a non-trivial effect on the conclusions we reach. Insofar as this is the case, it can be said that "experience" is constantly playing a significant role in theological reasoning and in theological persuasion, but it is doing so in a way that is clearly distinct from formal appeal to experience as a "source."

It is dynamics like these that Eliot is getting at in the example from *Janet's Repentance* referred to in the Introduction. The process by which Mr. Tryan's abstract theological ideas are transmuted into an affectively compelling, life-altering force in Janet Dempster's life—in short, their role in effecting her religious conversion—is inseparable, in Eliot's view, from their affective atmosphere and context. Without either the intensity of Janet's distress or the sincerity of Mr. Tryan's compassion, his soteriological ideas would remain "poor ghosts" and nothing more.[12]

Taken together, here we have two very different ways of thinking about the relationship between theology and "experience." We might call the first the *formal* function of experience in theological reasoning (the explicit theological procedure of appealing to a particular kind of experience to prove a point) and the second the *implicit* function of experience in theological reasoning (the irreducible affective and experiential texture of theological reasoning and persuasion for a given theologian as an embodied and historical being). Recognizing this distinction, it soon becomes clear that we cannot get rid of "experience" in theological discourse quite so easily as has sometimes been supposed. Even if we refuse to draw formally on experiences in theological argumentation, it is impossible for theologians to avoid being shaped implicitly by our experiences as embodied human beings with emotions, brains, and histories, who are always embedded in social and material environments.

The second conceptual clarification that needs to be made at the outset is to observe that formal theological appeal to experience can draw on what at least in theory are two distinct arenas of experience: (i) "religious experiences" that are understood to have God as their explicit agent or object; and (ii) human experience in the world in general, i.e. experiences that do not have God as their explicit agent or object.[13] Thus when Luther, defending his view that the will is bound, urges Erasmus to "Ask experience how impervious to dissuasion are those whose affections are set on anything!" he is making a theological argument that draws on "general" human experience rather than on an explicit experience of God.[14] By contrast, when the apostle Paul appeals to the Galatians' early experiences of the Holy Spirit in support of his views about justification and the law, he is appealing to "religious" experience, in that God is explicitly the agent, and the Spirit the object, of the experiences to which he refers.[15] There is more that can and must be said about "religious experience," but this basic distinction is useful enough for the moment.

---

[12] Indeed, in Eliot's hands the psychological and affective harmonics at work in the passage are yet more subtle than this, encompassing further factors such as Janet's implied distrust of men after years of abuse at the hands of her husband and her sense of safety at being in her mother's house and not her husband's.

[13] There are many further differentiations we could make within the broader category of "non-religious" experience; for now it is enough to acknowledge that theologically we are in quite different waters when an experience is attributed to or explicitly oriented to God than we are with forms of human experience where there is no explicit connection to God.

[14] *WA* 18:634; Martin Luther, *The Bondage of the Will*, trans. J.I. Packer and O.R. Johnston (Grand Rapids, MI: Fleming H. Revell, 1957), p. 103.

[15] In the passage, "God" is the one who "supplies" the Galatians with the Spirit (Gal. 3:5) and is thus its agent, and the experiences in question involve "receiving" the Spirit (Gal. 3:2), and the Spirit is thus the object of the experience. Often the distinction between God as "agent" and God

Together, these distinctions provide a useful preliminary map of some of the main forms that the relationship between theology and experience can take: experience can be appealed to formally in theological argument, and it can also shape theological reasoning in implicit and often unconscious ways; and experience can refer either to general human experience in the world or to experiences that are understood to be experiences of God in some sense. Over the course of this book, we will come across a number of ways in which these distinctions in fact become blurred in theology—for example, the ways in which theologians often understand the Spirit to be at work *incognito* in what otherwise appear to be "non-religious" or only latently religious experiences, or the way that no human experience of any kind is outside of the remit of God's providential activity—but for now they will help us avoid some of the main confusions and conflations that often plague theological discussions of experience. The value of the distinctions will become clear as we turn now to the history of theological engagements with "experience" in modern theology.

THE PROBLEM OF "EXPERIENCE" IN PROTESTANT THEOLOGY

In order to see why the constructive account of the relationship between theology and experience that will be offered in this book is necessary, and why it must take the shape that it does, it is important at this stage to examine why "experience" has become such a troubled and underutilized category in modern theology.

To do this, we must have some grasp of the modern history of debates about experience and theological subjectivism. As I indicated at the outset, this means first and foremost the fraught history of Protestant debates about experience. Anxiety and ambivalence about "experience" are by no means exclusive to Protestant traditions; an argument can be made that the origins of such debates are in the New Testament itself, especially in Paul's reflections on *glossolalia* and the gifts of the Spirit in 1 Corinthians and the Johannine author's discussion of pneumatological discernment in 1 John. But it is in a particular and highly influential strand of Protestant theology that arguments against experience have taken their most forceful and persuasive modern forms, and it is this legacy that continues to have the greatest impact on modern theological thinking about experience.

as "object" in religious experience is not so clear as it is in this passage, with its proto-trinitarian dynamics.

What is distinctive about Protestant theology in this respect, and the reason why debates over "experience" have been particularly intense for Protestants, is Protestantism's enduring rejection of what is perhaps the most coherent alternative approach to discernment of the Spirit: the idea of a magisterial teaching authority capable of making such discernments in history. Set in motion by a deep dissatisfaction with this Roman Catholic position, it is in Protestant theology that the theological authority or otherwise of personal and communal "experience" became a subject of particular urgency. It is therefore no surprise that it is within Protestant theology that the strongest arguments for suppressing and excising affectivity and experience in theological reflection have been articulated.

In fact, disagreement over the reliability and significance of Christian religious experience has been one of the most fundamental and enduring debates in Protestant theology from the 1520s to the present. Under the influence, first, of Martin Luther in his debates with "enthusiasts" in the 1520s, and then of Karl Barth in the early twentieth century, mainstream Protestant theology has long operated in the shadow of a deep distrust of subjective religious experience, viewing it as a phenomenon that is at best irrelevant to theology's task of the exposition of Scripture and at worst a pernicious false substitute for genuine divine revelation. Regardless of whether such experiences were understood to be subtle inner intuitions and impulses from the Holy Spirit, "unmediated" guidance from the Spirit in the interpretation of biblical texts, revelatory dreams and visions, or simply powerful affective experiences of intimacy with God, for Martin Luther and a great many later Protestants they all amounted to the same thing: "enthusiasm" or *Schwärmerei*, a chaotic and uncritical affirmation of the experiences of the human subject over and against God's objective Word.

At the same time, Protestantism has also consistently generated powerful and popular theologies and movements that have rejected Luther and Barth's suspicions of claims to such encounters with the Spirit, from radical reformers like Andreas von Karlstadt in the 1520s, through the pietist and revival movements of the eighteenth and nineteenth centuries, to modern Pentecostal and charismatic theologies. Because of the sharpness of Luther's initial formulation of the possible positions on spiritual experience in the "enthusiasm" debate, the debate over "experience" has tended to unhelpful extremes: either you view "experience" as the foundation for all dogmatic claims, as Schleiermacher allegedly did, or you exclude "experience" from the practice of theology entirely as hopelessly compromised by idolatry and sinfulness. In what follows I will trace, briefly, the history of this influential false dichotomy, and as I do so it will become clearer why a new approach is needed that can mediate between the two.

The Birth of Protestant "Experience" Polemic: Luther and the Enthusiasts

Woven through Martin Luther's and Karl Barth's arguments against theological appeals to "experience" is a fundamental question of how divine authority can be claimed for particular theological positions. As has been noted, at the eve of the Protestant Reformation, Catholic theology already had a sophisticated way of addressing the question of pneumatological discernment: the authority of the magisterial teaching office of the Church.[16] In sharp contrast, Protestants involved in debates over "enthusiasm" and "experience" had no such structures to which to appeal. Given their shared rejection of the magisterial-ecclesial solution to the problem, Protestants were forced from very early on to articulate alternate strategies for making theological discernments. The result was the emergence in Protestant theology of two major alternative approaches to authority and the discernment of the Spirit: the Bible and religious experience. At first, in the early theology of Martin Luther, these two sources of authority were closely interwoven, but by the mid 1520s they had been teased apart, and five centuries of Protestant debate over the value or otherwise of "experience" had been set in motion.

The earliest public Protestant formulation of an alternative doctrinal authority to that of the Catholic Church is to be found in the immediate aftermath of Luther's posting of the *Ninety-Five Theses*. Summoned to the Diet of Augsburg in 1518 for official judgment on the theses, Martin Luther was asked by papal legate Cardinal Cajetan to consider the statements on indulgences in Pope Clement VI's 1343 bull *Unigenitus*.[17] Here Luther found himself in the position of having to choose between the authority of the Catholic Church—represented by *Unigenitus*—and the authority of Scripture as he understood it.[18] As Luther described it shortly after the event, the bull "did not impress me as being truthful or authoritative for many reasons, but especially because it distorts the Holy Scriptures."[19] This was a point that Luther could not get past: "I did not possess the extraordinary indiscretion so

---

[16] In this view, the Spirit can be trusted to give guidance to the Church by means of its ordained authority structures, and so to provide satisfactory resolution to concrete questions of theological and pneumatological discernment that periodically face the Church. This position is expressed paradigmatically in the practice at the Council of Constance and the Council of Trent of beginning each session with an assertion of the Holy Spirit's involvement in the workings and conclusions of the Council: "This holy, ecumenical and general Council of Trent, lawfully assembled in the Holy Ghost." See H.J. Schroeder, ed. *Canons and Decrees of the Council of Trent: Original Text with English Translation* (St Louis: B. Herder Book Co., 1941), pp. 12, 15, 17, 21 (Latin: pp. 291, 294, 296, 300). For discussion, see Yves Congar, *I Believe in the Holy Spirit*, ii: *'He is Lord and Giver of Life'* (New York: The Crossroad Publishing Company, 1983), pp. 43–7.

[17] Specifically, the statements in the bull affirming the Church's possession of a treasury of merit that can be dispensed via indulgences.

[18] *WA* 2:12–13; *LW* 31:269–70.   [19] *WA* 2:8; *LW* 31:262.

as to discard so many important clear proofs of Scripture on account of a single ambiguous and obscure decretal of a pope who is a mere human being."[20] Faced with what he understood to be a clear choice between the teaching authority of the Church and that of Scripture, Luther opted decisively for the latter: "The Scriptures . . . are to be preferred to the bull in every case."[21] With this public statement, the Protestant approach to theological authority and discernment known as *sola scriptura* was born.[22]

Less often recognized is the fact that, in the same period that Luther was articulating this principle of the supreme authority of the Bible in matters of doctrine, he was also drawing in a concrete way on "experience" as a crucial aid in the interpretation of Scripture and the consequent development of doctrine—in this case, his development of the doctrine of justification by faith. As I have shown elsewhere, between 1513 and 1518 Luther drew increasingly on an analysis of his own inner life—what above we have called "general" rather than "religious" experience—to argue for a doctrine of the bondage of the will that was grounded in a belief in the insuperability of sinful affections in human beings through effort, practice, or habit.[23] This way of proceeding is evident in the 1518 "Explanation" attached to the *Heidelberg Disputation*. In a section arguing against one of Luther's favorite theological targets in medieval scholastic theology, the view that what is required of sinners to be saved is *facere quod in se est* ("to do what is in you"), Luther asks:

> Why therefore do we grant that lustful desire [*concupiscentiam*] is invincible? Do what is in you [*Fac quod in te est*] and do not lust [*non concupisce*]. But you cannot do that. Therefore you also do not by nature fulfil the law . . . Likewise, do what is in you and do not become angry with him who offends you. Do what is in you and do not fear danger . . . Do what is in you and do not fear death. I ask, what person does not shudder, does not despair, in the face of death?[24]

The rhetorical force of this characteristic argument depends on the reader assessing their own personal "experience" in relation to lust, anger, fear, and death, and then finding Luther's point empirically incontrovertible. The basis here is not least Luther's own experience of these affections, his own self-analysis leading to the discovery of what he thinks to be the insuperability of anger, lust, and so on.[25] Philip Melanchthon summarized this dimension

---

[20] *WA* 2:10; *LW* 31:266.   [21] *WA* 2:8; *LW* 31:262.

[22] For a full account of this episode, see Martin Brecht, *Martin Luther: His Road to Reformation 1483–1521*, trans. James L. Schaaf (Minneapolis: Fortress, 1985), pp. 246–61.

[23] See Simeon Zahl, "The Bondage of the Affections: Willing, Feeling, and Desiring in Luther's Theology, 1513–25," in *The Spirit, the Affections, and the Christian Tradition*, eds. Dale M. Coulter and Amos Yong (South Bend, IN: University of Notre Dame Press, 2017).

[24] *WA* 1:374; *LW* 31:69.

[25] On arguments from experience in Luther's writings, see also Zahl, "Non-Competitive Agency," pp. 212–16.

of early Lutheran theology of experience in his 1521 *Loci communes*: "Experience teaches that there is no freedom in the affections."[26] At this early stage in the history of Protestant theology, Scripture and "experience," especially affective experience, were seen to work together to provide a mutually reinforcing source of theological authority.

All this began to change in the mid 1520s as Luther began to encounter a more radically subjectivistic, "experience-oriented" approach to Protestant theology in the form of what he would famously dub "enthusiasm" or *Schwärmerei*. It is here, above all in Luther's attack on the theology of early Protestant radical Andreas Bodenstein von Karlstadt, that the enduring Protestant polemic against "experiential" theologies first took form. Luther came to believe that the theological essence of Karlstadt's position, like that of other "enthusiasts," is a privileging of inner experience, interpreted as experience of God's Spirit, over the external instruments of the Bible and the biblically authorized sacraments. This theology seems to have touched a deep nerve in Luther, and he accused Karlstadt and others like him of "devouring the Holy Spirit, feathers and all."[27]

The force of Luther's critique is that "enthusiasts" like Karlstadt are anthropologically naïve. They greatly underestimate the power of human sin to regard one's own desires and experiences uncritically as the activity of the Holy Spirit. By 1525, Luther had begun to argue in response that no inner experience of God's Spirit is likely to be authentic if it is not mediated through what he called the *verbum externum*, the external Word of biblical preaching and the sacraments of baptism and the eucharist. Luther summarizes this view in the *Smalcald Articles*:

> In these matters, which concern the spoken, external Word, it must be firmly maintained that God gives no one his Spirit or grace apart from the external Word which goes before. We say this to protect ourselves from the enthusiasts.[28]

According to Luther's new theology of the Word, inner experience of the Spirit, especially the experiences associated with coming to faith, is always ecclesially and biblically mediated, through scriptural preaching and the sacraments. You cannot have a saving experience of the Holy Spirit while hiking in the mountains or having a conversation with a friend. If you want to know where you stand with God, you must look to your baptism and to the Word that encounters you in church rather than to your inner experiences.

This position was first developed in an extended way in Luther's main treatise against Karlstadt, *Against the Heavenly Prophets*, one of the most

---

[26] *MW* 2.1:40; Melanchthon, *Loci communes 1521*, p. 59.   [27] *WA* 18:66; *LW* 40:83.

[28] *Smalcald Articles* 3.8.3 (*BSLK*, p. 453; *BC*, p. 322).

influential writings in the history of theological debate over "experience" of the Spirit.[29] The heart of Luther's analysis is the view that an "unmediated" pneumatology would give the *Schwärmer* wide license to make false attributions of the Spirit's guidance and agency in the lives of Christians, both consciously and unconsciously: "If you ask who directs them to teach and act in this way, they point upward and reply, 'Ah, God tells me so, and the Spirit says so.' Indeed, [for them] all idle dreams are nothing but God's Word."[30]

Prior to the debate with Karlstadt, as we have seen, Luther had not recognized a need for a strict distinction between "general" experience, which he had little problem with, and experience of God in particular, with the result that his theological references to experience were largely positive. In the *Dictata super Psalterium*, for example, he observes that "in tribulation [the exegete] learns many things which he did not know before; [likewise,] many things he already knew in theory he grasps more firmly through experience [*per experentiam*]."[31] It was only in 1525, in *Against the Heavenly Prophets*, that Luther began to write about Scripture and personal experiences of God as ultimately incompatible theological authorities that need to be carefully distinguished.

Importantly, in the vehemence of his reaction against appeals to divine experience, and in his conviction that the experiences in question were in fact general human experiences ("idle dreams") and emphatically *not* experiences of the Holy Spirit, Luther ended up unintentionally communicating a broader anxiety about human subjective experience as such. Luther's new, pessimistic view on subjective experience, which would eventually carry the day in confessional Lutheranism at the expense of the affective dimensions of his thought, is given classic expression in a 1532 sermon, where we can already see the polemic against "religious" feelings bleeding over into an anxiety about "feelings" and "the heart" *tout court*:

> [W]hen you no longer accord the Word greater validity than your every feeling [*all dein fuelen*], your eyes, your senses, your heart, you are doomed, and you can no longer be helped . . . [Y]ou must judge solely by the Word, regardless of what you feel or see.[32]

The message is clear: feelings and other inner perceptions cannot be trusted; only the Word can be trusted. "Experience" had become problematic for Protestants.

---

[29] Asendorf notes that it is here, "above all in the debate with the *Schwärmer*" that Luther "fully worked out his theology of the Spirit" (Ulrich Asendorf, *Heiliger Geist und Rechtfertigung* (Göttingen: V&R unipress, 2004), p. 29).
[30] *WA* 18:138; *LW* 40:148.   [31] *WA* 3:44; *LW* 10:49.   [32] *WA* 36:494; *LW* 28:70.

It is difficult to underestimate the impact of Luther's new anti-experiential theology of the Word and his corresponding critique of "enthusiasm" on later Protestantism. Luther's rejection of "enthusiasm" became even more influential in the seventeenth and eighteenth centuries, as Anabaptism failed to disappear and as pietism began to rear its head in reaction to a perceived spiritual coldness in Lutheran and Reformed Orthodoxy. Developing and expanding to encompass subjectivistic and radical theologies of all kinds, the term "enthusiasm" became the preferred pejorative term for a wide variety of non-mainstream Protestant theologies.[33] In the eighteenth century, as ways of thinking associated with the Enlightenment grew in power and influence, "enthusiasm" became as much a target for liberal Protestant Christians as it was for more conservative confessional Protestants. For liberals, the problem with "enthusiasm" came to be seen primarily in terms of its perceived "irrationality" rather than its failure to make the Bible adequately central.[34]

Representative here is the view of Charles Chauncy, an influential congregationalist minister in Boston in the mid eighteenth century. During the First Great Awakening in America, Chauncy criticized revivalist preacher George Whitefield and his followers, arguing that they "place their Religion so much in the *Heat* and *Fervour* of the *Passions*, that they too much neglect their *Reason* and *Judgment . . .* The Goodness that has been so much talked of [in the Awakening] is nothing more, in general, than a *Commotion of the Passions.*"[35] Here again we see the bleed that often took place from critiques of "religious experience" in particular to critiques of appeals to human subjectivity in general. Ultimately Chauncy's problem appears to be less with the idea that God is the source or kindler of these passions than it is with passions and emotions as such.

Whitefield responded to Chauncy's critique with a telling argument, which encapsulates a great deal of the perennial intra-Protestant debate about experience: "To Talk of . . . having the Spirit of God without feeling it, is really to deny the Thing."[36] In Whitefield's view, a theology that has no experiential purchase is not a theology at all, it is just a set of ideas about God, and indeed is implicitly atheistic. In the same period, John Wesley, too, emphasized the

---

[33] See Michael Heyd, *"Be Sober and Reasonable": The Critique of Enthusiasm in the Seventeenth and Eighteenth Centuries* (New York: Brill, 1995), p. 2.

[34] On the relationship between emotion and reason in Enlightenment-era philosophy, see Susan James, *Passion and Action: The Emotions in Seventeenth-Century Philosophy* (Oxford: Oxford University Press, 1997), especially pp. 1–4, 13–19, and 159–82 ("Passion and Error"). For the use of reason as a criterion for judging enthusiasm, as well as the use of medical science as an anti-enthusiastic discourse in the seventeenth and early eighteenth centuries, see Heyd, *"Be Sober and Reasonable,"* pp. 144–90.

[35] Charles Chauncy, "The Heat and Fervour of Their Passions," in *Religious Enthusiasm and the Great Awakening*, ed. David S. Lovejoy (Englewood Cliffs, NJ: Prentice-Hall, 1969), p. 79. Emphasis original.

[36] Whitefield, "Spirit of God," p. 106.

irreducible importance of experiential factors for Christian thinking, arguing that it is through personal encounter with the Spirit that we receive the "experimental knowledge" that "alone, is true Christianity."[37] It is no surprise that Wesley, like Whitefield, had to address charges of "enthusiasm" over the course of his career, leading to his extended refutation of the charge in the sermon "The Nature of Enthusiasm."[38]

In these developments, Protestant theological reflection on emotion and subjective "experience" continued to labor in the shadow of Luther's critique of Karlstadt. Despite contextual variations, the fundamental issue remained that of the reliability or otherwise of "unmediated" personal experience of God as a theological authority and source, and the basic contrast continued to be the one drawn by Luther: that of the "subjectivity" and hence unreliability of affective and revelatory experience as against the "objectivity" of alternative theological sources, initially that of the Bible and later also that of human reason.

Crucially, anti-enthusiastic critiques of claims to unmediated experience of God—critiques of "religious" experience—tended to mutate, often without theologians being fully aware of it, into critiques of theological appeals to "general" experience as well. This is because, in the view of anti-enthusiasts, claims to "unmediated" religious experience in fact refer to misidentified "non-religious" experiences rather than to real experiences of God, and this implies the unreliability of "non-religious" experience as well. In other words, in asserting that a putative experience of God is in fact an erroneous baptizing of some conventional human experience or set of experiences—as for example Chauncy's assertion that conversion experiences in the Great Awakening were a mere "Commotion of the Passions"—a question mark is being placed against conventional, "non-religious" experience too, in that the latter has shown itself to be unreliable and open to misidentification as experience of God.

In the late eighteenth and early nineteenth centuries, the pendulum swung back in favor of more "enthusiastic" positions as theologies that drew upon "experience" as a resource achieved a new mainstream acceptance through the

---

[37] John Wesley, "'Awake, Thou That Sleepest'. Sermon 3, 1742," in *John Wesley's Sermons: An Anthology*, eds. Albert C. Outler and Richard P. Heitzenrater (Nashville, TN: Abingdon Press, 1991), p. 92.

[38] On debates about "enthusiasm" in Britain, in addition to Heyd, *"Be Sober and Reasonable,"* see especially Phyllis Mack, *Heart Religion in the British Enlightenment* (Cambridge: Cambridge University Press, 2008); for America, see David S. Lovejoy, *Religious Enthusiasm in the New World: Heresy to Revolution* (Cambridge, MA: Harvard University Press, 1985); for developments on the Continent, see especially W.R. Ward, *The Protestant Evangelical Awakening* (Cambridge: Cambridge University Press, 1992). One of the most lastingly important works of eighteenth century theology, Jonathan Edwards' *Treatise Concerning the Religious Affections*, can be understood as an attempt to square the circle of affective and experiential religion on the one hand, and a high view of the Word on the other. See Jonathan Edwards, *Religious Affections* (New Haven, CT: Yale University Press, 1959).

work of Friedrich Schleiermacher. In the wake of Lessing's critique of the authority of the Bible and of Christian tradition, and Kant's attempt to establish a new foundation for religion on the basis of universal moral principles, Schleiermacher developed a sophisticated new vision of "experience" as the true foundation for Christian theological reflection. For Schleiermacher, religious "feeling," construed a certain way, became both the starting point for dogmatics ("Christian doctrines are accounts of the Christian religious affections [*christlich frommen Gemüthzustände*] set forth in speech"[39]) and its limit (where "the stirrings [*Erregungen*] of the religious self-consciousness . . . do not exist the doctrines cannot arise"[40]). In giving Christian theology this new starting point, Schleiermacher succeeded in meeting the Enlightenment challenge of providing a new basis for religious belief that was not simply a trust in reports of past experiences recorded in Scripture or in the teaching of the church. As a response to the sort of approach represented by Lessing ("contingent truths of history can never become the proof of necessary truths of reason"[41]), this approach was extraordinarily effective: Schleiermacher began not with assertions about the past but with "actually experienced facts" of present religious existence,[42] but at the same time, in a subversion of Lessing's worries about the authority of history, Schleiermacher simultaneously succeeded in providing compelling arguments for the connection between the present facts of religious experience and the historical activity of Jesus Christ.[43]

Schleiermacher's approach to experience resulted in a further problematizing of the distinction between "religious experience" and general, "non-religious" experience. In Schleiermacher's view, "piety" or the feeling of absolute dependence is fundamental to religious self-consciousness as such and in this sense is present, one way or another, in virtually the whole of the Christian person's experience in the world, in every dimension of "consciousness of sin" and "consciousness of grace." As he puts it, "the self-consciousness which accompanies all our activity, and therefore, since that is never zero, accompanies our whole existence . . . is itself precisely a consciousness of absolute dependence." And this self-consciousness is in fact religious: "the *Whence* of our receptive and active existence, implied in this self-consciousness, is to be designated by the word 'God'."[44] In other words, the

---

[39] Schleiermacher, *The Christian Faith* (1999), p. 76 (§15).

[40] Schleiermacher, *The Christian Faith* (1999), p. 78 (§15).

[41] Gotthold Ephraim Lessing, "On the proof of the spirit and of power (1777)," in *Philosophical and Theological Writings*, ed. H.B. Nisbet (Cambridge: Cambridge University Press, 2005), p. 87.

[42] Friedrich Schleiermacher, *On the Glaubenslehre: Two Letters to Dr. Lücke*, trans. James Duke and Francis Fiorenza (Oxford: Oxford University Press, 1981), p. 45.

[43] See Zahl, "Experience," pp. 180–3.

[44] Schleiermacher, *The Christian Faith* (1999), p. 16 (§4.4).

kind of "experience" Schleiermacher is interested in is clearly "religious experience," but at the same time it is religious experience redefined in such a way as to be a dimension of everything a religious person might feel and experience in their life—"all our activity," "our whole existence"—and thus of everything that we might otherwise think of as "general" experience.

Schleiermacher's approach proved to be immensely generative for theology for nearly a century, giving a new confidence and starting point for theologians as diverse as Samuel Taylor Coleridge in England, Horace Bushnell in America, and J.C.K. von Hofmann in Germany.[45] In the wake of Schleiermacher's success, by the late nineteenth century one of the most pressing issues for theology had become the relationship between the authority of individual religious experience and the findings of historical science, in light of the fact that religious experience always instantiates in historical time and therefore arguably cannot be understood in isolation from historical analysis.[46] Shaped by this debate, the theology of Ritschlian theologian Wilhelm Herrmann represented a kind of doubling down on individual religious experience against the claims of historical science: "Our certainty of God may be kindled by many other experiences, but has ultimately its firmest basis in the fact that within the realm of history to which we ourselves belong, we encounter the man Jesus as an undoubted reality."[47] But already the pendulum was beginning to swing back the other way. In the aftermath of the outbreak of the First World War, after a century of flowering, the tradition culminating in Herrmann, which believed "experience" could in some sense provide theological "certainty of God," came under withering assault at the hands of Herrmann's greatest student: Swiss theologian Karl Barth.

Before turning to Barth, it is important to treat in more detail an important theme in the narrative thus far: namely, the consistent and often unintentional slippage that has taken place between theological criticism of appeals to *religious experience* and theological anxiety about *subjective experience as such*. We have seen it in the Enlightenment-era discourse, represented here by Chauncy, which in order to criticize affectively charged renewal theologies ended up playing rationality against "the passions" as a whole; we have seen it in Schleiermacher's development of a concept of religious "feeling" that is in

---

[45] For an overview of the theme of "experience" in nineteenth-century Christian theology, including the contribution of Schleiermacher, see Zahl, "Experience."

[46] See Johannes Zachhuber, *Theology as Science in Nineteenth-Century Germany: From F. C. Baur to Ernst Troeltsch* (Oxford: Oxford University Press, 2013), Chapter 10 and Conclusion.

[47] Wilhelm Hermann, *The Communion of the Christian with God: Described on the Basis of Luther's Statements* (Philadelphia: Fortress Press, 1971), pp. 59–60. This was also the basic position articulated by Barth himself in his earliest writings. See Bruce L. McCormack, *Karl Barth's Critically Realistic Dialectical Theology: Its Genesis and Development, 1909–1936* (New York: Oxford University Press, 1997), pp. 68–77. On Hermann's influence on Barth, see ibid., pp. 49–68, and Kenneth Oakes, *Karl Barth on Theology and Philosophy* (Oxford: Oxford University Press, 2012), Chapter 1.

fact ingredient to most of what a Christian might expect to experience in the world; and we have seen it in the implications of the widespread reading of "enthusiastic" experiences from Luther onwards as nothing more than conventional, non-religious experiences that have been misidentified. Over and over, anxiety about religious experience has tended to mutate into anxiety about subjectivity and emotion *tout court*. When this happens, anxiety about the "formal" function of experience in theology starts to bleed into anxiety about "implicit" factors as well. Experience as such becomes problematic rather than just certain kinds of direct reflection on perceived encounters with God. In such cases, soon there is little left to fill the void for Protestant theologians but a highly conceptual appeal to reason and the Bible, shorn of attention to the affective atmosphere and context in which such reasonings in fact take place. This helps explain why, as Horace Bushnell once observed, Protestant theological method has so often devolved, in practice, into an unhappy choice of whether to be "rationalists *over* the scriptures" or "rationalists *under* them."[48] Certainly it has proven surprisingly difficult for Protestant theologians to maintain an anti-enthusiastic position that does not soon devolve into a de facto methodological rationalism of one kind or another. In such cases, affective and experiential factors do not of course disappear. They just go "underground," and continue their work unrecognized and unexamined, while dogmatics, unmoored from bodies and from time, drifts into realms of increasing abstraction and irrelevance, paving the way for yet another renewalist correction.

Karl Barth's Critique of "Experience"

It is in the theology of Karl Barth that the critical approach to "experience" that began with Luther received its most decisive and influential update. The influence of Barth's approach on modern theology has been enormous, and in many respects it remains alive and active today, shaping theological reflection even for those who are critical of Barth. As Sarah Coakley has rightly observed, "[Barth's] work, with its resounding '*Nein!*' uttered . . . against any attempts to moor theology in an analysis of the human, is probably still the dominating influence in new, contemporary attempts at systematic theology."[49]

The ignition point for Barth's position on "religious experience" is a theology of revelation that entailed a ferocious rejection of all theologies that take their starting point from a place other than divine revelation. In the

---

[48] Horace Bushnell, "Preliminary Discourse on Language," in *God in Christ: Three Discourses* (New York: Charles Scribner's Sons, 1876), p. 92. Emphasis original.

[49] Sarah Coakley, *God, Sexuality, and the Self: An Essay "On the Trinity"* (Cambridge: Cambridge University Press, 2013), pp. 39–40.

well-known narrative, which at this point is virtually modern theology's founding myth, the young Barth was shocked in early 1914 to see that all but one of his theological teachers had signed a public statement in support of the German military cause in the First World War. He saw in this ethical failure on the part of the German liberal theological establishment a mortal indictment of the entire liberal theological project inaugurated by Schleiermacher.[50] In Barth's powerful interpretation, liberal theology from Schleiermacher to Herrmann had taken its starting point from anthropology—from human experience, human reasoning, and human scientific and cultural achievements—and this had led to critical and ethical disaster.[51] As Barth saw it, theology needed to begin again, taking its starting point this time neither from history nor from experience but from God himself in his revelation.

In Barth's new view, one of the most pernicious false starting points for theology, inevitably a major option when theology begins with anthropology, is once again the broad domain of inner subjective experience. Barth emphasizes this point over and over in the second edition of *The Epistle to the Romans*. "Is there any connexion," Barth asks, "between those impressions of revelation which may be discovered in the events of history or in the spiritual experiences of men, and the actual revelation of the Unknown God himself? . . . May it not be that the perception of God as the Judge involves the denial of all connexion and relation between here and there?"[52] The answer to the first rhetorical question is clearly a resounding "no": "The truth [that the promises of God have been fulfilled in Jesus Christ], in fact, can never be self-evident, because it is a matter neither of historical nor of psychological experience."[53] To argue otherwise, in Barth's view, is to misunderstand the fundamental otherness of revelation and of God in relation to the world and human experience: "when the mercy of God is thought of as an element of history or as a factor in human spiritual experience, its untruth is emphasized."[54] The perception that a perceived religious experience might point even

[50] "Concluding Unscientific Postscript on Schleiermacher," in Karl Barth, *The Theology of Schleiermacher: Lectures at Göttingen, Winter Semester of 1923/24*, trans. Geoffrey W. Bromiley (Edinburgh: T & T Clark, 1982), pp. 263–4.

[51] Barth to Herrmann, on Nov. 4, 1914: "Especially with you, Herr Professor . . . we learned to acknowledge 'experience' as the constitutive principle of knowing and doing in the domain of religion. In your school it became clear to us what it means to 'experience' God in Jesus. Now however, in answer to our doubts [about the war] an 'experience' which is completely new to us is held out to us by German Christians, an allegedly religious war 'experience'; i.e. the fact that German Christians 'experience' their war as a holy war is supposed to bring us to silence. Where do you stand in relation to this argument and to the war theology which lies behind it? . . . Our relationship to you has become a mixture of great gratitude and complete antithesis." (Karl Barth to Wilhelm Herrmann, November 4, 1914, from Karl Barth and Martin Rade, *Karl Barth–Martin Rade: Ein Briefwechsel* (Gütersloh: Gütersloher Verlagshaus, 1981), pp. 114–15; extract trans. in McCormack, *Critically Realistic Dialectical Theology*, pp. 113–14.

[52] Barth, *Romans II*, p. 78.   [53] Barth, *Romans II*, p. 98.

[54] Barth, *Romans II*, p. 102.

in some small, contingent way toward truths about God and His relation to the world is therefore emphatically mistaken: "No, thy impress of revelation, thy emotion, thy experience and enthusiasm, are of this world, are flesh."[55] Indeed, efforts in this direction are always doomed to failure due to the very nature of divine revelation: "[The Holy Spirit] is invisible, beyond all psychological analysis...He is the subject of faith, which 'religious experience' reaches after and longs for, but never finds."[56]

In these statements we see an important difference between Luther's and Barth's characterizations of the problem of "experience." Whereas Luther was mainly worried about private revelations and about hermeneutical strategies that drew on religious experiences to justify interpretations of particular texts—what I have been calling "formal" appeals to experience in theological argumentation—Barth's language immediately expands the object of critique to include human subjectivity in all its dimensions. In Barth's early rhetoric, "all connexion" must be severed between the realm of the divine and the realm of human subjectivity; both historical experiences and human "psychology" itself are suspect in all forms. Thus a point that was often present only obliquely in earlier critiques of enthusiasm is now explicit in Barth: the "implicit" function of experience in theological inquiry is just as problematic as the "formal" function of experience.

In making these kinds of statements about "experience" in the *Epistle to the Romans*, what Barth had particularly in mind was the approach to theology taken by Schleiermacher and his heirs through to Hermann. But Barth's argument is not exhausted in the rejection of German theological liberalism. His critique also applies to theologies that emphasize personal experience of God in less philosophically sophisticated ways, including the pietist and "awakening" theologies that had flourished in the eighteenth and early nineteenth centuries in Europe and America and were still a significant feature of the early twentieth century German and Swiss religious landscapes. Commenting on "revival theology" a few years after *Romans*, in an essay from 1927, Barth asserts that such theology "has no principle of opposition between God and Man." As a result, and because it speaks "out of feeling and out of experience" [*Aus dem Gefühl, aus der Erfahrung, aus dem Erlebnis*] and focuses on "the Christian subject," "revival theology" is best understood as a "variation on the theology of that century classically represented in Schleiermacher," just in a "much more powerful and drastic" form.[57] With statements

---

[55] Barth, *Romans II*, p. 72.   [56] Barth, *Romans II*, p. 158.

[57] Karl Barth, "Das Wort in der Theologie von Schleiermacher bis Ritschl," in *Die Theologie und die Kirche. Gesammelte Vorträge*, ii (Zollikon-Zürich: Evangelischer Verlag, 1928), pp. 197–200. See also Karl Barth, *Die Christliche Dogmatik im Entwurf* (Zürich: Theologischer Verlag Zürich, 1982), pp. 402–13, and Eberhard Busch, *Karl Barth & the Pietists: The Young Karl Barth's Critique of Pietism and Its Response*, trans. Daniel W. Bloesch (Downers Grove, IL: InterVarsity Press, 2004), pp. 264–75.

like these, Barth's theology is carrying the torch for the Protestant tradition of anti-enthusiasm begun by Luther. For Barth, claims to subjective human experience, whether in terms of feelings and emotions, personal revelations, dispositions, inner intuitions, or any other "impress of the divine," and regardless of whether such experience takes a philosophically sophisticated Schleiermacherian form or a less complex pietist form, are utterly excluded as a valid starting point in theological reflection.

Barth's critical statements about "experience" often appear to imply, rhetorically, some alternative "starting point" that would not be subject to an idolatrous confusion of the experiences of human beings with the Word of God. Thus when, in a 1915 letter to Eduard Thurneysen, Barth describes the problem with Leonhard Ragaz's theology as being one of having the wrong "*Ansatz*,"[58] the implication appears to be that some alternative, better *Ansatz* exists and must be found. On the basis of statements like this, Bruce McCormack is not wrong to refer to Barth's theological shift in 1915 as the development of a "new starting-point,"[59] and there is little question that Barth believed his own way of doing theology, developed in its maturity in the *Church Dogmatics*, and for all his repeated assertions of its radical provisionality,[60] to be a qualitatively better way of doing things than the alternatives.[61]

But it would be a mistake to take this language of "starting points" and *Ansätze* too far. It need hardly be said that, insofar as Barth has a "starting point," already in the second edition of *Romans* it is one that dialectically entails its own negation. Barth's method is built around a deep conviction of theology's inability to "possess" revelation and therefore of the corresponding impossibility, from the human side, of its task: "The Word of God is the transformation of everything that we know as Humanity, Nature, and History, and must therefore be apprehended as the negation of the starting-point [*Verneinung seines Ausgangspunktes*] of every system which we are capable of conceiving."[62] Barth's early polemic against "experience" is thus caught up in a broader polemic against the very idea of "starting points" as they had previously been conceived in modern theology. In this sense, his radical

---

[58] Karl Barth, *Karl Barth—Eduard Thurneysen Briefwechsel,* i: *1913–1921* (Zürich: Theologischer Verlag Zürich, 1973), p. 69.

[59] McCormack, *Critically Realistic Dialectical Theology*, pp. 129, 130.

[60] "In both its investigations and its conclusions [dogmatics] must keep in view that God is in heaven and it on earth, and that God, His revelation and faith always live their own free life over against all human talk, including that of the best dogmatics" (Karl Barth, *Church Dogmatics I: The Doctrine of the Word of God*, Part 1, trans. G.W. Bromiley (London: T & T Clark International, 2004), pp. 85–6).

[61] In *Church Dogmatics* I/1, the main alternatives in view are the approaches to dogmatics taken in Roman Catholic and liberal Protestant theology, respectively. See Barth, *CD I/1*, pp. 248–75, *passim*.

[62] Barth, *Romans II*, p. 278.

anti-enthusiasm is just one dimension of a broader strategy for extricating theology from the modern dream of a methodologically unassailable "scientific" dogmatics.

Barth's rejection of theologies that affirm the theological importance of religious experience soon led to a further question: do real experiences of the Spirit ever actually take place at all for human subjects? By the time of the first part-volume of the *Church Dogmatics* in 1932, Barth had advanced and clarified his position on the revelation of the Word such that he could now answer this question, perhaps surprisingly, with a clear "yes." Revelatory encounter with God does in fact take place in particular human lives at particular times. As Barth puts it, "we must now make the positive statement that in faith men have real experience of the Word of God."[63] Barth continues: "Man does not exist abstractly but concretely, i.e., in experiences, in determinations of his existence by objects, by things outside him and distinct from him . . . If knowledge of God's Word can become possible for men, this must mean that they can have experience of God's Word."[64]

With statements like these, Barth clarifies his polemic against religious experience and feeling in *Romans* and elsewhere as being specifically about the procedure of making a certain kind of theological use of such experiences rather than about their existence or about the validity of experience of God as such. The problem only begins when

> the reality of this experience . . . is thought of in such a way that in it God hands something over to man in the sense that it really passes out of God's hands into the hands of man, or, from man's standpoint, in such a way that man receives something from God in the sense that it is really put in his hands.[65]

Indeed, in Barth's account, genuine experience of the Word necessarily and immediately communicates the complete inadequacy of such experience to the genuine divine revelation that is being experienced:

> [The person who encounters and believes God's Word] will indeed be called by God in his whole existence; 'with all his heart and soul and mind and strength' he will be involved. But not for a moment or in any respect will he think that his being involved is even approximately an adequate counterpart to the promise and claim confronting him . . . What acknowledgement of God's Word in our

---

[63] Barth, *CD I/1*, p. 238.

[64] Barth, *CD I/1*, p. 198; for Barth's extended reflection on this point, see pp. 198–227, "The Word of God and Experience," where Barth responds to the critiques of Georg Wobbermin. This point is brought out persuasively in Clifford B. Anderson, "A Theology of Experience? Karl Barth and the Transcendental Argument," in *Karl Barth and American Evangelicalism*, eds. Bruce L. McCormack and Clifford B. Anderson (Grand Rapids, MI: William B. Eerdmans Publishing Company, 2011).

[65] Barth, *CD I/1*, pp. 211–12.

experience is not unmasked and convicted by the Word of God even as it takes place, convicted not of its imperfection and inadequacy but of its total corruption and futility?... *In what acknowledgement of God's Word in our experience, then, can there be anything like a sure and necessary correspondence to the Word of God?*[66]

In the first part-volume of the *Church Dogmatics*, Barth thus affirms simultaneously the reality and power of Christian experience of God and the total separation of such experience from the practice of doing theology. "Correspondence to the Word of God" is secured only from God's side, in the gracious event of revelation, and can never be located, even indirectly, in the impact of that revelation, no matter how authentic the experience.[67] In this it remains always "mystery,"[68] an "impossible possibility."[69]

It is often pointed out that it is a mistake to reduce Barth's entire account of human subjectivity in its relation to the Word of God to critical statements like these.[70] In fact, Barth's vision elsewhere in the *Church Dogmatics* of reconciliation, of the sacraments, of prayer, and of many other topics involves a more interesting and nuanced account of subjectivity and experience than the core material on the subject in I/1 and I/2 would seem to suggest. Nevertheless, as Coakley indicates, it is still true that Barth has done more to problematize the category of "experience" for later theology than any figure since Luther. Partly this is because even his more sophisticated engagements with human subjectivity leave much to be desired. But it also has to do with the reception history of Barth's theology. The dimension of Barth's thought that has resonated most loudly through the years has not generally been the subtle dialectical revisions and symphonic multitextured constructive accounts of the later volumes of the *Church Dogmatics*. What theology instead heard and still hears from Barth, first and foremost, are the ferocious negations of the 1922 *Romans* and the "*Nein!*" against Brunner; the drama of his horror at his teachers signing "the horrible manifesto" defending Germany at the start of World War I; and the polemics against experience, against Schleiermacher, and against dogmatic appeal to the authority of human subjectivity in any form.

One reason for this is that, to a substantial degree, Barth's polemics against the dogmatic value of experience are framed in terms of his critique of liberal Protestant "apologetics," and this methodological framing has tended to

---

[66] Barth, *CD* I/1, p. 220, emphasis added. See also Barth, *Romans II*, p. 79.

[67] Thus Barth in *Church Dogmatics* I/2 makes the astonishing claim that there is "nothing specific that we can say" about the "work of the Holy Spirit" by which "subjective revelation... comes to man and is recognised by man." Karl Barth, *Church Dogmatics I: The Doctrine of the Word of God*, Part 2 (London: T & T Clark International, 2004), p. 239.

[68] Barth, *CD* I/1, p. 125.   [69] Barth, *Romans II*, p. 79.

[70] See e.g. Trevor Hart, "Revelation," in *The Cambridge Companion to Karl Barth*, ed. John Webster (Cambridge: Cambridge University Press, 2000), pp. 53–5.

swallow up the entire theological thematic of human experience.[71] The claim that experiences of revelation provide no "sure and necessary correspondence to the Word of God" is made in the context of an argument with a liberal Protestant search for Herrmann's "certainty of God." By consistently connecting the question of experience to the question of apologetics, Barth seems to assume that the only reason to attend to experience, theologically, would be for the sake of an apologetic attempt to secure dogmatic certainty from some Archimedean point outside of God's own revelation—a procedure Barth regards as idolatrous in its intentions and impossible in practice.

Accepting the validity of this characterization of the function of experience in "modernistic dogmatics,"[72] theologians in Barth's wake have often followed him in assuming that this one way of engaging with experience in theology— as an apologetic tool or as some kind of foundational human norm for assessing revelation—exhausts the theological significance and interest of the topic of "experience." John Webster's characterization of Barth's discussion of dogmatic prolegomena in *Church Dogmatics* I/1 illustrates this reductive dynamic:

> Prolegomenal discussion [in dogmatics] often seeks to construct a platform from which theology can be launched, establishing the possibility of talk of God by showing from outside the sphere of faith and church that, on the basis of general principles of knowledge, metaphysics or experience, there is some readiness for revelation on the part of humanity . . . [Here we see what] Barth had already found it necessary to repudiate in theological liberalism, namely, *the exchange whereby revelation became religious history and experience, grounded not in the freedom of God but in the wider human context of its occurrence.* In place of this, Barth sets out an understanding of dogmatics which derives its principles at all points from the active, speaking reality of the being of God.[73]

Here Barth's rejection of experience, as interpreted by Webster, is built upon a false dichotomy. The question of experience is reduced to the question of theology's "ground," and then forced into a theologically and rhetorically loaded choice: either we build theology on "the freedom of God" or we build it on "the wider human context of [revelation's] occurrence"; no third way between these poles is conceived or given.

As will be evident throughout this volume, the theological question of "experience" is hardly exhausted by modern questions of theology's apologetic

---

[71] For Barth's classic account of liberal theology as "apologetics," see Karl Barth, *Ethics*, trans. Geoffrey W. Bromiley (Edinburgh: T&T Clark, 1981), pp. 21–8; for discussion of this text, see Oakes, *Barth on* Theology, pp. 125–34.

[72] Barth, *CD* I/1, p. 36.

[73] John Webster, *Barth* (New York: Continuum, 2004), p. 54. Emphasis added.

"ground" or "platform."[74] The de facto eclipse of the experiencing subject in much Protestant theology after Barth was not some dogmatic inevitability; it was collateral damage downstream of Barth's great labor to drag theology out of its modernist cul-de-sac. To argue otherwise is to read the whole theological theme of "experience" through the narrow lens of the nineteenth-century liberal quest for a new basis for theology in the aftermath of Kant and the rise of historical criticism of the Bible. It is to ask the questions of the early twentieth century instead of those of the twenty-first.

On the topic of theological foundations, there is no question that theology is working in a very different methodological and epistemological environment today than it was a century ago when Barth was formulating his position on experience. For a host of reasons, starting with the influence of Barth himself, theology today is substantially less interested in "starting points" and foundations. Instead, much of the discipline's energy in recent decades has been focused on the many ways that doctrinal arguments and interpretations are always attuned to and shaped by their contexts to one degree or another—by cultural factors, by sociological factors, by confessional and liturgical factors, by particular cultural and religious histories. As Marcella Althaus-Reid has put it, theologians are not and never can be "neutral practitioners." We all have "ideological and geopolitical investments in our praxis," though some theologies are more self-aware about the fact than others.[75] Peter Phan makes the same point: "because theology is a social fact and because the theologian is not only a theoretician but also a social agent, theology is never neutral and the theologian is never socially uncommitted."[76] The result is that theologians today are much more likely than in the past to agree with Graham Ward's observation that "theological discourse always comes from somewhere, is spoken by someone, and is legitimated or delegitimated by some institution implicated in particular sets of social and cultural relations."[77]

---

[74] Indeed, chapter by chapter, the present monograph can be read as a sustained demonstration of the theological value and significance of "experience" apart from such questions.

[75] Marcella Althaus-Reid, "Queer I Stand: Lifting the Skirts of God," in *The Sexual Theologian: Essays on Sex, God and Politics*, eds. Marcella Althaus-Reid and Lisa Isherwood (London: T&T Clark International, 2004), p. 102. David Ngong's work, for example, has shown how the irreducibility as well as the power of such "investments" is impossible to ignore in a context like postcolonial Africa, where there is a history of Christian pieties whose effect has been "to keep Africans in thrall." In such a context, Ngong argues, it is particularly obvious that the "religious imagination" is never neutral, but can be either "liberating or enslaving," "salutary" or "unsalutary." See David Ngong, *Theology as Construction of Piety: An African Perspective* (Eugene, OR: RESOURCE Publications, 2013), pp. 16, 28.

[76] Peter C. Phan, "A Common Journey, Different Paths, the Same Destination: Method in Liberation Theologies," in *A Dream Unfinished: Theological Reflections on America from the Margins*, eds. Eleazar S. Fernandez and Fernando F. Segovia (Eugene, OR: Wipf and Stock Publishers, 2006), p. 150.

[77] Graham Ward, *How the Light Gets In: Ethical Life I* (Oxford: Oxford University Press, 2016), p. 116.

As we have become more aware of our locatedness, contemporary theology has also become less anxious than before about the irreducibility of the subjectivity of the theologian, and now tends to be very aware of the challenges involved in making straightforward, theologically normative claims on behalf of all of humanity. A consequence of this has been an increased epistemic humility in theology: a renewed recognition that, as Ward puts it, "the Church" (and we might also say, theology) "in its labouring to discern and in its passing of judgement has always to recall its ignorance, the fragility of its discernment, the necessary limitations of its judgements."[78] In statements like this we see that Barth's radical claims about the provisionality of dogmatics have become almost a standard operating assumption in the field. To put it another way, it is clearer than before that although theology does seek after truth, and although it can and should seek to articulate such truth and to distinguish it from falsehood, theology is also always doing its work *in media res*, intervening in more or less provisional ways at particular moments in a much larger ongoing history of Christian discourse about God and the world, and indeed of God's ongoing relationship with the world.

Contemporary resistance to the quest for idealized methodological starting points is fed by a number of other sources as well. Over the past fifty years critical theorists have developed a variety of powerful tools for showing how claims to universality tend to mask problematic power dynamics. Another important factor, especially for theologians, has been the legacy of an explicitly postfoundational vein in postliberal theology, which learned from Thomas Kuhn and Ludwig Wittgenstein, among others, about the difficulties in making universal theological claims. As George Lindbeck has put it:

> The issue is not whether there are universal norms of reasonableness, but whether these can be formulated in some neutral, framework-independent language. Increasing awareness of how standards of rationality vary from field to field and age to age makes the discovery of such a language more and more unlikely and the possibility of foundational disciplines doubtful.[79]

The effect of these intellectual trajectories on the discipline as a whole has been a general lessening of the traditional concern to establish the foundations for theology in advance. Corresponding to this skepticism about foundations has been an increased emphasis on theology as a procedure of pragmatic redescription and "repair," and as a discourse taking place within the ongoing "drama" of Christian history in all its particularities rather than from a putative neutral point outside of that "drama."

---

[78] Ward, *How the Light Gets In*, p. 224.
[79] George A. Lindbeck, *The Nature of Doctrine: Religion and Theology in a Postliberal Age* (London: Westminster John Knox Press, 1984), p. 130.

For the purposes of this chapter, this matters because the recent alleviation of the pressure on theology to establish its universal validity from first principles means that there is now more room than before to take the many dimensions of human subjectivity seriously without having to turn them into theology's "starting point" or apologetic basis. And this is particularly true in relation to "experience." When theology views its first task as establishing "a sure and necessary correspondence to the Word of God" in light of the assaults of modernity, it is no surprise that "experience" has so often been seen to be problematic, as it is far too messy, strange, contingent, and complex a category to bear such a burden. By contrast, today there is finally breathing space to examine the wide variety of ways that theology engages with and is shaped by experience without the distorting pressure of having to establish the legitimacy of theology as a *Wissenschaft*. When the universalizing and apologetic burden is lifted, and we are free to observe the ways that "experience" actually has functioned and continues to function in theology without the stakes being so high, it soon becomes clear that theology has always done its work in engagement with "experience," both explicitly and implicitly, and regardless of whether or not it "should" have done so.

EXPERIENTIAL ARGUMENTS IN THE HISTORY OF THEOLOGY

The idea that theology has ever actually succeeded in bracketing the experience of the church and of the theologian from its engagement with divine truth does not bear scrutiny. To start with, there is the obvious fact that the Bible itself is in large part a record of God's people's experiences of him over time, such that all theology that builds on Scripture is a kind of reflection on a rich and complex deposit of experience.

But Scripture draws on experience in theological reflection in quite direct ways too—indeed, in just the sorts of ways someone like Barth would be so worried about in other contexts.

Even limiting ourselves to New Testament examples of explicit pneumatological significance, the evidence is very clear. Is the church at Jerusalem not making a dogmatic judgment derived from experience when it concludes from the fact of the descent of the Spirit on the Gentiles at Caesarea that "God has given even to the Gentiles the repentance that leads to life" (Acts 11:18)? Is Peter not engaging in a kind of dogmatic reasoning—what Barth himself defines as the testing of the proclamation of the church by the criterion of the Word of God—when he argues from these same events, "Can anyone withhold the water for baptizing these people who have received the Holy

Spirit just as we have" (Acts 10:47)? Are not the key theological data at the Council of Jerusalem two sets of religious experiences: first, the fact that God "testified to [the Gentiles] by giving them the Holy Spirit, just as he did to us" (Acts. 15:8), and second, Barnabas and Paul's account of "all the signs and wonders that God had done through them among the Gentiles," to which the "whole assembly" listened in "silence" (Acts 15:12)? Turning to St. Paul, does not Paul give the Galatians a detailed practical description of the differences between the fruit of the Spirit and the deeds of the flesh in order that they might examine their own lives in light of his description, and thus to engage in a theological reflection in which their experiences play a vital role? And finally, is Paul not drawing on religious experience to make a theological argument when he defends his account of the relationship between justification and the law by asking the Galatians, "Did you receive the Spirit by doing the works of the law or by believing what you heard? . . . Did you experience so much for nothing?" (Gal. 3:2, 4)[80]

The idea of testing examples like these in light of Barth's concerns about "modernistic theology" is not a serious one. There is no question at Caesarea, in Jerusalem, or in Galatia of theological systems, of philosophical "apologet-ics," or of dogmatic prolegomena. It is simply taken for granted in these apostolic cases, via a kind of ad hoc pneumatological wisdom, that certain kinds of experience of the Spirit are both legitimate and useful for making core theological judgments in certain circumstances. A world in which an experi-ence like the Spirit's descent on the Gentiles at Caesarea must be utterly excluded from the practice of dogmatic discernment is a post-Reformation, indeed a post-Kantian, world, not the world of the New Testament. And to a significant degree it is an early twentieth-century world from which theology has now moved on.

Appeal to religious experience to help address fundamental dogmatic ques-tions did not end with the closure of the canon. For example, Larry Hurtado has made a strong case that, in the context of Jewish monotheism, the rapid adoption among early Christians of the conviction that Jesus was divine is difficult to explain apart from experiences of the risen Christ as one worthy of worship in the early church.[81] Similar to this is the increasing consensus in

---

[80] And this is not yet to mention the Old Testament. What of the sustained attention to subjective experience in the Psalms, which Luther called a "school and training ground for the affections" (*Cum enim psalterium sit non nisi affectuum quedam palestra et exercitium*)? (*WA* 5:46/*LW* 14:310)? What of the constant calls in the Old Testament for God's people to remember their past experiences of him? One could list a wide range of relevant texts here, including Ex. 13:3; Deut. 5:15, 7:18, 15:15; 16:3; 24:18; Judges 8:34; 1 Chron. 16:12; Ps. 77:11, 105:5, 143:5; Is. 63:7, 11; and Lam. 1:7.

[81] According to Hurtado, "Christ-devotion" in the early church "quickly amounted to what may be regarded as an unparalleled innovation, a 'mutation' or new variant form of exclusivist monotheism in which a second figure (Jesus) was programmatically included with God in the devotional pattern of Christian groups . . . [T]he most plausible factor for this is the effect of

biblical studies that belief in the deity of the Holy Spirit—the conviction the Spirit is not just a divine force but is the Spirit of Christ and thus God himself—was the outcome of a process of reflection on the widespread phenomenon of early Christian ecstatic experiences attributed to the Spirit, and indeed that this process of reflection and pneumatological specification is already clearly underway in the letters of Paul and in the Johannine writings.[82] A few centuries later, Augustine's mature theology of grace developed in significant part out of "bitter experience" of the stubborn reality of "Christian mediocrity," as Brown and Markus have shown.[83] And we have seen a fourth, much later example of this dynamic in the role played by reflection on affective experience in Martin Luther's development of the Protestant doctrine of justification by faith. These are not peripheral or minor examples. Here we are talking about theological engagement with "experience" in the development of fundamental church dogma in respect of Christology, pneumatology, and the doctrine of the Trinity, at the foundation of Latin theological reflection on sin and grace, and in the core soteriological doctrine of the Protestant Reformation. To argue for the exclusion of experience from formal dogmatic reasoning is to whitewash the history of the church in the name of modern methodological anxieties.

Implicit Experience and the Affective Salience of Doctrines

Over the course of Christian history, theologians have drawn on "experience" in many other ways as well. One of the most consistent methods for doing this has been a very widespread practice in the history of theological discourse of incorporating arguments about what I have elsewhere called the "affective salience of doctrines" in defenses and explications of dogmatic positions.[84] What I mean by arguments about "affective salience" are theological arguments that focus on the practical emotional valence and the anticipated experiential impact of doctrines.[85]

powerful religious experiences in early Christian circles, experiences that struck the recipients . . . as having revelatory validity and force sufficient to demand such a significant reconfiguring of monotheistic practice." See Larry W. Hurtado, *Lord Jesus Christ: Devotion to Jesus in Earliest Christianity* (Grand Rapids, MI: William B. Eerdmans Publishing Company, 2003), pp. 64–5.

[82] See Chapter 2 for a more extended discussion of this development. Particularly notable figures here are Jörg Frey, Gordon Fee, and James Dunn. See also N.T. Wright, *Paul and the Faithfulness of God* (London: SPCK, 2013), pp. 709–28.

[83] Peter Brown, *Augustine of Hippo: A Biography*, 2nd ed. (Berkeley: University of California Press, 2000), pp. 141, 139–50; R.A Markus, "Augustine: a defence of Christian mediocrity," in *The End of Christianity* (Cambridge: Cambridge University Press, 1991).

[84] Zahl, "Affective Salience."

[85] For a related set of observations about how doctrines and practices shape subjectivity, see Ngong, *Theology as Construction of Piety*, pp. 1–20.

A typical example of this phenomenon can be found in the disagreement between John Calvin and the authors of the Decree on Justification at the Council of Trent on the issue of election and assurance. In his argument in favor of predestination in the *Institutes*, Calvin asserts from the start that the value of the doctrine is not least that through it we come to "sincerely feel how much we are obliged to God." He argues that the doctrine should bestow upon those who understand and believe it "firmness and confidence" and "free [dom] from all fear." By contrast, "all those who do not know that they are God's own will be miserable through constant fear."[86] In other words, Calvin believes we should agree with him on election not just because of exegetical-theological arguments about a text like Romans 8:29–30, but because it is only through correct understanding of this doctrine that a certain kind of fear of God can be correctly managed and dealt with.

The authors of the Decree on Justification at the Council of Trent, in turn, argue the opposite case, but they too do so in part on affective and experiential grounds. Critical of the "vain and ungodly confidence" they consider Protestant views of assurance to be seeking, they argue that it is in fact perfectly appropriate, in light of human weakness and the limits of human knowledge, for a Christian to experience a certain "fear and apprehension concerning his own grace."[87] Overconfidence, not fear, is the affective sin to be avoided. What matters for our purposes is that, despite their disagreement, both Calvin and the Tridentines, like many others after them, are explicitly concerned in their arguments with the experiential consequences of the doctrine of predestination as they perceive it. That is, they are attentive to the felt, emotional effects they expect belief in the doctrine to have in human lives, both positively and negatively, and in this they ground the effectiveness of their arguments to a significant degree in arguments about experience.[88]

Another example of theological appeal to the affective salience of doctrines can be found in Augustine's *Homilies on the First Epistle of John*. In the Sixth Homily, Augustine argues that a number of heretical groups who claim to

---

[86] John Calvin, *Institutes* 3.21.1 (John Calvin, *Institutes of the Christian Religion*, trans. Ford Lewis Battles (London: Westminster John Knox Press, 2006), p. 922).

[87] Schroeder, *Canons and Decrees*, p. 314 (Eng.: p. 35). Sixth Session, Chapter 9.

[88] In a similar vein, John Wesley devotes half of his influential refutation of the doctrine of predestination (the sermon "Free Grace") to arguments about affective salience. According to Wesley, belief in the doctrine of predestination "has a manifest tendency to destroy holiness . . . for it wholly takes away those first motives to follow after it, [namely] the hope of future reward and fear of punishment"; it "naturally tends to inspire or increase a sharpness or eagerness of temper which is quite contrary to the meekness of Christ"; it "destroy[s] the comfort of religion, the happiness of Christianity"; and finally those who "hold this doctrine" often experience "a return of doubt and fears concerning [their] election and perseverance." There could hardly be a clearer example of theological argumentation based on the affective salience of doctrines than what we find in Wesley here. See John Wesley, "Free Grace. Sermon 110, 1739," in *John Wesley's Sermons: An Anthology*, eds. Albert C. Outler and Richard P. Heitzenrater (Nashville, TN: Abingdon Press, 1991), pp. 52–3.

affirm the doctrine of the incarnation in fact deny it with their deeds, and these deeds (what he has in mind are their specific actions causing church division) are in turn a reflection of their affections.[89] In Augustine's view, to believe rightly in the incarnation is to be filled with the affection of love:

> [Christ] came in the flesh, therefore, in order to die for us. But how did he die for us? "Greater charity than this no one has, than to lay down his life for his friends" (Jn 15:13). It was charity, then, that led him to the flesh. *Whoever doesn't have charity, therefore, denies that Christ has come in the flesh* . . . You [heretics] don't have charity because . . . you cause divisions in unity . . . How do you not deny that Christ has come in the flesh, you who break up the Church of God that he gathered together?[90]

As in the sixteenth-century debate over predestination, what we find here is an explicit rhetorical concern with the affective and therefore experiential consequences of a particular doctrinal position, in this case to do with the incarnation. According to Augustine, a correct view of Christ's "coming in the flesh" will result in a love for God and neighbor that will promote and resource the unity of the church, and an incorrect view will accomplish the reverse. Indeed, for him, affectively sourced behavior is more trustworthy than mere verbal consent to a doctrine, because, regardless of what a person says verbally, where the affection of love is not present, the incarnation is denied: "The Spirit of God, then, is he who says that Jesus has come in the flesh, who says it . . . not with words but by loving."[91]

We will see many further historical examples of this mode of argument on the basis of affective salience over the course of this book. One particularly influential and compelling example—Philip Melanchthon's extended explication of justification by faith in terms of its power for "consoling terrified hearts"—lies at the heart of my account of salvation and the experience of grace in Chapters 3 and 4. What these arguments about "affective salience" have in common is that they take for granted the importance of what I have called implicit experiential factors in theological reasoning. That is, they operate and draw their power from the premise that the affective shape and texture and impact of a doctrine is a key component of what makes it

---

[89] *Ep. Io. tr.* 6.12 (*PL* 35:2027; *WSA* I/14:100–1).

[90] *Ep. Io. tr.* 6.13–14 (*PL* 35:2028–9; *WSA* I/14:102–3). Emphasis added.

[91] *Ep. Io. tr.* 6.13 (*PL* 35:2028; *WSA* I/14:102). Although the meaning of "charity" for Augustine in these sermons is complex—what he has in mind is as much an ethic and disposition in relation to neighbor and world as it is a simple emotion—it is a complexity that clearly includes a deep sense of charity's affective character. This is evident in *ep. Io. tr.* 9.4–5 and 10.7, where Augustine explicates the meaning of charity in terms of a direct affective counterpoint to fear and anger. For more on this argument in Augustine, see Robert Dodaro, "'Omnes haeretici negant Christum in carne uenisse' (Aug., *serm.* 183.9.13): Augustine on the Incarnation as Criterion for Orthodoxy," *Augustinian Studies* 38, no. 1 (2007), pp. 163–74. See also the discussion of love and delight in Augustine in Chapter 5.

persuasive or otherwise in a given case. In this they represent one of the core ways in which the "implicit" function of experience in theology has been taken seriously and brought to the surface in the history of theology.

THEOLOGY AS EMBODIED PRACTICE

It should come as no surprise that experience has in fact played an important role in the history of theological debate, regardless of whether or not it "should" have done so. Human beings are not just rational creatures—we are animals, not angels[92]—and, like most human ideas, religious beliefs both arise and play out in a complex entanglement of arguments, feelings, social contexts, and practices. As Barth himself acknowledges, human beings "[do] not exist abstractly but concretely, i.e., in experiences, in determinations of [their] existence by objects, by things outside [them] and distinct from [them]."[93] Indeed, a good deal of recent theology can be characterized as a series of explorations into the role of subjectivity and "implicit" experience in theological knowledge-production from different angles and using different methods.

As a number of scholars have recently observed, the claim that theological ideas are shaped by the contexts in which they arise in the world has implications that extend beyond questions about why we are interested in the ideas that interest us, or why we are drawn to some theological ideas and resist others. Context and experience shape theology right down to the physical act of theological knowledge-production. Linn Tonstad, for example, builds on Marcella Althaus-Reid to call for attention to the way that theological writing is inescapably a "bodied practice," producing

> discourses of abstraction laboriously handwritten or typed, perhaps with aching wrists and shoulders... seated somewhere or other... Is there perhaps a child wailing to be fed? A domestic worker in the background, freeing the writer for a few hours? Has one gone to a library or coffee shop or bar or park to escape, or to be in the company of strangers, as an antidote for loneliness?[94]

Attending to the bodied dimensions of scholarly knowledge-production in this way helps draw attention to physical, economic, social, and psychological

---

[92] On this point, see Donovan O. Schaefer, *Religious Affects: Animality, Evolution, and Power* (Durham, NC: Duke University Press, 2015), p. 12, and Manuel Vásquez, *More Than Belief: A Materialist Theory of Religion* (Oxford: Oxford University Press, 2011), p. 5.

[93] Barth, *CD I/1*, p. 198.

[94] Linn Marie Tonstad, *Queer Theology: Beyond Apologetics* (Eugene, OR: Cascade Books, 2018), pp. 74–5.

factors that are always present, affecting our experience of writing and think-ing and helping to shape our patterns of attention, but which often go unnoticed and unacknowledged.[95]

In *The Christian Imagination*, Willie Jennings has demonstrated a different and more troubling dimension of the impact of embodiment, and histories of embodiment, on Christian theology. Over the course of the book, he makes a powerful argument for the deep but underrecognized significance of space, location, and dislocation in the construction of Christian theological imagin-ations. He shows how the effects of displacement to the New World on African as well as European bodies came to be inscribed in theology, resulting in "an abiding mutilation of a Christian vision of creation and our own creatureli-ness."[96] He argues that the failure of European traditions of theological reasoning to "discern its new special situation" in the New World rendered such traditions implicitly docetic, denying materiality and embodiment with-out being fully aware of the fact.[97] Here not only bodies but places and geographies have powerful shaping effects on the practice of theology, on what it notices and attends to, and on what it fails to see.

In recent anglophone theology, the importance of embodied subjectivity for theology has also been emphasized from a different angle, by attending to the connection between theology and spirituality. Sarah Coakley, for example, opens the first volume of her systematic theology, *God, Sexuality, and the Self*, with the assertion that "the questions of right contemplation of God, right speech about God, and right ordering of desire all hang together," and goes on to foreground the importance of contemplative prayer for the practice of theology.[98] In a related key, Lewis Ayres has made a strong case that under-standing the doctrine of the Trinity is as much or more about "shaping structures of the Christian imagination and habits of Christian speech"[99] as it is about the degree of technical correctness of particular propositions about the Trinity. The implication, he argues, is that "good continuing articulation of pro-Nicene orthodoxy is likely to involve us in being able to perform [intel-lectual and spiritual] practices that are in a high degree of continuity with those that sustained its original expression."[100] For theologians like Coakley

---

[95] For related discussions, see Kimerer L. LaMothe, "What Bodies Know about Religion and the Study of It," *Journal of the American Academy of Religion* 76, no. 3 (2008), p. 589, and Donovan O. Schaefer, "Beautiful Facts: Science, Secularism, and Affect," in *Feeling Religion* (Durham, NC: Duke University Press, 2018).

[96] Willie James Jennings, *The Christian Imagination: Theology and the Origins of Race* (New Haven: Yale University Press, 2010), pp. 293. See also pp. 37–8.

[97] Jennings, *The Christian Imagination*, pp. 112–13.

[98] Coakley, *God, Sexuality, and the Self*, pp. 2, 18–26.

[99] Lewis Ayres, *Nicaea and its Legacy: An Approach to Fourth-Century Trinitarian Theology* (Oxford: Oxford University Press, 2004), p. 299.

[100] Ayres, *Nicaea and its Legacy*, p. 397.

and Ayres, the practice of theology is deeply entangled with the spiritual life of the theologian.[101]

Writing from a Pentecostal perspective, Daniel Castelo, too, emphasizes the irreducibility of the life of the theologian in the practice of theological reasoning. He points out that for early Pentecostals, "the theologian . . . had to be located within a broader context and reality" in which "the life of piety is the essential and orienting ground for one's work of theological reflection." Specifically, a theologian "would need to have, and work out of, a 'personal Pentecost' because such an experience opened up theological horizons."[102] This helps explain why narrative and personal testimony are crucial theological genres for Pentecostals. The result is that Pentecostal theology tends to be resistant to "abstraction and decontextualization," testing its insights in "life experience," and taking for granted, like Coakley and Ayres, that theology is "directly related to spirituality."[103]

My own contribution to this movement to acknowledge and take account of the irreducibility of subjectivity in theological reasoning will be through an extended focus on the affective dimensions of embodiment as they relate to the practice of theology as well as to Christian experience more generally. As I will show over the course of the book, attention to affect and desire illuminates the irreducibility as well as the constructive power of reflection on embodied subjectivity for traditional dogmatic reasoning, especially in relation to salvation and sanctification.

Psychological Science and Implicit Experience

Given the fact that theological reasoning and writing are embodied practices that draw upon and engage the subjectivity of the theologian at a range of levels, theology today can also learn from recent developments in the psychological and cognitive sciences, which have given intriguing evidence for a number of specific ways in which the processes by which we reason, including theologically, are complexly interwoven with affective factors in particular. These developments provide, at least in a suggestive way, a kind of empirical evidence for what George Eliot already knew: that theological ideas are always operating in an affective-experiential atmosphere, and that we underestimate these implicit forces at our peril.

---

[101] For recent work on the relationship between theology and prayer, in particular, see Andrew Prevot, *Thinking Prayer: Theology and Spirituality amid the Crises of Modernity* (Notre Dame: University of Notre Dame Press, 2015) and Ashley Cocksworth, "Theorizing the (Anglican) lex orandi: A Theological Account," *Modern Theology* (2019).

[102] Daniel Castelo, *Pentecostalism as a Christian Mystical Tradition* (Grand Rapids, MI: William B. Eerdmans Publishing Company, 2017), pp. 20–1.

[103] Castelo, *Pentecostalism as Mystical Tradition*, pp. 30–1.

One interesting example, which has robust empirical support, is the set of phenomena that cognitive scientists call "mood congruence." A series of studies since the 1980s have demonstrated significant correlations between our current mood and the types of information we attend to, the sorts of information and memories we find easiest to recall, and the way that we process information. Forgas and Eich define "mood congruent cognition" as the empirically supported "observation that a given mood promotes the processing of information that possesses similar affective tone or valence." "Mood-congruent information" appears to "receive greater attention and be processed more extensively than affectively neutral and incongruent information."[104] Thus when we are sad or depressed we attend relatively more closely to sad or depressing information, and when we are happy we do the reverse. Perhaps especially intriguing for scholars is the data that evidence this effect on the way that we read and process texts: "people spend longer reading mood-congruent material, linking it into a richer network of primed associations, and, as a result, they are better able to remember such information."[105] In other words, we process reading material better and find it more interesting if it contains information congruent with our current affective state.

This does not of course mean that mood simply explains what we believe, whether theologically or otherwise—not by any means. These phenomena are much more subtle than that, playing just one part in the highly complex processes involved in different kinds of cognition. Furthermore, it is also empirically clear that the mood congruence effect varies a great deal in intensity depending on the kinds of thinking involved.[106] But, at the very least, studies like these do seem to put the lie, in a quite direct empirical way, to the idea that theological judgments are simply objective or neutral relative to our experiences or affective states, and to indicate that the way we think, the way we process new information and recall old information, and even the way that we read texts is constantly being shaped in subtle but significant ways by

[104] J.P. Forgas and E. Eich, "Affective Influences on Cognition: Mood Congruence, Mood Dependence, and Mood Effects on Processing Strategies," in *Handbook of Psychology*, 2nd ed., iv, eds. Irving B. Weiner, Alice F. Healy, and Robert W. Proctor (Wiley, 2012), p. 65.

[105] Forgas and Eich, "Affective Influences on Cognition," p. 65. For more on this see G.H. Bower and J.P. Forgas, "Affect, memory, and social cognition," in *Cognition and Emotion*, eds. E. Eich, F. Kihlstrom, G.H. Bower, J.P. Forgas, and P.M. Niedenthal (New York: Oxford University Press, 2000).

[106] For example, mood effects appear to be strongest when "tasks require a high degree of open and constructive processing, such as inferences, associations, impression formation, and interpersonal behaviors," and are significantly diminished when subjects are made to be more consciously aware of their internal state (Forgas and Eich, "Affective Influences on Cognition," p. 63). See also L. Berkowitz, S. Jaffee, E. Jo, and B.T. Troccoli, "On the correction of feeling-induced judgmental biases," in *Feeling and Thinking: The Role of Affect in Social Cognition*, ed. J.P. Forgas (Cambridge: Cambridge University Press, 2000).

the affective states we happen to be in.[107] In the terms of this book, "mood congruence" represents one small and suggestive example of how experiential factors—in this case, our moods—have at least some effect on our theological thinking whether we like it or not. To return to *Janet's Repentance*, phenomena like "mood congruence" are beginning to shed empirical light on what Eliot already knew: namely, that Janet Dempster's openness to theological persuasion cannot be fully disconnected from the complex psychological state in which she found herself as a result of the breakdown of her marriage.

Another set of examples has arisen in the field of the psychology of emotion, where the line traditionally drawn between "reason" and "emotion" has been profoundly blurred. As will be examined further in Chapter 3, there is wide agreement today among psychologists as well as empirically engaged philosophers of emotion that emotions are helpfully understood to differ from mood states above all insofar as they "involve cognitive appraisal as a defining feature,"[108] and thus possess an inherent "intentionality."[109] Unlike either moods or the continuous affective hum of human experience that psychologists call "core affect," emotions are "intentionally directed" at specific cognitive "objects, events, or states of affairs."[110] Thus a feeling of anger is always elicited in part through a set of cognitive judgments—for example that we have been wronged or mistreated in some way—and a feeling of religious anxiety can come about only in complex interaction with a set of beliefs about, say, sin or God's impending judgment. What this means is that emotion is always bound up in complex ways with cognitive judgments.

Sarah Coakley has noted quite rightly that such research has "yielded remarkably interesting challenges to the idea that reason and emotion can be regarded as an oppositional binary," and that these challenges are of "great intrinsic interest for theology."[111] For example, earlier we saw Charles Chauncy's argument against George Whitefield that revivalist theologies are to be rejected as irrational because they appeal to nothing more than a

---

[107] A related phenomenon is "mood-dependent memory," which is the observation that "information encoded in a particular mood is most retrievable in that mood, irrespective of the information's affective valence" (Forgas and Eich, "Affective Influences on Cognition," p. 61). In other words, when we are happy we remember information we learned when we are happy, even if what we learned was about sad things. Even our basic procedures of recalling information are affected by the mood we are in.

[108] Panteleimon Ekkekasis, *The Measurement of Affect, Mood, and Emotion: A Guide for Health-Behavioral Research* (Cambridge: Cambridge University Press, 2013), p. 41.

[109] See J.A. Russell and L. Feldman Barrett, "Core affect, prototypical emotional episodes, and other things called emotion: dissecting the elephant," *Journal of Personality and Social Psychology* 76 (1999), p. 806; and Ekkekasis, *Measurement of Affect*, p. 41.

[110] Julien A. Deonna and Fabrice Teroni, *The Emotions: A Philosophical Introduction* (London: Routledge, 2012), pp. 4–5.

[111] Sarah Coakley, "Introduction: Faith, Rationality and the Passions," *Modern Theology* 27, no. 2 (2011), p. 219.

"Commotion of the Passions." Viewed in light of contemporary cognitive science, Chauncy's argument is significantly weakened, since it is based on a perceived contrast between reason and emotion that in turn depends on a mistaken understanding of how both "rational" cognition and affective experience seem to work. In fact, given the complex inseparability of cognition and emotion, it would appear that most forms of theological reasoning are implicitly "experiential" in some minimal sense, in that the influence of mood states and affective factors on such reasoning cannot be avoided, at least not in any direct way.

That said, we should resist the temptation to take this point too far. Regardless of the irreducibility of such affective and experiential factors in any actual process of human reasoning, recent empirical psychology is also very clear that the relative importance of affective states on the cognitive conclusions we draw, and vice versa, varies a great deal depending on the kinds of cognition involved and the nature of the object of our reasoning. In particular, some emotions are much more cognitively complex than others: a feeling of fear that is the outcome of a cognitive judgment that a scary bear is attacking you is much less cognitively sophisticated than, say, an affective state of guilt and anxiety before God, which involves a host of more complex judgments about God's existence, about a moral standard that has been violated, about anticipation of a future judgment, and so on.[112] Likewise, research shows that some affective states actually reduce the phenomenon of mood congruence substantially (anxious people, for example, are less likely to demonstrate mood congruent effects[113]), while other states, like depression, seem to amplify them.

Certainly, the conclusions that we draw on the basis of cognitive processes in many cases can be shown to possess an objective force that is independent of the process by which such reasoning took place. Two plus two does equal four regardless of whether we are happy or depressed when we come to that conclusion. At the same time, most theological judgments are not of this kind, and do manifest the sort of complexity and appeal to an "open, constructive style of information processing"[114] that makes them likely to be implicated in phenomena like mood congruence. Theology does not do its work in a vacuum, but is engaged in an enormously complex process that integrates,

---

[112] On the special complexities of religious emotion, see Chapters 13 and 17 in Raymond F. Paloutzian and Crystal L. Park, eds. *Handbook of the Psychology of Religion and Spirituality*, 2nd ed. (London: The Guilford Press, 2013).

[113] See Forgas and Eich, "Affective Influences on Cognition," p. 65; M. Burke and A.M. Matthews, "Autobiographical memory and clinical anxiety," *Cognition and Emotion* 6 (1992); and J.V. Ciarrochi and J.P. Forgas, "On being tense yet tolerant: The paradoxical effect of trait anxiety and aversive mood on intergroup judgments," *Group Dynamics: Theory, Research, and Practice* 3 (1999).

[114] Forgas and Eich, "Affective Influences on Cognition," p. 64.

for example, hermeneutical judgments from Scripture or tradition, the wide-ranging implications of doctrinal claims like the two natures of Christ or the doctrine of creation from nothing, logical arguments about coherence and the connections between doctrines, concerns over the practical implications of a given doctrine for the life of the church, and, not least, the personal history and social embeddedness of the theologian, which determines to a very significant degree which sort of arguments or positions a given theologian or community of theologians believe to be most worthy of attention, repair, explication, attack, or support.

CONCLUSION

It is important to be clear at this stage what I am and what I am not arguing in relation to the importance of experience for theology. In the second half of this chapter I have been drawing attention to the ways that theology has, historically, been closely attuned to experience: in reflecting theologically upon experiences Christians have in the life of the church, in being attentive to the experiential implications of particular doctrinal positions, and in showing how intellectual reflection, including the forms of cognition involved in making theological arguments, is a "bodied" practice complexly interwoven with materiality in general and with affectivity in particular. In doing so, I am not arguing that "experience" should be privileged over other factors in any straightforward sense, or that there is no such thing as truth that exists independently of our experience. Attending to experiential factors does not mean that the theologian should not at the same time remain deeply attentive to reason, to tradition, to arguments from Scripture, and so on; indeed, much of what I have been saying about "implicit" experiential factors in human reasoning could as easily be labeled a thick description of reasoning as it is a form of "experience." What I am simply trying to show is that, unless we choose to define theology in such a way that it has no formal connection to actual processes of theological reasoning as they occur in bodies and in time, experiential factors not only should not but actually *cannot* be ignored. In other words, my purpose has not been to locate theology's "starting point" once again in experience and feeling, but instead to observe and explicate certain irreducible features of how theology actually functions in the world, and to argue that to exclude or excise these factors artificially is to work with an impoverished, ill-informed, and historically blinkered theological vision. That such attention can be constructively valuable, helping to advance our thinking in a number areas of major theological interest, will be demonstrated in the chapters below on the work of the Spirit in salvation and sanctification.

Before we can begin to make such arguments, however, the question now becomes: how exactly are we to go about taking this irreducibility of "experience" seriously in theology while avoiding the pitfalls rightly pointed out by Luther and Barth? My answer, which will be elaborated in Chapter 2, is that we must begin by defining "experience" in a particular sort of way. To do this theologically we must turn to the doctrine of the Holy Spirit as it has taken shape both in Scripture and in later Christian theological tradition.

2

Experiencing the Spirit

Almost wherever one starts, the discussion of Christian experience leads without much delay to some question about the Spirit of God.

—C.F.D. Moule[1]

In the previous chapter, I examined some of the main ways that theologians have understood the relationship between theology and "experience." I made a preliminary distinction between two different roles that experience can play in theology: the *formal* function of experience in theological reasoning, which refers to the explicit procedure of appealing to a particular kind of experience to prove a theological point; and the *implicit* function of experience in theological reasoning, which refers to the fact that our reception and inter-pretation of theological ideas, and whether or not we find them compelling, is affected in non-trivial ways by the affective texture and atmosphere in which we encounter them, by our personal history and temperament, by our physical and social environment, and even by our mood. I then identified a number of reasons why contemporary Christian theology stands in need of renewed attention to "experience," and showed how in the modern era a great deal of theological reflection on the topic has been caught up in a false choice between making "experience" into the ground and foundation of dogmatics and excluding it from theology entirely.

In light of these preliminary observations, how might we go about thinking through and repairing theology's relationship with "experience"? To answer this question, the task of the present chapter will be to determine more precisely what we mean when we use the term "experience" in relation to theology. In doing so, I take my cue from C.F.D. Moule's observation above about the close connection between questions of Christian experience and questions about the Holy Spirit. In what follows, I will argue that "religious experience" needs to be interpreted through the theological framework of pneumatology, and will demonstrate that theological accounts of the work of the Holy Spirit that cannot do justice to experiences of the Spirit that

---

[1] C.F.D. Moule, *The Holy Spirit* (London: Continuum, 2000), p. 7.

The Holy Spirit and Christian Experience. Simeon Zahl, Oxford University Press (2020). © Simeon Zahl.
DOI: 10.1093/oso/9780198827788.001.0001

are "practically recognizable" in bodies and in time are pneumatologically problematic.

One powerful approach to the question of how to understand Christian experience of God has come from the field of the study of religion. Since the publication of William James' seminal work on religion, *The Varieties of Religious Experience*, a great deal of intellectual energy has gone into the question of whether there can be said to be a discrete class of human experience that can usefully be identified as "religious experience" and thus distinguished from other, "non-religious" dimensions of human experience in the world.[2] The belief that there is indeed such a class of human experience and that it can be identified across cultures and across religious traditions is classically associated with the work of William James and Rudolf Otto in the early decades of the twentieth century. For James, although religious experience can be usefully discussed under a number of different topics and themes—for example, saintliness, conversion, or the experience of the "divided self"—its most interesting and meaningful form is "mystical." As he puts it, "personal religious experience has its root and centre in mystical states of consciousness." Furthermore, this "everlasting and triumphant mystical tradition" is a kind of human universal, "hardly altered by clime or creed," that can be located in "Hinduism, in Neoplatonism, in Sufism, in Christian mysticism, in Whitmanism," and so on.[3]

In Otto, the same point is made even more starkly: "If there be any single domain of human experience that presents us with something unmistakably specific and unique, peculiar to itself, assuredly it is that of the religious life."[4] Otto then identifies such religious experience as encounter with what he calls "the numinous": religious experience is a "state of mind" characterized by feelings like "awefulness," "overpoweringness," and "urgency," which "is perfectly *sui generis* and irreducible to any other."[5] Despite important differences between them, for both James and Otto such "mystical" or "numinous" experiences represent, in a minimal way, something universal about what it means to be human, because they occur across cultures and religions,[6] and appear to be tantalizing clues to deeper and more fundamental realities beyond the world of the mundane.[7]

---

[2] For an overview of the history of this debate in the discipline of religious studies, see Ann Taves, *Religious Experience Reconsidered: A Building-Block Approach to the Study of Religion and Other Special Things* (Princeton, NJ: Princeton University Press, 2009), pp. 3–12.

[3] William James, *The Varieties of Religious Experience* (New York: The Library of America, 1987), pp. 342, 378.

[4] Rudolf Otto, *The Idea of the Holy: An Inquiry into the Non-Rational Factor in the Idea of the Divine and Its Relation to the Rational*, trans. John W. Harvey (Oxford: Oxford University Press, 1950), p. 7.

[5] Otto, *The Idea of the Holy*, p. 7.

[6] As Otto says of "the numinous," "there is no religion in which it does not live as the real innermost core" (Otto, *The Idea of the Holy*, p. 6).

[7] James, *Varieties*, p. 385.

After a long period of influence, this tradition of analysis of "religious experience" fell under sustained criticism starting in the 1970s. A major shot across the bow came from Wayne Proudfoot, who argued in his book *Religious Experience* that the concept of "religious experience" at work in James and Otto has its roots in Friedrich Schleiermacher's theological appeal to religious feeling, and that this appeal is not critically "neutral" but was in fact developed for "apologetic purposes," as a "powerful protective strategy" for defending the claims of Christian theology against "critical inquiry from outside the religious life."[8]

The force of Proudfoot's argument is that Schleiermacher and those who came after him were naïve about the ways that all "experiences," religious and otherwise, are not just influenced by the language and concepts used to express them, but are fundamentally *constituted* by such language. That is, they failed to understand that there is no such thing as an "immediate" or "pure" religious feeling that precedes the concepts and beliefs we use to make sense of the experience. Rather, "such moments of experience are clearly dependent on the availability of particular concepts, beliefs, and practices."[9]

As a critique of an account of "mystical" or "numinous" experience as a human universal, this argument is a powerful one. Here we must distinguish between a weak version of Proudfoot's argument—the basic observation that religious experiences never exist in a "pure" state but are always shaped to some degree by the concepts and beliefs through which they are experienced and communicated—and the stronger version for which Proudfoot actually argues, whereby concepts and other signs actually constitute the experiences all the way down. In its strong form, the argument has many problems and is no longer tenable.[10] In its weak form, however, Proodfoot's insight has rightly

---

[8] Wayne Proudfoot, *Religious Experience* (University of California Press: Berkeley, 1985), p. xvi.

[9] Proudfoot, *Religious Experience*, pp. xv–xvi; see also especially pp. 63, 107, and 219. For a more recent "socio-rhetorical" version of this constructivist argument, see Russell T. McCutcheon, "Introduction," in *Religious Experience: A Reader*, ed. Leslie Dorrough Smith, Craig Martin, and Russell T. McCutcheon (Bristol, CT: Equinox, 2012), pp. 8–16.

[10] First, Proudfoot's account of religious experience depends very substantially on a set of experiments by psychologist Stanley Schachter in the 1960s that appeared to indicate that emotion is almost entirely constructed by the cognitive and conceptual "labels" we apply to states of physiological arousal (Proudfoot, *Religious Experience*, pp. 75–118, 218–21). Schachter's experiments, though influential, have never been replicated, and his radically constructivist account of emotion—upon which Proudfoot builds his radically constructivist account of religious experience—has not been taken seriously by psychologists for several decades (see Elaine Fox, *Emotion Science: Cognitive and Neuroscientific Approaches to Understanding Human Emotions* (New York: Palgrave Macmillan, 2008), pp. 150–1).

Second, the rhetorical force of Proudfoot's approach depends at key points upon a straw man conception of how "religious experience" actually functions in theological discourse. Proudfoot, like Scharf, McCutcheon, and to some degree Taves, assumes that any time a person attempts to draw upon claims to religious experience for theological purposes, they must be doing so for "apologetic" reasons (see Proudfoot, *Religious Experience*, pp. ix, xv, xvi, 2, 228, 229; for similar

been accepted quite widely by Christian theologians over the past forty years, though more through the influence of George Lindbeck than of Proudfoot directly.[11] For the purposes of the present inquiry, the lesson to be learned here is that we will not get much grip on the kinds of "experiences" that Christians understand to be encounters with God unless we do so in the context of the specific linguistic and theological matrix that helps shape such experience for Christians—in this case, that of pneumatology.

Despite the efforts of Proudfoot and others, the approach to religious experience from the perspective of religious studies continues to be influenced by Otto and especially James in other ways. One dimension of James' approach that appears to be alive and well in religious studies is his emphasis on *extreme* forms of "experience." Following a path set much earlier by Christian "anti-enthusiasts," who were especially troubled by the more unusual and bizarre features of eighteenth- and nineteenth-century revivalist spirituality,[12] James argued that we come closer to the "essence" of what is distinct about religious experience the more we focus on "those religious experiences which are most one-sided, exaggerated, and intense."[13]

arguments see Robert H. Scharf, "Experience," in *Critical Terms for Religious Studies*, ed. Mark C. Taylor (Chicago: The University of Chicago Press, 1998), p. 104; and McCutcheon, "Introduction," pp. 9–12). In other words, it is assumed that such experiences are of interest for theological inquiry only insofar as they can be seen as providing intellectual justification for the validity of religious belief in the face of critical and scientific inquiry.

Certainly something like this was true for a figure like Wilhelm Hermann in the late nineteenth century, and no doubt Rudolf Otto, too, was motivated to some degree by what Taves calls "a tacitly theological agenda of a liberal ecumenical sort" (Taves, *Religious Experience Reconsidered*, p. 3). But to characterize even Schleiermacher in this way is deeply misleading. Proudfoot and others do not seem to have taken on board the fact that Schleiermacher explicitly denied that his account of the feeling of absolute dependence was intended as a proof for the existence of God (*contra* Proudfoot's characterization of it as "a transcendental version of the cosmological argument" (Proudfoot, *Religious Experience*, p. 19)), or indeed the fact that his concept of dogmatics in the *Glaubenslehre* excludes any such apologetic argument at the outset ("But the view increasingly emerges that I wanted, as it is usually put, to demonstrate Christianity a priori . . . [This view] insufficiently distinguish[es] between the intent of the Introduction and that of dogmatics . . . [The method of the Introduction] does not provide anyone with a foundation" (Schleiermacher, *On the Glaubenslehre*, pp. 41–2)). Furthermore, Proudfoot and others also do not seem to be aware that, thanks to Barth, theologians have generally been deeply wary of both "experience" and apologetics for nearly a century (see Chapter 1).

Finally, it should be noted that the linguistic account of religion associated with Jonathan Z. Smith, whose basic premise Proudfoot and McCutcheon take for granted, is currently sinking under heavy fire in the field of religious studies, from the direction of affect theory as well as the "material turn" in religious studies. See especially Schaefer, *Religious Affects*, and Vásquez, *More Than Belief*. For further discussion of affect theory see Chapter 4.

[11] So Lindbeck: "We cannot identify, describe, or recognize experience qua experience without the use of signs and symbols . . . In short, it is necessary to have the means for expressing an experience in order to have it" (Lindbeck, *Nature of Doctrine*, pp. 36–7; see also pp. 17–18, 32–41). Lindbeck refers to Proudfoot's work in n. 31 on p. 29.

[12] See Zahl, "Experience," pp. 189–92.   [13] James, *Varieties*, p. 48.

Although there is some value in this approach, in the long run it can lead to an emphasis on the bizarre and the unusual in religious behavior at the expense of understanding the more mundane ways that "religious experience" actually functions in the lives of many religious practitioners. This is the major failing, for example, in Ann Taves' study of religious experience "from Wesley to James," *Fits, Trances, and Visions*, which focuses on "uncontrolled bodily movements," "spontaneous vocalizations," "unusual sensory experiences," and "alterations of consciousness."[14] In focusing her attention on these rather extreme forms of spirituality, which have rarely been viewed as normative even within heavily "experiential" Christian revivalist traditions and which even John Wesley believed to be adiaphora, Taves' narrative about religious experience has relatively little to say about more commonplace dimensions of "experience" like the kindling of feelings of love and joy, or spiritualities of day-to-day divine guidance.[15] Here again we see the importance of drawing our account of "experience" from the linguistic and conceptual resources of the tradition that shapes it rather than trying to examine it from an ostensibly external vantage point.

My proposal is that the question of "experience of God" in Christian theology is best addressed not via a general category of "religious experience," but by starting with Christian theology's own internal set of categories for addressing the theme. Christian theology has always been deeply interested in the question of experience of God, and it possesses a powerful set of resources for engaging with it. Above all, Christian theology tends to specify "religious experience" pneumatologically. That is, it holds that experience of God is to be understood and described first and foremost as experience of God the Holy Spirit.

There are a number of reasons for this traditional theological association between pneumatology and "experience," as will become clear over the course of this chapter. Perhaps most important is the fact that there is a strong tendency in the New Testament to associate experience of God in general with experience of God the Spirit in particular. The result has been a long-standing theological association of the "presence" of God in the lives of Christians with the presence of the Holy Spirit, and it is on this tradition that I will be building in what follows.

Specifying Christian "religious experience" as experience of the Holy Spirit has substantial ramifications for how experience of God is to be understood. Importantly, this specification means that, contra James and Otto, such experience is not finally a singular, unified phenomenon, and that, contra Taves, it hardly reduces to more obviously extraordinary dimensions of

---

[14] Ann Taves, *Fits, Trances, and Visions: Experiencing Religion and Explaining Experience from Wesley to James* (Princeton, NJ: Princeton University Press, 1999), p. 3.

[15] Taves, *Fits, Trances, and Visions*, p. 3.

religious life like "fits, trances, and visions." Rather, according to both biblical witness and theological tradition, there are a wide variety of facets and dimensions of experience of God's Spirit. The basic Christian language and grammar of experience of the Spirit is irreducibly pluriform and particular, encompassing not only the dramatic and episodic (e.g., conversion experiences), but also the Spirit's involvement in longer term affective-dispositional change (for example, the kindling of the affections and dispositions that St. Paul calls the "fruit of the Spirit"), as well as specific, less easily categorizable instances of guidance, gifting, calling, and healing. This variety of pneumatological encounter, in turn, implies that in order to engage with the topic of "experience" in a theological way we must do so through a set of extended engagements with the particular areas in which Christian theology specifies that the work of the Spirit is experienced. In this book, I will be focusing on the pneumatology of salvation and sanctification in particular.

THE SPIRIT, THE PRESENCE OF GOD

In focusing on the theme of Christian experience, the account of the Holy Spirit that follows can be located in a tradition of what have been called "pneumatologies of presence."[16] To a significant degree, the question of Christian experience of God is the question of God's presence as it is perceived in human lives in various forms and under various conditions and with various effects. The question of divine "presence," in turn, is closely related to the perennial theological and pastoral problem for Christians of how to understand the connection between eternal divine realities and the daily lives of particular individuals and communities in particular times and places.

This question of "presence" can arise from a number of different directions. One angle has to do with the fact that God is unseen. What does it mean to speak of a person's perception of the presence of God if that presence is invisible, cannot finally be tested, measured, or proven, and tends to elude attempts to pin it down or to generate experience of it on command? The Johannine author twice reminds us that "no one has ever seen God" (John 1:18; 1 John 4:12), and the apostle Paul urges us to remember that Christians "walk by faith, not by sight" (2 Cor. 5:7). And yet, even apart from Jesus's incarnate history, God is constantly described in Scripture as speaking directly to individuals, as kindling desires and affections, and as breaking into specific human situations and stories and causing transformative experiences of disruption, guidance, indwelling, and healing.

---

[16] Eugene F. Rogers, *After the Spirit: A Constructive Pneumatology from Resources outside the Modern West* (Grand Rapids, MI: William B. Eerdmans Publishing Company, 2005), p. 6.

Perhaps the most fundamental form of the question, however, is christo-logical: how does the life, death, and resurrection of Jesus of Nazareth in a small province of the Roman Empire 2,000 years ago relate to a life lived today? How is Gotthold Lessing's "broad, ugly ditch" between the recorded experiences of people one has never met and their contemporary moral force to be bridged, and how does what Jesus said and did then have any meaning for people in the contemporary world, living as we do in vastly different contexts and circumstances?

In an influential 1927 essay, Adolf von Harnack observed that Jesus's statement, "I am with you always, to the end of the age" (Matt. 28:20), raises with some urgency the question of *how* exactly Jesus is "with" us. In von Harnack's account, the early church's initial answer to the question was to identify its own experiences of the Holy Spirit since Pentecost as in some sense experiences of the presence of the risen Christ (what he dubbed the *Christus praesens*).[17] Thus, according to von Harnack, for early Christians perception of the presence of God rapidly became inseparable from the perception of the presence of Christ in experiences of the Holy Spirit.

The essential accuracy of von Harnack's basic observation has been borne out by more recent biblical scholarship on the pneumatology of the New Testament, in which a series of parallels between the ongoing presence and activity of Christ in the church and experiences of the Holy Spirit have been identified. Jörg Frey, for example, observes a gradual movement in Paul's thought towards the view that "Christ himself is present and effective in the Spirit and through the Spirit."[18] He cites a variety of evidence. Perhaps most important, in Frey's view, are the series of passages

> in which the work of the Spirit is set in an analogy with the work of the exalted Christ: God has sent the Spirit (Gal 4:6) as he also sent his Son (Gal 4:4). The Spirit indwells believers (Rom 8:9, 11) as does Christ (Rom 8:10; Gal 2:22). The Spirit intercedes for those who believe and pray in God's realm, as does the exalted Christ (Rom 8:34; cf. 1 John 2:1). It is striking that Paul articulates these parallels in relatively narrow textual units (esp. Gal 4 and Rom 8). This means that the correspondences are not accidental but programmatic.[19]

Frey is not alone in making this observation. James Dunn writes that passages like these in Romans and Galatians show that "Paul intended to represent the risen Christ as in some sense . . . becoming identified with the life-giving Spirit

---

[17] Adolf von Harnack, "Christus praesens - Vicarius Christi," in *Kleine Schriften zur Alten Kirche: Berliner Akademieschriften 1908–1930* (Leipzig: Zentralantiquariat der Deutschen Demokratischen Republik, 1980), p. 772.

[18] Jörg Frey, "How did the Spirit become a Person?," in *The Holy Spirit, Inspiration, and the Cultures of Antiquity: Multidisciplinary Perspectives*, eds. Jörg Frey and John R. Levison (Berlin: De Gruyter, 2014), p. 359.

[19] Frey, "How did the Spirit become a Person?," p. 359. For further examples see pp. 360–1.

of God."[20] Indeed, in Dunn's view this "redefinition, or tighter definition, of *the Spirit as the Spirit of Christ*... constitutes one of Paul's most important contributions to biblical theology."[21] Michael Wolter, likewise, asserts that "God's Spirit [for Paul] is the manner and method of the presence [*Anwesenheit*] of the transcendent God in the world and among human beings. Through his Spirit, God is experienced as present [*gegenwärtig*] and active in the world of human beings."[22] Eduard Schweizer makes the same point in a classic extended article on the meaning of *pneuma* in the New Testament,[23] and C.F.D. Moule agrees that "it is fair to say of the New Testament generally, that, even where 'Spirit' means no more than simply 'God present in and among his people', this is a presence conditioned by... the presence of the risen Christ."[24] And all of this is not yet to mention the close relationship in John's Gospel between Jesus and the Spirit who is sent in his place.

To make these observations is by no means say all that needs to be said about the relationship between Christ and the Spirit in New Testament pneumatology. For present purposes the above is intended simply to demonstrate that, as von Harnack observed, there is a very close connection in New Testament thought between three themes: the presence of God in general, the presence of the risen Christ among Christians, and early Christian experiences of the Holy Spirit. It is because of this connection that theologians like Rogers speak about "pneumatologies of presence," and it is because of this network of associations that Christian religious experience has long tended to be understood in primarily pneumatological terms. When we speak of God being made known in the experiences of his people, the natural mode of speech is that of pneumatology.

Influenced by von Harnack's essay, as well as by the New Testament, it has been common in theology in recent decades to understand the work of the Holy Spirit in terms of the mediation of divine "presence." Gerhard Sauter, for example, has described the Holy Spirit as "the structure or form by which the chronologically and spatially distant God [is] mediated across time and space. Thus the Spirit [is] as it were the bridge-principle of the distant God, the medium of his becoming present" and "the presence of God in his activity."[25] Khaled Anatolios has made the same argument from an explicitly trinitarian

---

[20] Dunn, *Theology of Paul the Apostle*, p. 262.

[21] Dunn, *Theology of Paul the Apostle*, p. 433. Emphasis original.

[22] Michael Wolter, "Der heilige Geist bei Paulus," *Jahrbuch für Biblische Theologie* 24 (2009), p. 95.

[23] Eduard Schweizer, "*pneuma, pneumatikos*," in *Theological Dictionary of the New Testament*, vi, ed. Gerhard Kittel and Gerhard Friedrich (Grand Rapids, MI: William B. Eerdmans Publishing Company, 1964), pp. 433–4.

[24] Moule, *The Holy Spirit*, pp. 38–9.

[25] Gerhard Sauter, "Geist und Freiheit. Geistvorstellungen und die Erwartung des Geistes," *Evangelische Theologie* 41 (1981), p. 215. Following this, Sauter calls the Spirit "God's becoming present" [*Das Gegenwärtig-Werden Gottes*].

direction: "The distinct role of the Spirit [is as] the one in whom the outward manifestation of the activity of the Father and the Son *is actualized in relation to us*... [The Spirit is] the point of contact between God and Creation."[26] Similar observations can also be found in Wolfhart Pannenberg ("The Holy Spirit is the medium of the immediacy of individual Christians to God"[27]), in H.J. Krauss (the Holy Spirit is "the confronting event of the efficacious presence of God"[28]), in Jürgen Moltmann (the Spirit is "a mode of [God's] presence in his creation and in human history"[29]), and in Maurice Wiles ("God as Spirit is God as present"[30]), amongst others.

But describing a crucial aspect of the Spirit's work as a "bridge-principle" and as "the medium of [God's] becoming present" is still rather vague. "Present" in what way, we might ask, and to whom, and for what purposes and with what effects? In a move that, as we have seen, can be traced back directly to the apostle Paul, theologians from a variety of confessional traditions have gone a step further by expressing the point about the Spirit's mediation of God's presence in specifically christological terms. Ernst Käsemann, for example, argues in a Johannine mode that "Jesus must always become newly present. This happens in the coming of the Paraclete."[31] Yves Congar agrees: "The Spirit makes it possible for us to know, recognize and experience Christ. This is not simply a doctrinal statement. It is an existential reality which comes from a gift and involves us in our lives."[32] The same point can be found in Jüngel ("in the Holy Spirit the absent Christ is present"[33]), Pannenberg ("it is always by the Spirit alone that the spiritual reality of the risen Lord is present to believers"[34]), Hendry ("in the experience of the Church the presence of the Holy Spirit was known, not as an alternative to, but as a mode of, the presence of the living Christ"[35]) and

---

[26] Khaled Anatolios, *Retrieving Nicaea: The Development and Meaning of Trinitarian Doctrine* (Grand Rapids, MI: Baker Academic, 2011), p. 142. Emphasis added.

[27] Wolfhart Pannenberg, *Systematic Theology*, iii, trans. Geoffrey W. Bromiley (London: T&T Clark International, 2004), p. 134.

[28] Hans-Joachim Kraus, *Systematische Theologie im Kontext biblischer Geschichte und Eschatologie* (Neukirchen-Vluyn: Neukirchener Verlag, 1983), p. 449.

[29] Jürgen Moltmann, *The Spirit of Life: A Universal Affirmation*, trans. Margaret Kohl (London: SMC Press, 1992), p. 11.

[30] Maurice Wiles, *Faith and the Mystery of God* (Philadelphia: Fortress Press, 1982), p. 123.

[31] Ernst Käsemann, "Geist und Geistesgaben im NT," in *Religion in Geschichte und Gegenwart*, 3. auflage, ii, ed. Kurt Galling (Tübingen: J.C.B. Mohr, 1958), p. 1278.

[32] Yves Congar, *I Believe in the Holy Spirit*, i: *The Holy Spirit in the 'Economy'* (New York: The Crossroad Publishing Company, 1983), p. 37.

[33] Eberhard Jüngel, "Zur Lehre vom heiligen Geist: Thesen," in *Die Mitte des Neuen Testaments: Einheit und Vielfalt neutestamentlicher Theologie*, ed. Ulrich Luz and Hans Weder (Göttingen: Vandenhoeck & Ruprecht, 1983), p. 108.

[34] Pannenberg, *Systematic Theology 3*, p. 321.

[35] George S. Hendry, *The Holy Spirit in Christian Theology* (London: SCM Press, 1957), p. 41.

Torrance ("through the Spirit . . . Christ himself returns to be present among us"[36]), amongst others.

For theologians from across a number of Christians traditions then, "the Spirit" has come to be understood as the best word for the agency that mediates the presence of God to human beings by establishing the connection between the risen Jesus and the faith and experience of Christians. In making such claims, theologians are formalizing and building upon a major theme in the pneumatology of the New Testament.

Understanding the Holy Spirit initially in terms of the mediation of divine presence raises further questions. Above all, what do we actually mean when we say that God, even God in Christ, is "present" through the Spirit? How is such presence experienced? In the quotations above, the concept of "presence" is employed for the most part in a curiously abstract way. "Presence" seems to be used simply as a solution to a logical or conceptual problem: that of a metaphysical gap between God and humanity and a related chronological-historical gap between the Jesus of history and the faith of contemporary Christians.

Criticizing this tendency, Eugene Rogers has asserted that "accounts of the Spirit that start with presence are boring, and fail to portray the Spirit with much distinctiveness."[37] The Spirit's role in such accounts seems to be simply to fill a perceived space rather than to display a distinctive identity, and this lack of specificity creates a danger that such pneumatologies will either collapse back into Christology or else revert to the sort of generic ideas about "religious experience" that we find in James and Otto. I will return to Rogers later in the chapter, but the main counterargument to his critique can already be stated: boring or not, the reason that so many pneumatologies begin with the question of "presence" is *scriptural*. Such approaches to the Holy Spirit have been found compelling by so many theologians not just because they solve an apparent logical problem, but because they also have strong foundations in the New Testament, especially in Pauline and Johannine pneumatology.

Nevertheless, Rogers is right to be worried about the potential flatness and contentlessness of the concept of "presence." In particular, pneumatologies of presence are prone to three basic problems. The first is vagueness. Often, the question of what an encounter with such presence is actually like—what we might call the phenomenology of experiences of divine presence—is simply not addressed, and the concept of "presence" becomes a theological abstraction that does not necessarily map onto any concrete experience or set of experiences that Christians actually seem to have. The second problem is an extension of the first: in their vagueness, theologies of presence tend to fail to address adequately the possibility of false claims about God's presence. That

---

[36] Thomas F. Torrance, "Come, Creator Spirit, for the Renewal of Worship and Witness," in *Theology in Reconstruction* (Eugene, OR: Wipf and Stock, 1996), p. 253.

[37] Rogers, *After the Spirit*, p. 6.

is, they do not engage sufficiently with the question of pneumatological discernment that is so important in both Pauline and Johannine theologies of the presence of the Spirit. The third problem is the one that seems to worry Rogers the most. It is that pneumatologies of presence risk failing to demarcate adequately the trinitarian distinctiveness of the Spirit, resulting in a collapse of the Holy Spirit back into Christology, or else leaving both Christology and pneumatology prone to annexation by an insufficiently trinitarian concept of the divine unity.

An instructive and influential example of each these dangers can be found in one of the most important works on the Holy Spirit in the past half century: Geoffrey Lampe's 1976 Bampton Lectures, published under the title *God as Spirit*. As probably the most robust and creative modern pneumatology to take its starting point from the categories of "experience" and "presence," this work is worth engaging in some detail. Doing so will further illustrate some of the most important potential weaknesses of experiential approaches to the Holy Spirit, and will thus help in mapping out some of the key obstacles to be navigated and pitfalls to be avoided in the approach to the Holy Spirit and Christian experience being put forward in this book.

CHALLENGES FOR PNEUMATOLOGIES OF "PRESENCE"

In *God as Spirit*, Geoffrey Lampe argues in favor of a deeply experiential interpretation of the theological term "Spirit." According to Lampe, "Spirit" is not "analytically descriptive of the structure of deity itself."[38] Rather, it should be understood as the most important in a series of biblical "bridge" terms whose "primary purpose is to describe a human experience: the experience of encounter with God."[39] Lampe further notes the "radical reinterpretation" that the Old Testament understanding of the term "Spirit" received in the New Testament: particularly in the thought of Paul and John, Lampe argues, "God's active presence in and with human beings was now understood in terms of Christ," such that the "central conviction of New Testament Christianity" became the view that "the phrases 'God as Spirit' and 'presence of Christ' are two alternative and interchangeable forms of words referring to the same experienced reality."[40] Thus, "the Spirit," for Lampe, is nothing more or less than "the mode in which Christ becomes present to believers."[41]

---

[38] Geoffrey Lampe, *God as Spirit: The Bampton Lectures 1976* (Oxford: Oxford University Press, 1977), p. 37.
[39] Lampe, *God as Spirit*, p. 36.   [40] Lampe, *God as Spirit*, p. 62.
[41] Lampe, *God as Spirit*, p. 145.

There are two major problems with Lampe's approach, each of which is representative of wider potential problems with pneumatologies of presence. The first follows from the fact that Lampe's understanding of experience as encounter with "the personal active presence of God" is still very general. Even if such "experience" is further specified as experience of Christ's presence, what are the particular contours of such experience? What is it like to have such "experiences," and what are their features? Here Lampe is more vague:

> [T]he answer to the question, "What reality is indicated by the analogy of 'Spirit'?" [is], "God: God experienced as inspiring, motivating, empowering, vivifying, indwelling, and acting in many ways which are difficult to analyse and describe in any precise fashion, but which are inherent in authentic human experience and are recognized by faith as modes of the personal active presence of God."[42]

Although Lampe's list of descriptors here is clearly derived from biblical pneumatology, his account of experience leaves crucial questions unanswered. Most importantly, what is it that actually constitutes the "authentic human experience" to which he refers? Can a person be "inauthentically" empowered, motivated, or inspired? And how exactly does "faith," as he puts it, "recognize" this personal presence of God, as distinct from human experience in which God is not present in this way? What are the conditions or criteria by which to "recognize" "authentic" divine presence? In short, Lampe gives us no clear guidance on how we are to discern true encounter with the Spirit from false. In its vagueness, Lampe's line of thinking gives us little purchase on the theologically and pastorally vital question of discernment of the Spirit.

The problem of discernment is not a small one, especially when it is viewed with an eye on the history of pneumatology. As we saw in Chapter 1, anxiety about the difficulties and dangers involved in discerning the activity of the Spirit directly from the raw material of human experience has led some of Christianity's most influential theologians to conclude that any starting point, like Lampe's, that draws conclusions about the nature of God from human claims to experience of God must be profoundly mistaken. T.F. Torrance has articulated a strong version of this view: according to Torrance, theologians should have "nothing to do with any attempt to reach an understanding of the Spirit beginning from manifestations or operations of the Spirit in creaturely existence, in man or in the world."[43]

A milder version of this claim can also be found in Rogers' *After the Spirit.* In his decision to sidestep questions of pneumatological "presence" in favor of questions of pneumatological "identity," Rogers states that he is following the

---

[42] Lampe, *God as Spirit*, p. 42.

[43] Thomas F. Torrance, *The Trinitarian Faith: The Evangelical Theology of the Ancient Catholic Church* (London: T&T Clark, 1997), p. 201.

path set out by Hans Frei, who "learned from Barth to be suspicious of nineteenth century theological subjectivism." In Rogers' account, the nineteenth century longed "for Jesus to be present to consciousness," and in this longing "theology made itself susceptible to Feuerbach's critique, and Jesus became a creature of human manipulation."[44] Although Rogers' phrasing indicates that his exposition is still caught in the long-standing Protestant false dichotomy on subjectivity and experience that was exposed and found wanting in Chapter 1—the idea that theology must either view experience as its foundation, or else avoid engaging with it at all—the suspicion of "subjectivism" is still a position with which any "experiential" theology must reckon. To take Luther and Barth's worries about idolatry and self-deception seriously in our theology of experience, we must do more than Lampe to address the problem of discernment. From the perspective of the history of pneumatology, in failing to provide an answer to the long-standing Protestant question about discernment and *Schwärmerei*, and in his related unwillingness to give further specifics about the nature of such "experience," Lampe's experiential approach would appear to fall at the first hurdle.

Another major problem with Lampe's approach is its metaphysical reductionism. According to Lampe, "'Spirit' properly refers, not to God's essence but to his activity."[45] Here he is taking a perfectly good insight about the importance of understanding the phenomenon of experience of God in pneumatological terms and bending it into a reductive and exclusionary principle. It is one thing to say that the most appropriate term for speaking of God as experienced by human creatures or as present to human creatures is the term "Spirit"—as we have seen, this approach has a long pedigree in Christian theology, and some form of this statement cannot really be avoided—but it is quite another to argue, as Lampe does, that this statement encompasses *all* that can and should be said about God's Spirit.

Lampe does not hesitate to draw the radical conclusions of his reductionist logic for the doctrine of the Trinity. As he puts it, "this 'Christ' is not other than the Spirit. The single reality for which these two terms stand is the one God in his relation to human persons."[46] The consequence, Lampe believes, is that "the Trinitarian model is in the end less satisfactory for the articulations of our basic Christian experience than the unifying concept of God as Spirit."[47] For Lampe, then, the doctrine of the Trinity is basically a mistake: the term "Spirit" is not "analytically descriptive of the structure of deity itself,"[48] and this means that the third person of the Trinity does not actually "exist" as such. The traditional Christian concept of the Spirit's eternal divine personhood is

---

[44] Rogers, *After the Spirit*, p. 5.
[45] Lampe, *God as Spirit*, p. 17.
[46] Lampe, *God as Spirit*, p. 118.
[47] Lampe, *God as Spirit*, p. 228.
[48] Lampe, *God as Spirit*, p. 37.

nothing more than a false hypostasization of human experience of God's presence in the world.

Lampe's reductionist argument is subject to criticism on two main fronts. The first has to do with the historical story he tells about the development of the doctrines of the personhood and deity of the Spirit, on which his rejection of trinitarian doctrine in part depends. In Lampe's account, these developments are to be understood entirely as late, patristic phenomena that have far more to do with safeguarding certain christological conclusions than they do with the actual pneumatology of the New Testament: "The emergence of the ultimate general consensus that the Holy Spirit is both a subsistent being and also fully divine was slow and uncertain . . . The disclosure of the Spirit's deity is . . . post-scriptural."[49]

It has become increasingly evident in scholarship on the pneumatology of the early church that Lampe's position is at best a drastic oversimplification. In a major recent study, "How did the Spirit become a person?," Jörg Frey has shown that, quite apart from the well-known smattering of proto-trinitarian statements in the New Testament such as the baptismal formula in Matthew 28:19, the most important conceptual building blocks for later understandings of the deity of the Spirit can be found already in the writings of Paul. As Frey explains, in Paul a "hitherto broad and 'somewhat nebulous concept' of the Spirit of God" is gradually clarified "through the novel understanding of the Spirit as being 'related to Christ.'" It is this christological clarification that then begins to provide "a functional criterion" for Paul to distinguish between the Christian Holy Spirit and other spirits.[50] This in turn spurs Paul gradually to develop "a view of the Spirit as a personal hypostasis"[51] such that the Spirit is "no longer simply an impersonal divine power,"[52] as often seems to be the case in the Synoptic Gospels. Frey then notes the further developments that take place in the Johannine writings. Unlike in Paul, where a gradual development as well as a certain degree of continuing ambiguity is discernible, in Johannine theology the Holy Spirit is a "predominantly personal figure" from start to finish.[53] It is ultimately "the Johannine statements on the Spirit [that] provide the most important Scriptural basis for the later view of the Spirit as a divine person in specific correlation with, and distinction from, the Father and the Son."[54] Frey concludes:

> The development towards the personality of the Spirit constitutes one of the decisive Christian developments . . . The personhood of the Spirit is the main aspect in which the Christian concept of the Holy Spirit differs from its biblical

[49] Lampe, *God as Spirit*, p. 217.   [50] Frey, "How did the Spirit become a Person?," p. 360.
[51] Frey, "How did the Spirit become a Person?," p. 358.
[52] Frey, "How did the Spirit become a Person?," p. 361.
[53] Frey, "How did the Spirit become a Person?," p. 368.
[54] Frey, "How did the Spirit become a Person?," p. 370.

and Jewish roots as well as from its Greco-Roman contexts, and it was predominantly triggered by the [Pauline and Johannine] correlation of the Spirit with the exalted Christ.[55]

If Frey is correct,[56] then Lampe's narrative requires substantial qualification. Certainly it is true that a full-fledged doctrine of the Spirit's deity as part of a triune Godhead did not exist in a mature form until the fourth century. But it is equally true that the most important conceptual building blocks of such a view—the use of personalist language to identify the Spirit as a relational agent rather than just as a power or a substance, and the increasing willingness to identify the Spirit with Christ while simultaneously maintaining a distinction between them—are already present at key points in the New Testament, at the very least in parts of Paul and in the Johannine writings. In light of this, Lampe's revisionist attempt to locate such developments entirely in the exigencies of later patristic theology rather than in the scriptural texts themselves, and his corresponding assertion that "the disclosure of the Spirit's deity is . . . post-scriptural," are weakened to the point of collapse, and his anti-trinitarian pneumatological reductionism loses one of its major supports.[57]

The second problem with Lampe's reduction of the Spirit to nothing more than a term for describing human experience of God in Christ is that he fails to take into account one of the most important features of the classical doctrine of the Trinity: the principle of the inseparability of the trinitarian operations. This traditional principle holds that the "external operations of the Trinity are indivisible" (*opera trinitatis ad extra indivisa sunt*), such that no external work of the Trinity in the economy is the work of one person alone. Related to this is the traditional doctrine of trinitarian "appropriations," which asserts that the undivided work of the Trinity in the economy can legitimately be ascribed to one particular person, for example on scriptural grounds, without denying the involvement of the other persons. Together these principles resource a very strong conception of the unity of the Trinity's work in the world.[58] In practice, this means that although Scripture and tradition do tend to associate certain activities with specific persons—the claim that it is the Spirit who sanctifies, for example, or that it is the Son who redeems—it is a mistake to try to identify the ultimate intratrinitarian distinctiveness of the persons through analysis of these general semantic associations. Technically speaking, it is not incorrect to say that the Son sanctifies or that the Spirit redeems.

---

[55] Frey, "How did the Spirit become a Person?," p. 371.

[56] His position appears to represent a growing consensus. See e.g., Wright, *Paul and the Faithfulness of God*, pp. 709–28; and Wolter, "Der heilige Geist bei Paulus," pp. 108–11.

[57] For further discussion, see Ayres, *Nicaea and its Legacy*, pp. 211–18.

[58] For an overview of these themes in "pro-Nicene" theology, see Ayres, *Nicaea and its Legacy*, pp. 297–300.

In Lampe's interpretation, the New Testament writers' established willingness at various points to elide Spirit-language and Christ-language should be taken as evidence that there is in fact no meaningful metaphysical distinction to be made between the two; both are simply different ways of speaking about the same unified divine reality. As Lampe puts it, "in Christian experience" we have to do "not [with] an experience of Christ being presented to us by, or through, another divine agency, but a single experience which can be described interchangeably in 'Christ' terms or 'Spirit' terms."[59]

A clue to Lampe's failure to take the inseparability of operations into account is the phrase "another divine agency." This choice of words indicates that Lampe views the doctrine of the Trinity he understands himself to be rejecting in terms of three separate divine agents acting in distinct but complementary ways, rather than as one divine agency manifested in three "persons." As Ayres has shown, this view of the Trinity is an historical and theological mistake. Summarizing the thrust of classical "pro-Nicene" trinitarian theology, Ayres explains that the doctrine of inseparable operations means that "if we were to imagine God as three potentially separable agents or three 'centres of consciousness' the contents of whose 'minds' were distinct," as Lampe appears to, "pro-Nicenes would see us as drawing inappropriate analogies between God and created realities and in serious heresy."[60] In light of this, the "problem" that Lampe identifies of a certain scriptural overlap and elision between Christ-language and Spirit-language in relation to human experience of God is not a problem for trinitarian theology at all. Such overlap is in fact fully consistent with traditional doctrines of appropriation and of the inseparability of the trinitarian operations, and can be interpreted equally well as a clear illustration of the trinitarian principle that "where Scripture attributes a work to one person all are involved."[61]

The examination of Lampe has allowed us to observe some of the principal dangers that can arise from pneumatologies that take "experience" and "presence" as their starting point: the tendency towards vagueness, which makes the concept of "presence" difficult to correlate with concrete human experiences in the world; the way that such approaches raise important questions about self-deception and about discernment between true and false experiences of the Spirit but fail to answer them clearly; and the difficulty that pneumatologies of presence have in articulating an adequately distinctive trinitarian vision of the Spirit's identity. The issue of discernment of the Spirit is a significant one. It is the primary theme of my previous monograph, where I deployed a pneumatological reading of Luther's theology of the cross as a framework for discernment that was simultaneously

---

[59] Lampe, *God as Spirit*, p. 117.   [60] Ayres, *Nicaea and its Legacy*, pp. 296–7.
[61] Ayres, *Nicaea and its Legacy*, p. 298.

experiential and critical.[62] A key task in the remainder of this chapter will be to provide a preliminary consideration of the other two issues: the problems of vagueness and of trinitarian distinctiveness. The initial answer to both will be to pay careful attention to the distinctive contours of experience of the Holy Spirit as it appears in the complex and multifaceted pneumatology we find in the Bible, above all in the New Testament.[63] This in turn will require a closer definition of "experience" and will indicate the key topics requiring extended consideration in the remaining chapters of this book.

Before turning to key areas in which the Holy Spirit is understood to be "experienced" in Scripture, it is necessary to explicate in more detail how doing this will help to answer the problems of vagueness and of trinitarian distinctiveness just described. The first point is the most obvious: the tendency towards vagueness in general accounts of experience of the presence of God through the Spirit, like Lampe's, cannot be sustained when compared with the wide variety of ways in which the Spirit is described as having effects on human lives in the New Testament. In acknowledging the pluriformity of tasks and experiences associated with the presence and activity of the Holy Spirit in the New Testament, and focusing on the particular experiences involved with salvation and sanctification, the account that follows will make significant headway towards addressing the problem of vagueness often found in pneumatologies of presence.

The problem of how to approach the trinitarian distinctiveness of the Spirit in the context of a pneumatology of presence is more complex. At its foundation is the difficult question of the relationship between Christ and the Spirit. This is because the vast majority of New Testament texts that express interest in the relation between the Spirit and the other divine persons refer more specifically to the relation between the second and third persons. And yet, as we have seen, one of the distinctive themes in many of these very texts is their willingness to attribute the same activities at times to Christ and at times to the Spirit (Gal. 4:4 and 4:6; Rom. 8:9–11; Luke 12:12 and 21:15), or else, in a more Johannine mode, to describe the ministry of the former as being carried on and expanded by the latter in the period after the ascension (John 14:16, 14:25–26, 16:7, 16:12–15).

---

[62] See Zahl, *Pneumatology and Theology of the Cross*, as well as Simeon Zahl, "Rethinking 'Enthusiasm': Christoph Blumhardt on the Discernment of the Spirit," *International Journal of Systematic Theology* 12, no. 3 (2010). The set of descriptions of key sites and contours of the work of the Spirit in salvation and sanctification that I give in Chapters 3, 4, and 5 below can be read as complementing and extending my earlier work on pneumatological discernment.

[63] For reflections on the question of pneumatological continuity and discontinuity between the Old and New Testaments, see John R. Levison, *Filled with the Spirit:* (Grand Rapids, MI: William B. Eerdmans Publishing Company, 2009), especially pp. 236–52; Frey, "How did the Spirit become a Person?," especially pp. 343–4, 369; and R. Kendall Soulen, *The Divine Names(s) and the Holy Trinity: Distinguishing the Voices* (Louisville, KY: Westminster John Knox Press, 2011), pp. 233–52.

From the perspective of trinitarian theology, texts like these appear to entail at minimum (i) a complex affirmation of simultaneous identity and distinction between Christ and the Spirit and (ii) an immediate chastening of even this paradoxical affirmation in light of the inseparability of operations and the doctrine of appropriations. This difficulty, which pertains to any robust attempt to establish the trinitarian distinctiveness of the Spirit in light of the issue of divine presence, has been summarized by Ralph del Colle:

> How to distinguish Christ and the Spirit in any aspects of presence . . . is problematic especially if we hold to the unity of the divine operation *ad extra*. Is the distinction between the *Christus praesens* and the *Spiritus praesens* anything beyond a nominal predication on the part of the theologian? If not, can we seriously hold to the hypostatic differentiation of the trinitarian persons in the realm of Christian practice, or simply consign such distinctions to an unrelated speculative theological enterprise?[64]

One way forward in light of the dilemma del Colle articulates is indicated by Ayres. Ayres draws on an extended analysis of the "pro-Nicene" fathers to articulate the following principle:

> Learning to speak of Father, Son, and Spirit as inseparably operating while still affirming that any one of the divine persons is not the other two, and that each possesses the fullness of the Godhead, does not so much lead us to an easy imagining of their diversity and unity as it defers our comprehension and draws our minds to the constantly failing (even as constantly growing), character of our interpretation of what is held in faith. The development of such attention to the mysteries of divine triunity is, ideally, the shaping of an ongoing process of analogical judgment, a process in which we learn to display a balance between admitting human inability to comprehend the divine and appropriately exploring the providentially ordered resources of the language of faith.[65]

Ayres' statement has two important implications. The first is that his close reading of fourth-century theologies of the Trinity does seem to confirm that any attempt to come up with some principle or set of principles that will allow an "easy imagining" of the diversity and unity of Spirit and Son is likely to be misguided in the sense that, even when done "well," such imaginings remain constantly subject to a kind of apophatic chastening.[66] The second is that reflection on the doctrine of the Trinity is more usefully framed as a kind of anagogic practice or spiritual pedagogy than as a neutral rational procedure of more or less accurate speculation into the nature of the Godhead. In other words, because of both the nature of the subject matter and the sheer difficulty

---

[64] Ralph del Colle, *Christ and the Spirit: Spirit-Christology in Trinitarian Perspective* (Oxford: Oxford University Press, 1994), p. 174.

[65] Ayres, *Nicaea and its Legacy*, p. 297.   [66] Ayres, *Nicaea and its Legacy*, p. 300.

of the problem, reflection on the Trinity is inseparable from the spiritual life and practice of the theologian doing the reflecting, and what is taking place in such inquiry is most fundamentally a "shaping [of the] structures of Christian imagination and habits of Christian speech."[67]

Importantly, the grammar and vocabulary of this trinitarian spiritual pedagogy—what Ayres calls "the providentially ordered resources of the language of faith"—is first and foremost that of Scripture itself. Following Gregory of Nyssa, Ayres indicates that the most meaningful way forward for trinitarian reasoning, such as it is, will be a procedure of

> inculcat[ing] a practice of speaking with Scripture, being attentive to where and how Scripture speaks and trying to mirror that speech in our own ... We speak with Scripture when we deploy scriptural titles and analogies in the light of Scripture's own dynamic of revealing and drawing.[68]

What this means for our purposes is that the path towards a better understanding of the trinitarian distinctiveness of the Spirit—at least so far as such a thing is to be attempted given the fact that the subject matter here is at the same time fundamentally "beyond our epistemic grasp"[69]—is to pay sustained attention to Scripture's own language, narratives, and claims about the Spirit's work. Rather than viewing Scripture's Spirit-language as a problem to be solved or a code to be cracked in light of a prior model of the Trinity, we should approach it instead as an opportunity to be shaped by Scripture's own patterns of speech and silence, concealing and revealing. In other words, good trinitarian theology should send us back to Scripture in all its particularities rather than away from Scripture and into a type of speculation untethered from close engagement with Scripture.

A good example of a recent pneumatology that takes Ayres' observations seriously is Rogers' *After the Spirit*. Taking as his starting point Hans Frei's approach to Christology, which seeks to explore the identity of the Son through a focus on scriptural narrative,[70] Rogers applies the Frei approach to trinitarian theology in general and to pneumatology in particular. The procedure, as Rogers explains, "is not so much to eschew [trinitarian] speculation (even ontological speculation, if ontology is at root a reflection on the conditions implied in a story) as to site it differently, in a narrative, scriptural place."[71]

On its own terms, *After the Spirit* is quite persuasive, and the attention I will pay throughout this book to the close relationship between the Holy Spirit and

---

[67] Ayres, *Nicaea and its Legacy*, p. 299.　　[68] Ayres, *Nicaea and its Legacy*, p. 298.

[69] Ayres, *Nicaea and its Legacy*, p. 300. On this point, see also Karen Kilby, "Is an Apophatic Trinitarianism Possible?," *International Journal of Systematic Theology* 12, no. 1 (2010).

[70] Hans Frei, *The Identity of Jesus Christ* (Eugene, OR: Wipf and Stock, 1997).

[71] Rogers, *After the Spirit*, p. 13.

bodies bears its influence. But Rogers' approach also indicates some of the significant limits involved in pneumatologies that focus first and foremost on the trinitarian *identity* of the Spirit rather than on my own theme of the experienced *presence* of the Spirit. In particular, Rogers' focus on the identity of the Spirit limits rather severely the range of pneumatological texts on which he is able to draw. For all the importance of the narrative events of annunciation, baptism, transfiguration, and resurrection, which are his focus, New Testament interest in the Spirit is by no means limited to these events. For example, it is very striking that two of the most important texts in the history of Christian pneumatology, Romans 5:5 ("God's love has been poured into our hearts through the Holy Spirit that has been given to us") and Galatians 5:16–25 (on living by the Spirit and the fruit of the Spirit) are not cited once in *After the Spirit*.

The reason Rogers does not engage with texts like these is that they do not meet his stated criterion of focusing on the Spirit's scripturally narrated interactions with the Son. In his view such texts are by definition unable, on the basis of the inseparability of operations, to tell us anything about the Spirit's distinctive trinitarian identity. But if Ayres' approach above is correct, an important part of understanding the identity of the persons of the Trinity is being attentive to and allowing oneself to be shaped by the full range of scriptural testimony about each divine person, not just the texts that speak more or less directly to the issue of the intra-trinitarian relations. According to Ayres, we learn about the Spirit by attending to how Scripture itself speaks of the Spirit, including in texts that focus on what the Spirit "does" to and for human beings rather than just on the question of who the Spirit is or how the Spirit relates to the Father and the Son. And Scripture itself does not seem to be particularly preoccupied in its pneumatology with trinitarian questions, at least not explicitly.[72] The New Testament authors as a whole are substantially more interested in the particular effects the Spirit has on human beings in the world, especially in salvation, in sanctification, and in mission. Given this, an excellent and not at all non-trinitarian way to be drawn into this rather different strand of biblical material is by inquiring into the activities of the Spirit that have strong experiential dimensions. Such an approach will not exhaust what can and should be said about the Spirit, any more than Rogers' approach does. What it will do instead is illuminate the further, equally important set of dynamics within Christian pneumatology that are our focus here: those that relate to Christian *experience* of God the Holy Spirit.

---

[72] By contrast, the Gospel of John, in particular, devotes substantial space to the question of the relation of the Father to the Son.

TOWARDS A PRACTICAL DEFINITION OF "EXPERIENCE OF THE SPIRIT"

At this stage in my inquiry into Christian religious experience three points have been established: first, that Christian theology specifies such experience above all pneumatologically, as experience of the Holy Spirit; second, that to ask how the Spirit is experienced is to a significant degree to ask how God revealed in Christ is "present" to Christians; and third, that the first step towards giving concrete specificity to this question and towards avoiding some of the main problems often exhibited by pneumatologies of presence is to explore the particular contours of such experience in the early church as described in the New Testament. In moving forward with this latter step, however, we are faced once again with the thorny problem of what we mean when we talk about "experience." If what we need to do next is to identify key varieties of experience of the Spirit in the New Testament, we must first have a clearer idea of what we mean by "experience."

A few possibilities can be ruled out immediately. First, to speak about "experience of the Holy Spirit" is to talk about something much more specific than the more general concept of "experience" that was at work in early modern philosophy. Philosophers like John Locke and Immanuel Kant were intensely interested in the topic of "experience," but for them the category was first and foremost an epistemological one, and their focus was on the possibilities and limits of "experience" as a source of knowledge, encompassing both the direct "experience" of the world via the senses and the mental procedures by which sensations are transmuted in the mind into knowledge.[73] Experience of the Spirit, by contrast, is much more specific than this: its remit is limited in the first instance to human encounter with God rather than human encounter with the world in general. Experience of the Spirit is by definition *religious* experience.

However, at the start of the chapter I also argued that a general concept of "religious experience" is equally inadequate for Christian theological purposes. The range of experiences that Christian tradition has associated with encounter with the Holy Spirit, and the internal Christian theological language and grammar for describing such experiences, is too pluriform and too particular to be encompassed by, or to be seen as ultimately deriving from, a singular phenomenon of "mystical" or "numinous" experience such as we find in William James or Rudolf Otto. At best such approaches can account only for the more dramatic, episodic, and individualistic dimensions of experience of the Spirit.

---

[73] See Martin Jay, *Songs of Experience: Modern American and European Variations on a Universal Theme* (Berkeley: University of California Press, 2005), pp. 28–77.

At the same time, it would be equally unhelpful simply to equate all descriptions of the activity of the Spirit upon Christians that we find in the New Testament and in later Christian theology with concrete Christian experiences in the world. A number of the most important works of the Spirit in relation to human beings are not obviously or straightforwardly "experiential." Many scriptural texts about the Holy Spirit that have shaped later theological tradition appear to blur the line between concrete experiences, on the one hand, and theological-metaphysical truths independent of experience, on the other.

An important example of this blurring is the attribution of the Spirit's agency to the process of transformation before God described in 2 Corinthians 3:18: "And all of us, with unveiled faces, seeing the glory of the Lord as in a mirror, are being transformed into the same image from one degree of glory to another; for this comes from the Lord, the Spirit." The burden of this deeply pneumatological passage appears first and foremost to be to describe a kind of ontological transformation taking place in human beings before God rather than in the world. Although it is certainly possible to draw connections between this general transformation or glorification and more concrete descriptions of Christian sanctification—for example, as a process of receiving new Christ-shaped affections, desires, and ethical dispositions from the Spirit—it would be a mistake to *reduce* the meaning of this Pauline text to a particular set of "experiences" in time or to specific perceptible changes in the affective and ethical lives of Christians.

Given these limits, in what follows I will define "experiential" scriptural texts as those which refer to activities of the Spirit that are *practically recognizable* in the lives of Christians and of Christian communities. This approach will be central to the broader sense in which "experience" is employed throughout this book, where it will be used to illuminate key issues to do with the Spirit's work in salvation and sanctification, so it is important at this stage to explain more closely what I mean by "practical recognizability."

Experience and the Problem of Theological Abstraction

Reflecting on the very wide variety of ways in which the term "experience" can be understood, Martin Jay has observed that "Rather than foundational or immediate, 'experience' itself [often proves to be] only a function of the counter-concepts that are posed against it in a discursive field."[74] A glance at the history of theological use of the term "experience" bears out the truth of

---

[74] Jay, *Songs of Experience*, p. 6.

this observation. So, for example, to understand what many pietists have meant in appealing to something called "immediate experience" of the Spirit, we have to understand the conception of mediation of the Spirit through the Bible and through the church with which such experiences were understood to contrast;[75] likewise, to understand Schleiermacher's use of the experiential term "Feeling" in the *Glaubenslehre* we need to bear in mind the contrast he understood to obtain between "Feeling," on the one hand, and "Knowing" and "Doing," on the other.[76]

In light of this principle, it is useful to ask what "counter-concepts" are at work in respect of my desire to focus on experiences of the Spirit that are "practically recognizable." We have already seen one important counter-concept—the early twentieth-century definitions of "religious experience" as a singular and individualistic human phenomenon identifiable across religious traditions. But the most important "counter-concept" to which my approach provides a corrective builds on the observations that I have been making about overly vague concepts of pneumatological presence. Perhaps the chief contemporary theological target in this book is a certain kind of *complacency with theological abstraction* that is often apparent in discussions of the Spirit, and indeed in doctrinal and dogmatic statements more generally. That is, my emphasis on the category of "practical recognizability" is intended to help correct or recalibrate a theological tendency to make general, often metaphysical, claims about the work of the Spirit in relation to human beings that stop short of specifying the specific practical implications of those claims and thus seal themselves off from the actual work of the Spirit in bodies and in the world. These statements require some explication.

In drawing attention to these problems I am following a path blazed in part by Karl Rahner. In two significant essays on religious experience Rahner observed that in neo-scholastic theology it was far easier to talk about the salvific effects of grace from the perspective of what he called the realm of "purely ontological reality" than it was to talk about the experience of grace in the more concrete and historical "realm of human consciousness."[77] He observed that we seem to know a great deal about what grace "does" to the soul and before God, but very little about what it does to the embodied human being in time, and he argued that this gap represents a significant problem.

---

[75] For examples and discussion of this phenomenon, see Zahl, *Pneumatology and Theology of the Cross*, pp. 87–93.

[76] Friedrich Schleiermacher, *The Christian Faith: A New Translation and Critical Edition*, trans. Terrence N. Tice, Catherine L. Kelsey, and Edwina Lawler (Louisville, KY: Westminster John Knox Press, 2016), pp. 8–18 (§3).

[77] Karl Rahner, "Religious Enthusiasm and the Experience of Grace," in *Theological Investigations, xvi: Experience of the Spirit: Source of Theology* (London: Darton, Longman, and Todd, 1979), p 37, pp. 35–51.

Rahner summarized his point with a question: "Have we ever actually experienced grace?"[78]

The more widely you read in modern theology, the more you notice that Rahner's question has purchase far beyond neo-scholasticism. Over and over, at just the point when you expect some attempt at a description of the experiential dimensions of the Spirit's work in, for example, salvation or sanctification, theologians make a kind of swerve into non-experiential, usually metaphysical, language. Instead of talking, as the New Testament so often does, about the effects of the Spirit's work on real bodies in time, theologians revert instead to ontological language about union with Christ, about salvific participation in the Godhead, or about deification and *theosis*. Through these strategies, the concrete historical experience of the Christian in the world quietly slides out of view. Such experience remains present in these cases only implicitly, in that presumably these concepts and images do at some point acquire existential purchase, but how exactly this happens the theologian does not say. At best, the "concrete" side of salvific experience gets swallowed up in the sheer bald fact of participation in baptism and the eucharist, regardless of how such participation "feels."

A good example of what I mean about making a swerve away from experience in favor of ontological categories can be found in T.F. Torrance's *The Trinitarian Faith*. Early in the volume, in answer to the question, what does the Spirit do in salvation, Torrance makes the following assertion:

> [W]e must regard the activity of the Holy Spirit as actualising our union and communion with God through Christ in the actual structure of our human, personal and social being.[79]

On its own terms, there initially appears to be little to object to in this claim. Torrance is expressing a theologically traditional, scripturally warranted view of the Spirit's work in unifying believers with Christ, and then asserting that this union will have concrete ("actual") implications in their lives. His claim furthermore fits well within the larger project, exemplified in *The Trinitarian Faith*, of recovering patristic language to deepen, enrich, and expand contemporary Protestant reflection on the doctrine of the Trinity. From the perspective of the argument of the present book, the problem here is not the content of the claim but the fact that Torrance then stops short of specifying what such changes to the "actual structure of our human, personal and social being" might look like *in practice*. Taken in isolation, language about the "actualising" of changes in the "structure" of our "being" is so vague that it could signify virtually anything: our affections and desires; our ethical conceptions; our

---

[78] Karl Rahner, "Reflections on the Experience of Grace," in *Theological Investigations*, iii: *The Theology of the Spiritual Life* (New York: Crossroad Publishing Company, 1982), p. 86.

[79] Torrance, *The Trinitarian Faith*, p. 9.

habits and virtues; a general sense of existential telos; deep psychological structures that affect how we engage in relationships with others; the sorts of practices in which we are drawn to engage—the possibilities are almost endless.

Viewed strictly from the perspective of practice and experience rather than theological "correctness," then, the sum of Torrance's claim is the banal and almost contentless assertion that union with Christ will entail deep unspecified changes in our "being." In its lack of specificity, it risks giving theological cover to all sorts of projection. We can potentially take anything we like and call it a form of "actualising our union and communion with God."

Given this indeterminacy, the effect of the choice of terms here is to create the *illusion* of an experientially integrated and pastorally attuned doctrinal claim, while deferring the greater theological challenge of operationalizing the claim for the life of the church. For example, what specific changes to the "structure" of our "being" are likely to take place? How do we know whether they have taken place or not, and how do we distinguish true changes from false in light of the reality of sin and self-deception? Torrance's account gives us little help in answering these important questions.

A second example of a problematically non-experiential account of the work of the Spirit can be found in Kathryn Tanner's short systematics, *Jesus, Humanity and the Trinity*, where Tanner makes the following claim about the connection between soteriology and sacramental participation:

> Our union with Christ must be nurtured through the workings of the Spirit. Baptized . . . into Christ, a struggle to shore up our oneness with him ensues; the character and quality of our union with Christ must be bettered, heightened from weak union to strong, for example, through the repeated performance of the Eucharist in the power of the Spirit.[80]

As with Torrance, what we have here is a series of claims and concepts about the work of the Spirit that at one level are difficult to contest—in terms of eucharistic theology, there is nothing here that we might not expect in a thoughtful contemporary Anglican account. In the context of the book, these statements furthermore succeed perfectly well in Tanner's larger purpose of describing how the "universal range of the incarnation's effects" can be articulated in terms that are simultaneously trinitarian and sacramental.[81]

From the perspective of "experience," however, Tanner's claims are so underspecified and abstracted from experience that they in no way answer the basic pneumatological question of how the Spirit makes salvation real to us other than through an undeveloped assertion that somehow this happens in

---

[80] Kathryn Tanner, *Jesus, Humanity and the Trinity: A Brief Systematic Theology* (Minneapolis: Fortress Press, 2001), pp. 55–6.

[81] Tanner, *Jesus, Humanity and the Trinity*, p. 54.

the sacraments. What does it actually mean for "the character and quality of our union with Christ" to "be bettered, heightened from weak to strong"? What form does this "bettering" and "heightening" and "strengthening" take? Does it manifest primarily affectively, in our feelings, or cognitively, in the way we think, or noetically, in what and how we know, or relationally, in the character and quality of our relationships to others, or what? How does participating in the eucharist actually change us in ways that might be observable in the world over time? What about discernment—can we ever know that our union with Christ really has been improved? And if such changes are never in fact observable—if they only take place in what Rahner calls the "realm of pure ontology"—then has any change actually taken place at all?

There may well be robust answers to these questions, but they are not evident in *Jesus, Humanity and the Trinity*, and on the subject of experience only a little more is added in Tanner's more extended discussion in *Christ the Key*. As we will see in Chapter 3, in her theology of participation Tanner generally tends to resist conclusions that could clearly map onto concrete experiences beyond general assertions about sacramental participation.[82] In her account of the work of the Spirit in sanctification, she mostly limits herself to more general language of the impartation and actualization of "new powers and capacities" and "new dispositions" in the Spirit,[83] and in *Christ the Key* she goes so far as to express explicit reservations about the value of thinking of the changes involved in sanctification in terms of what she calls their "psychological quality."[84]

My point in bringing up these examples is to draw attention to a widely used register of theological speech that relies on ontological language that may sound and even be theologically "correct" but which serves in practice to obfuscate the question of how doctrines actually come to have experiential impact in human lives. In my view, general statements about the Spirit "bettering" our union with Christ through the eucharist, or "actualizing" changes in our "being" through participation in the Godhead need to be tempered by some kind of theological attempt to show how these metaphysical realities actually relate to the lives of real people in time. Otherwise, the Holy Spirit—theoretically the agent of this saving and sanctifying union with Christ—risks being reduced to a generic divine power, banal, clinical, and dehistoricized. And our ontological statements risk becoming mere theological words that will "pass athwart us," "unable to make themselves felt"[85]—a register of

---

[82] For discussion of the sacraments, see Kathryn Tanner, *Christ the Key* (Cambridge: Cambridge University Press, 2010), pp. 198–204.

[83] Tanner, *Christ the Key*, pp. 82, 84.

[84] Tanner, *Christ the Key*, pp. 94–5. See the more extended discussion of Tanner's theology of participation in Chapter 3.

[85] Eliot, *Janet's Repentance*, p. 236. See the discussion of this novella in the Introduction.

theological speech that gives the illusion of having said what needs to be said but that is unable to address fundamental questions about the plausibility and practical meaning of theological claims.

To take the argument a step further, vague ontological assertions like the ones we have seen in Torrance and Tanner are particularly vulnerable to the problem of *projection*. Here I am influenced by Karen Kilby's demonstration, in a seminal article, that there is a "high degree of projection" that is "built into" a good deal of late-twentieth-century social trinitarian theology.[86] In my view, something similar is at work in accounts of salvation and sanctification that pay inadequate attention to the register of experience. Because the details are left so underdetermined, there is nothing in Torrance's account of the Spirit's work to prevent us from understanding these changes to the "actual structure of our human, personal and social being" in whichever way is most convenient to us or which matches concerns we have already determined in advance. Likewise, Tanner's language of "bettering" and "strengthening" our union with Christ through eucharistic practice is so vague that it could be used to justify any number of accounts of what might be taking place in the eucharist. Without further augmentation or experiential mooring, such language is unable to do much to bridge the divide between general theological claims and the way that doctrines actually function in the world. And if the Holy Spirit is indeed the bridger of such gaps, the actualizer of divine realities in the world, as I argued above, then profoundly pneumatological *loci* like soteriology and sanctification must engage directly and explicitly with the question of experience. We cannot hide behind either methodological anxieties or metaphysical generalities. To do so in these cases would be to eclipse the Spirit from our theology.

Of course, some theological topics are more prone than others to the experiential complacency and indifference that I am describing. In drawing attention to claims like those of Torrance and Tanner, my point is not that such claims are necessarily untrue on their own terms, or that they are always to be avoided, or that they are not valuable for solving quite different theological problems. Indeed, Scripture itself contains similar statements, such as Paul's description of the transformation of believers from glory to glory before God in 2 Corinthians 3. But biblical accounts tend to complement such *abstract* statements through sustained attention to more specific, practically recognizable *concrete* outcomes of the Spirit's work, such as the experiences connected with Christian initiation, the kindling of holy affections, specific prophetic guidance, healing and other gifts of the Spirit, and so on. In the New Testament, the Holy Spirit's primary sphere of operation is the concrete world

---

[86] See Karen Kilby, "Perichoresis and Projection: Problems with Social Doctrines of the Trinity," *New Blackfriars* 81, no. 957 (2000), pp. 439–43.

of embodied, historical human existence, not some idealized realm of the theologically "real."

The argument can be summarized as a theological principle: where purely ontological claims about God's relation to human beings in the Spirit are made without any attempt to identify connections and correlations between that relation and effects that are also recognizable in the world of bodies and in the sequence of historical events, then such claims are particularly vulnerable to the problem of projection. The same principle can also be stated positively rather than critically: in order to combat the problem of projection, theologians should seek to draw connections between metaphysical or otherwise abstract dogmatic statements about the status of believers before God in the Spirit and their phenomenological correlates, and where possible to refuse the distinction entirely. The remaining chapters of this book will be an attempt to do precisely this in relation to two key dimensions of the theology of the Holy Spirit: the work of salvation and the work of sanctification.

Experiences of the Spirit: Practical Recognizability

Having examined the key "counter-concepts" for the account of "experience of the Spirit" that follows—concepts of "religious experience" as a singular and monolithic human phenomenon and forms of theological abstraction that are vulnerable to projection—I am now in a position to clarify further what I mean by "practical recognizability" as a criterion for identifying "experiential" dimensions of the Spirit's work. The primary function of the term "practical recognizability" is to draw attention to experience of the work of the Spirit in the world, in bodies and in time, and to distinguish it from other forms of interaction with the Spirit that focus on effects taking place "before God," i.e., on a primarily ontological or eschatological plane. Thus, if we wish to correct a tendency towards abstraction in theological discussions of the Holy Spirit, an excellent way forward is to begin by focusing on the more concrete, experiential dimensions of the Spirit's work.

The value of narrowing my definition of "experience" to encounters that exhibit "practical recognizability" is now clear. In light of this, the question now arises: how are we to go about identifying experiences of the Spirit that exhibit "practical recognizability"?[87]

---

[87] The definition of "practical recognizability" that follows is influenced by James' pragmatic understanding of human experience as "sensible apprehensions of change...carrying practical consequences." Richard R. Niebuhr, "Williams James on Religious Experience," in *The Cambridge Companion to William James*, ed. Ruth Anna Putnam (Cambridge: Cambridge University Press, 1997), p. 219.

First, attending to "practical recognizability" means focusing on texts that speak of the effects of the Spirit's agency or presence in ways that are *temporally specific*—i.e., that take place at specific moments or over identifiable periods of time. Some straightforward biblical examples would be what happened to Peter and the group of Gentiles at Caesarea ("And as I began to speak, the Holy Spirit fell upon them just as it had on us at the beginning" (Acts: 11:15)), or else instances of revelatory or prophetic communication like the commissioning of Barnabas and Saul ("the Holy Spirit said, 'Set apart for me Barnabas and Saul for the work to which I have called them'" (Acts 13:2)) and the sending of Philip to speak with the Ethiopian eunuch ("the Spirit said to Philip, 'Go over to this chariot and join it'" (Acts 8:29)). More broadly, this feature of temporal specificity would be present in any New Testament description of sudden conversion, of miracles like healing, or of specific divine guidance, at least insofar as the description includes an attribution to the agency or presence of the Spirit. By contrast, the biblical statements that the Spirit "will glorify" Christ (John 16:14) or that the Spirit is the agent behind Christian transformation into the "image" of the Lord (2 Cor. 3:18) are not temporally specific.

The second feature to look for in terms of "practical recognizability" is *affective impact*. Very often in the New Testament, the presence of the Spirit is explicitly connected with particular emotional and emotional-dispositional outcomes, and this connection will be particularly important in the chapters that follow. The classic texts here are Galatians 5:16–25, which contrasts the "manifest" or "obvious" (*phanera*) desires and works of the flesh with those of the Spirit, and then provides a list of "fruit" of the Spirit that begins with three affections (love, joy, and peace), and Romans 5:5, with its description of the Spirit's pouring out of "love" into the hearts of believers. But the theme is not exclusive to these Pauline passages: Jesus "rejoiced in the Holy Spirit" in Luke 10:21; the result of being filled with the Spirit in Acts 4:31 is a disposition of "boldness"; in Acts 13:52 the disciples are "filled with joy and with the Holy Spirit"; 1 Thessalonians 1:6 speaks of "joy inspired by the Holy Spirit"; and so on.

Shaped by texts like these, it is no accident that later theological reflection has tended to identify a close connection between religious emotion and the work of the Spirit. Didymus the Blind, for example, refers to Galatians 5:16–25 and Romans 5:5 together to demonstrate that love, joy, and peace represent a mode of participation in God through the Spirit.[88] Augustine, likewise, refers to Romans 5:5 in *On the Spirit and the Letter*, in which he argues that God imparts righteousness to human beings not by "externally produc[ing] sounds

---

[88] Didymus the Blind, *On the Holy Spirit* 78–80 (Mark DelCogliano, Andrew Radde-Gallwitz, and Lewis Ayres, eds. *Works on the Spirit: Athanasius and Didymus* (Yonkers, NY: St Vladimir's Seminary Press, 2011), pp. 167–8, 157).

in our ears with the commandments of righteousness," but rather "internally," in a transformation of our affections and desires, by "pouring out love in our hearts by the Holy Spirit who has given to us."[89] Peter Lombard, too, refers to Romans 5:5 to claim, following Augustine, that "The Holy Spirit himself is the love or charity by which we love God and our neighbor."[90] Martin Luther makes much the same point in his preface to Romans: Christian holiness is impossible

> unless all that you do is done from the bottom of your heart. But such a heart is given only by God's Spirit, who fashions a man after the law, so that he acquires a desire for the law in his heart, doing nothing henceforth out of fear and compulsion but out of a free heart . . . This pleasure and love for the law is put into the heart by the Holy Spirit.[91]

In terms of practical recognizability, identifying the work of the Spirit through attention to affective impact is a particularly useful experiential indicator because, in contrast to effects of divine action like the transformation of believers "from one degree of glory to another" in 2 Corinthians 3, emotional experience is always embodied, and this means that it is always embedded in some sense in historical time. Because affects and desires like those described above possess irreducible psychological and physiological dimensions, affective speech always implies particular bodies responding to particular stimuli in time and space. In the case of specific emotions, this will often mean reasonably precise, short-duration "moments." But affective language can include longer term but still "practically recognizable" effects as well, such as when we talk about desire and its transformation, or long-term dispositional change that contains affective components, such as "hope" or "kindness" or "boldness." Thus, regardless of whether a text explicitly specifies when the emotional or emotion-related experience is actually occurring, affective language implies the element of temporal embeddedness referred to above.

The category of affect, which in my view encompasses both feelings and desires, is one of the central categories of this book. It will receive more extensive analysis and clarification in Chapter 4, in the context of a discussion of affect theory, and in Chapter 5, where I discuss the theological implications of the social and material embeddedness of affects, as well as the ways in which they resist efforts at analytical understanding. For now there are three preliminary points to emphasize, in anticipation of later discussions. The first is the close connection just referred to between affects and bodies. It is a core assumption of this book that for human beings there is no such thing as experience of fear or joy or delight apart from the physical body and brain,

---

[89] *Spir. et litt.* 25.42 (*PL* 44:226; *WSA* I/23:170).   [90] Peter Lombard, *Sentences* 1.17.2.
[91] *WA Deutsche Bibel* 7:4; *LW* 35:367–8. See similarly Melanchthon, *Loci communes 1521*, p. 112.

embedded in the material world. The assumption that affect is a category that is tethered to embodiment has implications for how I interpret theological texts about emotions and desires. It means that, unless otherwise noted, I will generally assume that the material body is implied in discussions of affective experience in scriptural and theological texts, even if it is not mentioned more directly or explicitly.

The second point to emphasize about affect and emotion is that they are particularly useful categories for mediating between theology and the insights of areas of intellectual inquiry outside of theology. On the one hand, discussion of affects and desires is everywhere in Scripture, as well as in the history of theology, such that they are a topic that is of unimpeachable interest and significance for theological discourse. On the other hand, many disciplines outside of theology have insights to offer about affects. In this book I will draw particularly on findings from critical theory and from the psychological sciences. In principle, however, attention to affects opens up dialogue with any field that is concerned with thinking about human emotion and desire.

Finally, the peculiar character of affects also helps to clarify an important question raised by the term "practical recognizability": who exactly is doing the "recognizing"? First and foremost, I understand this term to refer to experiences that in principle are open to recognition *by the experiencer*. But this point needs to be qualified in two ways. First, as embodied realities, recognition of affects is not strictly limited to the realm of 'inner" mental subjectivity. Affects are generated in and mediated through the feeling body, and their effects can therefore in principle be traced on bodies, at least to some degree, such that there is space here for acknowledging forms of "recognition" beyond that of the experiencing subject (for example, in the ways we can recognize emotional responses in others of which they may at times not be fully aware themselves). Second, as we will see in Chapter 5, part of what is interesting about affects is the way they can resist easy legibility, including for the experiencing subject. Often we do not know exactly what we are feeling, much less why we are feeling it. This dimension of affects builds a degree of epistemic humility into investigation of the practical recognizability of experiences. I will expand on this point in the final chapter.

Returning to pneumatology, my purpose in drawing attention to the "practically recognizable" effects of the Spirit's work in the world, and correspondingly to the substantial problems generated by certain kinds of theological abstraction, is not to dispute the value and indeed the necessity of more abstract, often ontological, claims in theology, including in pneumatology. My goal, rather, is *recalibration*. A good deal of contemporary theology has responded to the difficulties in talking about Christian experience in the shadow of Barth by erring on the side of metaphysical description, leaving the practical implications as well as sources of Christian doctrines under-specified in a way that contributes to a plausibility problem for Christianity in the contemporary world. In arguing for a reorientation of theology back to "experience" through careful attention to the contours of the doctrine of the Holy Spirit, I will have failed in my task if this is taken to mean a simple return to a "Schleiermacherian" account of experience as the primary foundation and ground of dogmatics.

Indeed, the wrong sort of focus on "practical recognizability" in relation to the work of the Spirit could generate new problems. Done badly, it could result in a kind of overspecification of the shape of the Spirit's work that would violate the fundamental pneumatological principle of the freedom of the Spirit, or in an overpsychologizing of Christian experience that becomes vulnerable to reductive accounts of such experience as explicable entirely in immanent, secular terms. Overspecification of the experiential shape of the Spirit's work can also risk doing a kind of violence to enormously complex and multivalent Christian experiences—a life-changing conversion, for example—by attempting to reduce them to a few simple emotional and motivational effects that are empirically available.

Given difficulties like these, my use of the criterion of "practical recognizability" for establishing what, in the terms of this book, is and is not an "experience of the Spirit" is not intended to provide an exhaustive principle for determining and analyzing the full scope and measure of the Spirit's experiential work in a given instance. In later chapters, I will deepen the texture and complexity of the concept of "experience of the Spirit," as well as of its "practical recognizability," by attending to some of the ways the Spirit works through ostensibly "non-religious" experiences. And no matter how subtle or comprehensive any particular account becomes, the activity of the Spirit, as divine work, will always resist exhaustive description. In light of this, my pneumatological method in what follows is more reparative than directly constructive; or, perhaps better, it is obliquely constructive, via a method of repair. That is, I will be drawing on major resources from within the Christian tradition—in this case the experiential dimensions of the doctrine of the Holy Spirit as they relate to soteriology—to provide useful correctives to a series of theological problematics by drawing attention to affective and temporally specific dimensions of "experience" which are of fundamental pneumatological importance, which have played a substantial role in the history of Christian theology, and which have tended in recent theology to be undervalued or ignored. This reparative work will clear the way for the more directly constructive retrieval of a particular soteriological outlook in the final chapters.

3

Salvation in the Spirit

Every metaphysic . . . must find its test in practical life.
—Ernst Troeltsch[1]

I turn now to two more specific sites where the Holy Spirit might be expected to be "experienced." My aim in the three remaining chapters is threefold. First, I will address the problem of vagueness that so often afflicts pneumatologies that take the experienced presence of God as their starting point, by looking at certain specific forms that such "experience" has been understood to take both in the Bible and in later theological reflection. The approach established in the previous chapter, of attending to "practically recognizable" effects of the Spirit that are located in time and have affective impact, can in principle be applied to any major dimension of the Spirit's work as described in Scripture. For the purposes of this book, I will focus on the Spirit's work in salvation and sanctification. This is because it is in relation to these themes that my approach has the most to contribute to contemporary theological debates, and because it is in relation to these topics that its critical as well as construct-ive power is most effectively modeled.

My second aim in the remaining chapters will be to provide, via the lens of pneumatology, a kind of extended case study for establishing the relation between "experience" and particular Christian doctrines that I identified in Chapter 1 as a pressing need in contemporary theology. The goal is to bring together, more closely than is usually the case, claims about the work of God's Spirit in the realm of theological ontology and claims about the effects of God's presence and agency in the Spirit that are "practically recognizable" in the lives of Christians. As Troeltsch observes in the quotation above, the most persuasive metaphysics are those that pass the test of "practical life."

My ultimate aim over the next three chapters, however, is constructive: to articulate the core features of a pneumatological soteriology that retains the

---

[1] Ernst Troeltsch, *Protestantism and Progress: A Historical Study of the Relation of Protestantism to the Modern World*, trans. W. Montgomery (New York: G.P. Putnam's Sons, 1912), p. ix.

The Holy Spirit and Christian Experience. Simeon Zahl, Oxford University Press (2020). © Simeon Zahl.
DOI: 10.1093/oso/9780198827788.001.0001

advantages of traditional Protestant disjunctive theologies of grace, which emphasize the work of the Spirit over and against the resistance of the sinful human agent and which seek to engage honestly and compassionately with the problem of moral non-transformation in Christians, while maintaining a robust connection between the saving work of the Spirit and embodied experience, thus avoiding the problems sometimes associated with "extrinsicist" models of grace. I will accomplish this through a constructive retrieval of key resources from early and pre-modern soteriologies, in dialogue with contemporary reflection on affect and emotion from disciplines outside of theology.

The next two chapters examine the pneumatological relationship between salvation and experience. Chapter 3 does this by engaging a major contemporary soteriological debate to show how that debate is advanced and reconfigured when viewed through the lens of experience of the Holy Spirit. It establishes the parameters for this reconfiguration through a series of critical soundings in contemporary and early modern approaches to the relationship between "justification" and "participation" as models of salvation. Chapter 4 will then build on these findings to give a constructive account of several key dimensions of how divine grace comes be to be experienced in practically recognizable ways.

Christian soteriology has been dominated in recent years by a two-fold movement: a critical turn away from Protestant soteriologies of justification by faith alone, and a multi-faceted recovery of what are broadly referred to as soteriologies of "participation." At the heart of the present chapter is the argument that a major engine behind the contemporary movement towards participatory soteriologies and away from soteriologies of justification by faith is a set of arguments about the relationship between theology and experience. Having established this, I will examine what are arguably the two most comprehensive and significant recent Protestant accounts of salvation through participation in Christ, those of T.F. Torrance and Kathryn Tanner, to see whether and to what degree they do in fact succeed in realizing the perceived promise of "participation" for reintegrating soteriology and experience in a Protestant key. It will become clear that even these highly sophisticated accounts have significant difficulties moving from the ontological to the experiential register. This is in part because they remain caught in the false choice about religious experience that has characterized so much Protestant theology since Luther, whereby "experience" must either be the primary ground of all theological claims or else excluded from theological method entirely. The degree to which Torrance's and Tanner's accounts fail adequately to engage with experience will be brought into further relief in a third section, where I show how accounts of sanctifying grace in recent neo-Thomist theology are substantially more successful in terms of my criterion of "practical recognizability," even as they generate significant new problems. The chapter culminates with an analysis of the soteriology of Lutheran Reformer Philip Melanchthon, which provides the foundations for a mediating account of salvation that preserves the best of both approaches. I will conclude by drawing on patristic discussions of participation and *theosis* to show how affective transformation is itself a mode of participation in God through the Spirit.

THE SOTERIOLOGICAL HORIZON

It is not difficult to demonstrate that there is a close connection in the New Testament between experiences associated with Christian initiation and a particular kind of activity of the Holy Spirit. In Acts 11, the fact that "the Holy Spirit fell upon all who heard the word" in Caesarea is interpreted by both Peter and the church at Jerusalem as a direct correlate of the acquisition of saving belief. Peter states that "God gave them the same gift [the Spirit] that he gave us when we believed in the Lord Jesus Christ" (Acts 11:7), and the church in Jerusalem then immediately interprets the fact of the Gentiles' receipt of the Spirit as evidence that they have received "the repentance that leads to life" (Acts 11:18). Likewise, the Corinthians' acquisition of "faith" as a result of Paul's "speech and proclamation" is described by Paul in 1 Corinthians as a consequence of their having experienced "a demonstration of the Spirit and of power" (1 Cor. 2:4–5). And in Galatians, Paul's rhetorical question as to whether the Galatians' early experience of the Spirit came about through "doing works of the law, or by your believing what you heard" (Gal. 3:5) explicitly situates their pneumatological experience of Christian initiation in the context of his broader soteriological argument in Chapters 2 and 3 about being "justified not by the works of the law but through faith in Jesus Christ" (Gal. 2:16). In speaking of "practically recognizable" experiences of the Spirit associated with Christian initiation in the New Testament, we have clearly moved into the realm of soteriology.

Spirit-language also plays a central role in New Testament soteriology more broadly, where a very close connection is maintained between receipt of the Spirit and salvation. To be saved is, among other things, to "receive the Spirit" (John 7:39, 20:22; Acts 2:38, 8:15, 8:17, 8:19, 10:47; Rom. 8:15; 1 Cor. 2:12; 2 Cor. 11:4; Gal. 3:2, 14), to be "born again of water and Spirit" (John 3:5), to become a "temple of the Holy Spirit" (1 Cor. 3:16, 6:19), to be adopted as God's children through the sending of "the Spirit of his Son into our hearts" (Gal. 4:4–7; Rom. 8:15–16); to follow the "law of the Spirit of life" rather than the "law of sin and death" (Rom. 8:2); and to be brought to "life" by the Spirit following the "death" of the "old self" (Rom. 6:3–6, 8:10–11). For the New

Testament writers, there is no question that one of the most natural and fundamental ways of talking about Christian salvation is in terms of the presence and work of the Holy Spirit.

In the previous chapter, I argued that one of the most important works of the Spirit is to build "bridges" between divine and human realities, and to "actualize" the work of the Father and the Son "in relation to us."[2] If this is the case, and given the close connection between the Spirit and soteriology, then one of the most important arenas where the Spirit accomplishes this "actualizing" should be in relation to salvation. In what follows, I test a series of accounts of salvation through the lens of this principle. Although I will be paying particular attention to ways in which Spirit-language is directly invoked in soteriological debate, it is important to note at the outset that, formally speaking, the whole topic of "experience" in relation to soteriology is at root a pneumatological one. To ask how salvation is "experienced" is by definition to analyze the character and contours of a major work of the Spirit.

Present Experience of Future Salvation

In addressing the question of how salvation is "experienced," we are soon confronted with the fact that salvation itself refers, in an important sense, primarily to a future rather than to a present reality. This feature of Christian soteriology has important implications for how we are to understand the concept of soteriological "experience," and it is necessary to pause at this point to unpack this relation in more detail.

Behind the multiplicity of images and concepts associated with salvation in the New Testament lies a more fundamental question: what exactly is it human beings are being saved from? What plight is being addressed and what situation is being rectified when Christians come to understand themselves as having been "adopted" as children of God through the Spirit, or when they speak of being "justified by faith," or of coming to "participate" in Christ's filial relation to the Father?

Historically speaking, the answer is relatively clear: the task of Christian soteriology is first and foremost to answer the question of how sinful and fallen human beings, alienated from God and each other and subject to the curse of death, can nevertheless come to spend eternity in the presence of a holy God. We see this basic schema in the Nicene Creed, which proclaims that when Christ "came down from heaven" and was "crucified . . . suffered, and was buried, and on the third day rose again," these events took place above all for soteriological reasons: Christ was incarnate "for us and for our salvation,"

---

[2] Anatolios, *Retrieving Nicaea*, p. 142.

so that we might receive "the remission of sins," take part in "the resurrection of the dead," and participate in "the life of the world to come." Although salvation language can and should be employed in a wider sense than this in theology, at its core Christian soteriology is concerned first and foremost with the specific problems of mortality and sin. As the creed indicates, it is these two interrelated obstacles that need to be overcome if human beings are to take part in the promised blessedness, joy, and reprieve of the "life of the world to come," and it is thus sin and mortality that are the chief initial concerns of any Christian soteriology that takes its lead from the witness of Scripture.

Viewing salvation through the lens of "experience," an interesting problem now arises. The issue is that from the perspective of the realm of "practical experience," which is always the realm of embodied human creatures embedded in historical time, in an important sense the salvation of believers in the sense of the Nicene Creed is a future, eschatological reality rather than something that has already taken place or is currently taking place in our present experience. Insofar as we understand soteriology to be about the overcoming of physical death and the final and complete transformation of sinful human beings into creatures capable of eternal communion with a holy God, then in this life Christians clearly are not there yet. Even the most faithful Christian still dies, and even the most holy saint is not completely free of sin in this life.

Martin Luther makes this point in the treatise *Against Latomus*, when he observes that the present Christian soteriological reality of having been set free from "the law of sin and death" (Rom. 8:2) and from the "reign and tyranny of sin and death" is demonstrably not identical with being set free from sin and death as such or in a final and complete way, for the simple reason that Christians still die. Although God "will . . . free us in the end," nevertheless it is simply a fact on the ground that "He has not freed us from death yet, nor yet from sin . . . for we have still to die and to labor in sin, [and] death faces us all."[3] Here Luther is simply repeating a point made in 1 Corinthians 15, where St. Paul contrasts the present tense of the fact that "all die in Adam" with the future tense of the fact that "all will be made alive in Christ" (15:22), and reminds us that the final overcoming of death is an event that will take place only in the eschatological future: "The last enemy to be destroyed is death" (15:26).

If rescue from the enemy of death lies very close to the heart of traditional Christian soteriology, and if the defeat of death and the resurrection of the dead remain fundamentally future events that by definition have not yet been experienced, then what does it mean to speak of "experience" of the saving

---

[3] WA 8:92; Martin Luther, *Luther: Early Theological Works*, trans. James Atkinson (Philadelphia: Westminster Press, 1962), p. 340. Emphasis added.

work of the Spirit? We can begin to answer this important question with the minimal statement that present soteriological experience is constituted to a significant degree by a future soteriological horizon. That is, such experience entails a proleptic participation in a future eschatological reality in some sense. Framing the question of soteriological "experience" in this way, it soon becomes clear that the New Testament makes use of several powerful concepts and images for describing just such a real and transformative relation in the present to future theological realities. Of particular importance here are the categories of hope (Acts 23:6; Gal. 5:5; Titus 3:7) and faith (Luke 7:50; Rom 3:24–25; Eph. 2:8; 1 Peter 1:9), and language that speaks about Christians engaging in a present-tense participation in Christ's death and resurrection in some sense (John 6:54–55, 58; Rom 6:4, 11; Gal. 2:19–20; 2 Cor 5:14; cf. John 14:19–20).

But to state that the resurrection of our bodies and the final eradication of sin are primarily future realities that can nevertheless be "experienced" in the present through hope, through faith, and through some form of participation in Christ, is to identify only the most basic features of the grammar of "experience" of salvation. In attempting to make use of these terms for contemporary soteriology, many questions arise. What precisely is the sequence of events by which believers come to have faith? Is faith a specific cognitive and affective event that takes place in bodies and brains, or is it better described as a kind of ontological reality in which we participate spiritually, before God, and whose practical correlates are underdetermined? What is the relationship between faith and the spiritual participation in Christ's death and resurrection that St. Paul describes? Is such participation primarily a model for our own ascetic practice, or is it more of a vicarious reality, one in which we "participate" simply by believing? How does participation in Christ relate to sacramental participation? And where does "grace" fit in—does grace describe the nature of the relation between the believer and God established through Christ, or is it a kind of ontological deposit through which believers are transformed to participate in Christ's own being, or is it somehow both?

There are a number of possible answers in each case. In asking such questions, it quickly becomes clear that "faith" and "participation," in particular, are categories that depend upon particular theological models of how salvation works. In the context of the present study, this means we will make little headway in analyzing the practical-experiential valence of such categories if we do not attend to the way they function within the broader soteriological frameworks to which they have given rise, including the way in which those frameworks were clarified and developed in later theology. With this in view, I turn now to a series of critical soundings in contemporary soteriology to see how several representative accounts fare when analyzed from the perspective of the relation between salvation and experience.

JUSTIFICATION AND PARTICIPATION IN CONTEMPORARY DEBATE

No soteriological issue has been the subject of greater exploration and con-troversy over the past four decades among both theologians and biblical scholars than the merits and demerits of traditional Protestant forensic and substitutionary accounts of salvation, on the one hand, and participation- and *theosis*-oriented accounts, on the other. Many scholars view the debate as being effectively over, at least in mainstream academic theology, having been resolved decisively in favor of participatory models. As Simon Gathercole has remarked, the idea that salvation takes place by means of some form of participation in Christ "has become an uncontroversial axiom in biblical scholarship and Christian theology," even as "substitutionary" models remain "highly contested."[4] Paul Fiddes has observed a similar trajectory, arguing that an understanding of the "goal of salvation as 'divinization' . . . is increasingly taking a central place in all modern systematic theology," both Eastern and Western, even as "it is no longer true, if it ever was, that Western theology is only interested in a forensic view of salvation, or the acquittal of human beings in a divine law court."[5]

From the perspective of the history of Protestant theology, this development constitutes a sea change of remarkable scope and rapidity. In forty short years, confident rejection of traditional justification-based models has become some-thing of a truism in contemporary theology. Even limiting ourselves to very recent major works, in no time at all we find Kathryn Tanner taking for granted the "obvious problems" with "vicarious satisfaction and penal substi-tution";[6] Douglas Campbell describing "Justification theory" as "bad theology" that is "incoherent," "contradictory," and "empirically false";[7] Frank Macchia arguing that "an *extrinsic* notion of justifying righteousness construed as a legal or quasi-legal transaction" neglects "the very heart and soul of justifica-tion," namely, "the more participatory and transformative aspects of salva-tion";[8] and John Milbank describing the Protestant concept of grace as "extrinsicist and judicial" and as reducing salvation to a "mere calculus."[9]

---

[4] Simon Gathercole, *Defending Substitution: An Essay on Atonement in Paul* (Grand Rapids, MI: Baker Academic, 2015), p. 13.

[5] Paul Fiddes, "Salvation," in *The Oxford Handbook of Systematic Theology*, eds. Kathryn Tanner, Iain Torrance, and John Webster (Oxford: Oxford University Press, 2007), p. 176.

[6] Tanner, *Christ the Key*, p. 252.

[7] Douglas A. Campbell, *The Deliverance of God: An Apocalyptic Rereading of Justification in Paul* (Grand Rapids, MI: William B. Eerdmans Publishing Company, 2009), p. 36; see pp. 36–166 for his explication of this judgment.

[8] Frank D. Macchia, *Justified in the Spirit: Creation, Redemption, and the Triune God* (Grand Rapids, MI: William B. Eerdmans Publishing Company, 2010), p. 39, emphasis original.

[9] John Milbank, *Beyond Secular Order: The Representation of Being and the Representation of the People* (Oxford: Wiley Blackwell, 2013), pp. 226, 63–4.

There are a number of reasons for this broad scholarly shift from forensic to participatory models of salvation. First, the shift has deep roots in biblical studies, especially Paul studies. Inspired by Albert Schweitzer's thesis that it is a kind of Christ-mysticism, rather than the legal and substitutionary imagery of justification, that lies at the heart of Pauline soteriology,[10] E.P. Sanders argued in *Paul and Palestinian Judaism* that "the realism with which Paul thought of incorporation in the body of Christ" is far more indicative of "the heart of his theology" than the theme of "righteousness by faith alone."[11] Although there remains much disagreement on the details, in the wake of Schweitzer and especially of Sanders there has been a strong turn in mainstream scholarship on Paul towards recognizing the centrality of imagery of participation and union with Christ in Pauline soteriology.[12]

In systematic theology, the shift has somewhat different sources. One important factor has been the twentieth-century ecumenical movement. Inspired by dialogues between Protestant denominations and the Roman Catholic and Orthodox Churches, Protestant theologians have rediscovered the riches of the major soteriological alternatives to Reformation-era theologies of justification, including especially the Thomist approach to participation and the soteriologies of deification and *theosis* associated with the Eastern churches.[13] Interest in participation and union with Christ among Protestants has produced a surge of studies of such themes in traditional Protestant figures, starting with Luther[14] and Calvin.[15]

[10] Albert Schweitzer, *The Mysticism of Paul the Apostle*, trans. William Montgomery (Baltimore: Johns Hopkins University Press, 1998).

[11] E.P. Sanders, *Paul and Palestinian Judaism: A Comparison of Patterns of Religion* (Minneapolis: Fortress Press, 1977), p. 434.

[12] See, e.g., Grant Macaskill, *Union with Christ in the New Testament* (Oxford: Oxford University Press, 2013), chapter 9, and Michael J. Gorman, *Inhabiting the Cruciform God: Kenosis, Justification, and Theosis in Paul's Narrative Soteriology* (Grand Rapids, MI: William B. Eerdmans Publishing Company, 2009). For an overview of the theme of participation in Paul and in Paul studies, see Susan Eastman, "Participation in Christ," in *The Oxford Handbook of Pauline Studies*, eds. Matthew V. Novenson and R. Barry Matlock (Oxford: Oxford University Press, 2014).

[13] Especially important have been the Lutheran-Catholic dialogues that culminated after many decades in the 1999 *Joint Declaration on the Doctrine of Justification*, and the dialogues between Finnish Lutherans and Russian Orthodox theologians that inspired the "Finnish Interpretation" of Luther.

[14] See especially Tuomo Mannermaa, *Christ Present in Faith: Luther's View of Justification* (Minneapolis: Fortress Press, 2005); Simo Peura, *Mehr als ein Mensch? Die Vergöttlichung als Thema der Theologie Martin Luthers von 1513 bis 1519* (Mainz: Verlag Philipp von Zabern, 1994); and Olli-Pekka Vainio, *Justification and Participation in Christ: The Development of the Lutheran Doctrine of Justification from Luther to the Formula of Concord* (Leiden: Brill Academic, 2008).

[15] See especially Todd Billings, *Calvin, Participation, and the Gift: The Activity of Believers in Union with Christ* (Oxford: Oxford University Press, 2007), and Trevor Hart, "Humankind in Christ and Christ in Humankind: Salvation as Participation in Our Substitute in the Theology of John Calvin," *Scottish Journal of Theology* 42, no. 1 (1989).

Another important dimension in the shift away from traditional Protestant approaches has been the critique, originating in feminist and womanist theology, of an affirmation of violence and an implicit valorization of victimhood and abuse perceived as a necessary consequence of atonement models that identify Christ's suffering and death as theologically necessary. The idea that Christ needed to die in order to restore full relationship between God and his creatures has been described as "cosmic child abuse,"[16] and as a tool for the powerful to justify exploitation.[17] Related to this has been the argument that traditional models of substitutionary vicarious atonement, including but not limited to theologies of forensic justification, depend on a problematic concept of God as a severe, even abusive figure who is willing to love human beings only once certain conditions have been met.[18] Although some of these arguments depend on social doctrines of the Trinity that have been challenged on theological and historical grounds,[19] probing questions about the symbolics as well as the mechanics of victimhood, sacrifice, and divine wrath in atonement theories continue to have a significant impact on soteriological debate.

The focus of the present discussion will be on another highly significant factor: a widespread perception that participatory models of salvation are capable of correcting a problematic coldness and abstraction associated with justification-based approaches. According to this argument, traditional Protestant theologies of justification, focused as they are on the "imputation" of Christ's righteousness to sinners through a decree offered in a putative divine "courtroom," offer no satisfying way of connecting what is happening objectively before God with subjective human experience in the world.[20] The connection, such as it is, is an abstract, intellectual one only—it is a conceptual game, a kind of shifting of counters in the sky, rather than a lived and livable reality. "Forensic" salvation, it is argued, is achieved through the exploitation of a legal loophole rather than through an actual participatory and transformative salvific engagement with the human creature. As a "reckoning" rather than an infusion or transformation, the doctrine is thus a "legal fiction" and a trafficking in "fantasies."[21]

---

[16] Rita Nakashima Brock, *Journeys by Heart: A Christology of Erotic Power* (New York: Crossroad, 1988), pp. 56, 53–7.

[17] See e.g., Delores S. Williams, "Black Women's Surrogacy Experience and the Christian Notion of Redemption," in *After Patriarchy: Feminist Transformations of the World Religions*, eds. Paula M. Cooey, William R. Eakin, and Jay B. McDaniel (Maryknoll, NY: Orbis Books, 1991), pp. 10–13.

[18] See e.g., Joanne Carlson Brown and Rebecca Parker, "For God So Loved the World?," in *Christianity, Patriarchy, and Abuse: A Feminist Critique*, eds. Carole R. Bohn and Joanne Carlson Brown (Cleveland: Pilgrim, 1989), pp. 7–9.

[19] See especially Kilby, "Perichoresis and Projection," and Ayres, *Nicaea and its Legacy*, pp. 292–3, 357–8, 407–10.

[20] The following section reproduces and extends arguments I make in Zahl, "Affective Salience."

[21] Clark H. Pinnock, *Flame of Love: A Theology of the Holy Spirit* (Downers Grove, IL: IVP Academic, 1996), p. 156.

Although in its basic form this critique is very old—a version of it is already implied in the Council of Trent's 1547 *Decree on Justification*[22]—the view that Protestant theologies of justification constitute a "legal fiction" has received substantial new attention under the influence of a particular genealogy of modernity in recent decades. This view holds that the problem with forensic, "extrinsicist" models can be traced to the univocal and nominalist legacies of John Duns Scotus and William of Ockham. Building on Etienne Gilson's critical account of the "dissolving influence" of Ockham's thought on medieval scholasticism,[23] Louis Bouyer argued in the mid twentieth century for a strong connection between nominalism and the view, which he attributes to Protestantism, that justification refers to a "merely extrinsic justice, which has nothing real to correspond with it in the person justified."[24] Parallel to this, Catherine Pickstock has argued more recently that Duns Scotus' account of metaphysical univocity necessitates a position in which "the space [of connection between God and humanity] is philosophically pre-determined as a space of facts or empirical propositions."[25] Building on analyses like these, John Milbank has connected Scotist as well as Ockhamist traditions with the development of Protestant theologies of salvation, arguing that Lutheran and Calvinist theologies of justification, insofar as they include significant forensic components, presuppose these rationalistic and anti-participatory scholastic metaphysical developments and are a natural consequence of them.[26] In Milbank's view, imputation-based soteriologies of justification, dependent as they are on a "nominalist univocal metaphysics" not only make a "real, inward reworking of our nature"[27] soteriologically unnecessary, they actually render

[22] The 1547 *Decree on Justification* explicitly criticizes Protestant language of "reckoning" and "imputation," and argues instead that in justification "we are not merely reputed [*non modo reputamur*] but are truly called and are righteous [*sed vere justi nominamur et sumus*], receiving righteousness within us." The word "truly" is vital here: if righteousness is not really present and infused, the Tridentine theologians contend, then it is essentially "untrue," i.e., fictional. See Council of Trent, Session 6, Chapter 7 (Schroeder, *Canons and Decrees*, p. 212).

[23] Etienne Gilson, *History of Christian Philosophy in the Middle Ages* (New York: Random House, 1955), pp. 489, 498–9.

[24] Louis Bouyer, *The Spirit and Forms of Protestantism*, trans. A.V Littledale (London: Collins, 1956), pp. 180–1, 184–200.

[25] Catherine Pickstock, "Duns Scotus: His Historical and Contemporary Significance," *Modern Theology* 21, no. 4 (2005), pp. 554, 553–6.

[26] Milbank's main discussions of Protestant forensic and judicial soteriologies can be found in Milbank, *Beyond Secular Order*, pp. 62–4, 79–80, 86, 225–6; John Milbank, "Knowledge: The theological critique of philosophy in Hamann and Jacobi," in *Radical Orthodoxy: A New Theology*, eds. John Milbank, Catherine Pickstock, and Graham Ward (London: Routledge, 1999), pp. 23–4; John Milbank, "Alternative Protestantism: Radical Orthodoxy and the Reformed Tradition," in *Radical Orthodoxy and the Reformed Tradition*, eds. James K.A. Smith and James H. Olthuis (Grand Rapids, MI: Baker Academic, 2005), pp. 27–33; and John Milbank, *Being Reconciled: Ontology and Pardon* (London: Routledge, 2003), pp. 110–11, 223.

[27] Milbank, *Beyond Secular Order*, pp. 79–80.

any claim to such inner change metaphysically incoherent. Salvation becomes "the pathetic gesture of 'faith'," a purely intellectual assent to "a neat set of propositions about [Christ's] saving significance,"[28] and in this "displace[s] the centrality of love in favor of themes of trust and hope."[29] Indeed, this "extrinsicist and judicial concept of grace"—which, in Milbank's account, Protestants share with later Counter-Reformation thinkers like Suarez—"was often deemed . . . to make no essential experiential difference to the human subject."[30]

The result is that forensic justification as it was articulated by the Magisterial Reformers has come to be viewed by a great many contemporary theologians as a "cold, abstract, logical, and judicial" doctrine that is far less plausible today than alternative accounts of atonement, especially those involving the categories of participation or *theosis*.[31] Tied to the mast of a narrative of theological and spiritual decline since Scotus, forensic justification has come to be seen as interwoven with the spiritual crisis of late modernity more generally. The association of justification by faith alone with nominalism and therefore with secular disenchantment has become something of a standard argument in accounts of the relation between theology and modernity in recent years, playing a central role in works by Brad Gregory, Hans Boersma, and Reinhard Hütter, amongst others.[32]

On the face of it, this line of critique can initially seem quite compelling. It seems to make good sense of the fact that classical Protestant theologies of forensic justification are indeed deeply concerned with the exclusion from soteriological consideration of any inner requirement of righteousness, of any inner subjective change that would be *formally necessary* to salvation. Although from the start theologians who held to a forensic view of justification usually took great pains to emphasize some form of inner

---

[28] Milbank, *Beyond Secular Order*, pp. 79–80.

[29] Milbank, "Alternative Protestantism," pp. 32–3.

[30] Milbank, *Beyond Secular Order*, p. 226.

[31] Thomas Coates, "Calvin's Doctrine of Justification," *Concordia Theological Monthly* 34, no. 6 (1963), pp. 333–4. Another commentator laments that, "In the present culture, to say that justification is primarily forensic is the rhetorical equivalent of saying that one teaches an implausible, cold, impersonal, and even arbitrary doctrine of justification" (R. Scott Clark, "*Iustitia Imputata Christi*: Alien or Proper to Luther's Doctrine of Justification?," *Concordia Theological Quarterly* 70, no. 3–4 (2006), p. 272).

[32] See Brad Gregory, *The Unintended Reformation: How a Religious Revolution Secularized Society* (Cambridge, MA: Harvard University Press, 2012), pp. 36–47, 145–52; Hans Boersma, *Heavenly Participation: The Weaving of a Sacramental Tapestry* (Grand Rapids, MI: William B. Eerdmans Publishing Company, 2011), pp. 68–99; and Reinhard Hütter, "'Thomas the Augustinian'—Recovering a Surpassing Synthesis of Grace and Free Will," in *Dust Bound for Heaven: Explorations in the Theology of Thomas Aquinas* (Grand Rapids, MI: William B. Eerdmans Publishing Company, 2012), pp. 252–62, 282; as well as Jennifer A. Herdt, *Putting on Virtue: The Legacy of the Splendid Vices* (Chicago: University of Chicago Press, 2008), pp. 92–4.

renewal or "fruit" consequent to justification or simultaneous with it—usually called sanctification—they took equal pains to separate that renewal formally from salvation itself.[33] Milbank speaks for many in being skeptical of this strategy: "Supposedly the Protestant elect *will* be charitable, and yet if they happen not to be, this does not really seem to matter all that much."[34] A true affection and *habitus* of love in the Christian believer is not just unlikely but finally precluded in his reading of the forensic model: in developing an "extrinsicist and judicial" theology of justification, "the Magisterial Reformers . . . compromised love as the heart of Christianity, replacing it with a loveless trust in an inscrutable deity."[35]

For the purposes of this chapter and the next, what is especially important about the "legal fiction" argument is that it is ultimately an argument about *soteriological experience*. Judicial and forensic models, it is contended, are unable to provide a compelling account of the experiential, transformative, and "effective" dimensions of the Christian encounter with divine grace, and it is precisely this weakness that gives urgency to contemporary retrievals of soteriologies focused around "participation." Implicit in the "legal fiction" critique is therefore a particular view of the relationship between "reason" and experience: traditional Protestant theologies of justification by faith are held to construe faith as "bare assent to propositions"[36]—above all the proposition that Christ's righteousness has been imputed to sinners *coram deo*—and thus to reduce soteriology to a procedure of rational assent divorced from non-cognitive dimensions of "experience."

Recent interpreters have tended to take for granted that participatory soteriologies integrate with experience more naturally and effectively than forensic and substitutionary models. Macchia, for example, seeks to escape forensic soteriologies that "confine the life-giving Spirit to the cognitive function of faith"[37] by turning to the more "relational and transformational" concept of participation in Christ,[38] while Allchin advocates a recovery of participation to move beyond theologies that have merely "theorised about [God] without being able to bring men and women to any living apprehension of his presence and his power."[39] But is this actually true? Do participatory

---

[33] See, e.g., the Solid Declaration of the *Formula of Concord* [1577]: "although renewal and sanctification are a blessing of our mediator Christ and a work of the Holy Spirit, they do not belong in the article or in the treatment of justification before God, but rather result from it" (Solid Declaration, Article 3.28; *BC*, p. 566); "in the justification of the sinner before God, faith relies neither on contrition nor on love or other virtues, but only on Christ and (in him) on his perfect obedience, with which he fulfilled the law for us and which is reckoned [*imputatur*] to believers as righteousness" (Solid Declaration, Article 3.30; *BC*, p. 567).

[34] Milbank, *Beyond Secular Order*, p. 225. Emphasis original.

[35] Milbank, *Beyond Secular Order*, pp. 63–5.   [36] Pinnock, *Flame of Love*, p. 156.

[37] Macchia, *Justified in the Spirit*, p. 39.   [38] Macchia, *Justified in the Spirit*, p. 234.

[39] A.M Allchin, *Participation in God: A Forgotten Strand in Anglican Tradition* (London: Darton, Longman and Todd, 1988), p. 1.

models succeed in integrating embodiment, practice, and experience back into soteriology? And is forensic justification in fact cold and rationalistic? In order to test these arguments, two core claims must be examined: the assumption that participatory soteriologies are basically successful at integrating transformation and experience, and the argument that Protestant theologies of justification by faith are problematically rationalistic and thus inherently anti-experiential. The examination of these claims will be the task of the remainder of this chapter.

In order to do this, in what follows I will analyze a series of accounts that exhibit enough detail and specificity to give further insight into the question of how salvation is "experienced," while still being broad enough to represent some of the main theological options. I begin with two major modern Protestant accounts of salvation as participation, those of T.F. Torrance and Kathryn Tanner. I will then contrast these with the Thomist model of participation as it has been articulated in recent Dominican theology, before turning to the approach of Philip Melanchthon, whose justification-based model, I will argue, contains a kind of implicit account of participation while still being deeply integrated with "experience." First, however, we need to discuss the definitional problems that have often beset discussions of participation.

THREE MODELS OF SOTERIOLOGICAL PARTICIPATION

What are the affective and experiential contours of the work of the Spirit in enabling Christians to "participate in Christ"? Turning to this question, we run into further challenges. The first is that there is a great deal of variation in understandings of what "participation" is. Broadly speaking, as a soteriology it refers to the idea that salvation comes through human beings coming to share in the divine life and thus to participate in God's being in some sense.[40] But beyond this matters become murkier. As Adam Neder rightly notes, there is "wide variety of opinion regarding the meaning of human participation in the being of God . . . not only across traditions, but in the patristic era itself."[41]

One issue is terminological. Up to this point, I have used the term "soteriological participation" rather than "deification," "divinization," or *theosis*. But in recent theology this cluster of terms has often been used more or less

---

[40] For an overview of the basic contours here, see Norman Russell, *The Doctrine of Deification in the Greek Patristic Tradition* (Oxford: Oxford University Press, 2004), pp. 1–2.

[41] Adam Neder, *Participation in Christ: An Entry into Karl Barth's Church Dogmatics* (Louisville, KY: Westminster John Knox Press, 2009), p. 87. See also Russell, *The Doctrine of Deification*, pp. 1, 8–9, and passim.

synonymously. Observing this, Daniel Keating makes a useful distinction between two varieties of creaturely participation in God. The first is general participation in the divine being by virtue of creaturely existence itself, which is true of all creatures simply by virtue of being created by God.[42] The second is a further participation in Christ "in the order of grace," which is "supernatural" and in which we "participate in the life and qualities of God through Christ and in the Spirit."[43] According to Keating, "deification" refers only to the latter, soteriological participation: it is "specifically our supernatural participation in God" through which "we enter into the personal communion of love of the Father, Son, and Holy Spirit."[44] It is thus reasonable, in Keating's view, to call participation "deification" or *theosis* insofar as it refers to soteriological participation in particular rather than to the general participation of all creatures in the being of God by virtue of their creation.[45]

One question that often comes up in this context is whether and to what degree Western concepts of soteriological participation and Eastern concepts of *theosis* are the same. Keating offers a series of arguments for fundamental continuity between the two.[46] These are relatively persuasive, at least in terms of how the various terms tend to be used in contemporary theology. But different views of salvific participation in Christ can still have very different emphases. Some theologians, like Athanasius, focus on participation in respect of particular divine attributes, such as "incorruptibility,"[47] while others focus

---

[42] Daniel A. Keating, *Deification and Grace* (Naples, FL: Sapientia Press, 2007), pp. 99–100. See, e.g., Acts 17:28.

[43] Keating, *Deification and Grace*, p. 100. Tanner makes a similar distinction between what she calls "weak" and "strong" participation (Tanner, *Christ the Key*, pp. 8–13).

[44] Keating, *Deification and Grace*, p. 100.

[45] Keating also shares A.N. Williams' view that the traditional distinction between Eastern and Western approaches to deification, relating to the Eastern tendency to distinguish between the essence and the energies of God, does not signify as fundamental difference between the two approaches as is often supposed, since both traditions seek to safeguard the Creator-creature distinction while maintaining a "real communion with God." See Keating, *Deification and Grace*, pp. 107, 104–7 and A.N. Williams, *The Ground of Union: Deification in Aquinas and Palamas* (Oxford: Oxford University Press, 1999), 171–2. For dissenting views, see Gösta Hallonsten, "*Theosis* in Recent Research: A Renewal of Interest and a Need for Clarity," in *Partakers of the Divine Nature: The History and Development of Deification in the Christian Traditions*, eds. Michael J. Christensen and Jeffery A. Wittung (Grand Rapids, MI: Baker Academic, 2007), pp. 286–7, and Paul L. Gavrilyuk, "The Retrieval of Deification: How a Once-Despised Archaism Became an Ecumenical Desideratum," *Modern Theology* 25, no. 4 (2009), p. 650.

[46] Lately there has been a push to avoid any easy conflation of soteriological participation in general with the Orthodox doctrine of *theosis* as such. Hallonsten, for example, distinguishes between *theosis* as a "theme" in a given theologian's writings and a full-fledged "doctrine of *theosis*" (Hallonsten, "*Theosis* in Recent Research," pp. 283–4; see also Gavrilyuk, "The Retrieval of Deification"). For a response from Keating, see Daniel A. Keating, "Typologies of Deification," *International Journal of Systematic Theology* 17, no. 3 (2015).

[47] Athanasius: "And thus he, the incorruptible Son of God, being conjoined with all by a like nature, naturally clothed all with incorruption" (*de Incarnatione* 9; Athanasius, "On the Incarnation of the Word," in *Christology of the Later Fathers*, ed. Edward Rochie Hardy (London: SCM Press, 1954), p. 63). See also Irenaeus, *Adversus haereses* 3.18.7.

on the epistemological implications of participation, for example in the growth of spiritual senses,[48] and on participation as growth in virtue.[49] Most draw close connections between participation and the sacraments of baptism and eucharist,[50] though others are more vague about the role of sacraments.[51] Most accounts emphasize the importance of human cooperation in deification,[52] but some (Protestants, in particular) seek to downplay or reframe this dimension.[53] Eastern Orthodox interpreters tend to follow Palamas in viewing the distinction between divine energies and the divine essence as central to safeguarding the Creator-creature distinction in *theosis*, while Western interpreters like Aquinas use the doctrine of analogy for this purpose.[54] And most serious interpretations of salvific participation do a number of these things at once.

Given this variety, it is important to engage in depth with specific accounts of participation. With this in view, I turn now to one of the most important modern Protestant accounts of soteriological participation, that of T.F. Torrance.

---

[48] For example, spiritual perception as a dimension of deification is an important theme in Maximus the Confessor. See Frederick D. Aquino, "Maximus the Confessor," in *The Spiritual Senses* (Cambridge: Cambridge University Press, 2011), pp. 104–20.

[49] "Infused virtues dispose man in a higher manner and towards a higher end, and consequently in relation to some higher nature, that is, in relation to a participation in the Divine Nature" (Aquinas, *Summa Theologiae* 1-2.110.3). See also Keating, *Deification and Grace*, pp. 78–82.

[50] Gregory Nazianzen: "Were the Spirit not to be worshipped, how could he deify me through baptism?" (*Or.* 31.28; Gregory of Nazianzus, *On God and Christ: The Five Theological Orations and Two Letters to Cledonius*, trans. Lionel Wickham and Frederick Williams (Yonkers, NY: St Vladimir's Seminary Press, 2002), p. 139). Aquinas: "For the food is not changed into the one who eats it, but it turns the one who takes it into itself . . . And so this is a food capable of making man divine and inebriating him with divinity" (*in Io.* 6:55 [972]; Thomas Aquinas, *The Commentary on the Gospel of St John*. Part 1, trans. J.A. Weisheipl and F.R. Larcher (Albany, NY: Magi Books, 1980), p. 386). For these and many other examples, see Keating, *Deification and Grace*, pp. 41–8.

[51] Thomas F. Torrance, *Atonement: The Person and Work of Christ* (Downers Grove, IL: IVP Academic, 2009), p. 387.

[52] Ware: "[W]e have been endowed with the divine quality of freedom. God created us free, and Christ has restored that freedom to us (Gal. 5:1). We *cannot* be saved without God's grace, but God *will* not save us without our voluntary consent" (Kallistos Ware, "Salvation and Theosis in Orthodox Theology," in *Luther et la réforme allemande dans une perspective oecuménique*, ed. W. Schneemelcher (Geneva: Éditions du Centre Orthodoxe, 1983), pp. 179–80. See also Keating, *Deification and Grace*, pp. 68–71, and Keating, "Typologies of Deification," p. 282.

[53] See e.g., the discussion of Torrance below.

[54] See Keating, *Deification and Grace*, pp. 104–7, as well as Williams, *The Ground of Union*, pp. 89, 171–2, and Gavrilyuk, "The Retrieval of Deification," pp. 650, 652. For further discussion of the range of images used to describe what is happening in *theosis*, see Williams, *The Ground of Union*, pp. 106–25.

Participation and Experience in T.F. Torrance

One of the most creative examples of a Protestant soteriology of participation and *theosis* in the past half century was also one of the first. As early as 1964, T.F. Torrance was advocating a Protestant "reconsideration . . . of what the Greek fathers called *theosis*."[55]

For Torrance, salvation at its core is neither something that happens "to" human beings, nor something that is applied to them "externally" as a result of an atoning transaction between the Father and the Son.[56] Rather, salvation is something that has already happened, fully and completely, in Christ, such that it is only by participating in Christ's own salvation that human beings are saved. Torrance is quite clear on the point:

> [T]he atoning mediation and redemption which [Christ] wrought for us, fall *within* his own being and life as the one Mediator between God and man. That is to say, the work of atoning salvation does *not* take place *outside* of Christ, as something external to him, but takes place *within* him, *within* the incarnate constitution of his Person as Mediator . . . [Thus the] vicarious efficacy [of the redemptive work of Christ] has its force through the union of his divine Person as Creator and Lord with us in our creaturely being, whereby he lays hold of us in himself and acts for us from out of the inner depths of his coexistence with us and our existence in him, delivering us from the sentence of death upon us, and from the corruption and perdition that have overtaken us.[57]

Thus, for Torrance, Christ "acts for us" in every dimension of salvation, regeneration, and sanctification, and his work on our behalf then becomes ontologically "ours" through our "union and communion" with him, the precondition for which is the hypostatic union.[58] This means that the holiness of the church is not "our" holiness, but rather "the holiness of Christ in which [the church] shares by grace" insofar as it is a "partaker of divine nature";[59] and even the faith by which human beings are justified is Christ's faith, not ours.[60] At every point and in every dimension, what is decisive for Torrance is

---

[55] Torrance, "Come, Creator Spirit"; see especially pp. 243–4. In his Protestant rehabilitation of *theosis* Torrance preceded both E.P. Sanders' revival of participation in Pauline studies and Tuomo Mannermaa's analysis of *theosis* in Martin Luther by more than a decade. Both Sanders' *Paul and Palestinian Judaism* and Mannermaa's initial article on *theosis* in Luther appeared in 1977.

[56] Torrance, *The Trinitarian Faith*, p. 158.

[57] Torrance, *The Trinitarian Faith*, pp. 155–6. Emphasis original. Although Torrance frames his discussion in *The Trinitarian Faith* as an exposition of a set of patristic sources, there is little question that he shares and commends the views he is expositing, as reviewers have noted. See e.g. David F. Ford, "Review of *The Trinitarian Faith*," *Scottish Journal of Theology* 43, no. 2 (1990), p. 263.

[58] Torrance, *The Trinitarian Faith*, pp. 9, 160, 166.   [59] Torrance, *Atonement*, p. 386.

[60] Thomas F. Torrance, "Justification: Its Radical Nature and Place in Reformed Doctrine and Life," in *Theology in Reconstruction* (Eugene, OR: Wipf and Stock, 1996), p. 160.

the sharing, via ontological participation, in what is already the case in Christ. This is why, in his view, "union with God in and through Jesus Christ" necessarily "belongs to the inner heart of the atonement."[61] Through ontological participation in Christ, we are taken "into the immediate presence of the Father" and "made partakers of God beyond ourselves."[62] It is thus perfectly legitimate, in Torrance's view, for a Protestant to use traditional patristic language of *theosis/theopoesis*, "deification," and "partaking of the divine nature" to describe Christian salvation.[63]

A clear benefit of this approach is that it allows Torrance to affirm language traditionally associated with "justification"-based models of salvation—"ransom, sacrifice, propitiation, expiation, reconciliation"[64]—while contextualizing and relativizing such language within a more fundamental participatory scheme. According to Torrance, such terms "refer, not to any external transaction between God and mankind carried out by Christ, but to what took place within the union of divine and human natures in the incarnate Son of God."[65] This union was "wrought out throughout the whole historical life of Jesus," including in and through his atoning death and resurrection.[66]

Fundamental for Torrance is what he calls the "objectivity" of salvation from the perspective of the Christian: "Justification has been fulfilled subjectively and objectively in Jesus Christ, but that objective and subjective justification *is objective to us*."[67] In Torrance's account, "our adoption, sanctification and regeneration have already taken place in Christ."[68] The salvation and regeneration of Christians takes place "not in ourselves but out of ourselves, objectively in him."[69]

---

[61] Torrance, *The Trinitarian Faith*, p. 159.

[62] Torrance, *The Trinitarian Faith*, pp. 181, 189.

[63] For the first three, see e.g., Torrance, *The Trinitarian Faith*, pp. 166, 184, 188–9; Thomas F. Torrance, "*Spiritus Creator*: A Consideration of the Teaching of St Athanasius and St Basil," in *Theology in Reconstruction* (Eugene, OR: Wipf and Stock, 1996), p. 214. For the latter, with its reference to 2 Pet. 1:4, see "Torrance, 'Come, Creator Spirit," p. 241–2; and Torrance, *Atonement*, p. 386.

[64] Torrance, *The Trinitarian Faith*, p. 168.

[65] Torrance, *The Trinitarian Faith*, p. 168. Elsewhere he calls this "the sanctifying and regenerating of our human nature that [has] already taken place in Christ" (Torrance, "Come, Creator Spirit," p. 254). In a sense, the whole of Torrance's soteriology can be seen as an attempt to think through the implications of the hypostatic union.

[66] Torrance, *Atonement*, p. 162.

[67] Torrance, "Justification," p. 160. Emphasis added. The context here is justification in particular, but for Torrance the point also applies more widely to salvation as such.

[68] Thomas F. Torrance, "The One Baptism Common to Christ and His Church," in *Theology in Reconciliation* (Eugene, OR: Wipf and Stock, 1996), p. 89. This paradox is captured well in Torrance's reference to "our own human nature, our own human flesh in Jesus" (Torrance, "Justification," p. 160).

[69] Thomas F. Torrance, "The Relevance of the Doctrine of the Spirit for Ecumenical Theology," in *Theology in Reconstruction* (Eugene, OR: Wipf and Stock, 1996), p. 238.

But how is this "objective" reality actually appropriated to Christians? If they are saved through a sharing in the objective salvation that has taken place in and through the person of Christ, how exactly do sinful human beings come to share in it? One answer is that such sharing is the work of the Holy Spirit:

> It is only through the communion of the Holy Spirit . . . that we may share in the saving, regenerating and sanctifying work in the life, death and resurrection of the Lord Jesus Christ, and thus share in his eternal offering of himself, and of us as redeemed and consecrated in him, to God the Father.[70]

For Torrance, the Holy Spirit is thus the agent of deification as it actually occurs in the lives of particular Christians,[71] and the prayer "Come Holy Spirit" is nothing less than "a prayer for participation in the divine nature."[72]

But what is such participation like from the perspective of the participant? When the Spirit "renews us by drawing us within the self-consecration of Christ made on our behalf and by assimilating us into his holiness," are there any practically recognizable experiential correlates to this process?[73] Does it change our feelings or desires or cognitions or behaviors? If so, how and in what ways?

Torrance makes no attempt to answer these questions. Again and again, he describes the saving activity of the Spirit in terms that could be read as implying some sort of experiential correlate, but then fails to specify what such experiences might be in practice. Thus Torrance is happy to say that the Holy Spirit "brings the impact of his divine power and holiness to bear directly and personally upon [Christians'] lives in judgement and salvation," but he then gives no indication of what such a "direct" and "personal" "impact" is actually like for embodied human beings and communities in the world.

From the perspective of a full-orbed pneumatology, this seems a deep weakness in Torrance's account. Faced with his near total silence on the relationship between participation and experience, and trying to understand the affective salience of his soteriological scheme, we are presented with two equally unsatisfactory possibilities: (a) the work of the Spirit in salvation never affects actual human bodies in time; or (b) there are experiential correlates of participation, but the task of theologically analyzing or describing them is so laden with problems that it should never be attempted. The first option is bad

---

[70] Torrance, *The Trinitarian Faith*, p. 4. See likewise Torrance, *The Trinitarian Faith*, p. 249, and Torrance, "Come, Creator Spirit," p. 250.

[71] Torrance, *The Trinitarian Faith*, p. 190: "the giving and receiving of the Spirit . . . constitutes the 'deifying' content of the atoning exchange in which through the pouring out of the same Spirit upon us we are given to participate."

[72] Torrance, "Come, Creator Spirit," pp. 241–2. See also p. 250; and Torrance, *The Trinitarian Faith*, p. 189 ("to have the Spirit dwelling in us is to be made partakers of God beyond ourselves").

[73] Torrance, "Come, Creator Spirit," p. 250.

pneumatology, and the second is problematic for the same reasons Luther's and Barth's false dichotomy on experience is problematic.[74]

Torrance sidesteps the question of how participation in Christ plays out in the world in a particular way. Faced with the question of how to describe the "actual" and "direct" work of the Spirit in salvation, Torrance consistently punts to ontological language, describing what Christ's work accomplishes for Christians in their "being" rather than anything that might happen in bodies and in time. Redemption, Torrance tells us, "is worked out in *the ontological depths* of the humanity which [Christ] made his own."[75] Christ "acts person-ally on our behalf . . . from within the *ontological depths of our human exist-ence* which he has penetrated and gathered up in himself."[76] What is decisive is Christ's "union . . . with us *in our creaturely being*, whereby he lays hold of us in himself and acts for us from out of *the inner depths of his coexistence with us and our existence in him*."[77] "[I]t is in *the inner depth of their personal being* that humanity must be reconciled to God and we must be healed of our enmity and contradiction to God."[78]

By describing the Spirit's mediation of Christ's saving work in ontological terms like these, the effect—intended or not—is a kind of rhetorical sleight of hand on the subject of experience. Because salvation and renewal are real events *coram deo*, Torrance is able to use highly actualistic and personalistic language to describe them—"direct," "personal," "actual," "confrontation," "lays hold of us," and so on—despite the fact that these events appear to bear no necessary relation to anything that happens in the embodied life of human beings in time, *coram mundo*. The reader perhaps assumes that all this will have concrete effects in the world of some kind, but Torrance does not spell out what these effects might be.[79]

---

[74] In Chapter 1 I argued that Luther and Barth's positions on "enthusiasm" and subjectivity, respectively, are caught up in a long-standing false choice in Protestant thought whereby it is assumed that "experience" must either be theology's foundation or else be distrusted entirely. I then argued that the attempt to excise experience and subjectivity from theological reasoning is problematic on biblical and theological grounds, and is impossible to achieve in practice.

[75] Torrance, *The Trinitarian Faith*, p. 181. Emphasis added.

[76] Torrance, *The Trinitarian Faith*, p. 156. Emphasis added.

[77] Torrance, *The Trinitarian Faith*, pp. 155. Emphasis added.

[78] Torrance, *Atonement*, p. 159. Emphasis added.

[79] Torrance's soteriology is full of this pattern of using language that appears to signal attentiveness to affective salience to describe events that in fact take place only in what Rahner calls the realm of "pure ontological reality." To list just a few: a good soteriology will "bear savingly upon the distorted and corrupt condition of man's actual human existence" (Torrance, *The Trinitarian Faith*, p. 156); "what he has actually done in penetrating into the dark depths of our twisted human existence" (Torrance, *The Trinitarian Faith*, p. 160); "Pentecost must be regarded . . . as the actualisation within the life of the Church of the atoning life, death and resurrection of the Saviour" (Torrance, *The Trinitarian Faith*, p. 190); the Spirit "open[s] us up within our subjectivities for Christ in such a radical way that we find our life not in ourselves but out of ourselves, objectively in him" (Torrance, "Relevance of the Doctrine of the Spirit," p. 238). In each of these cases we see the rhetoric of experience without its actuality.

In Torrance's hands, even ostensibly temporally specific events like baptism and the eucharist exhibit this dynamic. Baptism is an "unrepeatabl[e] initiation" into "the enduring reality" of a sanctification that is "already complete in Christ"; and "holy communion" is the means by which the church is "continually participant" in that reality.[80] The sacraments are thus modes of participation in an ontological reality, and the question of how such participation is perceived in experience is simply not addressed. Ziegler summarizes Torrance's "objective" understanding of salvation, and its implications for experience:

> Torrance understands Christian existence in Christ to be an objective ontological reality. Each Christian is brought within the circle of the life of Christ to share in the Son's communion with the Father through the Spirit. *Whether we recognize it or not*, the reality of who we are is not the sum of our individual acts and personal virtues, but the fact that we are hid with Christ in God. 'Strictly speaking,' Torrance remarks, 'Christianity is quite invisible.'[81]

From the perspective of pneumatology, this will not do. As I argued in Chapter 2, a purely "invisible" Christianity is one that does not take seriously the reality of the Holy Spirit. Torrance's framework for understanding *theosis* builds on important traditional and scriptural resources, and his approach is particularly successful at integrating cross and incarnation in a synthetic soteriological scheme. But absent any affectively and experientially plausible account of how *theosis* might play out in the world, Torrance's soteriology ends up operating, in practice, at the level of pure conceptuality. It functions as a kind of pneumatological Docetism: it has no real connection to bodies, just the appearance of such a connection.[82]

Why is Torrance's soteriology so oriented towards the "objective," and so devoid of reference to Christian experience? One reason appears to be that his thinking on subjectivity and experience is deeply shaped by the old Protestant false dichotomy on experience that was examined and found problematic in Chapter 1. We see this in a series of early articles Torrance wrote on the doctrine of the Holy Spirit, where he repeatedly articulates a critique of what he calls "Neo-Protestant subjectivism."[83] According to Torrance, "the persistent error . . . of Protestantism" is that it

---

[80] Torrance, *Atonement*, p. 387.

[81] Geordie W Ziegler, *Trinitarian Grace and Participation: An Entry into the Theology of T.F. Torrance* (Minneapolis: Fortress Press, 2017), p. 243. Emphasis added. The Torrance quotation is from an unpublished sermon on Colossians 3:3.

[82] On "pneumatological docetism," see Otto Weber, *Foundations of Dogmatics,* ii, trans. Darrell L. Guder (Grand Rapids, MI: William B. Eerdmans Publishing Company, 1983), pp. 237–8.

[83] Thomas F. Torrance, "A New Reformation?," in *Theology in Reconstruction* (Eugene, OR: Wipf and Stock, 1996), p. 279.

confounds the Spirit of God with the human spirit. Thus the knowledge of the Spirit is dissolved into the subjectivities of the consciousness of the . . . individual, and the products of this consciousness . . . are put forward as operations of the Holy Spirit.[84]

The focus on subjective experience is deemed to be particularly problematic when it comes to salvation: "We have become accustomed to think of the coming of the Holy Spirit far too much as the interiorizing in our hearts of divine salvation, with the result that the presence of the Spirit is so often identified with inward moral and religious states."[85] In Torrance's view, Protestant theology has erred precisely insofar as it has correlated salvation with particular experiences in or of the "heart."

In response, he prescribes the return to "objectivity" that we saw worked out above:

> What is required is a recovery of complete objectivity . . . that depends upon our being objectively related in worship, action and reflection to the transcendent objectivity of God. It can take place only when we allow God [to] open us up for truly objective relation toward himself.[86]

And it is just this objectivity that Torrance believes *theosis* can provide. In "*theosis*" the Christian is "raised up to find the true centre of his existence not in himself but in Holy God." In this, *theosis* represents "the antithesis of the nineteenth-century notion of 'the divine in man' . . . or of the man-centred emphasis of so many modern Protestants."[87]

Torrance's consistent prioritization of ontological over experiential language for describing the work of the Spirit in salvific participation is thus no accident. The value of *theosis* is precisely its ability to articulate an "objectivity" to the work of salvation that is free of the errors of "Neo-Protestant subjectivism." Unless theology restricts its soteriological speech to the level of ontology alone, Torrance believes it cannot but fall into an idolatrous "confusion between the Creator Spirit of Holy God and the creative spirituality of Christian man."[88] In this vision, ontological and experiential registers of soteriological speech seem to be mutually exclusive.

From the perspective of the present study, Torrance's argument is compromised by its uncritical acceptance of the old Protestant false dichotomy about religious experience. Like the early Barth, Torrance is unable to conceive of a middle position between a total excising of experience from theology and an equally total Schleiermacherian establishment of experience as the "ground" for all dogmatic claims. As I argued in Chapter 1, this is a false

---

[84] Torrance, "*Spiritus Creator*," pp. 227–8.   [85] Torrance, "Come, Creator Spirit," p. 242.
[86] Torrance, "Relevance of the Doctrine of the Spirit," p. 233.
[87] Torrance, "Come, Creator Spirit," p. 243.
[88] Torrance, "Come, Creator Spirit," pp. 244–5.

alternative, unsustainable on biblical, historical, dogmatic, and cognitive-scientific grounds. Far from reintegrating experience into theology, Torrance's account of participation simply reestablishes an earlier Protestantism's naïve anti-experientialism on a framework of deification.

We now see that Torrance's account of "union and communion" with Christ does not succeed in providing the kind of integration of transformation and experience that recent theologians have looked to participatory soteriologies to provide. It would seem that the mere fact of having a soteriology of participation and deification does not secure the integration of soteriology with embodied experience.

But is this a problem peculiar to Torrance, or does it represent a broader tendency in Protestant theologies of participation? I turn now to Kathryn Tanner's account of participation to see if her model fares any better when examined through the lens of pneumatology and experience.

Participation and Experience in Tanner's Christ the Key

Kathryn Tanner's *Christ the Key* is probably the most significant Protestant account of soteriological participation to appear since Torrance. Although the book touches on a number of themes, close to its heart is the relation between Christology and soteriology. Tanner's goal throughout *Christ the Key* is to show how a certain kind of reorientation of theology to Christ "throws fresh light on otherwise tired theological topics and opens up new avenues for approaching them by breaking through current impasses in the theological literature."[89]

I pose the same question of Tanner that I posed of Torrance: in what sense and to what extent in her scheme is saving "participation" something that is experienced by the participant in practically recognizable ways? In asking this question, Tanner's account serves as a useful contrast because, unlike Torrance, she is explicitly attentive at a number of points in the book to the subjective changes wrought in the Christian through participation in Christ, and because she associates such effects directly and programmatically with the work of the Holy Spirit.

In the first chapter of *Christ the Key*, Tanner distinguishes between "weak participation," which is characteristic of all created things at all times, and "strong participation," by which the creature participates in "what one is not," namely, "the divine image itself." It is this latter mode of participation that is soteriological: the purpose of this imaging is that human nature may be

---

[89] Tanner, *Christ the Key*, p. vii.

"healed and elevated, shaped and re-formed . . . in short, . . . re-fashioned in the divine image so as to become humanly perfect."[90]

What makes this reshaping through strong participation possible and what gives it its content is the incarnation, through which Christ attached himself permanently and irrevocably to human nature: "The humanity of Jesus has that perfect attachment or orientation to the Word in virtue of his being one with the Word . . . and we gain the capability of something like that through our connection to him."[91] Tanner continues: "Before Christ came, the divine image of the Word was simply foreign to us . . . Now that the Word has taken our humanity to be its own, the Word has become in a sense proper to us."[92] The consequence is that in the incarnation human beings are given the possibility of a healed and perfected human nature through participation in Christ's perfect and glorified humanity. Such participation "could simply be called grace."[93]

Tanner characterizes this salvific and sanctifying participation through a particular trope: "attachment to Christ."[94] She describes this in more detail in the second chapter:

> [W]hat we are given in Christ so adheres to us as to amount to a kind of redone internal constitution. Via the hypostatic union, we are wrapped around with something we cannot get rid of, something that therefore inevitably makes itself felt in all that we go on to become . . . We are given a new sufficiently strong tie . . . to what is life-giving and nourishing to counter our old bondage to what harms us.[95]

Strong participation, then, consists in a form of "attachment" that allows the transfer of the attributes of Christ's humanity—above all, the "life-giving power of the Word"[96]—to human beings in their nature, in such a way that sin and death are successfully combated and "humanity's entrance into trinitarian relations" is made possible.[97]

On the face of it, such attachment thus appears to have experiential and affective rather than just ontological consequences: it involves "becoming attached [to Christ] . . . with purity of attention, full commitment, and intense love";[98] or again, it is the function of the "power of the Spirit" to "attach us to [Christ], make us one with him, in all the intensity of faith, hope, and love."[99]

However, it soon becomes clear that there is in fact a typically Protestant distinction in Tanner's model between attachment to Christ per se, which she

---

[90] Tanner, *Christ the Key*, p. 17.   [91] Tanner, *Christ the Key*, p. 14.
[92] Tanner, *Christ the Key*, p. 36.   [93] Tanner, *Christ the Key*, p. 58.
[94] Tanner, *Christ the Key*, pp. 13, 14, 36, 40, 70, and passim.
[95] Tanner, *Christ the Key*, pp. 72–3.   [96] Tanner, *Christ the Key*, p. 269.
[97] Tanner, *Christ the Key*, p. 144.   [98] Tanner, *Christ the Key*, p. 13.
[99] Tanner, *Christ the Key*, p. 14.

associates with salvation proper, and the subjective dimensions like faith, hope, and love, which she ascribes to sanctification only:

> [S]tress on strong participation in God, through attachment to what one is not, encourages a very sharp, typically Protestant distinction between justification and sanctification. We are not justified in virtue of the righteousness we possess in and of ourselves by leading renovated lives under God's grace. This would make justification a matter of sanctification, a consequence of our own holiness. Instead, we are justified through our attachment to Christ, who is righteous as we are not. We are justified in being attached to him because of what he is and not what we are in ourselves.

Tanner continues:

> What . . . accounts for our being justified is simply the change of state we undergo in relationship to [Christ]. What justification refers to in us is the fact of our unity with him, our incorporation within his own life . . . Nothing about us, in and of ourselves, therefore has to change in order for us to be justified; it is the fact of our attachment to Christ, irrespective of anything else that might be going on with us, that accounts for God's declaring us just.[100]

In locating the foundation of salvation in "what he is and not what we are in ourselves," Tanner's model is similar to that of Torrance. For both theologians, a key advantage of understanding salvation as participation is that they believe it provides a way of thinking about salvation in terms that are simultaneously non-"extrinsic" *and* radically non-Pelagian. Tanner is even more explicit than Torrance that justification must do its formal work independent of its subjective effects in Spirit-enabled sanctification: "The fact that the gift of the Holy Spirit is part of what it means for us to be justified does not . . . make justification part of sanctification, as if we are justified to the extent that we are made just."[101] And again: "We are justified in this same sense whether or not, and whatever the degree to which, our lives have been made over through the power of the Spirit to conform to the pattern of the human life that Jesus lived."[102]

Having established a strict formal distinction between justification and sanctification, Tanner argues that the two are nevertheless profoundly connected:

> Sanctification refers to the good changes in us that attachment to Christ brings about. Sanctification is a matter of what happens in and to our humanity, what is different about the way we live, as a consequence of attachment to Christ.[103]

This sanctification is, furthermore, the particular work of the Holy Spirit, given to us in justification as a new "power": "In being attached to Christ, we gain the power of the Spirit to renovate our lives."[104]

---

[100] Tanner, *Christ the Key*, p. 86.
[102] Tanner, *Christ the Key*, p. 89.
[104] Tanner, *Christ the Key*, p. 87.

[101] Tanner, *Christ the Key*, p. 89.
[103] Tanner, *Christ the Key*, p. 87.

The language of "power" is central to Tanner's pneumatology in *Christ the Key*. The primary function of the gifting of the Spirit in her soteriology is

> [to] give rise to new powers and capacities in us; there are certain created correlates of the gift of the Holy Spirit in us—new human dispositions, for example, of faith and love—by way of which our whole life is renovated in Christ's image.[105]

Attachment to Christ thus really does have subjective consequences—"new powers and capacities" given by the Holy Spirit—and these consequences as they develop and grow over time are what she calls "sanctification."

At the same time, Tanner carefully distinguishes the new "powers" that all those who are attached to Christ have in principle from the *effects or manifestations* of these powers as they begin to change or "renovate" the human being in question. The reason, once again, is to preclude any possibility of inferring a person's status before God from the degree of empirical change evident in their lives as "the human consequences" of the work of the Spirit "unroll over time."[106] As she puts it, "the presence of the Holy Spirit might simply be the obverse of attachment to Christ"—and therefore an objective and irreducible given of such attachment—"but the human consequences are not. The Holy Spirit may be genuinely given to us, present within us, even when that fact is not visible in our changed dispositions and deeds."[107] This is important in her view because otherwise the Spirit's work could come to be considered in some sense our own possession or merit, and these are possibilities Tanner strictly rejects. Like Torrance, Tanner appears to be concerned that, in the history of Protestantism, "faith" itself has tended to become a kind of "work."

Is there then any formal connection between justification and "experience" for Tanner? Strictly speaking, the answer is "no," and this for distinctly Protestant reasons: absent a "sharp distinction" between justification and sanctification, in Tanner's view it is difficult to avoid making sanctification at least partially constitutive of salvation.

To see just how disconnected justification and experience are in Tanner's thought, it is helpful to examine her account of "faith." In her view, although faith "constitutes a form of attachment to [Christ],"[108] it nevertheless falls under the domain of sanctification, not justification. Although "from our side," i.e. the side of human subjectivity, faith is a "human act of turning away from self toward Christ in order to cling only to him,"[109] and is therefore fundamentally oriented towards christological "attachment," nevertheless

---

[105] Tanner, *Christ the Key*, p. 83.   [106] Tanner, *Christ the Key*, p. 89.
[107] Tanner, *Christ the Key*, p. 89.
[108] Tanner, *Christ the Key*, p. 92, or "act of attachment to Christ" (p. 91).
[109] Tanner, *Christ the Key*, p. 91.

"attachment to Christ does not come about because of our own dispositions of attachment to him such as faith."[110] Rather, saving attachment to Christ is grounded objectively, in the incarnation alone.[111] Tanner's conclusion is that "faith is a gift of the Holy Spirit, and as such part of our sanctification to new life. It should be placed on the side of sanctification rather than justification in that it is one human consequence of the latter."[112] Otherwise, Christians would inevitably interpret faith as "some kind of work by which we are justified."[113]

In its complete formal detachment from subjective effects and correlates, justification for Tanner is therefore fundamentally an ontological rather than an experiential reality. Like Torrance, Tanner in fact polices this line very carefully. "Attachment to Christ" is a metaphysical reality that can be described by the theologian, but *as justification* it can never be "experienced" directly.

At the same time, it would be an error to conclude that Tanner's soteriology is simply anti-experiential, for two reasons. The first is that there is one dimension of Tanner's participatory soteriology that is clearly "practically recognizable," at least in the sense of being temporally specific. In a later chapter on "Trinitarian life," Tanner notes that soteriological attachment to Christ does not just take place once and for all for humanity as a whole by virtue of the incarnation, as her earlier discussion had seemed to imply. Discussing the trinitarian dimensions of soteriological attachment as an ascension with Christ to the Father and descent back into the world from the Father through Christ and the Spirit, Tanner asks:

> What are we talking about more concretely here? What forms do such movements take in Christian lives? Our initial ascent to the Father with Christ requires us to be joined to Christ, to become Christ's own, through the power of the Spirit; and is therefore associated with baptism. The Spirit ministers to us at our baptisms to make us one with Christ, according to the Father's will.[114]

Attachment thus takes place, for Tanner, at a specific moment in time in the life of the Christian: when they receive the sacrament of baptism. Although the affective and experiential dimensions are not specific here, the moment of "attachment" is temporally specific.

The second reason her soteriology is not as anti-experiential as that of Torrance has to do with how closely she connects justification and sanctification. Even if at one level there is a "sharp distinction" between them, at another level the two categories are intimately related. The sanctifying presence of the Spirit is the "obverse" of justification. This means in practice—here

---

[110] Tanner, *Christ the Key*, p. 92. [111] Tanner, *Christ the Key*, p. 92.
[112] Tanner, *Christ the Key*, pp. 92–3. [113] Tanner, *Christ the Key*, p. 94.
[114] Tanner, *Christ the Key*, p. 198.

Tanner is reminiscent of traditional Reformed accounts—that a person can never be justified without at the same time receiving the Spirit's "powers" in sanctification.

Unlike Torrance, Tanner seeks to specify what this sanctification might entail with some care. She is very clear that sanctification involves new "dispositions" and "powers" and "capacities" from the Spirit, and these in turn have all sorts of "human consequences" that "unroll over time." Indeed, in one case Tanner asserts explicitly, via a quotation from Luther, that this includes affective changes.[115]

Yet despite these affirmations, overall Tanner reads as fundamentally ambivalent about these "human consequences." At one point she explicitly downplays the importance of concrete experiential and "psychological" effects of sanctification: "Faith and love are privileged . . . in virtue of the way they refer to God and therefore not because their own psychological character establishes their greater importance over other human acts and dispositions." Thus it is not because faith produces "gratitude for what God has done" or because love "gives one the desire to act in God's service . . . selflessly and without fear" that they are important, but rather because of their "own empty receptiveness to what comes to them from without," namely, "the divine power that remakes human lives."[116] In the crucial cases of faith and love, then, it is their orientation to ontological realities as distinct from psychological ones that explains their privileged status in relation to other dimensions of human subjectivity.

We might summarize as follows. On the one hand, Tanner claims that the purpose of the presence of the Spirit is to sanctify real human beings in all their historical and embodied particularity. Indeed, the central argument of the final chapter in *Christ the Key* is that the Spirit works "in and under the human," through "ordinary human operations" and in "sinful historical processes,"[117] and thus, presumably, through real human bodies. On the other hand, like many Protestants before her, Tanner also wants to secure the independence of salvation proper from the subjective appropriation or impact or experience of that salvation, however construed. And this means that there is a prioritization of the conditions of the possibility of such sanctification over its particular embodied outworkings. In her account, the "divine *power* to remake human lives" is more important, theologically, than any specific "remaking" that might take place.

---

[115] "[W]hen Christ is present he drives out 'lust, sadness of heart, fear of death, and the like '[, and] through the gift of his Spirit . . . 'creates new life and impulses in us'" (Tanner, *Christ the Key*, p. 88). The sections in single quotation marks are from Luther's *Lectures on Galatians* (*LW* 26:350 and *LW* 26:260 respectively).

[116] Tanner, *Christ the Key*, pp. 94–5.   [117] Tanner, *Christ the Key*, pp. 298, 274, 299.

In practice, this privileging of the possibility of sanctification over its actuality risks rolling back the affirmations of the importance of subjective outworkings of attachment to Christ that Tanner stresses at various points. Tanner's functional distinction between the conditions of possibility for human transformation and the experiential reality of actual transformation experienced in bodies does not hold up well in practice. What meaningful Christian concept of the "remaking" or "renovating" of "human lives" could there be if fostering "gratitude for what God has done" and giving "the desire to act in God's service" are not precisely the sort of forms that such remaking should take?

The answer thus seems to be similar to what we found in Torrance: such remaking can be described reliably only through ontological rather than experiential categories, through assertions about pneumatological "powers" and "capacities" rather than also through practically recognizable changes in bodies and minds. In Tanner's picture, it seems that you can be saved, you can participate in God through attachment to Christ, you can even have new "powers" and "capacities" for virtue from the Holy Spirit, without experiencing anything that is practically recognizable to others or indeed to yourself, beyond the sheer, bald fact of baptism: "The Holy Spirit may be genuinely given to us, present within us, even when that fact is not visible in our changed dispositions and deeds."[118]

In *Christ the Key*, salvation as participation in Christ is secured theologically as a mechanism by which God saves human beings by grace alone. This is done by drawing on and expanding traditional accounts of soteriological participation, especially that of Gregory of Nyssa. However, despite appearances and even some claims to the contrary, the divide between subjective and objective dimensions of soteriology has been bridged only in a reserved and ambivalent way. Consequently, it is difficult to say that Tanner's soteriology succeeds in truly doing justice to the pneumatological principle that the Spirit is the one who "actualizes" the work of Father and Son in the subjective experience of the Christian.

Why, despite efforts to the contrary, is Tanner's account of the effects of the indwelling of the Spirit in the Christian ultimately so ambivalent? Once again, the problem appears to lie with her concern, after the fashion of Barth, that any articulation of a more concrete connection between salvation and experience might necessarily turn such experience into the *ground* of salvation. This concern seems to be visible in her statement that "the fact that the gift of the Holy Spirit is part of what it means for us to be justified does not ... make justification part of sanctification, as if we are justified to the extent that we are made just."[119] Even faith itself cannot involve any subjective experience of

---

[118] Tanner, *Christ the Key*, p. 89.   [119] Tanner, *Christ the Key*, p. 89.

salvation in itself because this would make it "some kind of work by which we are justified."[120] In this Tanner, like Torrance, seems to be caught in the old Protestant false dichotomy about experience. Absent an alternative way of construing the affective salience of the work of the Spirit in salvation, the only non-Pelagian language left for describing salvation resides in purely onto-logical categories like "attachment to Christ" and the implantation of vague "powers" and "capacities."

It is now clear that Torrance and Tanner's accounts of salvific participation, while compelling and helpful in other ways, exhibit significant difficulties when examined from the perspective of pneumatological experience. In both cases these difficulties are substantially affected by their allegiance to one of the core convictions of classical Protestantism, that the only way to prevent a model of salvation from devolving into a subtle form of justification by works is to assert the strict objectivity of Christ's saving work in relation to the effects of that work on human beings. Both furthermore interpret this principle to mean that human faith, however construed, cannot be soteriologically de-cisive, because this would make faith into a work. Thus for Torrance it is not our faith but Christ's that saves us, while for Tanner faith as such does not save at all because it falls under the domain of sanctification.

From a Protestant perspective, these accounts leave us with a question: how might we take forward the valid concern to preserve the disjunctive and radically non-Pelagian character of grace while at the same time providing a thicker and more persuasive account of the fact that the Holy Spirit works in real bodies?

Participation and Experience in Neo-Thomism

I now turn to a third account of soteriological participation that provides an illuminating contrast to both Torrance and Tanner: the neo-Thomist vision of salvation that has been articulated in recent Dominican theology by figures such as Servais Pinckaers, Romanus Cessario, and Jordan Aumann.[121] Exam-ining these late twentieth-century interpreters of Aquinas will serve two purposes. First, it will provide further evidence, through contrast, of just how powerfully Torrance and Tanner are shaped by the Protestant either/or on Christian religious experience, despite their respective turns to the lan-guage *theosis* and participation. Second, an examination of the strengths as

---

[120] Tanner, *Christ the Key*, p. 94.

[121] Specifically, I will draw on three texts, all originally published between 1980 and 1996: Servais Pinckaers, *The Sources of Christian Ethics*, trans. Sr. Mary Thomas Noble (Washington, D.C.: The Catholic University of America Press, 1995); Romanus Cessario, *Christian Faith and the Theological Life* (Washington, D.C.: The Catholic University of America Press, 1996); and Jordan Aumann, *Spiritual Theology* (London: Continuum, 2006).

well as the weaknesses of these Dominican accounts will set up the basic problem that must be addressed by any experientially and pneumatologically integrated Protestant soteriology: how to describe the practically recognizable reality of the Spirit's saving work in such a way that it does not ultimately exclude the Protestant appeal to the radically unconditional and unearned character of grace.

I make no particular claim in what follows as to the accuracy of the modern Dominican accounts as interpretations of Aquinas himself, though it is clear that they function deep within his theological orbit. Furthermore, my interest is in broad commonalities between the work of Pinckaers, Cessario, and Aumann, rather than the differences between them. The purpose is simply to draw out the striking contrast that the modern neo-Thomist vision provides for Protestant soteriologies of participation such as those of Torrance and Tanner above, on the one hand, and the Melanchthonian account of justification by faith to follow, on the other, in light of the fundamental question of the relationship between ontology, experience, and the work of the Spirit.

Reading Pinckaers, Cessario, and Aumann, it is immediately clear that we are dealing with a much closer and less ambivalent connection between ontology and experience than is the case in either Torrance or Tanner. Pinckaers, glossing the apostle Paul, is typical here:

> Faith joins the believer so intimately to Christ that it transforms his inmost being, producing in him through baptism a death whence springs a new source of life . . . These are not simply dogmatic abstract statements; for St. Paul they are directly operative and effect a profound change in the personality and life of the Christian . . . This change is not in the purely ontological order, escaping perception.[122]

Cessario is equally clear: "God's action in the world results in real changes and produces real effects in people."[123]

At the core of this model is the notion that what makes a Christian a Christian is the infusion of the theological or supernatural virtues. This is because it is these that effect the Christian's participation in the divine nature: "the theological virtues of faith, hope, and charity . . . constitute the supernatural capacities given to the Christian that enable him or her to adhere personally to the triune God."[124] These virtues are bestowed directly and concretely in baptism,[125] such that baptism "imprints a lasting spiritual

---

[122] Pinckaers, *Sources of Christian Ethics*, p. 117. See also p. 116: "Personal union with Christ through faith and love has a direct and general effect on the moral life of the Christian."

[123] Cessario, *Christian Faith*, p. 31.

[124] Cessario, *Christian Faith*, p. 5. See also Aumann, *Spiritual Theology*, p. 67.

[125] "Baptism bestows on the recipient the life of sanctifying grace, the infused theological and moral virtues, and the gifts of the Holy Spirit" (Aumann, *Spiritual Theology*, p. 212). See also Pinckaers, *Sources of Christian Ethics*, p. 117, and Cessario, *Christian Faith*, p. 6.

character on the soul."[126] Furthermore, although they are distinct from the gifts of the Spirit proper,[127] the agent that infuses these virtues is still the Holy Spirit: "Infused virtues . . . are spiritual endowments that originate entirely in the sanctification that Christian theology attributes to the Holy Spirit."[128]

As in the Protestant accounts, the process of salvation is grounded ontologically in the first instance: grace is "a participation in God's own life" that "belongs to the inner reality of the soul."[129] Furthermore, in talking about "supernatural capacities" and "spiritual endowments" bestowed by the Holy Spirit, at first it appears that we might be close to Tanner's understanding of Spirit-given "powers" and "capacities" for sanctification. But a closer look reveals significant differences. Most importantly, Pinckaers, Cessario, and Aumann are all very clear that there can be no outworking of these infused virtues that does not directly take up and transform natural human affections, faculties, and actions, even as it always also transcends them. In contrast to the Protestant accounts, then, grace is connected very closely and without ambivalence to its concrete effects on bodies.[130]

Pinckaers describes this dynamic in relation to the theological virtue of charity. When the Spirit pours the love of God into our hearts (Rom. 5:5), this "fills the life of believers and takes over even the humblest human virtues and emotions." Importantly,

> this in no way precludes an interest in human forms of love, for far from destroying these, charity purifies, deepens, and strengthens them, even enhancing them with a divine dimension. We could say that charity is enfleshed in human affections . . . Nevertheless, charity springs from another source than human emotions, claims another essence.[131]

This is a typical example of the interweaving of the ontological and the experiential that is characteristic of neo-Thomist accounts of sanctifying grace. It is the real historical and embodied human being who is being transformed, but at the same time the supernatural source and character of the infused virtues means that this transformation "transcends ordinary thought and emotion."[132] In view here is a kind of transfiguration of the natural that opens human capacities to the divine and "shape[s] us . . . to our supernatural end."[133] As Aumann puts it, infused virtues "are supernatural in their essence but not in their operation."[134] The relationship between ontology

---

[126] Aumann, *Spiritual Theology*, p. 212.

[127] See Aumann, *Spiritual Theology*, pp. 92–3, 96–7; and Cessario, *Christian Faith*, pp. 159, 162–3.

[128] Cessario, *Christian Faith*, p. 3. See also Pinckaers, *Sources of Christian Ethics*, pp. 120–2, and Aumann, *Spiritual Theology*, pp. 92–3.

[129] Cessario, *Christian Faith*, p. 32.   [130] See e.g., Cessario, *Christian Faith*, p. 129.

[131] Pinckaers, *Sources of Christian Ethics*, pp. 122–3.

[132] Pinckaers, *Sources of Christian Ethics*, p. 117.   [133] Cessario, *Christian Faith*, p. 5.

[134] Aumann, *Spiritual Theology*, p. 82.

and experience is thus very close here, and it is articulated according to a particular system. The way that all this plays out in practice depends on a series of further distinctions amongst types of virtues and habits.[135]

Particularly illuminating for present purposes is the interplay in neo-Thomist theology between "infused" and "acquired" virtues in the lives of believers. Given the presence in the Christian of infused supernatural capacities for sanctified action, why do Christians still sin? The answer, as Aumann argues, is that infused virtues "give us the intrinsic power for supernatural acts but not the extrinsic facility for those acts." This is why "the repentant habitual sinner experiences great difficulty in the practice of virtue."[136] Baptism and the infused virtues do not simply remove the habits of vice acquired prior to conversion. As acquired habits, such vices can be removed and replaced only through the acquisition of virtue through a process of habituation over time. It is thus that "the notion of *habitus* . . . provides . . . a way of illustrating how grace transforms the principal psychological capacities of human nature."[137]

The particular way that the infused virtues function in all this is as "operative habits." What this means is that they operate as powers that genuinely *facilitate* virtuous action, but they do so in such a way that they do not bypass either the will or the natural processes of habituation through which human beings acquire virtue or vice. Talk of "operative habits" is thus a quite precise method of describing how a metaphysical reality can come to have recognizable physical effects. As Cessario explains, such virtue "shapes and energizes our human operative capacities, intellect, will, and sense appetites, so that a human person can act promptly, joyfully, and easily in those areas of human conduct that are governed by the Gospel precepts."[138] Aumann makes the same point: an operative habit "gives the subject facility for operation . . . [I]t causes delight in the operation because it produces an act that is prompt, facile, and connatural."[139] Likewise Pinckaers: supernatural virtues are "permanent qualities or dispositions, which ennoble our faculties and enable us to perform meritorious actions."[140] Infused virtues thus (i) grant the theoretical capacity to perform supernatural and meritorious actions, and (ii) as operative habits, make it easier for the Christian to perform them. Broadly speaking, in any given instance their mode of operation is thus facilitation rather than force; they always require the cooperation of the free human will as well as other

---

[135] E.g., between "theological" and "moral" infused virtues; between "entitative" and "operative" habits; and between infused virtues and the gifts of the Holy Spirit proper. On these distinctions, see Cessario, *Christian Faith*, pp. 2–12, 37, and 162–9, respectively.

[136] Aumann, *Spiritual Theology*, p. 84; see also pp. 82, 268–9.

[137] Cessario, *Christian Faith*, p. 129.

[138] Cessario, *Christian Faith*, p. 5. Here Cessario is speaking of the infused moral virtues in particular.

[139] Aumann, *Spiritual Theology*, p. 81.

[140] Pinckaers, *Sources of Christian Ethics*, pp. 283–4.

natural faculties to achieve their ultimate end. The result is that the saving transformation of the human being is a process that necessarily takes place in bodies, in history, and over time.

This all-too-brief discussion reveals a profoundly different understanding of the relation between ontological and experiential realities in salvation than we saw in either of our Protestant theologies explored above. Indeed, in a sense the entire neo-Thomist vision of grace and sanctification in terms of virtue and habit can be understood as a theological system for describing the connection in salvation between the order of being and the order of experience. The operation of grace through the Holy Spirit really and necessarily changes people in their bodies and in their particular moral actions, and it does so both through concrete historical participation in baptism and eucharist and through processes of habituation that are at work every time a human being engages in morally valenced behavior.

One result is that, in striking contrast to Protestant accounts of deification, in this Catholic vision there is little anxiety about an inappropriate psychologization of the effects of the Spirit's work. Cessario, for example, is quite blunt about the way the gifts of the Spirit "shape the psychological powers of the believer"[141] and the fact that grace "transforms the principal psychological capacities of human nature."[142] Aumann, likewise, spells out at some length the effects of the infusion of grace and the acquisition of virtue on the specific and highly psychological issue of the Christian's mastery over the passions.[143] These are real effects on creatures' bodies and minds that take place in the context of a larger transformation whose foundation and final end are nevertheless "supernatural." The neo-Thomist vision of the role of the Spirit in the process of salvation is thus both deeply embodied *and* not simply reducible to what happens in bodies.

Does all this not represent just the sort of third way on salvation and experience that we have been seeking? In an illuminating passage, Pinckaers reflects on the difference between the Thomist vision of salvation and the "extrinsic" understanding of salvation he associates with classical Protestant soteriology. Most fundamentally, Pinckaers explains, "Protestantism . . . refused to admit that the grace of Christ and justification could find any foothold or penetrate and abide within the human person in a lasting manner."[144] He continues:

> [In the theology of justification by faith,] justice could not operate internally, within us, for in this case we might think of claiming it as our own. It remained external, "forensic." Justice belonged only to Christ who attributed it to us . . . [Furthermore, there] was no such thing as sanctifying grace, touching and

---

[141] Cessario, *Christian Faith*, p. 163.   [142] Cessario, *Christian Faith*, p. 129.
[143] Aumann, *Spiritual Theology*, p. 186.
[144] Pinckaers, *Sources of Christian Ethics*, p. 283.

transforming us in our souls, in the depths of our being, as St. Thomas had thought. Nor were there any supernatural virtues, conceived as permanent qualities or dispositions, which would ennoble our faculties and enable us to perform meritorious actions.

It appears from this that Pinckaers understands the difference between classical Protestant and Roman Catholic theologies significantly in terms of the inability of Protestant accounts to affirm a real transformation of the sinner in the substance of their inward being, rather than simply in their relationship to God *coram deo*. In this his critique of "forensic" models is not all that far from my own critique of Protestant theologies for failing to bridge the divide between ontological and experiential registers in soteriological claims, and it also dovetails with some of the critiques of forensic justification referred to earlier in the chapter.

Particularly interesting in light of what we have seen in Torrance and Tanner above is Pinckaers' claim that Protestant soteriologies preclude the possibility of Christians being changed or transformed "in our souls, in the depths of our being." Whether this claim is in fact true of traditional justification models will be addressed later, but it is certainly *not* true of the modern Protestant soteriologies of participation examined above. Indeed, the primary burden of both Torrance and Tanner's accounts is to establish just such a connection to Christ in the "ontological depths" of human nature, and to locate salvation in this ontological transformation. In this respect at least, recent Protestant soteriologies of participation have succeeded in articulating an account of salvation that avoids the classic charge of extrinsicism that Pinckaers articulates. For both Tanner and Torrance, salvation now involves real change at the ontological level, through the mechanism of participation.

However, my analysis of Torrance and Tanner has indicated that the charge of extrinsicism has been avoided in their cases more in theory than in practice. Pinckaers takes for granted that a change in the soul must result in new "permanent qualities or dispositions" that "ennoble our faculties," generating concrete effects on our bodies and our behavior rather than just in our "being." Torrance's account, as we have seen, strongly resists this sort of language. Tanner's account, with its concern for the gift of new "powers" and "capacities" and "dispositions" through the indwelling Spirit, is somewhat more open to it. But the similarities only go so far: for Pinckaers, as for Cessario and Aumann, such powers and capacities take the form of a concrete deepening and transfiguration of natural human faculties—"the principal psychological capacities of human nature," "ordinary thought and emotion," "human forms of love," and so on.[145] As we have seen, Tanner is resistant to speaking of

---

[145] In Aumann's words, the purpose of the infused virtues is "to supernaturalize the faculties" (Aumann, *Spiritual Theology*, p. 81).

sanctification at this level of embodied and experiential specificity lest the "strict separation" between justification and sanctification be dissolved. Indeed, her concern in maintaining that separation appears to be to avoid precisely what does in fact happen in neo-Thomist theology, where the long-term cultivation of and growth in sanctifying grace is what fits the Christian to their supernatural end in God, and thus in an important sense is what "saves" them.

To anticipate a discussion in Chapter 5, it can be pointed out that even the neo-Thomist accounts do not succeed at integrating ontology and experience at every level. As we will see, the procedure through which the theological virtues are initially infused in their accounts is still a sudden and miraculous irruption into the world of bodies and time in baptism. For present purposes it is enough to note that, even so, there is little question that a neo-Thomist model is substantially more friendly to practically recognizable experience than what we have seen above in the positions of Torrance or Tanner.

Overall, it would seem that the soteriology we find in late twentieth-century neo-Thomism largely succeeds in a key area where modern Protestant soteriologies of participation are substantially less successful. In conceiving the Spirit's transformation of human beings in Christ as necessarily including (even as transcending) real changes in Christian bodies and minds over time— changes which furthermore are closely connected to sacramental acts that take place at specific times and places and which can be articulated with some precision and affirmation—this sort of Catholic soteriology does seem to provide an account of the Spirit's work in salvation that is practically recognizable to human experience.

The problem is that in doing so Dominican theology articulates an understanding of the shape and purpose of the Christian life that is deeply at odds with a number of core concerns of classical Protestant theology. In enumerating these briefly here, my purpose is simply to explain why a pneumatology like the one being articulated in this book, grounded as it is Protestant history and in historically Protestant theological concerns, cannot finally accept the neo-Thomist model, even as it recognizes and seeks to learn from neo-Thomism's relative success at integrating pneumatology, salvation, and experience.

The first significant worry, from the perspective of Protestant concerns, is that in connecting participation in God so closely with the category of virtue, there is a risk in the neo-Thomist model that moral questions will come to determine the theological interest of every dimension of human existence. Even fundamental Christian affects like joy and love risk subversion into mere facilitating energies in the process of growth in sanctifying grace. Pinckaers offers a striking example of this sort of annexation of all Christian action by a strictly moral vision of Christian actions. Early in his discussion of the Protestant view of justification by faith he makes the remarkable claim that the Protestant view entails a "systematic refusal of any personal participation in justification by way of works or merit and, consequently, the denial of any value to human actions... through which a person might glorify himself before God."[146] In making this claim, Pinckaers seems to be working with an assumption that the only way theology can conceive of human moral action as having ethical significance is if it is interpreted in the context of a soteriological scheme in which such action can be reconfigured in terms of "works or merit." In other words, Pinckaers seems to think that a denial that salvation takes place through a progressive growth in sanctifying grace is tantamount to denial of the possibility of a plausible Christian ethics. But no Protestant would say that human action after justification is devoid of ethical meaning. The classical Protestant claim is rather the much narrower one that there is no *soteriological* value to such actions as "works or merit" before God. The result is that Christian ethics is interestingly reconfigured and reconstructed on new grounds, liberated from concerns about salvation, rather than simply abolished.

The fact that this distinction is not persuasive to Pinckaers shows just how deeply his view of Christian life is shaped by a very particular moral and soteriological viewpoint. In the neo-Thomist vision, it is difficult to avoid the conclusion that all human action is soteriologically freighted in a more or less direct way, such that the stakes in moral action for the Christian at any given moment are enormously high. In this respect, we can understand the traditional Protestant worry that Christian affective life will be characterized in such a scheme by a state of persistent, or at least recurring, moral anxiety. Indeed, criticizing the "vain and ungodly confidence" they believe will be generated by Protestant views of the assurance of faith, the theologians at the Council of Trent seem to affirm this conclusion explicitly, arguing that a Christian should indeed experience a certain "fear and apprehension concerning his own grace."[147] From a Protestant perspective, such recurrent "fear and apprehension" is difficult to square with the New Testament emphasis on the way that salvation specifically liberates Christians from the anxieties of traditional moral and soteriological striving.

A second problem with the neo-Thomist model is that it takes for granted a particular moral psychology that views graced habituation as the primary mechanism for generating human moral change. Historically, most Protestants have not shared either this view of moral change or the view of human nature it implies. For both exegetical and experiential reasons, Luther and other Protestants in the sixteenth century were deeply unconvinced by the theological anthropology implied in Thomist and scholastic understandings of virtue, with their particular configurations of the relationship between reason,

---

[146] Pinckaers, *Sources of Christian Ethics*, pp. 283, 282, 286. Emphasis added.
[147] Council of Trent, Session 6, Chapter 9 (Schroeder, *Canons and Decrees*, p. 314; Eng: p. 35).

appetites and desires, and the will. Indeed, Protestantism's foundational experience, as it were, was Martin Luther's years in the monastery of trying and failing to become more holy through conventional medieval Catholic methods for cultivating virtue and destroying vice.[148]

More specifically, from Luther onwards Protestants have argued that one of the chief problems with the sort of model articulated in neo-Thomist soteriology is that it is fundamentally overoptimistic about Christian ethical transformation. The Protestant argument against a soteriology focused on the ontological infusion in the Christian of sanctifying grace is that, for all its intellectual elegance and coherence, it simply does not work very well in practice, and certainly not well enough to function as the core dynamic through which salvation comes about. Protestant spirituality is traditionally focused very substantially, especially where salvation is concerned, on what we might call the "rhetoric of passivity." What I mean by this is the sense that much of the force of the Christian message is precisely its efficacious protest, in and through the work of Christ, against the natural human tendency to freight our day-to-day actions and feelings with soteriological or crypto-soteriological significance. It is just this freighting, basic to the neo-Thomist vision, that Martin Luther found punishing and terrifying rather than inspiring or transformative or productive of meaning.[149]

In sketching these traditional Protestant critiques of virtue-based theories of salvation, my purpose has not been to provide a large-scale rebuttal of Roman Catholic soteriology. My goal has been simply to explain why neo-Thomist accounts are not satisfactory from the perspective of this book, working as it does from within a broadly Protestant horizon, despite the relative effectiveness of such accounts on the subject of practically recognizable experience of the Spirit in salvation.

Problems and Parameters for a Protestant Soteriology of Participation

The conclusions thus far in this chapter can be summarized as follows. First, even the best Protestant models of soteriological participation are shaped by an anxiety about religious subjectivity that leads them to resist integrating

---

[148] See Zahl, "Non-Competitive Agency," pp. 212–14.

[149] Protestant concerns about such models are not assuaged when reading assertions like the following, which Aumann makes in the context of a discussion of what is needed "to arrive at the intimate union with God in which sanctity consists": "A prudent organization of all our psychological resources can result in a near-perfect control of our passions...There is no doubt that there are great difficulties at the beginning, but gradually the individual can achieve self-mastery." This is an astonishingly optimistic claim to make. See Aumann, *Spiritual Theology*, pp. 177, 185.

ontological claims with experiential dynamics. In this they do not succeed in achieving what much contemporary rhetoric around the virtues of participation assumes or hopes they will achieve. At the same time, neo-Thomist models indicate why Torrance's and Tanner's concerns about giving a robust place for experiential effects in salvation might be justified. The alternative articulated by Pinckaers, Cessario, and Aumann is an anthropologically optimistic soteriology that puts a very substantial emphasis, practically and experientially, on Christian moral agency, in a way that is at odds with core Protestant convictions about human nature and the relation of sanctification to salvation.

Is this the price that must be paid for an experientially integrated pneumatology of salvation? I do not believe it is. From a Protestant perspective, what seems to be needed is an alternative that does not entail the metaphysical and moral optimism of the neo-Thomist model but at the same time is not forced, in obeisance to worries about theological "foundations" carried over from the early twentieth century, to exclude experience from soteriological description.

One option here would simply be an exercise in repair: to expand and revise an account like Tanner's in such a way that the core model is preserved but closer and more explicit attention is paid to questions of affective salience, and a more robust and clearly articulated account is given of how the "dispositions and deeds" attendant upon receipt of the Spirit play out in bodies and in time. If the effect of the foregoing analysis is simply to foster newer, better Protestant accounts of soteriological participation, then much will have been achieved.

However, to do the above would be to articulate a Protestant soteriology that has jettisoned what historically has been one its most powerful engines for growth and pastoral effectiveness: the doctrine of justification by faith, understood experientially. In seeking a Protestant account of salvation that is not simply fighting a long retreat before the forces of secular modernity, and that might help resource creative, plausible, and compelling ministry and mission in this context, I am convinced that something more directly emotionally compelling and affectively engaged is necessary.

The result of my analysis to this point is that participation does not seem to be the silver bullet for solving the problems currently facing Protestant soteriology that it has recently appeared to be. These problems include how (i) to provide a clear affirmation, grounded in the reality of the Spirit, that salvation is not simply a propositionalist abstraction but affects real bodies in time; (ii) to acknowledge the continuing pastoral and theological power of core Protestant concerns about the unconditional character of saving grace and the ongoing reality of sin in the Christian life; and (iii) nevertheless to take seriously the participatory language we find in New Testament soteriology. To these concerns, which to one degree or another can be found in Torrance and Tanner, a fourth can be added. In late modern cultural contexts where

Christianity is often seen to be increasingly implausible, a contemporary theology of salvation needs (iv) to be able to inform and resource Christian ministry that is experientially powerful and emotionally compelling, doing creative justice to both the dramatic and the more "ordinary" dimensions of the Spirit's work in salvation and in Christian life.

PHILIP MELANCHTHON'S SOTERIOLOGY OF CONSOLATION

I believe that the foundations for a soteriology that succeeds on all four counts can be developed through a retrieval of early Lutheran soteriology, and in particular the soteriology developed by Philip Melanchthon in the first decade of his career. As I have demonstrated elsewhere, Luther's early soteriology was profoundly focused on affect and desire as core dimensions of human experience that are of particular significance in life before God.[150] In this, Luther's soteriology functions quite differently than critics of classical justification models have tended to assume. The affective and desiderative dimension of Luther's thought was initially expanded and formalized by his colleague Philip Melanchthon in the 1521 edition of his early Protestant systematics, the *Loci communes theologici*, but it received its most extensive and mature exposition a decade later, in the *Apology of the Augsburg Confession*.

In the present section, I will examine three key dimensions of the theology of justification that Melanchthon presents in the latter text. These are its description of the mechanics of Christ's saving work, its pneumatology, and its account of the relationship between justification and affective experience. I will then argue, against Milbank and others, for the psychological plausibility of Melanchthon's account in light of some basic insights from psychological science.

Published in 1531, Melanchthon's *Apology* was arguably the most influential single text on justification in the first generation of the Protestant Reformation.[151] Careful analysis of Melanchthon's soteriology and pneumatology in this text will serve two key purposes. First, it will demonstrate that the critical characterization of justification by faith alone as a disembodied, implicitly rationalist "legal fiction" is simply false. Melanchthon will be shown to provide a highly specific and psychologically sophisticated account of salvation as a "practically recognizable" experience of God's Spirit in the world, and thus to meet the requirements for a properly pneumatological account of Christian

---

[150] See Zahl, "Bondage of the Affections."
[151] See Alister E. McGrath, *Iustitia Dei: A History of the Christian Doctrine of Justification* (Cambridge: Cambridge University Press, 2005), pp. 237–41.

religious experience that were outlined in Chapter 2. Second, Melanchthon's account gives intriguing evidence that one powerful way to integrate the best insights of justification by faith with the category of "participation" is to recognize that transformative affective experience of salvation is itself a mode of participation in Christ through the Spirit. Third, and ultimately, Melanchthon's soteriology provides parameters for a contemporary soteriology that preserves concerns about the disjunctive character of grace while still affirming the reality of practically recognizable effects of the Spirit's work in salvation.

The *Apology of the Augsburg Confession* was conceived as a clarification and defense of positions that Philip Melanchthon had articulated more briefly in *The Augsburg Confession*, a confessional document written in 1530 in anticipation of the Diet of Augsburg and published in German and Latin editions in 1531.[152] The *Apology* sought to respond to arguments made in the *Confutatio Pontificia*, the official Catholic response to *The Augsburg Confession*. On the question of justification, the core of the *Confutatio*'s critique concerns the issue of whether good works are soteriologically "meritorious." The *Confutatio* repeatedly condemns the Lutheran rejection of the view that "the merits that men acquired by the assistance of divine grace"[153] are meritorious in relation to forgiveness: when it comes to "the remission of sins," it observes, "it is entirely contrary to Holy Scripture to deny that our works are meritorious."[154] The particular catalyst for Melanchthon's "forensic" account of justification in the *Apology* was thus the question of whether believers' good works, made possible "by virtue of Christ's passion" and on the basis of a grace communicated through sacramental participation, play any role in meriting the remission of sins.

However, more is at stake in the disagreement between Melanchthon and the authors of the *Confutatio* than a narrow dispute over the nature of "merit." At work are two very different visions of Christian salvation and of the relationship between salvation and Christian life after conversion. If good works are to be regarded as meritorious in any way for the remission of sins, then it follows that the whole of the Christian's life is soteriologically significant, and that grace-enabled transformation lies at the heart of Christian

---

[152] These in turn were drawn from the 1529 Schwabach Articles and the Marburg Articles of the same year. See *BC*, p. 28. On the historical background and circumstances of the *Apology*, see Gunther Wenz, *Theologie der Bekenntnisschriften der evangelisch-lutherischen Kirche*, i (Berlin: Walter de Gruyter, 1996), pp. 486–98; on the theology of justification in the *Apology* in relation to other Lutheran confessional documents, see Wenz, *Theologie der Bekenntnisschriften*, ii, pp. 59–235.

[153] *Confutatio Pontificia*, response to Article 4 ("Confutatio Pontificia." (1530): http://www.gutenberg.org/files/853/853-h/853-h.htm, accessed 21 June 2019).

[154] *Confutatio Pontificia*, response to Article 4; see also the response to Article 20 ("Confutatio Pontificia.").

salvation. In the "forensic" model, by contrast, the sole formal basis for salvation is Christ's own merit, "reckoned" or "imputed" to sinners, rather than any concrete transformation that actually takes place in the lives of Christians.

Melanchthon's most explicit response to the *Confutatio* on the question of merit can be found in Article 21 of the *Apology*, in a paragraph which has gone down in history as a foundational text for the Protestant doctrine of forensic justification:[155]

> The second qualification for a propitiator is this: his merits must be authorized to make satisfaction for others who are given these merits by divine imputation [*imputatione divina*] in order that through them, just as though [*tamquam*] they were their own merits, they may be reckoned righteous [*iusti reputentur*]. It is as when a person pays a debt for friends, the debtors are freed by the merit of the other, as though [*tamquam*] it were by their own. Thus, Christ's merits are given to us so that we might be reckoned righteous [*iusti reputemur*] by our trust [*fiducia*] in the merits of Christ when we believe in him [*in eum credimus*], as though [*tamquam*] we had merits of our own.[156]

Here we see several of the key themes of classical accounts of justification by faith alone: the focus on the question of "righteousness" [*iustitia*], the financial image of debt repayment on behalf of another, the invocation of Anselmian language of "making satisfaction," and the centrality of "trust" [*fiducia*] and "believing" [*credere*] as indicating the mechanism through which the divine imputation is made effective for the believer. Although no "courtroom," lawyer, or judge is mentioned here, some sort of legal or forensic context is implied in the ideas of "divine imputation" and "authorization to make satisfaction," as the presumed metaphorical context in which debt-paying on behalf of another must take place.[157]

Along with "imputation," two further terms are particularly important: "reckoning," and "as though" [*tamquam*]. The "legal fiction" critique of justification by faith is at root a critical commentary on the dynamics Melanchthon seeks to describe by these terms. This is especially the case with regard to his repeated invocation of the term *tamquam*, which indicates in no uncertain terms that Christians are treated in justification "as though" they had a quality—saving righteousness—that they do not in fact have, but are only "regarded" as having by God.

---

[155] See McGrath, *Iustitia Dei*, pp. 240–1.   [156] *Ap* 21.19 (*BSLK*, p. 320; *BC*, p. 240).

[157] McGrath makes a strong case that the most significant source of legal language informing Melanchthon's forensic conception of justification in the *Apology* is in fact Erasmus' gloss, in his critical edition of the New Testament, on the Pauline term *logizomai*, which Erasmus interprets in light of procedures for debt repayment in Roman law courts. See McGrath, *Iustitia Dei*, pp. 239–40.

The paragraph from Article 21 constitutes the clearest exposition of the "forensic" logic at the heart of Melanchthon's soteriology, but the question of the imputation of Christ's merit is just one piece in the larger picture of the doctrine of justification in the *Apology*. Earlier on in Article 4, the article on justification itself, Melanchthon gives a much fuller account of justification in the context of the human plight before "the law":

> Therefore, because people cannot by their own powers live according to the law of God and because all are under sin and guilty of eternal wrath and death, we cannot be set free from sin and be justified through the law. Instead, what has been given us is the promise of the forgiveness of sins and justification on account of Christ, who was given for us in order to make satisfaction for the sins of the world, and who has been appointed as the mediator and propitiator. This promise is not conditional upon our merits; it freely offers the forgiveness of sins and justification, just as Paul says.[158]

But how is this "promise" received, and how is "justification" made effective for the Christian? The answer, Melanchthon continues, is through "faith":

> [T]he promise cannot be grasped in any other way than by faith ... [T]his faith does not bring to God trust in our own merits, but only trust in the promise of the mercy promised in Christ. Therefore it follows that personal faith—by which an individual believes that his or her sins are remitted on account of Christ and that God is reconciled and gracious on account of Christ—receives the forgiveness of sins and justifies us.[159]

Here we see that justification by faith has a number of key features for Melanchthon. First, its context and starting point is a particular view of human nature in relation to the law of God. Drawing on texts like Romans 3:23 ("all have sinned and fall short of the glory of God"),[160] Melanchthon asserts that human beings are required by God to live in a way that is holy and righteous, but at the same time that they are incapable doing so because their lives take place "under sin": "people cannot by their own powers live according to the law of God" and therefore "all are under sin and guilty of eternal wrath and death." Second, God has addressed this plight through the atoning death of Christ, "who was given for us in order to make satisfaction for the sins of the world, and who has been appointed as the mediator and propitiator." Third, the way that this satisfaction or propitiation is appropriated by human beings is through "personal faith," which "receives the forgiveness of sins and justifies us." And finally, as something that is appropriated through "faith" alone, justification is not "conditional" but "freely offer[ed]." What Melanchthon

---

[158] *Ap* 4.40–41 (*BSLK*, pp. 167–8; *BC*, pp. 126–7).

[159] *Ap* 4.43–45 (*BSLK*, p. 168; *BC*, p. 127).

[160] *Ap* 4.32 (*BSLK*, p. 166; *BC*, p. 125). Cf. Romans 3:9: "all, both Jews and Greeks, are under the power of sin."

means by this is that human beings are radically passive in relation to their justification. Justification is not dependent on any willed, meritorious action or cooperation on their part, but is instead a consequence of a gift that they simply receive. The purpose and effect of all this is the same as it is in other traditional soteriologies: the rescue of human beings from an otherwise inevitable death, the gift of eternal life, and the creation of a reconciled relationship between human beings, born in sin, and a holy God.

Reading Melanchthon through these excerpts, taken out of context, we might be forgiven for simply stopping here, as many later interpreters of justification by faith seem to have done. Here the doctrine of justification and its specific function as a mechanism for accomplishing the salvation of sinners have been described as clearly and succinctly as they ever were in the first generation of the Reformation, and there is already plenty of material to work with in assessing the strengths and weaknesses of such a doctrine. Reading just these excerpts from Article 21 and Article 4 in the *Apology*, the places in the text where Melanchthon articulates the doctrine of justification by faith alone most clearly and succinctly, we find several of the foundations for later debates over Protestant understandings of justification, including the appeal to Pauline discussion of justification,[161] and the focus on the "objective" mechanism of salvation before God. Looking at just these texts, we might also observe, in keeping with the concerns of later interpreters, that the sole point of contact with human "experience" is the apparently rather abstract phenomenon of "faith," through which sins are theoretically forgiven through a sheer belief in the fact of Christ's saving significance.

On this basis, we might see good reasons for the critical positions exposited earlier: Milbank's reference to this doctrine as a "mere calculus" that reduces salvation to an intellectual assent to "a neat set of propositions about [Christ's] saving significance";[162] or Macchia's lament that such accounts neglect the "participatory and transformative aspects of salvation" that in his view constitute "the very heart and soul of justification";[163] or Campbell's assertion that in such accounts justification is an "individual, rational (if not rationalistic), largely cognitive... process";[164] or Pinnock's characterization of forensic justification as "engaging in fantasies... based on bare assent to propositions."[165]

The problem with such readings is that they cannot actually be sustained from the text. To interpret Melanchthon in this way is to draw conclusions deeply at odds with his actual exposition of the doctrine of justification. The

---

[161] Melanchthon presents the doctrine as a straightforward interpretation of Paul's thought in Romans, focusing especially on Rom. 4:14, 4:15, 3:21, and 11:6.

[162] Milbank, *Beyond Secular Order*, pp. 64, 79–80.

[163] Macchia, *Justified in the Spirit*, p. 39. Emphasis original.

[164] Campbell, *The Deliverance of God*, p. 128.   [165] Pinnock, *Flame of Love*, p. 156.

point is not difficult to demonstrate. Here is the final sentence of the last excerpt above, now cited together with the sentence that follows:

> Therefore it follows that personal faith—by which an individual believes that his or her sins are remitted on account of Christ and that God is reconciled and gracious on account of Christ—receives the forgiveness of sins and justifies us. *Because in repentance, that is, in terrors, faith consoles and uplifts hearts, it regenerates us and brings the Holy Spirit that we might then be able to live according to the law of God, namely, to love God, truly to fear God, truly to assert that God hears prayer, to obey God in all afflictions, and to mortify concupiscence, etc.*[166]

Here we see that faith, as Melanchthon understands it, is not an abstract rational procedure, but can take hold only in a particular experiential and affective context, namely "in terrors." We see furthermore that faith "consoles and uplifts hearts," producing concrete affective consequences of "love" and the proper "fear" of God. And we learn that, according to Melanchthon, the Holy Spirit is the agent of this real transformation by which Christians become "able to live according to the law of God."

Such claims are not just secondary asides in the context of a largely "objective" account of justification. The practically recognizable and profoundly "experiential" work of the Spirit in "consoling terrified hearts" and in kindling a genuine and transformative love towards God and neighbor is in fact the dominant theme in Melanchthon's exposition of the doctrine of justification by faith. It appears on almost every page in the discussion of justification in Article 4 of the *Apology*, and it is consistently paired with an explicit critique of the idea that faith is a matter of mere "knowledge" or assent to propositions.[167] In its earliest and most influential form, the doctrine of forensic justification by faith is not at all what its modern critics believe it to be.

Pneumatology in the Apology

Fundamental to Melanchthon's exposition of justification by faith in the *Apology* is the work of the Holy Spirit. Melanchthon identifies what initially appear to be two distinct works of the Spirit in relation to justification. First and foremost, the Spirit is the source and giver of saving faith itself. Melanchthon makes this point already in the *Augsburg Confession*: "through the Word and the sacraments . . . the Holy Spirit is given, who effects faith where and when it pleases God."[168] This claim is then repeated at various points in the

---

[166] *Ap* 4.45 (*BSLK*, pp. 168–9; *BC*, p. 127). Emphasis added.

[167] See e.g., *Ap* 4.115: "faith is no idle knowledge . . . but it is a work of the Holy Spirit that frees us from death and raises and makes alive terrified minds" (*BSLK*, p. 183; *BC*, p. 139).

[168] *Augsburg Confession* 5 (*BC*, p. 41), Latin version. The German version is very similar: "the Holy Spirit produces faith, where and when he wills" (*BC*, p. 40).

Apology: to be saved is to be "born anew through the Holy Spirit,"[169] and the "faith" that saves is "a work of the Holy Spirit" who "frees us from death [and] produces new life in our hearts."[170]

Here Melanchthon is building on his own account of faith in the 1521 first edition of his influential theological summary, the *Loci communes*, where he describes "faith" as a "constant assent to God's every word" through "God's Spirit renewing and illuminating our hearts."[171] For Melanchthon, as an ongoing "assent" to God's promise that is deeply experiential and transformative, the faith that saves is itself a gift and work of the Holy Spirit. We cannot understand what it means to be justified by faith without understanding that the Holy Spirit is the source and agent of the faith that justifies.[172]

At the same time, the Holy Spirit is not just the source of faith in the *Apology*. The indwelling of the Spirit in the believer is also simultaneously a *consequence* of faith, in the sense that it is precisely "by faith in Christ" that "the Holy Spirit is received."[173] According to Melanchthon, "because . . . faith consoles and uplifts hearts, it regenerates us and brings the Holy Spirit that we might then be able to live according to the law of God, namely, to love God, truly to fear God."[174] The affective and regenerative efficacy of the Spirit is thus an outcome or effect of faith. This is a claim that Melanchthon makes

---

[169] *Ap* 4.31 (*BSLK*, p. 166; *BC*, p. 125).   [170] *Ap* 4.64 (*BSLK*, p. 173; *BC*, p. 131).

[171] *MW* 2.1:92; Melanchthon, *Loci communes 1521*, p. 119. See also Melanchthon's virtually identical claim in the later 1543 edition of the *Loci* (Philip Melanchthon, *Loci communes 1543* (St. Louis: Concordia Publishing House, 1992), p. 98).

[172] On this point Melanchthon is in full agreement with the other Magisterial Reformers. See e.g., Calvin, *Institutes* 3.1.4 (Calvin, *Institutes*, p. 541), and Huldrych Zwingli, "Of Baptism," in *Zwingli and Bullinger*, ed. G.W. Bromiley (London: Westminster John Knox Press, 1953), p. 137. It has sometimes been argued that Martin Luther is an exception here, in that he rarely ascribes the acquisition of faith directly or explicitly to the work of the Spirit. Certainly Luther usually prefers to speak instead either of both faith and the receipt of the Spirit as consequences of hearing the Word, or of the receipt of the Spirit as a consequence of both the Word and of faith (for the former, see e.g., *WA* 18:136; *LW* 40:146; for the latter, see e.g., *WA* 40.1:343; *LW* 26:213). On these grounds, Reinhard Flogaus criticizes Luther's tendency to prioritize a christological understanding of the Word in relation to faith as a "pneumatological . . . deficit" (Reinhard Flogaus, "Luther versus Melanchthon? Zur Frage der Einheit der Wittenberger Reformation in der Rechtfertigungslehre," *Archiv für Reformationsgeschichte* 91 (2000), p. 14).

There is some merit to this critique. Luther does seem to go out of his way to avoid certain kinds of appeals to Spirit-language in places where such an appeal would be the obvious theological move to make. At a deeper level, however, Luther's difference from Melanchthon, Calvin, and Zwingli on this issue is more apparent than real. This is because the Word itself, which in Luther's view is the primary means through which both faith and the Spirit are given, is a deeply pneumatological category. For the Luther, the "external Word" is the sole instrument through which the Spirit's salvific work takes place and thus there can be no real encounter with the Word where the Spirit is not also present and efficacious. The connection between faith, Word, and Spirit is made explicit in the treatise *Against the Heavenly Prophets*: "Before all other works and acts you hear the Word of God, through which the Spirit convinces the world of its sin (John 16 [:8]). When we acknowledge our sin, we hear of the grace of Christ. *In this Word the Spirit comes and gives faith where and to whom he wills*" (*WA* 18:139; *LW* 40:149; emphasis added).

[173] *Ap* 4.133 (*BSLK*, p. 186; *BC*, p. 141).   [174] *Ap* 4.45 (*BSLK*, pp. 168–9; *BC*, p. 127).

again and again in the *Apology*: "faith truly brings the Holy Spirit and produces a new life in our hearts";[175] "we cannot truly keep the law until we have received the Holy Spirit through faith";[176] "faith alone regenerates (for by faith alone the Holy Spirit is received)."[177]

In identifying Melanchthon's willingness to describe the work of the Spirit as simultaneously the source and the consequence of the gift of faith—or, which is the same thing, to describe faith as simultaneously a gift of the Spirit and the precondition for receiving the Spirit—we have arrived at a fundamental issue for understanding the relationship between faith and experience in the doctrine of justification. On the face of it, Melanchthon's double claim appears to indicate a problematic circularity in the relationship between these two main elements of the pneumatology of justification. As Reinhard Flogaus has argued, in the *Apology* "a circular relationship between Spirit and faith is evident: on the one hand, the Spirit is that which effects the faith which justifies, but on the other hand the Spirit is also the gift attained through this very faith."[178]

One possible explanation for this circularity would be to say it is a consequence of Melanchthon engaging in a plain reading of St. Paul, where a similar dynamic can be observed. In Galatians 3:2–5, the gift of the Spirit is described as the consequence of "believing what you heard," while in 1 Corinthians 12:8 and Galatians 5:22 the order is reversed and faith (or "faithfulness") is described as itself a "manifestation" and "gift" of the Spirit. According to Gordon Fee, these texts indicate that for Paul "faith itself, as a work of the Spirit, leads to the experienced reception of the Spirit that also comes through the same faith . . . [T]he Spirit is thus both the cause and the effect of faith."[179]

However, careful investigation of the *Apology* indicates that there is more at work here than a willingness to live with an unresolved pneumatological "circularity" on the basis of Pauline authority. Examining the role of affective experience in Melanchthon's account, it soon becomes evident that the experience of justification—the Spirit's gift of faith that consoles terrified hearts—is so closely interwoven with the experience of "regeneration"—the Spirit's kindling of love and peace and new desires to follow God's law—that a strict distinction between the two simply cannot be maintained. In the context of the

---

[175] *Ap* 4.125 (*BSLK*, p. 185; *BC*, p. 140). The Quarto edition of the *Apology* has the same turn of phrase in *Ap* 4.116 (*BC*, p. 139, n. 118).

[176] *Ap* 4.132 (*BSLK*, p. 186; *BC*, p. 141).

[177] *Ap* 4.172B (*BC*, p. 149). For further examples see *Ap* 4.64 and *Ap* 21.15.

[178] Flogaus, "Luther versus Melanchthon?," p. 15. Wengert identifies a similar "inconsistency" and "hermeneutical circle" in Melanchthon's final commentary on Romans. See Timothy J. Wengert, *Defending Faith: Lutheran Responses to Andreas Osiander's Doctrine of Justification, 1551–1559* (Tübingen: Mohr Siebeck, 2012), p. 334–5.

[179] Gordon D. Fee, *God's Empowering Presence: The Holy Spirit in the Letters of Paul* (Grand Rapids, MI: Baker Academic, 1994), p. 853.

contemporary debate between justification- and participation-based models of salvation, the collapse of this distinction in Melanchthon's theology of justification is deeply significant.

Experiencing Faith and Regeneration in the Apology

The acquisition of faith for Melanchthon is a deeply experiential, affective phenomenon. In justification, says Melanchthon, "we are not talking about an idle knowledge, such as is also to be found in the devils, but about a faith that resists the terrors of conscience and which uplifts and consoles terrified hearts."[180] Indeed, he writes, "we insist that faith justifies and regenerates inasmuch as it frees us from our terrors and produces peace, joy, and new life in our hearts."[181] In fact, faith cannot come into existence at all for Melanchthon outside of the context of an existential, affective experience of anxiety and fear before God: "faith . . . is conceived in the terrors of the conscience that experiences the wrath of God against our sin and seeks forgiveness of sins and deliverance from sin."[182] In Melanchthon's view, soteriology always begins with a particular set of what in the next chapter I will call "affective predicates": in his account, all human beings, as soon as they begin to reflect on their nature and their relation to God, live with a kind of existential guilt and terror of judgment.[183] He explains this situation in detail in the section of the *Apology* on "Repentance":

> In these terrors the conscience experiences the wrath of God against sin, something unknown to those who walk around in carnal security . . . [The conscience] flees the horrible wrath of God because human nature cannot withstand it unless sustained by the Word of God . . . [H]ow will anyone love God in the midst of such real terrors when they experience the horrible and indescribable wrath of God? What else do [scholastic theologians] teach than despair, when in the midst of such terrors they present only the law?[184]

In light of these affective predicates of fear, guilt, and sorrow before God, the significance of a specifically forensic account of justification for Melanchthon

---

[180] *Ap* 4.249 (*BSLK*, p. 209; *BC*, p. 158).

[181] *Ap* 12.60 (*BSLK*, p. 263; *BC*, p. 197). See also *Ap* 4.100 ("faith . . . produces peace, joy, and eternal life in the heart"); *Ap* 4.225 ("Therefore after we have been justified and reborn by faith, we begin to fear and love God . . . [and] to love our neighbor"); and *Ap* 4.316A ("Love necessarily follows regeneration" despite the fact that "even after our renewal we are regarded as righteous on account of Christ").

[182] *Ap* 4.142 (*BSLK*, p. 188; *BC*, p. 142).

[183] See especially *Ap* 4.204 ("in genuine terror . . . they end up in despair"); *Ap* 4.244 ("the terrors of sin and death"); *Ap* 12.38, 44 ("the anxious heart"; "anxieties, and the terrors of sin and death"); and *Ap* 12.48 (the sentence of the law "is perceived only in the midst of genuine sorrows and terrors").

[184] *Ap* 12.32–34 (*BSLK*, pp. 257–8; *BC*, p. 192).

is that it alone can convincingly relieve that terror and provide peace and joy for the troubled human soul. "[T]he position we defend ... brings the surest consolation to godly consciences."[185]

For Melanchthon, the key to understanding forensic justification lies above all in understanding the powerful affective salience he perceives it to have for fearful human beings with troubled consciences.[186] The acquisition of faith is not "idle knowledge"—a mere rational assent to a set of propositions—nor is it arbitrary or random or abstract, a pneumatological bolt from the sky. Rather, Melanchthon suggests, "faith arises and consoles in the midst of those fears."[187] Faith thus represents a key moment, inspired by the Holy Spirit, in a practically recognizable affective sequence of moving from existential terror over sin and death to a new state of consolation, peace, and joy in the Holy Spirit. And as a set of affective experiences, and therefore something irreducibly dependent on human embodiment, the sequence is not just conceptual or metaphorical: it is something that takes place in time, in the actual historical experience of a given individual. In the terms of this book, the acquisition of faith is in this way a "practically recognizable" experience of the Spirit.

But what about the other dimension of the relationship between faith and the Holy Spirit in Melanchthon, the sense in which the Spirit is also conceived as a gift received as a consequence of faith, who continues to dwell in Christians following the experience of justification? I have already noted one of Melanchthon's key comments on this topic: "Because ... faith consoles and uplifts hearts, it regenerates us and brings the Holy Spirit that we might then be able to live according to the law of God, namely, to love God, truly to fear God."[188] The same point is repeated a few pages later: "when we are consoled by faith through hearing the gospel and the forgiveness of sins, we receive the Holy Spirit, so that we are now able to think righteously about God, to fear God, and to believe him, etc."[189] Clearly Melanchthon understands this

---

[185] *Ap* 4.393A (*BC*, p. 173). Wengert has shown that this theme of consolation remained close to the heart of Melanchthon's theology twenty years later during the Osiandrian controversy—and indeed that it lay close to the heart of Lutheran theology more broadly well into the 1550s, when it was widely understood to be the key issue at stake in the debate with Osiander. See Wengert, *Defending Faith*, pp. 9, 79–82, 100, 325–6, and 349–51.

[186] On Melanchthon's affective theology, see especially Karl-Heinz zur Mühlen, "Melanchthons Auffassung vom Affekt in den Loci communes von 1521," in *Humanismus und Reformation*, eds. Michael Beyer, Günther Wartenberg, and Hans-Peter Hasse. (Leipzig: Evangelische Verlagsanstalt, 1996), pp. 327–36; Markus Höfner, "The Affects of the Soul and the Effects of Grace: On Melanchthon's Understanding of Faith and Christian Emotions," in *The Depth of the Human Person*, ed. Michael Welker (Grand Rapids, MI: William B. Eerdmans Publishing Company, 2014); and Wilhelm Maurer, *Der junge Melanchthon zwischen Humanismus und Reformation. ii: Der Theologe* (Göttingen: Vandenhoeck & Ruprecht, 1969), pp. 244–61.

[187] *Ap* 4.62 (*BSLK*, p. 172; *BC*, p. 130).　　　[188] *Ap* 4.45 (*BSLK*, pp. 168–9; *BC*, p. 127).

[189] *Ap* 4.135 (*BSLK*, p. 187; *BC*, pp. 141–2).

indwelling of the Spirit consequent to the acquisition of faith to have affective consequences as well.

In the *Apology*, Melanchthon identifies the essence of pneumatological regeneration first and foremost in terms of a changed relationship to the demands of the divine law. In Melanchthon's view, "it is impossible to keep the law without the Holy Spirit."[190] At the same time, the change in the believer's relationship to the law takes place primarily at the level of affect and desire. "[The] heart of the divine law" consists in "affections of the heart [*affectus cordis*] toward God" that "cannot be rendered without the Holy Spirit."[191] Following the law, for Melanchthon, is thus ultimately less about doing the deeds it proscribes than about having a heart that desires to keep the law, such that the deeds then follow naturally.

Above all for Melanchthon, this means truly to love God, and such love is something he believes is impossible until through faith it is understood that God is no longer angry over sin and the violation of his commandments:

> [H]ow can the human heart love God as long as it believes that he is terribly angry...? However, the law always accuses us; it shows that God is angry. Therefore God is not loved until after we grasp his mercy by faith. Not until then does he becomes someone who can be loved.[192]

Here love, which is the essence of the law, is not primarily a kind of ontological substance infused in the believer, as it is in the theology of Melanchthon's Catholic opponents. Rather, it is first and foremost an *affection* that replaces the equally concrete affection of fear over God's anger at sin. In this sense Melanchthon interprets regeneration primarily in experiential rather than ontological terms. Love, like faith, does not arrive by divine fiat or out of nowhere. It arises through concrete processes that occur in bodies and in time, in the context of the larger affective sequence associated with justification.

Indeed, one of Melanchthon's chief criticisms of his opponents' position is that in his view they turn the regenerating gift of the Holy Spirit into a mechanical, purely "theological" concept, a metaphysical reality that need not have any direct connection to the embodied affective experience of the Christian. The authors of the *Confutatio*, claims Melanchthon, "imagine that the sacraments confer the Holy Spirit *ex opere operato* without the recipient

---

[190] *Ap* 4.126 (*BSLK*, p. 185; *BC*, p. 140). Likewise: "the law cannot be kept without Christ and without the Holy Spirit" (*Ap* 4.135; *BSLK*, p. 187; *BC*, p. 142).

[191] *Ap* 4.130 (*BSLK*, p. 186; *BC*, p. 141). Luther makes the same point about the Spirit and the law in his preface to Romans: "no one can satisfy [the law] unless all that you do is done from the bottom of your heart. But such a heart is only given by God's Spirit, who fashions a man after the law, so that he acquires a desire for the law in his heart, doing nothing henceforth out of fear and compulsion but out of a willing heart" (*WA Deutsche Bibel* 7:5; *LW* 35:367).

[192] *Ap* 4.128–129 (*BSLK*, pp. 185–6; *BC*, pp. 140–1).

being favorably stirred[,] as if in actual fact the bestowing of the Holy Spirit were without any effect."[193]

Overall in Melanchthon, the regenerating work of the Spirit that is a consequence of the acquisition of faith constitutes a real change in the believer that begins with changes in the affections and results in new behaviors. He writes: "Because faith truly brings the Holy Spirit and produces a new life in our hearts, it must also produce spiritual impulses in our hearts."[194] What are these impulses? After the Christian has "been justified, reborn, and received the Holy Spirit," they really do "begin to fear and love God, to pray for and expect help from him, to thank and praise him, and to obey him in [his] afflictions."[195] Melanchthon is perfectly willing to describe the latter as "outward good works," with the caveat that in his view such works are not meritorious for the forgiveness of sins and thus, for the purposes of salvation, are not related to the fulfillment of the law.[196]

At the same time, Spirit-sourced regeneration remains substantially limited and provisional over the course of a Christian's life: "in this life we cannot live up to the law, because our sinful nature does not stop bringing forth evil affections [*malos affectus*], even though the Spirit resists them."[197] This is an important and complex topic, which will receive more extended treatment in Chapter 5, in the context of a discussion of the issue of "non-transformation" in the lives of Christians.

It is now clear that for Melanchthon both the Spirit's justifying work in giving the gift of faith and the Spirit's work in regeneration are understood very substantially in affective terms. Together they constitute overlapping elements in a single affective sequence: a movement from fear and anxiety before God to a love, peace, and joy that are a consequence of God's gracious solution of the problems—sin and the threat of death—that generated the fear and anxiety in the first place. Regeneration, for Melanchthon, is therefore not extricable from justification. It is the psychologically inevitable outcome of the experience of justification.

What this means is that Melanchthon's account of the pneumatology of justification is not in fact "circular," as Flogaus suggests. Rather, the work of the Spirit in justification and the work of the Spirit in regeneration ultimately

---

[193] *Ap* 4.63 (*BSLK*, p. 172; *BC*, p. 131).

[194] *Ap* 4.125 (*BSLK*, p. 185; *BC*, p. 140). Calvin, likewise, describes the renewal that comes from faith in both pneumatological and affective terms, though he characteristically adds a cognitive dimension as well: regeneration is a "vivification of the Spirit" which only "comes to pass when the Spirit of God . . . imbues our souls, steeped in his holiness, with both new thoughts and feelings" (*Institutes* 3.3.8; Calvin, *Institutes*, p. 600). Zwingli, too, attributes all "works" in Christians to the "unceasing . . . activity and operation" of "the Spirit himself" (Huldrych Zwingli, "An Exposition of the Faith," in *Zwingli and Bullinger*, ed. G.W. Bromiley (London: Westminster John Knox Press, 1953), p. 272).

[195] *Ap* 4.125 (*BSLK*, p. 185; *BC*, p. 140).   [196] *Ap* 4.136 (*BSLK*, p. 187; *BC*, p. 142).

[197] *Ap* 4.146 (*BSLK*, p. 189; *BC*, p. 143).

constitute a single work. Melanchthon repeatedly identifies saving faith directly with the experience of consolation rather than seeing consolation as a side effect of justifying faith, and consistently attributes regeneration directly to faith itself rather than seeing it as a simultaneous but theologically distinct work of the Spirit. Insofar as Melanchthon does distinguish between them, the distinction is not between discrete works of the Spirit so much as different moments in a single diachronic work of the Spirit that encompasses the whole affective sequence from fear and despair to joy, peace, and love for God and neighbor.

In refusing a clear distinction between justification before God and the regeneration that takes place in the world, Melanchthon's soteriology appears to be in some tension with many later Protestant accounts. Largely in response to the Osiandrist controversy in the 1540s and 1550s, later Protestants came to parse these dimensions of the Spirit's work as logically distinct steps in the theological event by which faith is kindled, absolution applied, and the regenerating Spirit received.[198] In Melanchthon's own Lutheran church, by the time the *Formula of Concord* was approved in 1577, the work of the Spirit in regeneration and sanctification had been formally separated, theologically, from the locus of justification: "although renewal and sanctification are a blessing of our mediator Christ and a work of the Holy Spirit, they do not belong in the article on the treatment of justification before God but rather result from it."[199] According to the Concordists, justification refers solely to formal absolution, or "pronounc[ing] free from sin," and is to be distinguished from both "the contrition that precedes justification" and "the good works that follow it." The subjective dimensions of what the *Formula* calls "conversion" (as distinguished from "justification"[200]), which include both the experience of repentance that precedes the arrival of faith and the experience of joy and gratitude that result from justification, are real and important, but they "do not belong in the article on justification before God."[201] For example, "love is a fruit that certainly and necessarily results from true faith," but it is the result of a distinct work of the Spirit in "renewal and sanctification" rather than being part and parcel of justification itself.[202] The work of the Spirit in justification proper, according to this later Lutheran view, is "objective" and takes place *coram deo* only, while the subjective effects or correlates of this event are separate works of the Spirit *coram mundo*, logically distinct from justification.

The authors of the *Formula* appear to have been aware that in making such claims their account of the relationship between justification and experience

---

[198] On the development of the distinction between justification and sanctification in Lutheran theology in response to the Osiandrian controversy, see Wengert, *Defending Faith*.

[199] *Formula of Concord*, Solid Declaration, Article 3.27 (*BC*, p. 566).

[200] *Formula of Concord*, Epitome, Article 3.8 (*BC*, pp. 495–6).

[201] *Formula of Concord*, Epitome, Article 3.11 (*BC*, p. 496).

[202] *Formula of Concord*, Solid Declaration, Article 3.27 (*BC*, p. 566).

was in some tension with that of the *Apology*. Fascinatingly, they even went so far as to provide hermeneutical guidance on this issue for Lutherans reading the *Apology*. According to the Concordists, when Melanchthon says "regeneration" readers should usually understand him to mean "justification" rather than "the renewal of the human being."[203] As I have shown, to interpret the *Apology* this way is a misreading that is at odds with Melanchthon's own refusal of the "objective"/"subjective," *coram deo/coram mundo* distinction in justification. The formalization of the distinction between justification and sanctification represented in the *Formula* thus created the conditions in which "experience" often came to be evacuated from justification itself in later Protestant theology. From the perspective of pneumatology and experience, this distinguishes later Lutheran theology in important ways from Melanchthon's view in the *Apology*.

The formal shifting of the experiences that Melanchthon, like Luther, associated with justification over to the separate "article" of sanctification appears to have had significant downstream effects upon Protestant reflection on experience. This is because the move is more than just a redrawing of the conceptual map in soteriology. From a Protestant perspective, such a move also communicates an implicit *value judgment* about such experiences. Although sanctification is an important and necessary theological and biblical category for Protestants, justification is far more than this. Luther called justification by faith the doctrine without which "everything is lost,"[204] and later Protestants referred to justification as "the article by which the church stands or falls" (*articulus stantis et cadentis ecclesiae*)[205] and the "material principle" of Protestantism.[206] In such a context, to remove the embodied, experiential dimensions of salvation from the article on justification is to render them substantially less theologically significant, in comparative terms, even if that was not the intention at the time. In the long run, this revaluation of the importance of experience did much to pave the way for the enduring power of the ambivalence about religious experience in Protestantism that was discussed in Chapter 1—including for the sorts of anxiety about subjectivity we saw so explicitly in Torrance's thought, and which also seems to have influenced Tanner's ambivalence about even sanctification as an embodied experience.

---

[203] "When in place of [the terms justification and absolution] the words *regeneration* and *vivificatio* . . . are used as synonyms of justification, as happens in the Apology, then they are to be understood in this same sense. Otherwise, they should be understood as the renewal of the human being and should be differentiated from 'justification by faith' (*Formula of Concord*, Epitome, Article 3.8; *BC*, p. 495–6).

[204] *The Smalcald Articles*, First Article (*BC*, p. 301).

[205] J.H Alsted, *Theologia scholastica didactica* (Hanover: 1618), p. 711.

[206] On the sources of the widespread view that justification by faith alone is the "material principle" of Protestantism, see Albrecht Ritschl, "Über die beiden Principien des Protestantismus," in *Gesammelte Aufsätze* (Freiburg & Leipzig: J.C.B. Mohr, 1893).

The Psychological Plausibility of Melanchthon's Account

In light of the alternative path taken by later Protestants in distinguishing more sharply between justification and regeneration, there is an important question to be asked of Melanchthon's approach in the *Apology*. It is clear that Melanchthon himself did not consider a forensic account of the mechanism of justification to be at odds with understanding justification at the same time as a kind of "experience," and that his own understanding of the doctrine is hardly "cold," disembodied, or "propositional." But is Melanchthon's inter-weaving of the two in fact coherent? Might he not be attempting to force "experience" onto an implicitly rationalistic forensic logic in a way that does not hold up to theological scrutiny? Given that his account of justification as "consolation" is to a significant degree a psychological one, is it plausible to contend that the noetic conviction that Christ's righteousness has been im-puted to sinners by faith should have the kind of affective-experiential conse-quences that Melanchthon attributes to such faith? Or has Melanchthon failed to recognize that his conceptualities are not as successful as he thinks at holding the objective forensic mechanism together with its subjective, affective effects, and that in fact, as Milbank argues, the presence or otherwise of these embodied effects ultimately "does not appear to matter all that much"?[207]

Although Milbank and others pose this question in metaphysical terms, the question is first and foremost a psychological one. In arguing that forensic justification is a rationalistic affirmation of "propositions" and therefore divorced from human experience, a claim is being made about the relationship between doctrines and concrete human experiences. Viewing the question in this way, it becomes clear that the question is best answered in dialogue with contemporary psychological science—an area that has had significant success in recent decades in illuminating the complex relationship between emotional states and cognitive judgments. The next task, then, is to test the plausibility of Melanchthon's account of the affective salience of forensic justification in relation to contemporary empirical understandings of the emotional dimen-sions of cognition, specifically the relation between "cognitive objects" and the elicitation of emotion.

There is wide agreement today among psychologists and empirically engaged philosophers of emotion that emotions are helpfully under-stood to differ from mood states above all insofar as they "involve cognitive appraisal as a defining feature,"[208] and thus possess an inherent

---

[207] Milbank, *Beyond Secular Order*, p. 225.
[208] Ekkekasis, *Measurement of Affect*, p. 41. Ekkekasis is drawing here on N.H. Fridja and K.R. Scherer, "Emotion definitions (psychological perspectives)," in *The Oxford Companion to Emotion and the Affective Sciences*, eds. D. Sander and K.R. Scherer (Oxford: Oxford University Press, 2009), pp. 142–4; as well as R.S. Lazarus, "Cognition and motivation in emotion,"

"intentionality."[209] Unlike either moods or the continuous affective hum of human experience that psychologists call "core affect," emotions are "intentionally directed" at specific cognitive "objects, events, or states of affairs."[210]

In one particularly useful philosophical account, drawing on and interpreting the broad consensus on the subject in empirical psychological research, Julien Deonna and Fabrice Teroni describe this intentionality of emotion as meaning that emotions always have some sort of "cognitive basis" (i.e., some kind of cognitive object that elicits them). As they put it, echoing an overview of the psychological literature on emotion by Panteleimon Ekkekasis,[211] "emotions differ from moods in virtue of being intentionally directed at specific objects." They continue:

> [E]motions can equally well be directed at objects, events, or states of affairs with which the subject is presently in perceptual contact ("Ben is afraid of this lion"), with which she had previously been in perceptual contact ("Mary regrets having met Ben in the jungle"), with which she has never been in such contact ("Louis is disappointed that Napoleon lost the Battle of Waterloo"), also with states of affairs with which perceptual contact is impossible ("Rebecca hopes she will travel to Atlantis") . . . [E]motions necessarily rely on other mental states in order to be intentionally directed at something. Emotions, unlike perceptions, are always grounded in some other mental state that is also about the object the emotion is directed at.[212]

Importantly, this intentionality in relation to cognitive objects means that there is an irreducibly imaginative element involved in emotion—an "imagination-based expectation . . . about a relevant event"[213]—and this explains why we can be sad in the present about things that we have access to only through memory, and why we can hope for things that are impossible.

If we apply this contemporary understanding of the basic building blocks of emotion to Melanchthon's account of forensic justification, it gives us an excellent way of understanding how it is that a shift in doctrine—even a shift as abstract as a change in God's relation to a person on the basis of the

---

American Psychologist 46 (1991), and Gerald L. Clore and A. Ortony, "Appraisal theories: how cognition shapes affect into emotion," in *Handbook of Emotions*, 3rd ed., eds. Michael Lewis, Jeannette M. Haviland-Jones, and Lisa Feldman Barrett (New York: The Guilford Press, 2008). For an updated overview of this literature, see Gerald L. Clore and Alexander J. Schiller, "New Light on the Affect-Cognition Connection," in *Handbook of Emotions*, 4th ed., eds. Lisa Feldman Barrett, Michael Lewis, and Jeannette M. Haviland-Jones (New York: The Guilford Press, 2016).

[209] As Feldman Barrett and Russell put it, a "prototypical emotional episode" is "a complex set of interrelated subevents concerned with a specific object," and such objects can be, in Ekkekasis' words, "a person, an event, or a thing; past, present, or future; real or imagined" (Russell and Feldman Barrett, "Dissecting the elephant," p. 806; and Ekkekasis, *Measurement of Affect*, p. 41).

[210] Deonna and Teroni, *The Emotions*, pp. 4–5.

[211] Ekkekasis, *Measurement of Affect*, pp. 33–51, especially pp. 40–3.

[212] Deonna and Teroni, *The Emotions*, pp. 4–5.

[213] Deonna and Teroni, *The Emotions*, pp. 4–6.

reckoning of Christ's merits to them in a perceived divine law court—might in fact have a strong and plausible connection to particular emotional, psychological states. The event of coming to faith can be characterized as an imaginative shift in one's present and/or future relation to a perceived or postulated divine judgment. When the "doctrine" changes—in the case of forensic justification from something like "God judges sinners like me" to "in Christ God accepts me fully and will judge me no longer"—this entails a change in the "cognitive basis" of the emotion of terror. Such a change, if it actually takes place, cannot but result in specific and plausible affective consequences—the dissolution of feelings of fear and the kindling of feelings like peace, joy, and gratitude.

In this interpretation, Melanchthon's consistent interweaving of descriptions of a doctrinal mechanism—forensic justification—with shifts in affective state, far from entailing an inherent contradiction and a failure to recognize the seeds of a disembodied theological rationalism, becomes psychologically plausible, even sophisticated and necessary, and *a putative opposition between "propositionalism," on the one hand, and "embodiment" and affectivity, on the other, is resolved.* In terms of cognitive psychology as well as contemporary philosophy of mind, the idea that a conceptual framework like forensic justification would somehow preclude or prevent affective engagement and participation, that it would be affectively blind and experientially unengaged, is a non-starter. In fact, cognitive frameworks like this are an irreducible component of most normal human affective processes.

The implication is that although Milbank and others who have critiqued justification by faith as a "legal fiction" are correct that such inner, affective change is viewed by Melanchthon and many of those who followed him as playing no formal role in the saving imputation of Christ's righteousness to the sinner, they are not correct to think that it therefore will not actually happen or that it will not matter whether or not it does. Indeed, we might say that it is psychologically *necessary* for some such deep affective response to take place, *if* real belief in the doctrine in relation to the believer's own life is involved. And it is precisely this that Melanchthon is claiming in the *Apology*, where he at no point conceives of faith as something that can come to exist outside of a particular kind of affective-experiential sequence.[214]

In concluding this examination of Melanchthon, we are now in a position to reflect more explicitly on what in the context of the long history of Protestant theologies of justification is perhaps the most unusual feature of Melanchthon's

---

[214] Wengert identifies the same dynamic in Melanchthon's later writings. According to Wengert, it is clear in the controversy with Osiander that "Melanchthon derives his theology and its method from the experience of the justified" in comfort and consolation, and furthermore that it was this "experiential theology [that] provided the heart of Melanchthon's rejection of Osiander's teaching" (Wengert, *Defending Faith*, p. 349).

account, and what for the purposes of this book is the most important: the apparent collapse of the distinction between "objective"/ontological and "subjective"/experiential dimensions of justification.

I have argued that one of the greatest challenges for a pneumatology of Christian experience is to avoid the temptation to split theological-metaphysical claims about the Spirit's work from practical-experiential claims about the Spirit's work: i.e., to refrain from separating the Spirit's work in our *being* and in our *bodies* into discrete and only indirectly related spheres. It is not easy to do this, and from the standpoint of the history of theology, it is in the arenas of salvation and sanctification that this difficulty is often most acute.

It is just this error that John Milbank, for example, accuses "extrinsicist and judicial" theologies of justification of generating. As we have seen, later Lutheranism did in fact formalize a strict distinction between the two spheres in the *Formula of Concord* in a way that seems to have opened the door for such problems later on to some extent. Whether the emphasis is on a divine courtroom separate from human experience, a participation in Christ's faith and righteousness that never crosses over into embodied experience, or an ontological infusion of a habit of charity that is unavailable to conscious awareness, Christian theology has a long record of generating soteriologies in which salvation and experience cohere very poorly.[215]

Not so Philip Melanchthon. I have shown that Melanchthon's theology of justification is driven by a passionate opposition to the idea that faith is simply "vain," "idle," "historical" knowledge about Christ's saving work. In this it constitutes a sustained attempt to articulate the fundamental unity, in the Spirit, of the saving work of Christ before God and the experiential effects of salvation in bodies and in history. It is precisely this integration that Melanchthon is after when he claims again and again that "*only* that which brings peace to consciences justifies before God";[216] that "in justification . . . consciences *must* find peace with God";[217] and that "faith justifies and regenerates *inasmuch* as it frees us from our terrors and produces peace, joy, and new life in our hearts."[218]

---

[215] It is the same error of separating the spheres that Karl Rahner laments in neo-scholastic accounts of the relationship between nature and grace: the problem "for this school," Rahner argues, is that in it "the proper reception of the justifying Spirit of God . . . [is conceived as taking place] beyond conscious awareness and is a purely ontological reality" (Rahner, "Religious Enthusiasm and the Experience of Grace," p. 37). Fascinatingly, in making this critique Rahner is echoing quite precisely Melanchthon's own concern about earlier scholastic soteriology in his argument in the *Apology* that a purely ontological understanding of the Spirit being communicated through the sacraments *ex opere operato* occurs "without the recipient being favorably stirred[,] as if in actual fact the bestowing of the Holy Spirit were without any effect" (*Ap* 4.63 (*BSLK*, p. 172; *BC*, p. 131).

[216] *Ap* 4.180A (*BC*, p. 146). Emphasis added.

[217] *Ap* 4.224A (*BC*, p. 154). Emphasis added.

[218] *Ap* 12.60 (*BSLK*, p. 263; *BC*, p. 197). Emphasis added.

I have also shown that these claims are not idle conjunctions or mere rhetorical flourishes in Melanchthon's thought. Melanchthon's conviction that a genuine faith in Christ's atoning work not only can but "must" have concrete experiential consequences—that it really does console terrified hearts—accords remarkably well with current understanding in empirical psychology of the relationship between cognition and the elicitation of emotional states. Psychologically speaking, Melanchthon's account of the relationship between theological and experiential realities is both plausible and coherent, even as it preserves the deeply disjunctive and "incongruous" character of divine grace about which Tanner is rightly concerned.

In Melanchthon's theology of justification, then, we have just the sort of experientially integrated and yet recognizably Protestant soteriology we did not succeed in finding in Torrance, and which we found only in muted and somewhat ambivalent form in Tanner. The account of justification in the *Apology* is a master-class in the dismantling of easy boundaries between the realm of ontological claims and the realm of human experience. In Melanchthon's hands, there is finally no durable distinction between salvation as an ontological event and the experience of Christian initiation in bodies and in time.[219] To separate the two is to revert salvation into an "idle knowledge" rather than something that can actually happen to a person. In the Melanchthonian picture, the divine courtroom of forensic justification is not "out there," in heaven, in the eschaton, or in some other idealized space of the theologically "real." The sphere of operation for the Spirit's saving work is precisely the entanglement of concepts, desires, judgments, and affective states that constitutes the experience of the embodied Christian soul.

AFFECTIVE TRANSFORMATION AS PARTICIPATION

It is now clear that Melanchthon's theology of justification points the way toward an understanding of salvation in the Spirit that satisfies the first and second requirements outlined earlier in the chapter. It is an account of the work of the Spirit to save that both affects real bodies in time and preserves a traditional Protestant emphasis on the unconditional and unilateral character of the grace of God in light of the reality of sin. But what of the third requirement, that of taking into account the importance of union with Christ and other participatory language in the New Testament?

A more elaborated account of life in the Spirit will be given in Chapter 5. In concluding the present chapter, it will be enough to draw out the core

---

[219] For analysis of the same dynamics in Melanchthon's later writings, see Wengert, *Defending Faith*, pp. 334–5, 338–41.

theological connection between Melanchthon's affective soteriology of justification and participation in God more broadly. Although the fact has not yet been adequately recognized in the recent Protestant "turn" to participation, traditional accounts of deification take for granted that the body, as the locus of emotions and desires, is one of the core sites where such participation takes place. As we will see, both Eastern and Western patristic accounts understand soteriological participation to entail the transformation and reordering of the affections. And this transformation and reordering is not a mere side effect or symptom of a more fundamental participation taking place at the level of ontology. Rather, the primary initial site of such participation simply is the feeling and desiring body, which prior to death is always located in communities and in the world.

A classic version of this argument can be found in Didymus the Blind's *On the Holy Spirit*. This text provides one of the clearest and most persuasive fourth-century arguments for the deity of the Spirit by focusing on the Spirit's role as "Sanctifier." According to DelColgliano, Radde-Gallwitz, and Ayres, the foundation of the work is the "fundamental argument" that "the Spirit is the source of all sanctification in which Christians . . . participate, and thus a priori cannot be a created reality participating in goodness."[220] As Didymus puts it:

> [All created] realities are capable of participating in wisdom, the other virtues, and sanctification. On the contrary, this substance we are now discussing [i.e., the Holy Spirit] produces wisdom and sanctification . . . [T]he Holy Spirit, as all acknowledge, is the immutable sanctifier, the bestower of divine knowledge and all goods. To put it simply, he himself subsists in those goods which are conferred by the Lord.[221]

What are these goods? Didymus argues that they include all Christian "virtues," including not least the sanctified affections of hope, joy, and peace, which he contrasts with the unvirtuous disorder of "the passions":

> God, the bestower of goods, in the power of the Spirit grants the hope he promised to those who have the Spirit. With joy and peace he fills those who possess undisturbed, peaceful thoughts, and have minds joyful and calmed from every storm of the passions. Now whoever obtains the aforementioned goods in the power of the Holy Spirit also obtains the correct faith in the mystery of the Trinity.[222]

---

[220] Mark DelCogliano, Andrew Radde-Gallwitz, and Lewis Ayres, "General Introduction," in *Works on the Spirit: Athanasius and Didymus* (Yonkers, NY: St Vladimir's Seminary Press, 2011), p. 45.

[221] Didymus, *On the Spirit* 10–11 (DelCogliano, Radde-Gallwitz, and Ayres, *Works on the Spirit*, p. 146).

[222] Didymus, *On the Spirit* 43–44 (DelCogliano, Radde-Gallwitz, and Ayres, *Works on the Spirit*, p. 157).

For Didymus, salvific participation is thus a participation in specific divine goods and virtues. As such, deification consists not least in a process of affective transformation that takes place in bodies. The calming of the passions and the generation of joy and peace and hope are not side effects of, or incidental to, participation in the Spirit. Rather, they are precisely the sorts of things in which participation in God through the Spirit actually consists.

A more elaborate version of the same vision can be found in Maximus the Confessor. In *Ambiguum 7*, Maximus draws on Gregory Nazianzen to establish emotion and desire as fundamental characteristics of creaturehood. They are the motors by which "rational creatures . . . are moved from their natural beginning in being, toward a voluntary end in well-being. For the end of the motion of things that are moved is to rest within eternal being itself."[223] In Maximus' view, even the motion of intellect in the soul is ultimately a desiderative motion:

> If an intellective being is moved intellectively . . . then it will necessarily become a knowing intellect. But if it knows, it surely loves that which it knows; and if it loves, it certainly suffers an ecstasy toward it as an object of love.[224]

Crucially for Maximus, desire and love of this sort are always caught up in corporeal realities. Reflecting on Gregory's lament about our "struggle and battle with the body," Maximus develops a sophisticated vision of the irreducibility of the body on the path of divinization:

> God in His goodness made man as a union of soul and body, so that the soul which was given to him, being rational and intellectual . . . should, on the one hand, by means of its desire and the whole power of its total love, cling closely to God through knowledge, and, growing in "likeness to God", be divinized; and, on the other hand, through its mindful care for what is lower . . . it should make prudent use of the body, with a view to ordering it to the mind through the virtues . . . itself mediating to the body the indwelling presence of its Creator, making God Himself—who bound together the body and the soul—the body's own unbreakable bond of immortality.[225]

For this reason, in Maximus' view there is no such thing as deification of human beings that does not directly involved the material body. As Constas explains, "any desire for God that does not mindfully engage the senses and the material world has no reality in the soul . . . Just as God descended to man through the flesh, so too does man's ascent to God involve not a rejection of

---

[223] Maximus, *Ambigua 7* (1073C; Maximos, *On Difficulties in the Church Fathers: The Ambigua: i: Maximos the Confessor*, trans. Nicholas Constas (Cambridge, MA: Harvard University Press, 2014), pp. 86/87. This edition includes both the Greek and the English. For references to this book here and below, the first page number is the Greek and the one after the forward slash is the English).

[224] Maximus, *Ambigua 7* (1073C; Maximos, *The Ambigua*, pp. 86/87).

[225] Maximus, *Ambigua 7* (1092B; Maximos, *The Ambigua*, pp. 118/119).

matter but a necessary passage *through* matter."[226] At the same time, the process of divinization is always a pneumatological one: "This occurs through the grace of the Spirit."[227]

Most importantly for our purposes, a major feature of this passage through matter is therefore the transformation of affects and desires through ascetic practice. As Maximus explains in *Ambiguum* 10, to undergo divinization is to be among those who are "dominated neither by anger, nor envy, nor rivalry . . . nor desire [*epithumia*] for the seemingly splendid things in life, nor any other vice from the wicked swarm of the passions [*pathon*] . . . so that, filled with joy, they might be united with the principles of those very virtues that they had come to know, or rather with God."[228] For Maximus, then, a fundamental dimension of deification is the mastery of the body with its passions, and the generation and cultivation of affections and desires that drive the creature to its final end in God.[229]

The idea that soteriological participation consists to a significant degree in the transformation of bodily affects is not just an Eastern one. To anticipate the extended discussion in Chapter 5, for Augustine Spirit-enabled participation in God consists above all in participation in divine love, which has been "poured into our hearts by the Holy Spirit" (Rom. 5:5). He describes this in *On the Spirit and the Letter*:

> [Human beings] receive the Holy Spirit so that there arises in their minds a delight in and a love for [*que fiat in animo eius delectatio dilectioque*] that highest and immutable good that is God . . . By this [love] given to them like the pledge of a gratuitous gift, they are set afire with the desire to cling to the creator and burn to come to a participation in that true light [*inardescat inhaerere creatori atque inflammetur accedere ad participationem illius veri luminis*], so that they have their well-being from him from whom they have their being.[230]

Similar to Maximus, the engine of participation in God is thus transformed desire—desire for "that highest and immutable good that is God." And once again this participation is not least an embodied and practically recognizable

---

[226] Nicholas Constas, "Introduction," in *On Difficulties in the Church Fathers: The Ambigua*: i: *Maximos the Confessor*, ed. Nicholas Constas (Cambridge, MA: Harvard University Press, 2014), p. xviii.

[227] Maximus, *Ambigua* 7 (1076C; Maximos, *The Ambigua*, pp. 90/91).

[228] Maximus, *Ambigua* 10.51 (1205B; Maximos, *The Ambigua*, pp. 342/343).

[229] According to Blowers, "For Maximus the various strands of the therapeutics of desire—the stretching, diversifying, educating, and consolidating of desire—converge and culminate in the mystery of deification." (Paul M. Blowers, "The Dialectics and Therapeutics of Desire in Maximus the Confessor," *Vigiliae Christianae* 65, no. 4 (2011), p. 442). For more on this in Maximus, see especially *Ad Thalassium* 1 ("On the utility of the passions"). For secondary discussion, in addition to Blowers and Constas, see Demetrios Bathrellos, "Passions, Ascesis, and the Virtues," in *The Oxford Handbook of Maximus the Confessor*, eds. Pauline Allen and Bronwen Neil (Oxford: Oxford University Press, 2015).

[230] *Spir. et litt.* 3.5 (*PL* 44:203; *WSA* I/23:145).

reality. For Augustine, there is no such thing as non-affective, disembodied human participation in divine love. To love something is always to delight in it and to take joy in it, to be drawn to it and compelled by it as an embodied creature in the world that God has created. "One only loves, after all, what delights one."[231]

In the context of the present argument, the key point is that soteriological participation and *theosis* are conceived in all three cases—Didymus, Maximus, and Augustine—as something that involves the transformation of affects and desires in the framework of the feeling body. Indeed, the importance of Christian *ascesis* in Maximus and beyond depends on the idea that divinization is a phenomenon that begins in bodies (even as it does not reduce to what happens in bodies).

There are two implications that follow from this. The first relates to the desire in contemporary theology to recover premodern theologies of soteriological participation. It is that, insofar as such retrievals fail to give a robust and plausible account of how affects and desires come to be transformed in practically recognizable ways, they will have departed from the patristic vision. Theologians like Didymus, Maximus, and Augustine are representatives of a Christian thought-world that simply did not recognize the sort of clear distinction between experiential and ontological realities that is operative in so much modern theology.

The second implication is the most significant for the argument of this chapter. It is that, insofar as Melanchthon's theology of justification provides a plausible account of how the Spirit effects affective and desiderative transformation in Christians, *it is also an account of participation*. Indeed, in this respect it is actually more persuasive *as an account of participation* than what we found in Torrance or indeed Tanner—even if Melanchthon never uses the word. At its core, Melanchthon's theology of consolation is about the establishment of a new affectively salient relation of love between Christ and the sinner. It is also, as we will see in the next two chapters, about the way that the divine words of law and gospel function as a mechanism for freeing the Christian from sinful desiderative attachments and for generating new sanctified energies of joy and delight in God and his ways. Although there are quite substantial differences between the affective soteriology we find in Melanchthon and the theology of deification in a figure like Maximus, it is also clear that there is one major, and perhaps unexpected, commonality as well: the fact that both understand salvation to involve, irreducibly, desiderative transformations that are legible in experiences taking place in bodies.

---

[231] *Serm.* 159.3 (*PL* 38:869; *WSA* III/5:122). In his Romans commentary, Aquinas remarks similarly on the Spirit's gift of charity being a participation in God that involves subjective transformation, including affective transformation. See Aquinas, *in Rom.* 5.1.392.

In the remaining chapters I will sketch in more detail what a contemporary account of salvation and sanctification in this key might look like. For now it is enough to summarize the findings of this chapter. I have been interrogating the truth of two premises that are widely held in contemporary soteriology: (i) that participatory soteriologies tend to be effective at integrating soteriology with experience, and (ii) that classical Protestant theologies of justification tend to be very ineffective at integrating soteriology with experience.

In relation to (i) we have found that it is by no means a given that a soteriology based around participation will succeed at such integration. This is especially true of accounts in a Protestant key that seek to preserve the disjunctive and unconditional character of divine grace. The widespread assumption that the answer to problematically "cold," propositional accounts of salvation is to reject forensic accounts in favor of participatory ones does not seem to bear scrutiny.

In relation to (ii) we have found that the premise is simply false. The most influential early Protestant account of forensic justification in fact provides a highly sophisticated and cognitively plausible theory of the relation between salvation and experience.[232]

Overall, we have found that questions about the experiential power of a given soteriology, and about the effectiveness of a given soteriological model in generating practically recognizable effects, simply do not map onto a distinction between forensic and participatory models. Insofar as a great deal of recent soteriology has taken this premise as an operating assumption, it seems to have been premised on a great mistake.

---

[232] It is no accident that one of the most durable and pastorally effective liturgies in the history of the church, the Anglican *Book of Common Prayer*, was shaped around an affective account of justification by faith that was directly influenced by Melanchthon. On Cranmer's affective soteriology, see Ashley Null, *Thomas Cranmer's Doctrine of Repentance: Renewing the Power to Love* (Oxford: Oxford University Press, 2000), pp. 120–33, 174–84; on Melanchthon's influence on Cranmer, see pp. 99–102, 130–1, and 219–20.

4

Grace as Experience

The tale of the Divine Pity was never yet believed from lips that were not felt to be moved by human pity. And Janet's anguish was not strange to Mr Tryan.

—George Eliot, *Janet's Repentance*[1]

In the previous chapter, I analyzed four major accounts of Christian salvation in the Spirit through the lens of "experience." In T.F. Torrance and Kathryn Tanner I found modern attempts to articulate a soteriology based on participation in Christ while holding on to the classical Protestant concern to ensure that salvation is in no way conditioned on human response and thus cannot be reduced to a process of sanctification. Both were shown to preserve the disjunctive character of salvation, but at the price of significantly problematizing the constructive connection between salvation and Christian experience. In Dominican neo-Thomist accounts we found something close to the reverse: a model of salvation that succeeds reasonably well at holding metaphysical and experiential realities together, but at the price of making salvation contingent on a lifetime of cooperation with grace. I then turned to Philip Melanchthon's affective account of justification by faith alone as a model of soteriology that succeeds on both fronts. I showed that Melanchthon develops just the sort of plausible and psychologically sophisticated account of the relationship between theological and experiential realities that was missing in Torrance, and only partially present in Tanner, while preserving the unilateral and disjunctive character of the saving grace that encounters human beings. And I concluded by arguing, with the help of Didymus the Blind, Maximus the Confessor, and Augustine, that affective change of the sort envisioned by Melanchthon can reasonably be construed as a mode of "participation" in Christ through the Spirit, helping to square the circle in recent soteriological debates about justification and participation.

[1] Eliot, *Janet's Repentance*, p. 226.

The Holy Spirit and Christian Experience. Simeon Zahl, Oxford University Press (2020). © Simeon Zahl.
DOI: 10.1093/oso/9780198827788.001.0001

What allowed Melanchthon's account to succeed where more recent Protestant soteriologies of participation fail was his close attention to the mediating categories of affect and desire. To speak of the work of the Spirit in the transformation of human affects and desires is to use a traditional biblical and theological vocabulary that can make sense of real bodily change without needing to appeal to the deliberate and conscious cooperation of the one in whom the Spirit is working. It is thus theological attention to affect and desire that makes it conceptually possible for Melanchthon to preserve the unilateral quality of grace and the correspondingly more pessimistic view of natural and graced human powers that is a core concern of classical Protestant theology, without having to evacuate the body and its experiences from theological description of salvation.

For Melanchthon, the primary mode by which the saving work of Christ is "actualized in relation to us" by the Spirit is through a practically recognizable affective sequence, moving from experiential plight through consolation to new feelings of joy and freedom. We might call his description of this sequence a kind of "pattern" of experience of divine grace.

The present chapter builds on the soteriological vision we found in Melanchthon to examine in greater depth how the doctrine of grace in this construal is much more than just a theoretical *description* of an affective pattern associated with salvation. It is also a kind of structure for interpreting, shaping, and generating patterns of Christian experience, in light of the intransigence of sinful affects on the one hand, and the transforming agency of the Holy Spirit on the other. The chapter does this by examining from the perspective of "affective salience" two core dimensions of a theology of grace following Luther and Melanchthon: accounts of sin and plight, and the distinction between the law and the gospel.

Within the constraints of a single chapter it will not be possible to discuss every dimension of this theology of divine grace, or to address all possible critiques of early Lutheran accounts of justification by faith. The goal here, rather, is two-fold. The first is methodological: to further demonstrate, through two extended examples, the power of the perspective on pneumatology and Christian experience being advanced in this book to illuminate and reconfigure debates about sin and grace in contemporary theology. The second is the constructive counterpart of this: to show, using resources from the theology of Martin Luther as well as contemporary affect theory, how this perspective provides compelling grounds for the rehabilitation of a more "disjunctive" theology of salvation than has recently been fashionable, and to begin to perform such a retrieval.

The choice to focus on accounts of sin and plight and the instruments of the law and the gospel means that the examination of grace in what follows will focus to a substantial degree on "legal" images in soteriology (law and judgment, forgiveness, and the relationship between divine grace and the "worth" of its recipients). There are a number of reasons for my focus on these dimensions of grace in particular. One is that they lie at the heart of the Melanchthonian soteriology that was found to be pneumatologically and experientially compelling in the previous chapter. Another is my conviction of their contemporary diagnostic and liberative power in the context of a world that tends to reduce the value of human beings to their economic performance and "worth."[2] A third, to which I will turn in a moment, is the recent recovery and new creative emphasis on these dimensions of grace that has been made possible by John Barclay's analysis of the "incongruous" character of divine grace in the theology of Paul, which underscores that there continue to be excellent biblical reasons for focusing on these topics.

It needs to be stated at the outset that although I do consider such themes to have substantial diagnostic traction and religious power in the contemporary world, across a variety of contexts and localities, and although I do view them as having a certain theological primacy in discussions of divine grace, I do not understand these sorts of imageries to be exhaustive of the topic. Above all, the theme of grace as liberation—not just from guilt or fear of worthlessness but also from concrete situations of suffering and oppression that are external to the sufferer—is a significant one for any biblically and traditionally serious soteriology. In Chapter 5 I will draw out certain political and social dimensions of the theology of grace presented here, though a full account of the relationship between grace and liberation from the affective and pneumatological perspective being developed here lies beyond the scope of the present book.

THE INCONGRUITY OF GRACE

The explorations that follow are resourced in part by recent work on the theology of grace in Paul studies by John Barclay. Barclay has made a compelling case that much confusion in this field can be cleared up by recognizing that "grace" is a variegated concept in the New Testament period. Barclay shows that accounts of divine grace can be differentiated by mapping them according to six distinct "perfections" of grace: superabundance, singularity, priority, incongruity, efficacy, and non-circularity.[3] Thus, for example, a given account of grace may be very clear on the "priority" of grace (the idea

---

[2] On the critical power of a Christian theology of grace to diagnose and subvert this reduction of human worth to economic value, see Kathryn Tanner, *Christianity and the New Spirit of Capitalism* (New Haven: Yale University Press, 2019), especially Chapters 2 and 3.

[3] John M.G. Barclay, *Paul and the Gift* (Grand Rapids, MI: William B. Eerdmans Publishing Company, 2015), pp. 70–5.

that God must always take the initiative in giving the gift of grace) without any commitment to belief that grace is "incongruous" (given without regard to the worth of the recipient).

Examining Paul's theology of grace through this lens allows Barclay to make better sense than is often the case of why Paul can be uncompromising in his view that grace is always given without regard to the moral, social, or religious worth of the recipient (this is its "incongruity") while at the same time expressing expectation that these unworthy recipients will nevertheless have their lives reconfigured and transformed in light of the gift. In Barclay's terminology, Paul's view of divine grace is most distinctive in the way it emphasizes the perfection of incongruity while still carrying "expectations of obedience," and thus rejecting the perfection of non-circularity.[4]

Paul and the Gift is particularly persuasive in demonstrating how comprehensively Paul's worldview and expectations are shaped by the perfection of incongruity. The typology of perfections of grace allows Barclay to isolate just how radical and uncompromising Paul is in his Christian subversion of value systems that presuppose the importance of moral, social, or religious worth for successful participation in the system.[5] A typical example for Barclay is Romans 5:6–10:

> Paul goes out of his way [in this text] to underline the total absence of worth on the human side: it was while we were weak (*astheneis*) ... that Christ died, on behalf of the ungodly (*asebeis*; 5:6); God proves (*sunistesin*; cf. 3:5) his love, in that "while we were still sinners" (*hamartoloi*), Christ died for us (5:8); it was when we were enemies (*echthoi*) that we were reconciled to God (5:10). The variety of terms, portraying the absence of value from multiple perspectives, seems designed to underline as emphatically as possible that the conditions for the gift were anything but positive. This is not the giving of covenants to the worthy ... [N]o fitting features can be traced in the recipients of God's love, not even in their hidden potential.

In demonstrating the centrality of the category of "incongruity" in Paul's interpretation of the Christ-gift, Barclay provides biblical support for the idea that themes like the "unworthiness" of human beings to receive grace and the subversion in Christ of a divine judgment that would otherwise obtain are of continual importance for any theological account of divine grace that seeks to take its lead from the witness of the New Testament. Again, this does not mean that such themes are the only significant dimensions of divine grace as described either in Scripture or in later theological traditions. For present

---

[4] Barclay, *Paul and the Gift*, p. 569.
[5] See e.g., Barclay's exposition of Romans 12–15 as a comprehensive description of a mode of communal life predicated upon "unconditioned welcome," i.e., that is not predicated on the worth or standing of its members according to some criterion or other. See Barclay, *Paul and the Gift*, pp. 508–16.

purposes, the implication is simply that there are excellent biblical reasons for a theology of Christian experience *to seek to make experiential sense of what it is like to encounter a transformative grace that one does not deserve.*

Elsewhere I have argued that Barclay's account of the transformative effects of the incongruous character of grace in Paul, while persuasive in explaining the revolutionary social and communal dimensions of such incongruity, needs to be complemented and extended through an equally textured account of how the incongruity of grace functions to pattern Christian experience in more rapid, experiential ways as well.[6] The present chapter provides an extended account of these dynamics in the context of contemporary questions about soteriological "plight," on the one hand, and traditional Protestant understandings of the distinction between the law and the gospel, on the other.

AFFECT THEORY AND THE NATURE OF DOCTRINE

An important resource in what follows will be the theoretical approach to emotion and desire known as "affect theory." Before proceeding with the discussion of grace and its patterns, it is necessary to introduce affect theory and to establish its relevance for discussions of the nature and function of Christian doctrine.

I have already referred at various points to the idea that theological doctrines are not just truth claims, but also function to shape and generate patterns of affective experience. From the standpoint of theories of doctrine, what makes Melanchthon's approach to soteriology particularly interesting is that it provides a way of conceiving of a genuinely significant relation between doctrine and experience without having to presume a false or naïve account of the plasticity and constructedness of affective experience under the influence of the interventions of Christian doctrinal discourse or indeed of religious practice.

The idea that doctrines, including soteriological doctrines, play a role in the construction and regulation of Christian experience is not new. George Lindbeck argued decades ago that "human experience is shaped, molded, and in a sense constituted by cultural and linguistic forms," including doctrines. To "become religious" is to learn not only how to act and think, but also how to "*feel* . . . in conformity with a religious tradition."[7] For Lindbeck, it is doctrines that generate experiences rather than the other way around. "Religious experiences in the sense of feelings, sentiments, or

---

[6] Simeon Zahl, "Incongruous Grace as Pattern of Experience," *International Journal of Systematic Theology* 22, no. 1 (2020).

[7] Lindbeck, *Nature of Doctrine*, pp. 34–5. Emphasis added.

emotions...result from...conceptual patterns[,] rather than being their source."[8] Here linguistic and cultural concepts like doctrines are the raw material of religion, and emotions and other experiences are a kind of downstream effect of a prior linguistic and symbolic "grammar" as it plays out in the world.

A good example of this sort of discourse-led account of the life of faith can be found in Gregory Jones' discussion of Christian moral life in *Transformed Judgment*. In Jones' view, the primary way that Christian transformation occurs and Christian identity is constituted is through the formative influence of Christian stories, doctrines, and practices. It is through "formation...in the Christian tradition [that] people learn to describe themselves, their actions, and the world."[9] Through "such practices as baptism, eucharist, forgiveness-reconciliation, and 'performing' the Scriptures...people are enabled to acquire the habits and skills reflective of the pattern discovered in Jesus Christ."[10] Jones' convictions about the importance of practices that draw us into narratives are grounded in Lindbeckian assumptions about the primacy of language in the shaping of human identity and behavior: "Because the human subject is constituted by language, the ability to deconstruct the old identity and refashion a new life in Christ pivots on the possibility of discovering a disruptive and creative language."[11]

The social and linguistic constructivism undergirding the cultural-linguistic model of religion that we see theorized in Lindbeck, and put into practice in Jones, has been heavily criticized in recent years. The chief problem with "strong" constructivism of this kind is that it underestimates the power of nondiscursive factors in shaping experience, and places a weight on language and discursive practice that they cannot bear. Manuel Vásquez, a theorist of religion, summarizes the point:

> [A]lthough our experience of the world [as human beings] is mediated through our discursive and nondiscursive practices, we cannot reduce to human texts the materiality of our bodies and the world in which and through which we live...Nature...is not opposed to culture...as a mere passive or empty surface upon which we inscribe our meanings. Nor is nature a mere artifice of reiterated, reified discourses. These attitudes betray a Cartesian dualism and the underlying anxiety to establish human exceptionalism, both of which have fed modernity's and religious studies' somatophobia.[12]

As Vásquez points out, text, language, and culture are not all-powerful in shaping religious life. Bodily and material conditions are constantly molding

---

[8] Lindbeck, *Nature of Doctrine*, p. 39. Emphasis added.

[9] L. Gregory Jones, *Transformed Judgment: Toward a Trinitarian Account of the Moral Life* (Eugene, OR: Wipf and Stock, 1990), p. 156.

[10] Jones, *Transformed Judgment*, p. 112.   [11] Jones, *Transformed Judgment*, p. 141.

[12] Vásquez, *More Than Belief*, pp. 321–2.

what we think and feel and how we think and feel it. Language and cultural practice are always operating within such conditions, and these conditions have substantial power to limit, skew, energize, redirect, and resist the effects of discourses and cultural practices. The result is that, *contra* the cultural-linguistic model of doctrine, if we seek to alter some problematic attitude or situation in religious life, it is not enough to change which doctrines we subscribe to or to revise the practices through which religious ideas are inscribed into habit. Such revisions may still encounter powerful resistance in the form of the material and natural conditions to which bodies in the world are always subject.

Theology and Affect Theory

One of the most important material "conditions" or limitations on the power of cultural practices to effect change is the cluster of embodied phenomena referred to in recent critical discourse as "affects." "Affect theory" refers to a set of theoretical positions that developed out of gender studies and queer theory in the 1990s and that has had a wide impact across the humanities. It arose as a response to the way that critical theory had been dominated since the 1960s by a focus on texts, language, and discourse. It characteristically attends to the ways that human behavior, politics, economics, culture, and religious life are shaped by forces other than discursive practices, with a particular focus on the realms of feeling, emotion, and desire. Its origins lie to a significant degree in reflections on the variability, strangeness, and inscrutability of desire—its "queerness"—pioneered especially by queer theorists.

From its foundational articulations in the work of Eve Kosofky Sedgwick, affect theory has been positioned against the view, popularized in the 1960s and 1970s by the psychologist Stanley Schachter, that physiological arousal[13] "is infinitely malleable by a fully acculturated cognitive faculty," such that the emotions we experience are always the direct product of "discursive social construction."[14] In a seminal essay, Sedgwick and her collaborator Adam Frank diagnose deep problems with the commitment to a Schachter-esque social constructivism that characterized critical theory at the time. The essay focuses especially on such theory's radical suspicion of appeals to non-constructed factors in the explanation of difference. Sedgwick and Frank argue that the immediate dismissal of any appeal to non-discursive influences

---

[13] In psychological science arousal is a technical term referring to a state of physiological activity, alertness, and attentiveness.

[14] Eve Kosofsky Sedgwick and Adam Frank, "Shame in the Cybernetic Fold: Reading Silvan Tomkins," in *Touching Feeling: Affect, Pedagogy, Performativity* (Durham, NC: Duke University Press, 2003), p. 113.

in human experience as simply "essentialist" has resulted in "the loss of conceptual access to an entire thought-realm."[15] What they mean is that social constructivism is unable to make sense of, and to a significant extent unable even to see, dimensions of experience and knowledge that are neither plastic nor fixed but lie in between. In its thrall to the essentialism/non-essentialism binary, and its firm conviction that meaningful difference is always the product of social construction, such theory is

> like a scanner or copier that can reproduce any work of art in 256,000 shades of gray. However infinitesimally subtle its discriminations may be, there are crucial knowledges it simply cannot transmit unless it is equipped to deal with the coarsely reductive possibility that red is different from yellow is different again from blue.[16]

It is in this context that Sedgwick began to leverage the concept of "affect" for its value in making sense of formations of power that are neither unchanging universals nor pure artifacts of discursive construction.[17]

Of particular interest from the perspective of theology and religious studies is the way that affect theorists are interested in sites where what people "believe" and what they do diverge. As Donovan Schaefer puts it, "affect theory ... is designed to profile the operations of power outside of language and the autonomous, reasoning human subject."[18] He continues,

> affect theory points to a flaw at the heart of traditional ideology critique, which takes as given that language is a sort of computer program, an intrinsically compelling system of information/force ... The linguistic fallacy presupposes that language is an apparatus of command that effortlessly articulates with bodies.

[15] Sedgwick and Frank, "Shame in the Cybernetic Fold," p. 108.

[16] Sedgwick and Frank, "Shame in the Cybernetic Fold," p. 114.

[17] Although "affect" in this sense describes motive forces that are more general, and usually more durable, than the states and experiences that psychologists call emotion, in practice the body encounters these affects primarily in the realms of feeling, emotion, and desire. Lauren Berlant provides a classic definition of affect from the perspective of affect theory: "sensual matter that is elsewhere to sovereign consciousness but that has historical significance in domains of subjectivity" (Lauren Berlant, *Cruel Optimism* (Durham, NC: Duke University Press, 2011), p. 53).

At the same time, affect theory is not singular. A particularly important divergence within affect theory has to do with whether affects are understood in a Deleuzian fashion as "something like unstructured proto-sensation," and therefore distinct from emotion, or as something more closely mapped to bodies, such that an "easy interchangeability of *affect* with terms such *emotion* and *feeling*" is legitimate (Donovan O. Schaefer, *The Evolution of Affect Theory: The Humanities, the Sciences, and the Study of Power* (Cambridge: Cambridge University Press, 2019), pp. 1–2). The former approach is associated especially with Brian Massumi; the latter is associated with Eve Sedgwick as well as Sara Ahmed and Ann Cvetkovich, amongst others. The vision of affect associated with Sedgwick and Ahmed is the one that will be taken here. For an analysis of the differences between these approaches, a persuasive case for the advantages of the latter approach, and a full bibliography, see Schaefer, *The Evolution of Affect Theory*, pp. 1–53.

[18] Schaefer, *Religious Affects*, p. 23.

It has no sense of how discourses attach to bodies and get them to move, and is baffled when bodies sincerely "believe" one thing and do another.[19]

Affect theory's starting point is thus the observation that procedures of discourse and rationality, including the cultural practices by which we seek to inscribe discursive insights into behavior and experience through habituation, are significantly limited in their ability to make sense of what human beings actually feel and do—to explain what "makes bodies move."[20]

More specifically, affect theory targets post-Enlightenment convictions of the autonomy of the individual rational subject, pointing to the phenomenology of emotion to expose the "myth of our own sovereignty over our emotions."[21] To talk about affects in this way is to draw attention to how bodies are subject to forces that have real power to shape what we feel and do, but which at the same time are capable of offering powerful resistance to efforts to alter them through changes of language and cultural practice.

Schaefer has applied this approach to religion:

> Affect theory . . . highlights how animal forces disrupt the abstract prerogative of the reasoning, calculating, talkative subject and attach bodies to complex structures of feeling that cut against not only external appraisals of the right things for bodies to do, places for them to go, ways for them to believe and feel, but the sovereign self's own assessment of its best course of action . . . [U]nderstanding religion [from this perspective] means pulling humans out of the domain of the angelic—which means out of the domain of self-determination through sovereign reason—and into the bodily, the material, and the animal.[22]

This is in sharp contrast to influential accounts of religion, following in the tradition of Jonathan Z. Smith, which Schaefer argues reduce religious phenomena "to 'language-like systems'."[23] In fact, "affect saturates experience, cognition, and behavior at every level," such that "language," including religious and theological language, "never even begins to diverge from the . . . seams of affect that stick meanings to words."[24]

What makes affects an unusually worthwhile site for theological investigation is the fact that they are relatively *intransigent* features of religious life, in the sense that they are core dimensions of religious life that are much more difficult to shift than doctrines or religious practices.[25] At one level, the point is

---

[19] Schaefer, *Religious Affects*, p. 35.

[20] Donovan O. Schaefer, "You Don't Know What Pain Is: Affect, the Lifeworld, and Animal Ethics," *Studies in Christian Ethics* 30, no. 1 (2016), p. 19.

[21] Schaefer, *Religious Affects*, p. 93. See also the discussion of "nonsovereignty" in Lauren Berlant and Lee Edelman, *Sex, or the Unbearable* (Durham, NC: Duke University Press, 2014).

[22] Schaefer, *Religious Affects*, p. 105. Here Schaefer is building on the work of Vásquez.

[23] Schaefer, *Religious Affects*, p. 11.   [24] Schaefer, *Religious Affects*, p. 45.

[25] As cognitive scientist Elaine Fox has observed of the related category of emotion, one of the defining empirical characteristics of emotions is that "they are less susceptible to our intentions than other psychological states." See Fox, *Emotion Science*, p. 25.

obvious. We see this resistance to intentionality in our experience all the time: in the way a bereaved person does not "choose" the pattern, duration, or intensity of their grief; in the experience of falling powerfully in love; in the way that the fears of the severely anxious are rarely allayed through "rational" reflection; in the resistance of political convictions to transformation through political argument; in the phenomenon of addiction.[26]

Similar phenomena can be observed in an explicitly theological key. It is because sinful desires and dispositions are so stubbornly resistant to top-down efforts at transformation that when the New Testament authors want speak about the ethical transformation of Christians, they very often attribute such change to an external, divine agency, the Holy Spirit. Likewise, the intensity of monastic and ascetic practice in the history of Christianity is a *de facto* acknowledgement of just how difficult it is to engage in truly effective pedagogies of desire.[27] Although affects are by no means immune to discursive influence and manipulation, nevertheless they are very often encountered as dimensions of human experience "that we, in our individual histories, can't necessarily push against."[28]

The insights of affect theory have significant implications for a theory of doctrine like Lindbeck's. By pointing to the irreducibly material, embodied, and animal dimensions of human experience and behavior, affect theory pushes back against the idea that meaning and experience are primarily culturally constructed through discursive practices. This is not to say that affect theory is anti-linguistic. As Schaefer points out, "the medium of this redistribution of affects across bodies . . . is often language, making linguistic analysis an indispensable critical tool."[29] But it does view discursive practice as substantially less effective at "making bodies move" than is often assumed. Language and reason are just two dimensions in a play of many powerful forces, and they acquire power primarily insofar as they become attached to affects.

For theology, what this means is that although it is true that doctrines and other forms of theological language play a role in the shaping and generating of affects, especially insofar as they get attached to religious practices of various kinds, the nature of that role is itself shaped by the fact that affects have substantial power to resist such change, often much more than theologians acknowledge. In other words, it is true that theological doctrines and religious practices do shape and form affects, and it is no less true that affects

---

[26] In relation to the latter, Schaefer analyzes the phenomenon of "compulsion" as a further dimension of how affects function that extends and parallels the insights about intransigence. See Schaefer, *Religious Affects*, pp. 92–119.

[27] For a remarkable analysis of these dynamics in medieval monastic practice, see Talal Asad, "On Discipline and Humility in Medieval Christian Monasticism," in *Genealogies of Religion: Discipline and Reasons of Power in Christianity and Islam* (Baltimore: Johns Hopkins University Press, 1993).

[28] Schaefer, *Religious Affects*, p. 58.   [29] Schaefer, *Religious Affects*, p. 30.

tend to resist such shaping and forming. Attention to the complex interaction of these two insights is a key dimension of the account of "grace as experience" that follows below.

The usefulness of affect theory for theological reflection on experiences associated with the Holy Spirit is substantial. First, it provides a sophisticated theoretical vocabulary for describing a set of dynamics that lie close to the heart of Christian experiences of sin, salvation, and sanctification. To talk about affects in the way that affect theorists like Sedgwick, Schaefer, or Lauren Berlant do, in terms of "nonsovereignty," "animality," "intransigence," "materiality," "plasticity," "power," "nondiscursivity," and "compulsion," is to make use of a subtle and powerful theoretical language for articulating a middle way between social constructivism and a naïve and ahistorical essentialism. In this, affect theory gives a kind of critical lens to help theologians focus their attention on affective dynamics that are already powerfully present in Christian theological discourse, and provides a toolkit of concepts for describing what we find.

A second way that affect theory is valuable for theology is that it raises cautionary questions about the widespread optimism in contemporary Christian theology about the transformative power of religious practices to shape religious behaviors via mechanisms of habituation. Affect theory's vision of religious life as more than a mere "play of language" mediated through cultural-linguistic practices has significant synergies with the vision of salvation we found in early Lutheran theology in the previous chapter, which was born out of sustained reflection on the intransigence of affects and on the limits and failures of late medieval religious practice in generating holiness.[30] Basic to early Protestant anthropology and soteriology are the Augustinian observations that sin is primarily a matter of disordered desire, that mere knowledge of the sinfulness of a desire (knowledge of God's law) does not give the Christian power to change their heart, and that the motivations of the heart are characterized by a complexity that strongly resists straightforward legibility or control. When Luther in his critique of the transformational efficacy of late medieval religious practices argued instead that human beings "cannot possibly change their hearts by the power of their own nature without the grace of God,"[31] and urged Erasmus to "ask experience how impervious to dissuasion are those whose affections [*affecti*] are set on anything!,"[32] and when Melanchthon claimed that "the Christian will acknowledge that nothing is less in his power than his heart,"[33] they were making much the same observation about the intransigence of affects that we find in many affect

---

[30] See Zahl, "Non-Competitive Agency."   [31] *WA* 7:355; *LW* 32:35.

[32] *WA* 18:634; *LW* 33:64–5. See also *WA* 7:448/*LW* 32:93 and *WA* 7:145.

[33] *christianus agnoscet nihil minus in potestate sua esse quam cor suum* (*MW* 2.1:16; Melanchthon, *Loci communes 1521*, p. 36).

theorists. For example, in their jointly authored volume, *Sex, or the Unbearable*, Lauren Berlant and Lee Edelman discuss at some length the affective forces that "keep . . . us, as subjects, from fully knowing or being in control of ourselves and that prompt . . . our misrecognition of our own motives and desires," such that we "encounter ourselves as nonsovereign."[34] Here Tonstad rightly draws attention to the affinities between "typically Protestant worries" about sin and self-deception and "basic insights in queer theory regarding the disunified status of the self, human capacity for self-deception, and misrecognition of the relation between our desires and their objects, the human tendency of scapegoating and abjection of others."[35] Indeed, the critical power of contemporary discourse about affect in the humanities seems to lie in part in its unknowing rearticulation of the Lutheran doctrine of the bondage of the will under the guise of critique of the post-Enlightenment "fantasy of sovereignty."[36]

Building on these observations, I turn now to the theology of grace as it functions to structure and interpret Christian soteriological experience. In the next section, I examine the question of Christian experience of soteriological plight and ask about the degree to which Christian understanding of sin is tied up with certain kinds of feelings and experiences rather than just discursive judgments about moral transgression. I then show how the law and the gospel, the theological instruments that lie at the heart of classical Protestant theologies of justification by faith, function in practice to effect a kind of affective pedagogy whose agent is the Holy Spirit. I conclude by drawing out the implications of this account of the law and the gospel for understanding the relationship between divine law and human moral standards, and for understanding the connection between the loss of an experiential account of sin and perception of the Spirit's absence in the contemporary world.

Particularly notable in what follows is the way that each dimension of this theology of grace is not naïve about the plasticity of affects or about the power of language to alter desires. In each case, the theology of grace is able to describe a plausible patterning of Christian experience precisely in light of and in engagement with affective intransigence.

AFFECTIVE PREDICATES OF SALVATION

The experiential valence of classical Protestant soteriology depends to a significant degree on the supposition that those who are to be saved will

---

[34] Berlant and Edelman, *Sex, or the Unbearable*, p. viii.
[35] Linn Marie Tonstad, "Everything Queer, Nothing Radical?," *Svensk Teologisk Kvartalskrift.* Årg. 92 (2016), pp. 126–7.
[36] Berlant and Edelman, *Sex, or the Unbearable*, p. viii.

possess a consciousness of personal sin and of plight before God as an experiential fact on the ground. From the perspective of pneumatological "experience," this leads to an important challenge to appropriating an account of salvation like Melanchthon's today: the fact that Melanchthon's understanding of faith as something that "consoles and sustains the anxious heart" is unlikely to be compelling unless it has "anxious heart[s]" of some kind to console and sustain.[37] For this to be the case there needs to be some sort of felt experience of sin and plight with which the doctrine can engage. I call these "affective predicates" of soteriological experience.

But are such predicates something to which people can still relate in the twenty-first century? Do people today still worry about God's judgment, and do they still need consolation in "anxieties, and the terrors of sin and death"?[38] For an increasing number of theologians, the answer appears to be "no." Jonathan Linman speaks for many when he claims that "traditional preoccupation with . . . the forgiveness of sins no longer speaks with immediate intelligibility in our current milieu. The challenge of our age is not individual sin but isolation, alienation, and broken . . . community life."[39] David Yeago makes much the same point: the problem with "developing the theology of grace in terms [of] the experience of the troubled conscience" is that the modern world possesses an "increasingly short supply of troubled consciences."[40] Wolfhart Pannenberg agrees, arguing that "consciousness of personal sinfulness" is a "presupposition" that has "lost its self-evident status."[41] For these theologians as for many others, late modern people are far less likely to be explicitly worried about God's wrath against sin than early moderns such as Melanchthon and his readers would have been. The result, they infer, is that a theology like justification by faith that proclaims consolation for "anxious consciences" is unlikely to be widely compelling today. For the Christian message to remain plausible what is needed instead are approaches that address more contemporary problems like isolation and yearning for community, such as soteriologies of participation and *theosis* (Linman and Yeago) or a eucharist-focused spirituality (Pannenberg).

Perhaps the most influential critique of the normativity of early Protestant accounts of the "terrified heart" was articulated by Krister Stendahl in his

---

[37] *Ap* 12.38 (*BSLK*, p. 258; *BC*, p. 191).   [38] *Ap* 12.44 (*BSLK*, p. 259; *BC*, p. 193).

[39] Jonathan Linman, "Martin Luther: 'Little Christs for the World': Faith and Sacraments as a Means of *Theosis*," in *Partakers of the Divine Nature: The History and Development of Deification in the Christian Traditions*, eds. Michael J. Christensen and Jeffery A. Wittung (Grand Rapids, MI: Baker Academic, 2007), p. 197.

[40] David Yeago, "Martin Luther on Grace, Law, and Moral Life: Prolegomena to an Ecumenical Discussion of *Veritatis Splendor*," *The Thomist* 62 (1998), pp. 165–6.

[41] Wolfhart Pannenberg, "Protestant Piety and Guilt Consciousness," in *Christian Spirituality and Sacramental Community* (London: Darton, Longman, and Todd, 1983), p. 24. See also Gerald McKenny, "Karl Barth and the Plight of Protestant Ethics," in *The Freedom of a Christian Ethicist: the Future of a Reformation Legacy* (London: Bloomsbury T&T Clark, 2016), p. 18.

seminal 1963 essay "The Apostle Paul and the Introspective Conscience of the Modern West." Stendahl's argument is that a great deal of interpretation of the theology of Paul since the Reformation had been predicated on an unjustifiable projection of modern experience back onto Paul. In assuming, following Luther, that Paul's soteriology is driven by reflection on a "timeless" human plight of the "plagued conscience," and that Paul's reflections on justification and faith in Romans and Galatians are therefore concerned with an eternally valid divine response to this "common human predicament," Western scholarship has deeply misread Paul.[42] In Stendahl's view, Paul's true concern in his reflections on justification was "the possibility for Gentiles to be included in the messianic community," and nothing more. It was in no way a "quest for assurance about man's salvation out of a common human predicament."[43]

Stendahl's position has been hugely influential.[44] But it is also increasingly recognized to have been built upon a false dichotomy. As Barclay observes, it is of course true that "Paul's notion of the incongruous Christ-gift was originally part of his *missionary theology*, developed for and from the Gentile mission." But at the same time, Paul himself was well aware that this theology had consequences not just for the particular issues that had come to the fore in the Gentile mission, but for "*every* pre-existent classification of worth."[45] Barclay concludes:

> Because the Christological event of grace is both highly particular and impacts on *any* criteria of worth that are not derived from the good news itself, Paul's theology does not remain encased within its first-century context. One does not have to find "timeless principles" by extracting general truths from particular historical debates: Paul himself saw the general relevance of a theology of grace that reconfigured the map of reality.[46]

Despite this, Stendahl's assumption about the primacy of contextual factors in shaping Christian experience of grace remains widespread among biblical scholars and theologians. According to Stendahl, what lies behind modern Paul scholarship's putative exegetical errors is the assumption, held paradigmatically by Bultmann, that "man is essentially the same through the ages,

---

[42] Krister Stendahl, "The Apostle Paul and the Introspective Conscience of the Modern West," *Harvard Theological Review* 56, no. 3 (1963), pp. 205–6.

[43] Stendahl, "Introspective Conscience," p. 206.

[44] See, e.g., Sanders, *Paul and Palestinian Judaism*, pp. 436–7; Wright, *Paul and the Faithfulness of God*, pp. 747–8; and James D.G. Dunn, *The New Perspective on Paul* (William B. Eerdmans Publishing Company: 2008), pp. 101–2, 120, 195–6. For recent engagement with Stendahl's thesis, which is still being discussed more than fifty years after its publication, see Barclay, *Paul and the Gift*, pp. 160–2; Stephen J. Chester, *Reading Paul with the Reformers: Reconciling Old and New Perspectives* (Grand Rapids, MI: William B. Eerdmans Publishing, 2017), pp. 341–6; and John D. Koch, *The Distinction Between Law and Gospel as the Basis and Boundary of Theological Reflection* (Tübingen: Mohr Siebeck, 2016), pp. 97–102.

[45] Barclay, *Paul and the Gift*, pp. 566–7. Emphasis original.

[46] Barclay, *Paul and the Gift*, p. 573. Emphasis original.

and that this continuity in the human self-consciousness is the common denominator between the New Testament and any age of human history."[47] In Stendahl's view, by contrast, whether or not we possess an "introspective conscience" and are plagued by feelings of guilt over sin depends primarily on our particular cultural histories. Human experience, at least of the kind that has informed much modern Christian soteriological reflection, is far more plastic than "universal."

For the purposes of the present chapter, Stendahl's argument raises the question of whether and to what degree we can speak theologically about human experiences of plight that inform, and to some degree precede, practically recognizable encounters with divine grace. As we have seen, the experiential valence of Melanchthon's soteriology depends to a substantial degree upon an account of salvation that has a particular set of "affective predicates": anxiety about God's love and mercy, fear of death, terror at the prospect of divine judgment, felt experience of the burden of guilt. Our contemporary critics reject this sort of Lutheran account on the grounds that it represents a set of experiences that are not "universal" but context-bound, and indeed are shared neither by Paul (Stendahl) nor by twenty-first century people (Linman and Yeago).

From the perspective of affect theory, we can see that these critiques depend on problematic assumptions about the relationship between culture and experience. They take for granted that sociocultural context has enormous power to shape the deep experiences of human bodies. Specifically, they consider this power to be decisive enough to validate the theological judgment that early Protestant understandings of sin and salvation are no longer theologically compelling in late modern contexts. Stendahl, for example, finds it reasonable to assert that a set of powerful experiences associated with something called "the introspective conscience" could characterize a great deal of post-Augustinian Western Christian religious experience, while still being deeply foreign to Paul's experience. Thus, according to Stendahl, "the West for centuries has wrongly surmised that the biblical writers were grappling with problems which no doubt are ours, but which never entered their consciousness."[48]

Affect theorists, by contrast, argue that such accounts of the power of discursive practice to shape experience and behavior are naïve. As Schaefer puts it, "religious practices tap embodied histories, activating coalitions of bodily technologies that have been shaped by long evolutionary timescapes." This does not mean that affects are not also "spun and manoeuvered by systems of signification." But attention to the embodied character of affects reminds us that the emotions and desires related to experiences of divine grace

---

[47] Stendahl, "Introspective Conscience," p. 208.
[48] Stendahl, "Introspective Conscience," p. 214.

are very unlikely simply to reduce to artifacts of language and culture. In fact, they are much more likely to "have semistable effects across cultures—at least as stable as discursive regimes."[49] Thus it is not nearly so obvious as Linman, Yeago, Pannenberg, and Stendahl assume that there are theologically decisive gulfs between the soteriological experiences of the apostle Paul, of Philip Melanchthon, and of the putative late modern westernized Christian. Even where there really are substantial differences at the discursive level, many such differences will prove to be superficial in comparison to the "semistable, species-wide, embodied"[50] affective and material structures that precede, saturate, skew, and exceed discourse.

Consider the fear of death. For Melanchthon, one of the most important affective predicates of salvation, one of the key experiences for which Christ's justifying work is perceived as consoling, is what he calls "the terrors of death." Writing 1,400 years earlier, the author of Hebrews makes what appears to be a very similar claim: Christ's saving work serves to "free those who all their lives were held in slavery by the fear of death" (Heb. 2:15). And there is a significant scientific literature on the phenomenon of "death anxiety" as an empirical reality for people today.[51] The question arises: when Melanchthon, the author of Hebrews, and contemporary researchers like Jong and Halberstadt[52] talk about human fear of death, are they talking about the same thing? Affect theory allows us to give a nuanced answer here. Reflecting on this question in light of recent neuroscientific work as well as affect theory, Schaefer concludes:

> Do all human bodies fear death in the same way? No, but we all fear or have feared, and the reconfiguration of that fear can be accomplished using a set of practices that can span historical epochs . . . Discursive practices of religious traditions intersect with animal embodied histories . . . [W]e need to consider the possibility that although the distribution, significations, and permutations of bodily practices (including discourses) are varied, they nonetheless can yield more or less consistent effects and affects across bodies.[53]

To say more than this would require a much more detailed examination than is possible here of what is meant in a given case by "fear of death" and "death anxiety," as well as an examination of the complex physiological, psychological, and neurological structures involved in fear-response in humans and other animals. For present purposes, the point is simply to question the assumption

---

[49] Schaefer, *Religious Affects*, p. 56.   [50] Schaefer, *Religious Affects*, p. 55.

[51] For an overview and discussion of the many complexities involved in assessing death anxiety from an empirical perspective, see Jonathan Jong and Jamin Halberstadt, *Death Anxiety and Religious Belief* (London: Bloomsbury, 2016), pp. 85–113. According to Jong and Halberstadt, initial evidence suggests that the fear of death, and of things that might cause death, is something that many twenty-first-century people do experience, though some other types of fear are often more salient than mortality-related fears.

[52] Jong and Halberstadt, *Death Anxiety and Religious Belief*.

[53] Schaefer, *Religious Affects*, pp. 57, 50–60.

undergirding many contemporary critiques of early Protestant soteriology that, because discursive factors can and do affect the shape of affective experience in particular ways in particular cases, it follows that such experiences are culturally constructed from top to bottom. It is one thing to note that we do not all fear death the same way, and it is quite another to claim an incommensurable gulf between the experiences referred to by the author of Hebrews, the experiences of early sixteenth-century European Christians like Melanchthon, and contemporary instances of "death anxiety." And yet the rhetorical power of Stendahl's essay depends on just this sort of reasoning. For Stendahl, either "man is essentially the same through the ages," or else religious "introspection" and the experience of having of a "plagued conscience" are so culturally constructed that they can obviously be bracketed from any worthwhile exegesis of Paul.

Affect theory gives us parameters for articulating a more persuasive middle path. Affects are neither ahistorical "essentials" nor pure artifacts of cultural construction. Rather, they are complexly intransigent, "neither essentially plastic nor static."[54] Religions are always "submerged in bodies, composed out of a suite of embodied forms that, at least in part, precede discursive determination."[55]

"The Feeling of Sin"

Viewing the matter this way helps us to see why the claim that twenty-first-century Western and westernized people no longer experience sin as an urgent existential burden, at least not on anything like the scale they would have done in the early and pre-modern West, may be less true than it appears.

In referring to the doctrine of sin what I have in mind is the broad view that human beings are born into a condition of fundamentally disordered willing from which they cannot extricate themselves by their own powers, which is closely connected with much of the suffering that is experienced in the world, and which is in some sense in violation of a morally good order created by God. What is it about the doctrine of sin that has made it so implausible, and even offensive, to modern people? This is a major question, and I can sketch only the beginnings of an answer here. In the excellent study *Bound to Sin*, Alistair McFadyen has put his finger on one key issue. According to McFadyen, the most significant problem is that "the traditional doctrine of original sin appears to run counter to the most fundamental affirmations of modernity's turn to the subject: that the individual is autonomous, and that autonomy is the sole basis for establishing responsibility and guilt."[56] In the

---

[54] Schaefer, *Religious Affects*, p. 49.   [55] Schaefer, *Religious Affects*, p. 55.
[56] Alistair McFadyen, *Bound to Sin: Abuse, Holocaust and the Christian Doctrine of Sin* (Cambridge: Cambridge University Press, 2000), p. 27.

centuries since the Enlightenment, McFadyen observes, more and more importance has been placed on the moral philosophical conviction that "freedom is a prerequisite for there to be a moral accounting of behaviour" such that "I may only be held responsible for that which I am the cause of; which I could have willed to do otherwise; which is a product of my own freedom in action and not an outcome of determining conditions."[57] From this perspective, moral transgression can be said to have occurred only where it is the product of deliberate action by a basically free and autonomous moral agent.

What is new in the modern era has been the way that this conviction about the relation between freedom and moral responsibility has been coupled with a new optimism about human moral powers: the view that "freedom," understood as "the capacity for unforced and undetermined choice," in fact "belongs to the basic structure of human being."[58] According to such anthropologies, human beings in principle have substantial power to avoid moral transgression, and therefore can rightly be held to account for such transgression; but at the same time they should not be held to blame for actions that are not in their power. A consequence of these assumptions is deep discomfort with conceptions of morality and of human nature that violate these premises, either by viewing human freedom as innately compromised, or by attributing moral blame to people in situations where free choice is absent or at least significantly delimited.

McFadyen's account operates at a relatively general level, but if it contains any measure of truth then it is no wonder that a traditional Christian conception of sin, and especially of inherited sin, has become problematic. Where today we tend to assume that all moral transgression that is generative of culpability occurs as the consequence of deliberate choices by unconditioned human agents, in a Christian framework sin is instead first and foremost a condition that precedes the transgression and informs it. For McFadyen, "sin . . . is not in any simple way a *phenomenon of*, but is *prior to* individual freedom." Because it is a fundamental disorder of the will, "sin *pre-conditions* freedom . . . [and] lies *behind* action, in the basic intentionality of the agent (indeed, in the biological and social processes which lie behind that), and not only in the acts themselves."[59] The Christian doctrine of sin thus violates the premise about intrinsic and unconditioned moral freedom by positing "a total and universal moral collapse which makes avoidance of sin impossible," and it violates the premise about culpability obtaining only in cases of free and deliberate transgression by asserting "that we are yet accountable for . . . our individual acts of sin which this situation pre-conditions us to commit."[60]

Even apart from directly theological concerns, understanding moral behavior and moral culpability primarily in terms of individual freedom has

---

[57] McFadyen, *Bound to Sin*, p. 21.   [58] McFadyen, *Bound to Sin*, pp. 25–6.
[59] McFadyen, *Bound to Sin*, p. 28. Emphasis original.
[60] McFadyen, *Bound to Sin*, pp. 21–2.

significant problems. As McFadyen demonstrates in heartbreaking detail, modern assumptions about freedom and its relation to morality are unable "to bring to comprehensive expression the depth dynamics of concrete pathologies."[61] Such frameworks reduce moral discourse to "the tracking of moral culpability," and are then baffled by pathological situations that cannot be reduced to the deliberate willing of free moral agents. As McFadyen shows, when you begin to analyze any given set of evils/pathologies, it soon becomes clear that many factors beyond conscious decision-making by bad actors are usually involved: economic, social, and institutional forces that apply massive pressure on individual willing; biological predispositions and physiological habituations; the shaping effects of the cultures and environments in which we are raised as children; and so on.[62]

What is particularly important for present purposes is the fact that contemporary narratives about the implausibility of the Christian doctrine of sin tend to take for granted the modern idea that a concept like "sin" is primarily meaningful insofar as it aids in the moral-philosophical project of establishing *culpability*—that the category of "sin" is basically a tool for adjudicating about morality. What this in turn means is that morality is primarily a matter of discourse and language. It is about the labeling of acts and behaviors as either "good" or "bad," in order to establish how transgressors are to be treated (politically, religiously, culturally).

But in the history of theology the value of the category of sin is by no means limited to its usefulness for establishing culpability for immoral actions. This is particularly true in the era that produced Melanchthon's affective theology of justification. For early modern Protestants like Luther, Melanchthon, or Thomas Cranmer, sin is not just *attributed*; it is also *experienced*. These theologians took for granted that crucial signs of the presence of sin in the world are particular patterns of psychological and affective anguish experienced by individuals and communities. These painful affects, while not necessarily "sins" themselves in the sense of generating moral culpability, were nevertheless understood to be the chief point of contact with the reality of sin from the perspective of Christian ministry. As Luther puts it,

> this knowledge of sin, moreover, is not some sort of speculation or an idea which the mind thinks up for itself. It is a true feeling, a true experience [*verus sensus, vera experientia*], and a very serious struggle of the heart . . . The knowledge of sin is itself the feeling of sin [*cognitio peccati est ipse sensus peccati*].[63]

---

[61] McFadyen, *Bound to Sin*, p. 42.

[62] See McFadyen, *Bound to Sin*, pp. 57–129. For a related discussion of the inescapability of sinful structures into which we are born, see Serene Jones, *Feminist Theory and Christian Theology: Cartographies of Grace* (Minneapolis: Fortress Press, 2000), pp. 116–19.

[63] *WA* 40.2:326–7; *LW* 12:310.

What sort of feelings and experiences are we talking about here? In the *Apology*, Melanchthon is quite clear about the experiences that are evidence of the reality of sin. As we go through our lives, Melanchthon says, we experience "genuine terror" and "end up in despair."[64] He talks about "the anxieties and the terrors of sin and death,"[65] and the way that we learn the truth about God's law "only in the midst of genuine sorrows and terrors."[66] He quotes Psalm 6: "Be gracious to me Lord, for I am languishing; O Lord heal me, for my bones are shaking with terror."[67] And Melanchthon interprets these affects as the consequence of the evidence of God's wrath against sin. In "such real terrors," the conscience experiences "the horrible and indescribable wrath of God."[68]

A similar dynamic is evident in the Anglican *Book of Common Prayer*, a work substantially influenced by Lutheran theologies of consolation.[69] Representative here is the language used to describe sin in the General Confession: "We . . . are heartily sorry for these our misdoings, the remembrance of them is grievous unto us; the burden of them is intolerable."[70] In the *Prayer Book*, as in Melanchthon, the concept of sin that is at work does not reduce to questions about moral culpability. This is sin that weighs on the conscience and on the body, that grieves a person, and that is experienced as an "intolerable burden." It is this sort of experience that Luther had in mind when he said that we only truly know our sin when we feel it.

The reason all this matters is that, despite the refrain from theologians and biblical scholars that late-modern people no longer possess "troubled consciences," many of the core *feelings and experiences* that early modern theologians associated with life under the condition of sin appear to be just as rampant as they were in the early and premodern world. People today still experience powerful fears of being judged, of being found to be unworthy by some criterion or other.[71] People still experience relational alienation and desire for reconciliation. People are still subject to deep worries about being loved and accepted rather than rejected and still experience debilitating

---

[64] *Ap* 4.204 (*BSLK*, p. 199; *BC*, p. 151).   [65] *Ap* 12.44 (*BSLK*, p. 259; *BC*, p. 193).

[66] *Ap* 12.48 (*BSLK*, p. 261; *BC*, p. 195).   [67] *Ap* 12.31 (*BSLK*, p. 257; *BC*, p. 192).

[68] *Ap* 12.33–34 (*BSLK*, pp. 257–8; *BC*, p. 192).

[69] On the influence of Melanchthon, in particular, on Cranmer see Null, *Thomas Cranmer's Doctrine of Repentance*, pp. 99–102, 130–1, and 219–20.

[70] *Book of Common Prayer* (1662) (*The Book of Common Prayer: The Texts of 1549, 1559, and 1662*, ed. Brian Cummings (Oxford: Oxford University Press, 2011), p. 399). Or, likewise the exhortation that anyone who "cannot quiet his own conscience . . . but requireth further comfort and counsel" should come "open his grief" to "some discreet and learned Minister" for the "quieting of his conscience" (pp. 396–7).

[71] Barclay views this dimension of Paul's theology of grace to be particularly well-suited to application beyond its original social and cultural context: "Because the Christological event of grace is both highly particular and impacts on *any* criteria of worth that are not derived from the good news itself, Paul's theology does not remain encased within its first-century context" (Barclay, *Paul and the Gift*, p. 573).

feelings of anxiety. We still encounter the world as a place full of large-scale injustice and structural evil, and we still long for healing and repair on societal as well as individual levels. And we still experience "death anxiety," when we have not distracted ourselves too much to think about it.

Viewed from the perspective of the "semistable" character of affects, the most important difference from the early modern era may thus be not that these affective experiences, these sufferings and fears and debilitations, are no longer felt, but rather that we now label and interpret them differently. It is not so much that we no longer undergo the sorts of experiences that earlier Christians associated with the burden of sin, the desire for forgiveness, or the longing for redemption and healing. It is that we tend not to associate these experiences with God or with sin anymore.

I am now able to state more precisely what I believe has changed as our concept of sin has narrowed down to questions of moral culpability only. The understanding of sin as conscious and deliberate moral transgression identified by McFadyen presupposes a primarily *linguistic* and *discursive* understanding of moral transgression that has become disconnected from bodies and from experiences. Where sin was once understood to encompass both a set of feelings, experiences, and desires, *and* questions of moral responsibility, now it appears to have become largely if not exclusively an artifact of discourse alone. The fact that we seem to think that a mere relabeling is adequate to have transformed sin from a widely plausible category for making sense of human experience into an old-fashioned term that is no longer compelling would appear to be evidence of this. You know you are working with a primarily discursive understanding of a phenomenon when you believe that changes in how you label it have the power to determine whether it exists.

To return to Linman's observation that concerns about the forgiveness of sins no longer speak with "immediate intelligibility" today, we can see now that his error is to take for granted an overly tight connection between our experiences and our explicit interpretations and articulations of those experiences. As we saw at the start of the chapter, affect theory gives a vocabulary for understanding how the experiences of bodies often take their own course and possess their own "bullying agency," regardless of explicit beliefs and labels.[72] Indeed, it is precisely the indifference they often exhibit to the vagaries of discursive description that makes affects so interesting.

In this section I have made two arguments. The first is that attention to affects problematizes common assumptions about the power of contextual and cultural difference to generate theologically decisive affective differences, particularly the idea that affective experiences described in the past, whether in the New Testament or in the early sixteenth century, are likely to be deeply if

---

[72] Schaefer, *Religious Affects*, p. 106.

not irretrievably alien to the experiences of a given late-modern reader. Attention to the "semistable" character of affects, which are "neither essentially plastic nor static," authorizes a kind of hermeneutical assumption of a basic affective continuity in the experiences of bodies across contexts and eras, including between the New Testament and the present. This does not mean that there are no discontinuities, or that discursive cultural factors are incapable of having meaningful and interesting effects on our experience of the world, or that we should naïvely project late-modern concerns onto ancient texts, or indeed that we should not be alert to the subtle differences involved in particular affective instantiations. But it does suggest that the most substantial differences generated by discursive and cultural factors are likely to be located at the secondary level of how we interpret our affects, and which sorts of objects our affects latch onto, rather than at the more primary level where affects are material forces that move across and between bodies.

Second, I have argued that contemporary assumptions about the relative implausibility of a traditional Christian doctrine of sin are problematized when we pay attention to the relationship between affects and the "experience" of sin. The idea that a soteriology like Melanchthon's is no longer theologically compelling because people today tend not to think of themselves as sinners liable to divine judgment depends on a narrow and problematic view of sin as a primarily discursive idea that is conceptually and pastorally separable from the affective experiences of bodies in which it is embedded and which both precede and exceed discursive conceptualization. Insofar as traditional Christian accounts of sin are in fact very substantially about desires and feelings, not just behaviors, and insofar as such desires and feelings often exhibit what affect theorists call "intransigence," then the cluster of affective predicates Melanchthon associates with encounter with divine grace are unlikely simply to have vanished as a result of changing cultural assumptions about human agency and moral culpability. As deep engines of human behavior and experience that emerge out of material bodies that have been shaped by evolutionary timescales, affects are simply not that plastic.

This in turn implies that contemporary perceptions of the implausibility of early modern accounts of soteriological plight are theologically superficial. It suggests that the contemporary theological and pastoral challenge is to show how the Christian doctrine of sin can help us to recognize, understand, interpret, reconfigure, and make use of affects that bodies are already experiencing, rather than to try to generate a feeling of plight from scratch where it does not already exist. To put it another way, the doctrine of sin in the sense that Luther or Cranmer understood it is in significant part a theological language for understanding affects we are always already experiencing.

I turn now to explore how these dynamics play out more precisely in relation to the doctrine of justification by faith.

LAW AND GOSPEL AS AFFECTIVE PEDAGOGY

In the previous chapter, I described the general pattern of pneumatological experience that Melanchthon understood the doctrine of justification by faith to generate. For Melanchthon, the doctrine functions to a significant degree as a mechanism for engaging and transforming negative affects: for surfacing and acknowledging them, for rendering them coherent by placing them within a narrative and symbolic system, and for providing a real therapy for them, transforming painful and troubling affects into joy, peace, and the desire to serve others. In the remainder of the chapter I seek to describe the mechanisms that produces this pattern more precisely in terms of the distinction between the law and the gospel. Here my focus will be especially on the theology of Martin Luther. Luther's soteriology is very similar to Melanchthon's, but, as we will see, his account of the law-gospel distinction is more extensive and more affectively subtle. After providing an account of how the law and the gospel function to shape and generate affects, I will conclude by drawing out implications of this framework for understanding the relationship between divine and human laws, and for the relationship between the plausibility of the doctrine of sin and perception of the Spirit's presence in the world.

At root, the Lutheran approach to distinguishing between the law and the gospel is a way of describing how exactly the faith that justifies is evoked by the Spirit and what faith does to the person in whom it is evoked. As Ebeling explains, although it is often mischaracterized as a flat-footed hermeneutical principle, for Luther the law-gospel distinction is first and foremost a theological tool for describing how a person comes to have a pastoral and experiential relation to God's Word. "[H]ow should the biblical word be interpreted so that it speaks directly to the reader, affects him and comes to life in his heart?"[73] To answer this question, the distinction thus seeks to describe the relation "between what [the Word] *says* and what it *effects* [in] the situation in which it is uttered."[74] As Luther himself explains in relation to the law, "when one treats the law, then one treats the nature and power and effect of the law [*de natura et vi et effectu legis*], what it can work by itself [*quid ipsa per sese possit*]."[75] In pneumatological terms, we might say that the law-gospel distinction describes the primary pattern by which the Holy Spirit mediates between the text and message of Scripture and the experience of the

---

[73] Gerhard Ebeling, *Luther: An Introduction to his Thought*, trans. R.A. Wilson (London: Collins, 1972), p. 110.

[74] Ebeling, *Luther*, p. 119. Emphasis original.

[75] Martin Luther, *Solus Decalogus est Aeternus: Martin Luther's Complete Antinomian Theses and Disputations*, trans. Holger Sonntag (Minneapolis, MN: Lutheran Press, 2008), p. 176/177. This edition includes both the original Latin and an English translation. For references to this book here and below, the first page number is the Latin and the one after the forward slash is the English.

contemporary reader to bestow the gift of faith and to make the saving grace of God experientially salient. The distinction between the law and the gospel is thus a particularly powerful principle for making sense of the relationship between metaphysical and experiential realities in salvation.

How do the instruments of the law and the gospel accomplish this mediation? For both Luther and Melanchthon, they do this most substantially and directly by effecting a pedagogy of the affections. Luther makes the point in the gloss to thesis 16 of the *Heidelberg Disputation*: "For this reason the law makes us aware of sin so that, having recognized our sin, we may seek and receive grace . . . The law humbles, grace exalts. The law effects fear and wrath, grace effects hope and mercy."[76] Likewise in the 1531/35 Galatians lectures: "the law was given to terrify and kill the stubborn and to exercise the old man"[77] and to "drive [the conscience] to despair";[78] while the gospel brings about a condition in which its hearers "feel . . . no terror or remorse of conscience, no terror, no sadness[, and there is] full and perfect joy in the Lord and peace of heart."[79] Melanchthon's summary is the pithiest: "The Law terrifies; the Gospel consoles."[80]

A particularly important text for both Luther and Melanchthon on this theme is 2 Corinthians 3, where Paul discusses the "ministry of death" and the "ministry of condemnation," on the one hand, and "the ministry of the Spirit" and the "ministry of justification," on the other. Melanchthon makes the connection explicit: "The Law is the ministry of death, which confounds, terrifies, and kills the conscience by exposing and revealing sin. The Gospel is the ministry of the Spirit . . . which consoles, strengthens, uplifts, and gives life to minds that were previously made to tremble in terror."[81]

Luther and Melanchthon are thus interested not just in what the law and the gospel "say"—not just in the content of particular laws or the theological substructures that undergird a message of grace—but also, and particularly, in what the law and the gospel *do* as they are encountered by human beings. And what they do in significant part is to interpret and generate particular kinds of affective experience.

Because "the law" is the dimension of this dynamic that is most often misunderstood, it is necessary to explain further what it is and how it operates for Luther and Melanchthon. Although its *function* is relatively clear, as in the above quotations, substantially more complex is the question of what they believe the law actually *is*. Part of the reason that Luther, in particular, is so often misunderstood on this point is that the conception of the law with which

[76] *WA* 1:360–1; *LW* 31:50–1. Emphasis added.   [77] *WA* 40.1:44; *LW* 26:6.

[78] *WA* 40.1:42; *LW* 26:5.   [79] *WA* 40.1:47; *LW* 26:8–9.

[80] *Lex terret, evangelium consolatur. Lex irae vox est et mortis, evangelium pacis et vitae. MW* 2.1:83; Melanchthon, *Loci communes 1521*, p. 108.

[81] *MW* 2.1:78; Melanchthon, *Loci communes 1521*, p. 103.

he is working is in fact quite complex. If we are to get further purchase on what it might mean to talk about the law and the gospel as effecting an affective pedagogy then some basic clarifications about Luther's understanding of the law are now needed.

Broadly speaking, when Luther uses the term "law" in the "theological" sense, as that which confounds the sinner, terrifies them, drives them to despair, reveals their sin, and so on,[82] he is drawing on a semantic ecology that has a series of overlapping but distinguishable dimensions.

The first is particular biblical laws, i.e., concrete scriptural commands of divine origin, such as the Ten Commandments or Jesus's exhortation to love one's neighbor, usually articulated in the imperative mood.

The second sense in which Luther talks about the law is in terms of God's more general will for the moral life of human beings. The law in this sense is the divine blueprint for how human beings should behave and what the world should be like. As Luther puts it, "the law commands and requires us to do certain things . . . For God speaks through the law, saying, 'Do this, avoid that, this is what I expect of you.'"[83] The divine will is communicated to human beings primarily, and most precisely, by means of concrete scriptural commandments, as above. But it is not reducible to such commandments. For one thing, Christ is himself the ultimate revelation of the divine will in a way that does not always reduce to explicit commandments. For another, Luther believes that the divine will, which he distinguishes from those dimensions of the "Mosaic law" that applied only to Israel, has also been written "by nature" in every person's heart: "Thus, 'Thou shalt not kill, commit adultery, steal, etc.' are not Mosaic laws only, but also the natural law written in each man's heart, as St. Paul teaches (Rom. 2[:15])."[84] Finally, it is important to note that the first sense of the law often bleeds into this second one via scriptural commandments whose scope is particularly expansive, such as the exhortation to love, the call to follow Christ, and the prohibition against idolatry.

Another dimension of what Luther means when he speaks about "the law" is what we might call the psychology of moral demand. This aspect of the law refers to the psychological dynamics involved in the belief that key goods can be obtained, and negative consequences avoided, only on the condition that a person behaves in certain ways and not others. Usually this is understood more specifically in terms of relational goods between moral agents, as in the belief that God or others will love you and value you only if you follow certain rules or meet certain expectations, or the belief that you will be punished in

---

[82] This is as distinct from his discussions of the "civil" use of the law, which is a different topic entirely.

[83] *WA* 16:366–7; *LW* 35:162.

[84] *WA* 18:80; *LW* 40:97. Luther continues: "Why does one then keep and teach the Ten Commandments? Answer: Because the natural laws were never so orderly and well written as by Moses." See also *WA* 16:372; *LW* 35:164.

some way by God or others if you fail to follow such rules or to meet such expectations. We are speaking, in other words, about the psychological dimensions of the attempt to achieve "justification by works." Crucially for Luther, this dynamic is virtually always experienced as debilitating and crushing.

The psychological dimension of the law is often discussed with reference to the category of conscience, but its most widespread language is that of affective consequence.[85] Luther describes these dynamics in the Second Disputation against the Antinomians:

> When we speak about the law, we speak about the law's proper effect, which it can have or perform in this corrupt nature . . . [W]e all experience that it can work nothing but despair. The law does not make me better, neither in loving, nor hoping, nor obeying . . . For by itself the law cannot do anything but afflict, ruin, and agitate consciences.[86]

A final dimension of Luther's understanding of the law is as a quasi-metaphysical principle of experience. Ultimately for Luther, "the law" refers to a structure of relation that is written into the human heart after the Fall whereby human beings in all contexts and circumstances tend towards debilitating fear of judgment of some kind, and are prone to generating new criteria of worth to which to submit themselves. This sense of "the law" is a bit like a natural law in that it is universal and inescapable, transcending any particular instantiation. But it is also a bit like a principality or power, in the sense that it is often experienced as possessing a kind of agency—it "condemns and drives us."[87] This fourth sense of the law thus overlaps with the third, the psychology of moral demand, but it does not quite reduce to it because its explanatory structure is ultimately theological rather than psychological. It also overlaps with the second, God's general moral will for humanity, in the sense that it is most often located in "the heart." But it goes beyond the latter somewhat in the

---

[85] For the role of affective language and terminology in Luther's early theology, see Zahl, "Bondage of the Affections."

[86] Luther, *Antinomian Theses and Disputations*, p. 176/177.

[87] Luther, *Antinomian Theses and Disputations*, p. 192/193. This sense of the agency of the law is memorably captured by John Bunyan in *The Pilgrim's Progress*, when Faithful recounts his encounter with the law personified: "Now when I had got about half way up [the Hill of Difficulty], I looked behind me, and saw one coming after me, swift as the wind . . . So soon as the Man overtook me, he was but a word and a blow: for down he knockt me, and laid me for dead. But when I was a little come to myself again, I asked him wherefore he served me so? he said, Because of my secret inclining to *Adam the First*; and with that, he strook me another deadly blow on the brest, and beat me down backward; so I lay at his foot as dead as before. So, when I came to myself again I cried him mercy; but he said, I know not how to show mercy, and with that knocked me down again" (John Bunyan, *Grace Abounding to the Chief of Sinners and The Pilgrim's Progress from this World to that which is to come* (Oxford: Oxford University Press, 1966), p. 196; emphasis original).

fact that it cannot be summed up through specific rules or commands. In the latter sense it is more like the principle of moral demand as such.

It is the fourth aspect of the law that lies behind Luther's illuminating assertion that there is no such thing as a true antinomian. Antinomianism, the belief that the law ceases to be operative for Christians, is an "impossible" position because, as a principle of fallen existence, the law does not cease to function in people's lives just because it is no longer preached to them in church, or because they are otherwise in a position where they no longer formally encounter scriptural commandments.[88] In Luther's view, the reality is that it has been "put in their hearts by nature,"[89] such that "it is impossible to remove the law totally. For even if you were to remove these letters: L-E-X, which can be very easily deleted, the handwriting etched into our hearts, which condemns and drives us, nonetheless remains."[90] In fact, only death itself brings an end to this power of the law.[91]

Although these four dimensions of Luther's rhetoric when he speaks about the law can be distinguished conceptually, in practice they are usually blended together very closely for Luther. We might summarize Luther's account by saying that when he talks about the law effecting fear and wrath and driving the conscience to despair, he is usually talking about a particular range of psychological and affective experiences that are interpreted as the action of God in the life of the individual, which prepare a person for experientially and soteriologically efficacious encounter with the gospel, and which are instantiations of a more general principle of human experience in a fallen world still subject to the rule of death. These experiences are most often occasioned by biblical teaching or preaching that seeks to apply particular divine standards to the lives of its listeners. But they are also experienced more broadly in human lives whenever sin is revealed, no matter how or when or by what means it happens. As Luther puts it, "whatever shows sin, wrath, and death exercises the law . . . For to reveal sin [*revelare peccatum*] is nothing else—nor can it be anything else—than to be law or to be the effect and power of the law in the most proper sense [*quam esse legem, seu effectum et vim legis propriissimam*]."[92]

Given the dogmatic connection between the Holy Spirit and experience, it is not surprising that Luther and Melanchthon both understand experiential encounter with the law in terms of the agency of the Holy Spirit. When the law is "used" to reveal sin and effect terror, the "user" is God the Spirit. Luther is especially clear on this in the Antinomian Disputations: "No one understands the law unless he is touched by its feeling and power in the heart [*sensu et vi*

[88] Luther, *Antinomian Theses and Disputations*, p. 242/243.
[89] Luther, *Antinomian Theses and Disputations*, p. 108/109.
[90] Luther, *Antinomian Theses and Disputations*, pp. 190/191, 192/193.
[91] Luther, *Antinomian Theses and Disputations*, p. 244/245.
[92] Luther, *Antinomian Theses and Disputations*, p. 136/137.

eius in corde]. This touch or feeling of the law is divine. Therefore, the law does not convict of sin without the Holy Spirit [*legem sine Spiritu sancto non arguere peccata*]."[93] Melanchthon makes the same point in the 1521 *Loci communes*: "the beginning of repentance consists in this work of the Law by which the Spirit of God regularly terrifies and confounds consciences . . . For the mortification, judgement, and dismay that come about by the Spirit of God through the Law are the beginning of man's justification and of his true Baptism."[94]

They also use pneumatological language to speak about the function of the gospel, which follows once the way has been prepared by the law. As the primary pattern by which God makes salvation experientially salient to Christians, it is not just that the Spirit works through the law to reveal the truth of a person's plight. It is the same Spirit who then responds to comfort and console the sinner in their plight by making Christ's saving work subjectively meaningful for them in their particular situation. As Luther puts it, "the Holy Spirit as God terrifies in the law, but consoles, sanctifies, and vivifies as gift."[95] It is through these specific dynamics that the Holy Spirit, in this view, can be said to bestow the gift of faith. To experience divine grace is thus to experience consolation, peace, and joy in the context of concrete experiences of suffering and plight which have been interpreted and rendered acute through encounter with the Spirit working through the law. Through faith in the promise, "the Spirit makes the heart glad and free."[96] Ultimately, then, the function of both the law and the gospel must be understood in pneumatological terms.

The pneumatological character of God's use of the law and the gospel also emerges in Luther's comments about how much harder it is to understand the law-gospel distinction in practice than in theory:

---

[93] Luther, *Antinomian Theses and Disputations*, p. 86/87. Luther repeats the point throughout these disputations. See pp. 54/55, 56/57, 90/91, 138/139, and 224/225. That the "user" of the law is the Spirit is a point widely recognized in German Luther scholarship. See Oswald Bayer, *Martin Luther's Theology: A Contemporary Interpretation*, trans. Thomas H. Trapp (Grand Rapids, MI: William B. Eerdmans Publishing Company, 2008), p. 247; Ebeling, *Luther*, p. 138; and Ulrich Asendorf, *Die Theologie Martin Luthers nach seinen Predigten* (Göttingen: Vandenhoeck & Ruprecht, 1988), p. 248.

[94] *MW* 2.1:81; Melanchthon, *Loci communes 1521*, p. 106. The connection between the law and the Spirit is not just recognized by Lutherans. This is due especially to the claim in John 16:8 that the Spirit "will convict the world of sin and righteousness and judgment." John Wesley, for example, explains that "the first use of [the law,] without question, is to convince the world of sin. This is indeed the peculiar work of the Holy Ghost, who can work it without any means at all, or by whatever means it pleaseth him . . . But it is the ordinary method of the Spirit of God to convict sinners by the law . . . By this the sinner is discovered to himself." See John Wesley, "The Original, Nature, Properties, and Use of the Law. Sermon 34, 1750," in *John Wesley's Sermons: An Anthology*, ed. Albert C. Outler and Richard P. Heitzenrater (Nashville: Abingdon Press, 1991), p. 263.

[95] Luther, *Antinomian Theses and Disputations*, p. 224/225.

[96] *WA Deutsche Bibel* 7:7; *LW* 35:368.

Therefore let everyone learn diligently how to distinguish the Law from the Gospel, not only in words but in affections and experience [*non tantum verbis, sed etiam ipso affectu et experientia*], that is, in the heart and in the conscience . . . For so far as the words are concerned, the distinction is easy. But when it comes to experience, you will find the Gospel a rare guest but the Law a constant guest in your conscience, which is habituated to the Law and the sense of sin.[97]

Ultimately, Luther believes, to "use" the law and the gospel correctly is something that only the Holy Spirit can do, and the Spirit is free. "There is no person living on earth who knows how to distinguish rightly between the law and the gospel. We may think we understand it when we are listening to a sermon, but we're far from it. *Only the Holy Spirit knows this art.*"[98]

At the same time, the Spirit's communication of the gospel is never less than a christological event as well. To believe the promise of the gospel in and through the Spirit is at the same time to receive the gift of Christ. It is to "encounter and recognize Christ as a gift and present, which is given you by God."[99] To believe in the reality and efficacy of Jesus's "actions and sufferings" on your behalf is to trust in them "just as closely as if you had done them yourself . . . as if you were this very Christ." The message of divine grace is thus not a generic word of forgiveness but a specific, christologically ordered gospel, which is experienced as a "joyful, good, and comforting message."[100] In this way, "the Holy Spirit . . . teaches us to understand this deed of Christ . . . helps us receive and preserve it, use it to our advantage and impart it to others, increase and extend it."[101]

Melanchthon provides an excellent summary of how the law-gospel pattern plays out in practice as a pedagogy of the affections:

The people are thus to be urged and exhorted to fear God, to repent and show contrition, lest their ease and life of false security be punished. Therefore Paul says in Rom. 3[:20]: "Through the law comes . . . knowledge of sin" [After this,] it is important that faith be preached. Whoever experiences grief and contrition over his sins should believe that his sins are forgiven, not on account of his merits, but on account of Christ. When the contrite and fearful conscience experiences peace, comfort, and joy on hearing that his sins are forgiven because of Christ, then faith is present—the faith that makes him righteous before God . . . True faith brings comfort and joy and we do not feel such comfort and joy where there is no repentance or fearfulness[.][102]

---

[97] *WA* 40.1:209; *LW* 26:117.
[98] *Solus Spiritus Sanctus hoc scit. WA Tischreden* 2:1; *LW* 54:127. Emphasis added.
[99] *WA* 10.1:11.   [100] *WA* 10.1:11.   [101] *WA* 26:506; *LW* 37:366.
[102] This is from Melanchthon's "Instructions for the Visitors of Parish Pastors" (*LW* 40:276–7). See also p. 294, "For true faith cannot exist where there is not true contrition and true fear and terror before God."

The basic affective pattern of experience of divine grace in the Spirit in a Lutheran and Melanchthonian mode is now clear. But there is a kind of psychological bluntness to these sorts of descriptions, and an early modern taking for granted of certain ideas about the fear of God and the person of Christ, that can stand in the way of understanding how these dynamics might plausibly play out in contemporary contexts. In order to render the present account of this affective patterning more intelligible to twenty-first-century ears, a bit more translation is in order.

Law, Gospel, and Affect Theory

One way to get further traction on the sort of "affective pedagogy" I am describing is to view it through the lens of affect theory and its chastened view of the power of discursive practice to "make bodies move." Viewed from this perspective, the law and the gospel can be seen as having several different functions.

The first function of the law and the gospel is to bestow a new kind of coherence upon certain common forms of affective suffering by placing them within the interpretive structure of a particular religious narrative. The law is particularly important here. Building on the sorts of experiences Luther and Melanchthon tend to refer to, we can say that these affects tend to cluster in two broad areas: fears and anxieties related to judgment, loss of relation, and loss of control; and terrors evoked by recognition of mortality, with its grim promise that efforts to generate and maintain well-being are all doomed to fail in the end.

In the context of such experiences, the theological distinction between the law and the gospel, and the broader soteriological grammar that is implied in it and fans out from it, provide a set of interpretive labels for making sense of such affects in light of a larger story about human life taking shape under a moral and experiential condition called sin, and about a loving God's response to that condition. So, for example, day-to-day anxieties about judgment, failure, and rejection can be mapped onto a deeper moral and theological reality about sinners standing before a holy God, and about atonement, reconciliation, and forgiveness. Efforts to control our circumstances and to persuade others to love and value us can be interpreted in relation to the divine prohibition against idolatry, as the morally problematic (and inevitably inefficacious) attempt to be gods unto ourselves, and to secure our sense of worth before God and others by "works" rather than by faith. And fears about death are first rendered more acute, and then dramatically reconfigured, by being interpreted in light of the death and resurrection of Jesus, the eschatological defeat of death, and the promise of eternal life.

While they are not exhaustive, examples like these indicate how we might think of procedures of discursive labeling—in this case, interpreting certain common affective experiences within a particular theological narrative and symbol-system—as genuinely having an impact on how we experience these affects, without having to make over-strong claims about the power of discourse either to generate affects from scratch or to overcome affective intransigence in a straightforward manner. In some cases, the theological framing might plausibly ease the suffering associated with the affects in some way, for example by giving us a language that helps us make sense of our experiences of ourselves, diminishing confusion and tapping new resources of compassion for ourselves and others, and reconfiguring which objects such affects latch onto in a way that opens up new possibilities of hope. But the core sinful desires do not necessarily change through this process of interpretation. As I have argued throughout this chapter, as material rather than just discursive artifacts, the most problematic affects are unlikely to be so easily manipulated through discourse. But the way we experience and understand them may well change.

So the first dimension of the affective pedagogy effected by the Spirit through the instruments of the law and the gospel is to label and make sense of existing problematic and painful affects, and to create space for accepting and interpreting key dimensions of our experience of ourselves and the world that would otherwise be less understandable and less subject to conscious awareness. In this sense, the distinction between the law and the gospel provides a discursive diagnostic instrument for interpreting affects that bodies already feel and for bringing greater awareness, through a kind of process of excavation, to forces and feelings that are present in the body but which have hitherto been shrouded, misinterpreted, or numbed. To label and excavate these experiences through the encounter with divine law, in particular, is a significant part of what Luther is talking about when, interpreting the Pauline claim that "through the law comes the knowledge of sin" (Rom. 3:20), he says that the purpose of the law is to "reveal sin" (*revelare peccatum*). It is through this labeling and this excavating that "the sinner is discovered to himself."[103]

A second, related mode in which the Spirit deploys the instruments of the law and the gospel to effect an affective pedagogy is the phenomenon by which encounter with the "force or power" of the law "increases transgression" (Rom. 5:20; 7:7–13) and causes "sinful passions" [*ta pathemeata ton hamartion*] to be "aroused" (Rom. 7:5). A core conviction for Luther, as for Melanchthon, is that encounter with the interpretive framework of divine law often renders problematic affects more acute in the first instance. To read our lives and experiences through a hermeneutic of law and gospel is in part to

---

[103] Wesley, "The Nature and Use of the Law," p. 263.

recognize that our efforts to justify ourselves to the world, our attempts to hide our flaws or to blame external circumstances or other people for them, our labors to manipulate relations with others to guarantee love, our unwillingness to resist oppressive and destructive structures of power out of fear of losing perceived benefits to ourselves, and so on, are not morally neutral. Within a theological frame practices like these, and the desires that compel them, come to be seen as indicative of a core concern for ourselves at the expense of the well-being of others and of a deep ingratitude before the gift of our existence, which cannot finally be hidden and which are ultimately subject to judgment. In this way the feelings of guilt, the fears of being found out, the anxieties about loss of relation, and so on, are often intensified rather than alleviated through the theological grammar of law, at least in the first instance. Our fears, sufferings, and anxieties are not just unpleasant; they are also indicative of deep moral problems embedded in our experience of ourselves and of the world. We discover that our situation is significantly worse than we thought— and that the stakes are significantly higher. It is not surprising that the initial response might often be to rage against it all the more and to double down on what is not working.

It will be helpful at this stage to give a concrete example of how these first two modes of affective pedagogy might work out in practice. Affect theorist Lauren Berlant has written about a phenomenon of experience that she calls "cruel optimism." She defines cruel optimism as "the condition of maintaining an attachment to a significantly problematic object,"[104] and as the situation that obtains "when something you desire is actually an obstacle to your flourishing."[105] She gives the example of punishing attachment to the expect-ation "that *this* time, nearness to *this* thing will help you or a world to become different in just the right way," no matter how often it does not actually work out that way.[106] Later she describes cruel optimism similarly as naming situations where "the loss of what's not working" in a person's life is experi-enced as "more unbearable than the having of it."[107] A relation of cruel optimism can obtain in relation to all sorts of objects: "it might involve food, or a kind of love; it might be a fantasy of the good life, or a political project," and it can also "rest on something simpler . . . like a new habit that promises to induce in you an improved way of being."[108] Describing "cruel optimism" Berlant is thus observing and analyzing a particular way in which human beings participate irrationally and compulsively in the generation of their own suffering. The phenomenon of "cruel optimism" exhibits the affect-ive reality of what Berlant calls "nonsovereignty"—the fact that appeals to conscious agency often have so little power to explain what "makes bodies

---

[104] Berlant, *Cruel Optimism*, p. 24. [105] Berlant, *Cruel Optimism*, p. 1.
[106] Berlant, *Cruel Optimism*, p. 2. Emphasis original.
[107] Berlant, *Cruel Optimism*, p. 27. [108] Berlant, *Cruel Optimism*, p. 1.

move." And it identifies such nonsovereignty as fundamentally problematic, caught up as it so often is in patterns of personal and social self-sabotage.

From the perspective of a theological framework of law and gospel, we might interpret Berlant's observations about "cruel optimism" as an incisive non-religious analysis of certain experiential outcomes of the fact that human existence unfolds under a condition that Christians call "sin." Theologically speaking, one core outcome of the Fall is that human beings are prone to trying to locate answers to their problems in objects in the world that by definition cannot deliver on the "salvation" they promise. As Augustine argues, a key implication of the doctrine of creation from nothing is that objects in the world are not designed to provide lasting satisfaction or to help us in our deepest needs. They are meant to be "used" for the sake of enjoying God, from whom their goodness derives, rather than to be "enjoyed" as ends in themselves.[109] The ontology of creation is such that created things will always fail us when treated as ends in themselves; the nature of sin is such that we will keep trying to treat them as ends in themselves anyway.

Understood in this Christian theological frame, we have a way of making a different kind of sense of the fact that, as Berlant observes, humans beings so often maintain attachments to "significantly problematic object[s]." Theology gives a different language for speaking about the ways we cannot help getting trapped in Sisyphean hopes that "*this* time, nearness to *this* thing will help you or a world to become different in just the right way," no matter how often it proves not to be the case. Interpreting the phenomena Berlant identifies through a theological lens does not necessarily change the problematic attachment directly. Berlant is talking about just the sort of affective attachments that prove to be so painfully intransigent, and which tend to resist easy transformation through discursive labeling, even theological labeling. We can imagine her echoing Luther's exasperated response to Erasmus, "Ask experience how impervious to dissuasion are those whose affections are set on anything!"[110]

But a theological framework can and does make a new and different kind of sense of these problematic attachments over which we experience so little power.[111] It renders them less inchoate and less baffling. It can make them *worse*, adding the dread of divine judgment to our own self-critique and our perceptions of the critiques of others. And it can also render the cost of acknowledging our problematic attachments less acute by placing them within a frame of meaning in which there is a real possibility of efficacious help from

---

[109] See Chapter 4, n. 122 below.   [110] *WA* 18:634; *LW* 33:64–5.

[111] Cf. Riis and Woodhead on "emotional ordering" ("Religious emotional regimes help to order and pattern emotional life"); as well as "emotional transcendence-transition" ("religion often facilitates emotional transition"). See Ole Riis and Linda Woodhead, *A Sociology of Religious Emotion* (Oxford: Oxford University Press, 2012), pp. 76, 82, 76–88.

outside, a help whose deep orientation is precisely to those who find themselves trapped in problems of their own making ("Those who are well have no need of a physician, but those who are sick; I have come not to call the righteous but sinners" (Mark 2:17)).

From a Christian perspective we can thus say that in describing the phenomenon of "cruel optimism," Berlant has accurately and compassionately analyzed a major contemporary instantiation of the experience of life before the law, and of the idolatrous treatment of objects in the world as ends in themselves. But we can also suggest that understanding "cruel optimism" and similar experiences through theological language about creation, sin, idolatry, and the salvific intervention of God in history does have power to reconfigure how we experience these experiences.

Ultimately, however, the theological framing goes one step further than this. It also introduces a new possibility within the closed system of self-inflicted suffering that Berlant describes: the possibility of hope for a deliverance that originates outside the system. The law-gospel hermeneutic interacts with the givens of our experiences as bodies in the world—in this case painful unwillingness to detach from things that harm us and others even when we can see perfectly clearly that this is what is happening—to testify that there may be a door in the wall after all. It is when "the sinner is discovered to himself" in the encounter with the law that he becomes open to the possibility of encounter with divine grace.

The Gospel as Experience

Here we arrive at the third mode in which the Spirit effects an affective pedagogy through the law-gospel pattern: the transformative effects of the gospel itself. As Melanchthon and Luther both stress over and over, the gospel is more than just an explanatory label. It really does function as a pastorally efficacious response to the affectively experienced plight revealed and rendered acute by the law. I examined this dynamic in some detail in the previous chapter, where I demonstrated the cognitive scientific plausibility of Melanchthon's belief that forensic justification can effect a genuine affective transformation in those who come to have faith in Christ and his saving work. As I argued there, it makes psychological sense to think that when a person living in fear of judgment becomes convinced that God no longer stands in judgment over them on account of their sins—a position rendered emotionally as well as conceptually compelling through a particular kind of account of the atonement—they might well experience "consolation" in their fear as well as affects of joy and gratitude and a new sensation of freedom and even empowerment. Likewise, it makes psychological sense that a person who is anxious over whether they are loved and who is exhausted from trying to secure love from others would find powerful affective relief in a message that their core belovedness is secured by a loving God rather through anything they have done or might do. And it makes sense that someone living in terror of their own mortality—what Berlant calls "the panic we might feel at the prospect of becoming exhausted or dead before we can make sense of our-selves"[112]—might find that fear profoundly reconfigured in being assured by a trustworthy source that in Jesus death has lost its sting and the grave its victory. In each of these respects, the Christian gospel is understood to be genuinely transformative for human beings who find themselves trapped in a web of painful and disordered affects.

At this point I must sound a note of caution. The fact that the sorts of deep transfigurations of powerful affects I have described as outcomes of experience of divine grace are *plausible* does not mean that they are easy to generate or manipulate—and certainly not by way of efforts built upon a discursive understanding of the law-gospel pattern![113] What we are talking about first and foremost are the sorts of affective transformations that take place com-paratively rarely: for example, in a life-changing conversion, or in some other watershed religious experience of crisis and liberation. The heavy resistance of problematic affects to our efforts to effect their transformation is part of why the acquisition of this sort of faith, faith that has a deep affective impact, is attributed ultimately to the agency of the Spirit—"Only the Holy Spirit knows this art." Here it is appropriate to speak of the freedom of the Spirit, particu-larly the freedom of the Spirit to resist instrumentalization (John 3:8).

And what of affective intransigence? What of the enduring power of the deep affects that the New Testament associates with the human plight before the law: "the desires of the flesh" [*epithumian sarkos*] (Gal. 5:16), being "enslaved to desires and various pleasures" [*douleuontes epithumiais kai hedonais poikilais*] (Tit. 3:3), being subject to "the flesh with its passions and desires" [*ten sarka ... sun tois pathemasi kai tais epithumiais*] (Gal. 5:24), the "fear [of] punishment" (1 John 4:18), and being "held in slavery by the fear of death" (Heb. 2:15)? The fact that descriptions of life-altering affective trans-formations lie close to the heart of most Christian soteriologies does not mean that such affects and desires are not still experienced first and foremost as something that "we, in our individual histories, can't necessarily push against."[114] The prospect of deep affective transformation through encounter first with the law and then with the gospel, as Luther and Melanchthon describe it, is a prospect whose horizon emerges precisely through experience

---

[112] Berlant, *Cruel Optimism*, p. 125.
[113] Cf. Berlant's critique of Edelman for implying that "acknowledgement of nonsovereignty" has "transformative potential" as a "path toward affect's redistribution" (Berlant and Edelman, *Sex, or the Unbearable*, p. 84).
[114] Schaefer, *Religious Affects*, p. 58.

of the stubborn resistance of powerful affects to manipulation through top-down discursive efforts. To encounter the law as that which gives "knowledge of sin" (Rom. 3:20) is not to ignore or downplay the intractability of the "desires of the flesh." In the first instance, it is simply to bring that intractability to awareness and render it acute. The gospel is good news precisely for people who find themselves "captive to the law of sin that dwells in [their] members" (Rom. 7:19, 23). Affective intransigence is not the end of the story here, but the mode of affective transformation we are talking about is one that takes the reality of affective intransigence precisely as its starting point. I will return to the question of affective transformation in such a mode in Chapter 5.

Divine Law and Human "Laws"

Before concluding this discussion of the affective pedagogy described and effected by the law and the gospel, it is necessary to draw out an important implication of the argument to this point. This is the fact that from a soteriological perspective there is less of a difference than there might appear between affective predicates that arise in our day-to-day encounters in the world—fears and guilt and anxieties in general—and affective predicates that arise in the encounter with divine law more concretely—fear of *God's* judgment, guilt over *sin*, anxiety about what happens *when we die*. In other words, the differences are largely operative at the levels of labeling and interpretation, and in terms of which cognitive objects affects become attached to. But is this true? In making such claims, do we not risk watering down the specificity and unique power of the divine law? Do we not risk turning the judgment and salvation of God into a mere therapeutic principle?

Gerhard Forde makes a version of this case as a way of responding to the argument we have already seen about the obsolescence of the law-gospel paradigm in an era with an "increasingly short supply of troubled consciences."[115] In Forde's view, the "theological" function of the divine law so outstrips anything that could be captured in merely "psychological" terms that any articulation that risks conflating the two is deeply dangerous.[116] He writes: "The preaching of the law is not dependent upon anxious consciences or ready-made guilt feelings. The preaching of the law is the use of the text to cut in upon and slay old beings."[117] Likewise, the promise of the gospel "is not a Word searching merely for those few who somehow 'feel the need' for it. It is a word that goes on the attack to create its hearers out of the nothing of our sin."[118] In Forde's analysis we see some of the problems that can recur

---

[115] Yeago, "Martin Luther on Grace, Law, and Moral Life," pp. 165–6.
[116] Gerhard Forde, *Theology is for Proclamation* (Minneapolis: Augsburg Fortress, 1990), p. 151.
[117] Forde, *Proclamation*, p. 154.　　[118] Forde, *Proclamation*, p. 155.

when Protestants get uncomfortable about the language of psychology and experience: the turn to ontological language to describe what is "really" happening and overdrawn rhetorical contrasts between ontological and experiential realities.

Forde's comments raise a fundamental question about the relation between divine laws (love God and neighbor; do not murder, lie, or commit adultery; do not worship other gods) and merely human moral and relational "laws" (you must be beautiful and successful, you must be a good parent to your children, you must have the right politics, you must satisfy the demands of your boss, you must keep up with the Joneses). What is the relation here? From the perspective of the Holy Spirit and Christian experience, a very strict distinction between these two instantiations of "law" in its condemning function simply cannot be sustained. Forde's rejection of the idea that the law makes use of "ready-made guilt feelings" and that the gospel speaks to those who "somehow 'feel the need' for it" is an overreaction to the threat that the existence of non-religious therapies for various forms of human suffering might render the Christian gospel irrelevant to modern people. Although Forde is right to affirm that the experience of divine grace does not reduce to an immanent therapeutic process, he goes too far in pressing for a strong distinction between encounter with divine law and encounter with human "laws." What meaningful form could the former take for an embodied human being that would not look and feel in practice like the latter? As we have seen in Melanchthon, these sorts of strict contrasts between ontology and experience are soteriologically unnecessary and pneumatologically unsustainable.

The point can be demonstrated on a number of grounds. Paul Zahl makes the first and crucial argument. Raising the question of what he calls "the relation between 'the Law' and laws, the relation between God's law absolutely given and understood, and the infinite forms of this law that are embodied in numberless 'laws' or standards under which people suffer," Zahl concludes,

> what we have to do to relate the concept of unbending divine law to human experience is to speak from analogy . . . We can state this as a thesis: the principle of the divine demand for perfection upon the human being is reflected concretely in the countless internal and external demands that human beings devise for themselves. In practice, the requirement of perfect submission to the commandments of God is exactly the same as the requirement of perfect submission to the innumerable drives for perfection that drive everyday people's crippled and crippling lives . . . *Law and laws constitute a unity in their effect!*[119]

In the terms of this book, the "unity of effect" that Zahl describes is to a substantial degree an affective unity. Powerful affects like fear are semi-stable

---

[119] Paul F. M. Zahl, *Grace in Practice: A Theology of Everyday Life* (Grand Rapids, MI: William B. Eerdmans Publishing Company, 2007), pp. 28–9. Emphasis added.

structures of power that are grounded in material realities that both precede and exceed discursive manipulation. From an affective perspective, fear of divine judgment on your sin and fear of your boss's judgment on your work performance are experienced in the same bodies, using the same material, physiological, and psychological structures. As *feelings*, the guilt an unfaithful spouse might feel in relation to their partner or children and the guilt they might feel before God are not fully separable. The logic of the incarnation, with its affirmation of embodied existence as the primary site of soteriological participation in Christ in this life, implies that divine grace must get purchase on bodies. In order to accomplish this, it must do so through the same biological and psychological structures of feeling and desiring that are at work in "non-religious" experience.

As I have been arguing throughout this chapter, this does not mean that differences in how we label and interpret affective experiences are therefore trivial. There really are quite significant *theological* differences between the judgment of God and the judgment of our boss, our spouse, or our parents, and these in turn will have effects on how we "experience our experience." But such differences are nowhere near decisive enough to sustain the sort of distinctions between psychological and theological-ontological experience that Forde's account of the law implies. Forde's position could only work if the operation of divine grace is at its core disconnected from everyday bodies and ordinary experience, generating experience miraculously, "from nothing." By contrast, for a theology that takes bodies seriously Zahl's point holds: affectively-speaking, "Law and laws constitute a unity in their effect."

The argument can also be made on historical grounds, from Luther himself. That is, this is a view that Luther himself seems to express at a number of points. As we saw above, Luther is very clear that God's law is written on the heart in such a way that it functions to judge and condemn us quite apart from formal and explicit encounter with scriptural commandments, even if its primary mode of action is through the preaching of the Word. This is why antinomianism is an "impossible" position for Luther, a heresy played out in "an empty theater."[120] It is also why Luther believed that religious rules that he regarded as human inventions, from priestly celibacy and monastic dietary rules to radical Protestant prohibitions on vestments and images, still function to weigh down the conscience, creating an affective context in which the liberation of the gospel becomes compelling. For example, he writes: "For although the matter of images is a minor, external thing, when one seeks to burden the conscience through it, as through the law of God, it becomes the most important of all ... [E]ating and drinking are also minor, external things. Yet to ensnare the conscience with laws in these matters is death for the soul."[121]

---

[120] Luther, *Antinomian Theses and Disputations*, p. 244/245.
[121] *WA* 18:73; *LW* 40:90–1.

A final reason that the distinction between divine law and human "laws" becomes blurry from the perspective of Christian experience derives from the divine prohibition against idolatry:

> You shall not make for yourself an idol, whether in the form of anything that is in heaven above, or that is on the earth beneath, or that is in the water under the earth. You shall not bow down to them or worship them; for I the Lord your God am a jealous God[.] (Exodus 20:4–5)

Here we have a divine law that, for all its scriptural specificity, has a scope so expansive that it implicates the whole of a person's relation to the created world. As Augustine argues, it shows that what makes a thing an idol is not its substance or the form it takes but the way we treat it: whether we treat it as an object of worship, "enjoying" it for its own sake rather than "using" it for the sake of enjoying God through it.[122] The prohibition against idolatry thus inscribes *every* attempt we make to find satisfaction or meaning outside of God within the circle of divine command and the fear of judgment it elicits. It shows that to be confronted with the reality of our sin, to locate the affective predicates of salvation in our experience, we must look in the first instance to how we view the created realities with which we are constantly engaged from day to day (our job, our money, our family, our beauty, our health, our social status, etc.). It reveals the possibility that debilitating fears of professional failure, or sexual rejection, or loss of financial security, or loss of cultural power, might be products of a relation of worship and caught up in questions about idolatry. The site of encounter with this explicit divine law is thus not restricted to church or to some other formally "religious" context. The cosmic reality of the divine law written on the heart instantiates in practice as the debilitating psychology of moral demand, regardless of whether or not in a given case we have yet interpreted that demand in explicitly religious terms.

An Eclipse of the Spirit

The final implication to draw out here is pneumatological. Earlier in the Chapter I argued that contemporary perceptions of the implausibility of traditional ideas about sin depend substantially on a disembodied and discursive understanding of sin in which the doctrine is reduced to a category for establishing culpability. I have also shown, on the basis of John 16:8 and traditions that have built upon it, that the conviction of sin is a work proper

---

[122] *Doctr. chr.* 1.3.3–1.5.5 (*PL* 34:20–1; *WSA* I/11:107–8). See Simeon Zahl, "Tradition and its 'Use': the Ethics of Theological Retrieval," *Scottish Journal of Theology* 71, no. 3 (2018), pp. 318–19, and Rowan Williams, "Language, Reality, and Desire in Augustine's *De Doctrina*," *Journal of Literature and Theology* 3, no. 2 (1989), pp. 138–45.

to the Holy Spirit. It is in this work of the Spirit that "the sinner is discovered to himself"[123] as the Spirit exposes and diagnoses the reality of sin through the instrument of the law. And in Chapter 2 I argued that accounts of the Spirit's work that cannot do justice to practically recognizable experiences of that work are pneumatologically problematic. As Rogers rightly states, "to think about the Spirit, you have to think materially [because the Spirit] has be-friended matter for Christ's sake on account of the incarnation."[124] Included in this "matter" that has been "befriended" is the biological matter through which affects circulate in and between bodies.

Bringing these three points together, we get further insight into why reduction of the doctrine of sin to a discursive framework for establishing culpability has rendered both the doctrine of sin and the doctrine of grace increasingly implausible. To eclipse the body and its experiences from our understanding of sin is also, to a substantial degree, to sever hamartiology from pneumatology. If the Spirit is the one who mediates God's presence by "actualizing" the work of the Father and the Son "in relation to us,"[125] and if a crucial site of this actualization is the material body, then insofar as we are failing to look for the Spirit's work of conviction in the realm of bodily experience we have blinded ourselves to a major site of pneumatological activity. It is no wonder the Spirit might thus appear to be absent from the world. And it is no wonder that the concept of sin, severed from the one who alone can accomplish true conviction, can seem like a bizarre abstraction. Cut off from the Spirit by being cut off from bodies, it is no wonder that the idea of sin can be viewed as hollow and moralizing, and can get co-opted for use in human power games. It is only in the Spirit that the *revelatio peccati* is put in its proper context of divine love, as an instrument of compassionate diagnosis that is always ordered to an infinite grace.

CONCLUSION

Recognizing the law-gospel pattern as an affective pedagogy, effected by the Spirit, does much to overturn claims in recent theology that the doctrine of justification by faith alone and the theology of sin that informs it are relics of an obsolete cultural and religious past. The relationship between the law and the gospel proves to provide a widely applicable description of how divine grace comes to be a transforming power in the real experience of human beings in bodies and in time, taking up pervasive forms of affective suffering, making sense of them, and transforming them in practically recognizable

[123] Wesley, "The Nature and Use of the Law," p. 263.
[124] Rogers, *After the Spirit*, p. 58.   [125] Anatolios, *Retrieving Nicaea*, p. 142.

ways. It shows how the incongruity of divine grace that is so central to Paul's understanding of the Christ-event changes much more than just the social ethics of Christian communities. The incongruity of divine grace also patterns Christian affective experience in powerful, disruptive, psychologically plausible ways that can make as much sense today as they did in the past. As we shall see in the next chapter, this soteriological pattern does not just describe the experience of conversion. It also continues to be crucial in the generation of transformation throughout the life of the Christian.

5

Desires of the Spirit

The entire life of a good Christian is a holy desire.
—Augustine, *ep. Io. tr.* 4.6[1]

One only loves, after all, what delights one.
—Augustine, *serm.* 159.3[2]

The previous two chapters examined the work of the Spirit in salvation from the perspective of practically recognizable experience. In the present chapter I turn to the work of the Spirit in the transformation and sanctification of the justified Christian. I begin by drawing attention to certain problems that emerge in conventional accounts of sanctification when viewed from the perspective of practically recognizable experience. I then draw on the pneumatology of Augustine in the early anti-Pelagian writings to resource what I call an "affective Augustinian" account of Christian transformation that avoids these difficulties, and which is centered on the category of "delight." As we see in the chapter epigraphs above, for Augustine all Christian life and all Christian holiness are shaped by dynamics of desire, and there is no love of God or neighbor that is not fundamentally an experience of delight. In the remainder of the chapter, I build on these insights to extend Augustine's account and demonstrate its contemporary theological power. I do this by examining four major advantages of the affective Augustinian model: its ability to take seriously the variability of experience and the mystery of the self; its ability to preserve a role for Christian practice and habituation in sanctification without attributing an efficacy to them that they do not possess; its resources for attending to social and political dimensions of the Holy Spirit's work; and its ability to account for the phenomenon of non-transformation and spiritual "mediocrity" in the lives of Christians.

---

[1] *Tota vita christiani boni, sanctum desiderium est. PL 35:2008/WSA I/12:69.*
[2] *PL 38:869; WSA III/5:122.*

The Holy Spirit and Christian Experience. Simeon Zahl, Oxford University Press (2020). © Simeon Zahl.
DOI: 10.1093/oso/9780198827788.001.0001

THE HOLY SPIRIT AND CHRISTIAN TRANSFORMATION

One of the primary works ascribed to the Holy Spirit in the New Testament is the work of sanctification. 1 Peter is addressed to those "who have been chosen and destined by God the Father and sanctified by the Spirit." 2 Thessalonians 2:13 refers to "sanctification by the Spirit and through belief in the truth," and Romans 15:16 speaks about Gentiles who have been "sanctified by the Spirit." In 2 Corinthians 3:18, the transformation of Christians into the image of Christ is attributed to the work of the Spirit. Perhaps most extensively and influentially, the ideal pattern of Christian life is described in Galatians 5 in terms of the "fruit of the Spirit," as contrasted with the works of the flesh. On the basis of such texts, when theologians speak about the work of God in generating holiness in Christians, we rightly turn to pneumatology to describe this work.

In the context of the present study, we might therefore expect that one of the main sites where the Spirit will be "experienced" in practically recognizable ways will be in the events and processes by which the Christian is transformed and sanctified by God. The work of the Spirit in sanctification thus raises the question of the relationship between ontological realities and the experiences of Christians in a particularly stark way. It is not controversial to state that in salvation Christians receive the Spirit in a new mode that is qualitatively distinct from the general presence of the Spirit to all of creation. It is equally uncontroversial to assert that the thus indwelling Spirit becomes the agent and power of Christian holiness insofar as such holiness comes to exist in this life. But to speak of Christian holiness in New Testament terms is also to speak, irreducibly, of something that finds purchase and expression in bodies and in time. Across a range of scriptural texts, new affects, dispositions, practices, and patterns of relation in human lives are attributed directly to the agency of the Holy Spirit working in and through Christians. What then is the relationship between the "theological," spiritual, ontological reality of the indwelling Spirit and the concrete and embodied outworkings of this in-dwelling in the experience of Christians?

This question has been answered in a number of different ways in the history of theology. As with salvation, the problem is particularly acute for Protestants, who traditionally wish to emphasize the strongly disjunctive character of the operation of justifying grace and therefore seek to preserve a distinction between Christian transformation of this kind and salvation proper. Torrance's approach gives a representative example of these difficul-ties, exhibiting the same problems we saw in his interpretation of participation in Chapter 3. In Torrance's account, the regenerating work of the Spirit has "the effect of healing and restoring and deepening" us,[3] and of "healing [our] corrupt human nature."[4] But this healing and restoring and deepening is in fact "worked out" "objectively," "in the ontological depths of [our] humanity," rather than in the realm of practically recognizable experience.[5] What is needed, Torrance argues, is to establish what is "objectively real" in sanctification, precisely in contrast to "our own subjective conditions and states."[6] But what meaningful definition of love, or joy, or kindness, or self-control (Gal. 5:22–23) could there be that does not involve "subjective conditions and states"?

John Webster takes a more illuminating approach. In an article on mortification and vivification, Webster negotiates the relationship between ontology and experience in sanctification in a classic way.[7] In contrast to Torrance, Webster asserts that the objective work of the Spirit to sanctify does take subjective form. This happens through a fundamental transformation of human ethical powers in baptism.[8] Subsequent to this initial event, and building upon it, the transformation of our powers then plays out in the Christian's life over time. Webster explains:

> [T]he Spirit imparts [a] new nature by uniting corrupt creatures to Christ's death and resurrection, [through] which . . . the new self is brought into being. This gift of the new nature includes a gift of powers and habits: "power" in the sense of the orientation, inclination, or disposition of our new nature to regenerate living. Such powers and habits are not acquired by practice but are infused by the Spirit, laid into the mind, will and affections, and preserved by God.[9]

Here Webster seeks, in a Protestant key, to preserve the disjunctive character of the Spirit's gift—"such powers and habits are not acquired by practice but are infused by the Spirit"—while continuing to stress the embodied reality of the changes thus effected.

It is the last line that is the most important for our purposes. For Webster, the place where ontology and experience meet in sanctification is in the way that the infusion of new powers by the Spirit is "laid into the mind, will and affections." But what does it mean to have new powers and habits "laid into the mind, will and affections"? Webster appears to be saying that when we receive the Spirit our fundamental capacities of thinking and willing and

---

[3] Torrance, *The Trinitarian Faith*, p. 230.   [4] Torrance, *The Trinitarian Faith*, p. 175.

[5] Torrance, *The Trinitarian Faith*, p. 181; Torrance, "Relevance of the Doctrine of the Spirit," p. 234.

[6] Torrance, "Relevance of the Doctrine of the Spirit," p. 233.

[7] John Webster, "Mortification and Vivification," in *God Without Measure: Working Papers in Christian Theology*, ii: *Virtue and Intellect* (London: Bloomsbury, 2016).

[8] Webster, "Mortification and Vivification," p. 106.

[9] Webster, "Mortification and Vivification," p. 107. Similarly, "The Spirit heals our disrupted and weakened nature, restoring created powers of life and directing them in obedience to God" (p. 113).

feeling are altered in such a way that we are more capable than before of living, thinking, and willing according to the pattern of the Spirit. Building on this fundamental shift in our ethical powers, he goes on to describe a variety of specific practices by which this "new nature" takes hold more and more through processes of mortification and vivification, including through a kind of epistemic sanctification via "recollection of Jesus Christ," "contemplating" and "studying" him.[10]

In Webster, then, unlike Torrance, the work of the Spirit to sanctify has real subjective effects in the sense that core capacities of our minds, our wills, and our affections are transformed by the indwelling of the Spirit. This then plays out concretely as we make use of these sanctified capacities in our lives and in the world. But the fundamental problem of how to relate ontological and experiential realities has not really been resolved. The problem has just been isolated to a very particular point: the point at which the Spirit infuses these new powers in baptism. To talk as concretely as Webster wishes to about transformed willing and desiring and about changed reasoning capacities is to talk about things that happen to a substantial degree in the realm of the body and the brain. But what, exactly, is being changed here, and how? If we are talking about lasting changes in our capacities for desiring and feeling (say, greater power to resist sinful desires and a stronger and more efficacious longing for the things of God) and in our epistemic faculties ("the sanctifica-tion of reason"[11]) should such changes not also be taking place at the level of neurology and physiology and brain chemistry? If so, how do these psycho-logical and bodily changes take place? Does the Spirit miraculously intervene in the natural world to reconfigure these features of our biology and our cognitive faculties at the moment of baptism? Alternatively, if the changes involved in the receipt of new powers in the Spirit do not in fact take place at that level—if they do not actually map onto some sort of instantaneous alteration of embodied capacities in baptism—then can the changes involved in sanctification be said to have taken place at all?

The same issue can be observed in neo-Thomist accounts of sanctification, which connect ontological and experiential realities through the categories of virtue and habit, as we saw in Chapter 3. Here the neuralgic point is even more precise. The way the Spirit operates to sanctify human beings in the concrete realities of their lives in this perspective is above all through the mechanism of the infused theological virtues. These virtues are what are called "operative" habits, which means that their function is to facilitate and energize virtuous behavior, but never in such a way as to override the cooperative action of the human will. As Romanus Cessario observes, as operative habits, these virtues

---

[10] Webster, "Mortification and Vivification," p. 112.
[11] John Webster, *Holiness* (Grand Rapids, MI: William B. Eerdmans Publishing Company, 2003), p. 8.

"shape . . . and energize . . . our human operative capacities, intellect, will, and sense appetites, so that a human person can act promptly, joyfully, and easily in those areas of human conduct that are governed by the Gospel precepts."[12] Here the language about implantation of new powers and capacities is framed in the language of habit as a kind of Spirit-given tailwind for facilitating virtuous action. It describes a kind of affective atmosphere that quietly energizes our natural capacities and that opens them to supernatural ends without overriding or annihilating them. But once again the question of how this energy of facilitation actually comes to push upon our bodies in the first place is only really answered in metaphysical rather than experiential terms: it is the product of an infusion of supernatural virtue that occurs paradigmatically in baptism.[13]

It is worth pausing here to ask: is there anything actually wrong with these sorts of approaches to sanctification? Why not simply acknowledge that the challenge of articulating the connection between spiritual and experiential realities is part of the mystery of the Spirit? Do we really need to say anything more, theologically, than that it is the character of the Spirit's work to bridge the gulf between the realms of ontology and experience? Why does it matter if there is a point where this bridging has the character of a mystery and resists further explanation?

Although I am sympathetic to this sort of reply, I do not think it is ultimately adequate to sustain a full-orbed theology of sanctification. This is for several reasons. The first is that there are reasons to want to avoid simply punting to mystery when things get difficult in theology. In too-easy appeals to mystery, theologians risk giving pious-sounding cover for what is in fact theological failure or incoherence. For example, a skeptical theologian might point out that the above accounts of the work of the Spirit in sanctifying bodies have structural similarities to the god-of-the-gaps arguments that have sometimes appeared in relation to natural science. Indeed, a cynic might argue that even the most sophisticated versions end up using the sacrament of baptism as a kind of pneumatological version of Descartes' pineal gland, his postulated site in the brain where body and soul interact. Each of these cases ultimately says, "Look, here. This is the place where something happens that can be described only in ontological terms, even though it has material effects. This is the spot where the Spirit mysteriously changes bodies."[14]

---

[12] Cessario, *Christian Faith*, p. 5. Here he is speaking of the infused moral virtues in particular.

[13] For a critical analysis of such approaches along similar lines, see Rahner, "Religious Enthusiasm and the Experience of Grace," p. 38.

[14] Here my concern is similar to Tanner's in emphasizing the working of the Spirit "in and under the human" and through "the operations of our usual faculties" (Tanner, *Christ the Key*, pp. 298, 276), as well as to Schleiermacher's resistance to what he calls "magical" theories of redemption, whereby the redemptive influence of Christ is "mediated by nothing that is natural"

The second reason the above answers are unsatisfactory follows from the argument I made in the first two chapters. There I showed that an account of the work of the Spirit in and upon Christians that cannot affirm and describe the material, corporeal, and experiential dimensions of the Spirit's work is pneumatologically deficient. To address this problem by locating one supposed moment where ontological and experiential realities are bridged when the Spirit is received, whether it is in baptism or in the moment when faith arises, is to isolate it rather than to resolve it.

The third problem with such accounts of sanctification is that by locating the key moment in the Spirit's sanctifying action in what is ultimately a sheer implantation of powers and facilitating capacities, we risk becoming theologically committed to a relative optimism about the moral powers of the Christian, as differentiated from the non-Christian, and to a degree of expectation of long-term growth in holiness, that may not in fact be legible from the lives Christians actually lead. Although the above accounts do leave some room for ongoing sin in Christians, there is nevertheless a fundamental orientation towards progressive growth in holiness that I am not convinced is borne out in Christian experience. As I have shown elsewhere, it is not an exaggeration to say that it was the failure of scholastic models of graced virtue-acquisition to "work" for Martin Luther and many of his peers that gave rise to the Protestant Reformation.[15] Luther famously did not find himself to be substantially less prone to sinful desire after a decade in the monastery than he was before. Whatever we make of Luther's experience, by grounding the work of the Spirit in sanctification in a basic shift in human powers that is grounded in a purely ontological reality, we commit ourselves to a non-falsifiable assertion of a substantial moral difference between Christians and non-Christians. Insofar as this difference may often be much smaller than we like to think, if it exists at all, in my view such accounts are vulnerable to fostering hypocrisy and inauthenticity amongst Christians.

What is needed now is a compelling alternative account of how the Spirit sanctifies Christians that is not subject to these problems. In search of such an account, I turn at last to the pneumatology of Augustine.

As will become evident, Augustine's theology of sanctification bears close similarities to the affective soteriologies that we found in Melanchthon (Chapter 3) and Luther (Chapter 4). These similarities are not surprising: Augustine, and especially the Augustine of early anti-Pelagian writings like *On the Spirit and the Letter* and *On the Grace of Christ and Original Sin*, was

---

(Schleiermacher, *The Christian Faith* (2016), pp. 627–8 (§100.3)). See likewise Gerald McKenny's argument, via Barth, for the importance of affirming that grace engages with the creature in the context of the "full integrity" of "her creaturely nature" (McKenny, "Karl Barth and the Plight of Protestant Ethics," p. 33).

[15] See Zahl, "Non-Competitive Agency."

the most important theological influence on early Lutheran soteriology out-side of the Bible. Indeed, many of the insights we have found most worthwhile in Melanchthon and Luther are simply creative receptions of Augustine in the conditions of early modernity.[16]

Why then have I waited until the present chapter to turn to Augustine himself? The answer follows from that fact that, although the ultimate aims of the present book are constructive, its constructive affirmations are argued for in dialogue with twenty-first-century questions, insights, and debates. Against this backdrop, the non-chronological ordering of major dialogue partners has seemed to make the most argumentative and conceptual sense. Thus, it is Melanchthon's affective theology of forensic justification that provides the most interesting and effective intervention in current debates about soterio-logical participation; it is Luther's sophisticated account of the law-gospel distinction that provides the most useful dialogue partner with affect theory as well as the most thoughtful corrective to cultural-linguistic theories of doc-trine; and it is Augustine, I will now argue, who provides the thickest and most compelling account of Christian transformation due to the metaphysical depth of his approach as well as his deployment of the affective category of delight.

PNEUMATOLOGY AND DESIRE IN AUGUSTINE

At the core of Augustine's mature understanding of sanctification, as ex-pressed during the period from the composition of *Ad Simplicianum* to his death, is the belief that to be sanctified by the Spirit is to have one's desires changed by God, such that desire to sin is superseded and conquered by desire to love God and do his will.[17] This position comes out most clearly and precisely in the early anti-Pelagian writings, and it is Augustine's position in this period that will be my primary focus here.[18] For Augustine, the primary method by which the Holy Spirit sanctifies us is by "substituting good desire for evil desire, that is, pouring out love in our hearts."[19] Augustine's theology

---

[16] For accounts of Luther's early reception of Augustine, see Ľubomír Batka, "Sin," in *The Oxford Encyclopedia of Martin Luther*, iii, eds. Derek R. Nelson and Paul R. Hinlicky (Oxford: Oxford University Press, 2017), pp. 349–51, and Albrecht Beutel, "Luther," in *Augustin Handbuch*, ed. Volker Henning Drecoll (Tübingen: Mohr Siebeck, 2007).

[17] On the importance of *Ad Simplicianum* in the development of Augustine's theology of grace, see especially James Wetzel, *Augustine and the Limits of Virtue* (Cambridge: Cambridge University Press, 1992), pp. 155–60, and Volker Henning Drecoll, *Die Enstehung der Gnadenlehre Augustins* (Tübingen: Mohr Siebeck, 1999), pp. 199–250, 358–9.

[18] The core model continues to lie behind Augustine's later anti-Pelagian writings like *Against Julian*, but it receives its clearest and most constructively compelling articulation in these earlier writings.

[19] *Spir. et litt.* 4.6 (*PL* 44:203; *WSA* I/23:146–7).

of sanctification in this period is deeply shaped by a series of Pauline texts, especially Galatians 5:16–26, with its characterization of the whole of the Christian life in terms of a struggle between the desires of the Spirit and those of the flesh, and Romans 5:5, Paul's assertion that "God's love is poured into our hearts by the Holy Spirit that has been given to us."[20]

What sets Augustine's account of Christian transformation apart from the more static, infusion-based models represented in different ways by Webster and neo-Thomism is the use he makes of the category of "delight" (usually *delectatio/delectare*[21]). For Augustine, the transformation of desire does not take place simply by divine fiat, or through a mysterious ontological implantation of a new capacity for desiring God. Rather, it happens through a providentially ordered process of God attracting and persuading the sinner to hate sin and love righteousness in the context of the particularities of their life. God sanctifies by operating in the life of the Christian to make himself delightful and by causing sin to delight no longer. Augustine gives a classic description of this process in *On the Spirit and the Letter*:

> We, on the other hand, say that the human will is helped to achieve righteousness in this way: [human beings] receive the Holy Spirit so that there arises in their minds a delight in and a love for [*que fiat in animo eius delectatio dilectioque*] that highest and immutable good that is God, even now while they walk by faith, not yet by sight. By this [love] given to them like the pledge of a gratuitous gift, they are set afire with the desire to cling to the creator and burn to come to a participation in that true light [*inardescat inhaerere creatori atque inflammetur accedere ad participationem illius veri luminis*], so that they have their well-being from him from whom they have their being.[22]

Here we have a multilayered account of sanctification in which experiential and ontological dynamics are interwoven in a highly sophisticated way. To acquire "righteousness" is to be possessed with delight in "that highest and immutable good that is God." It is to live a life of "well-being" and delight in goodness through deep affective attachment to the one who is the source of all being. And this delight, this affective attachment, is a form of "participation"

---

[20] For Gal. 5:16–26, see e.g., *nat. et gr.* 50.58, 53.61, 57.67; for Rom. 5:5, see e.g., *spir. et litt.* 3.5, 17.19, and 25.42; *nat. et. gr.* 17.18, 42.49, 57.67, 64.77, 66.79, 70.84; and *gr. et. pecc. or.* 1.9.10, 1.26.27, and 1.30.31. Also important for Augustine in this respect are 1 Cor. 4:7 ("What do you have that you did not receive?"); Phil. 2:13 ("It is God, after all, who produces in you the willing and the accomplishment [*to thelein kai to energein*]"); and the Vulgate version of Rom. 7:25 (particularly the phrase "the grace of God, through Jesus Christ our Lord").

[21] For the category of delight in Augustine, see especially Mark F.M. Clavier, *Eloquent Wisdom: Rhetoric, Cosmology and Delight in the Theology of Augustine of Hippo* (Turnhout: Brepols Publishers, 2014), pp. 16–22, 145–252; Carol Harrison, *Beauty and Revelation in the Thought of Saint Augustine* (Oxford: Clarendon Press, 1992), pp. 247–61; and John Burnaby, *Amor Dei: A Study of the Religion of St. Augustine* (Eugene, OR: Wipf and Stock Publishers, 2007), pp. 220–6.

[22] *Spir. et litt.* 3.5 (*PL* 44:203; *WSA* I/23:145).

in the "true light" that is God.[23] This dovetails well with Augustine's earlier account of sin in *On Christian Teaching*, where the paradigmatic sin is to find delight—"enjoyment"—in creation for its own sake rather than using creation as an instrument for "enjoying" the Creator.[24] To be freed from sin and made righteous is to have the object of one's desires and delights reordered to the one in whom alone creation can find its "well-being."

Most significant for our purposes is the term *delectatio*. It is through the category of delight that Augustine takes the idea that the Spirit implants new capacities and desires in the Christian and fills it out into something that is practically recognizable, that takes place in the embodied experience of particular Christians, even as it is indexed to God's being as love and to the ordering of creation to Creator. As Burnaby argues, "the Pelagian controversy compelled Augustine to . . . develop a psychology of grace, an account of the actual working in the human heart of God's redemptive love. The keyword of this anti-Pelagian psychology is 'delight in righteousness' [*delectatio iustitiae*]."[25]

What are the details of this "psychology"? It begins with Augustine's basic theory of human action. Wetzel describes the broadly Ciceronian shape of Augustine's views, which are articulated most programmatically in *City of God* 14. For Augustine, as for Cicero, Wetzel writes,

> the soul is moved in one of two basic ways: by attraction or by repulsion. When the soul anticipates what attracts it, it experiences desire; when its desire is satisfied, it feels joy. When the soul shrinks from what repels it, it feels fear; when its fear is realized, it knows grief. The four cardinal movements of the soul are desire and joy, the two modes of attraction, and fear and grief, the corresponding modes of repulsion.[26]

When it comes to sin and righteousness, however, it is "delight" that matters most of all. Indeed, Peter Brown asserts that for Augustine "'delight' is the only possible source of action, nothing else can move the will."[27] When we sin,

---

[23] See the discussion in Chapter 3 of affective transformation as a mode of participation in Augustine as well in Didymus the Blind and Maximus the Confessor.

[24] *Doctr. chr.* 1.3.3–1.5.5 (*PL* 34:20–1; *WSA* I/11:107–8).

[25] Burnaby, *Amor Dei*, p. 221. Brown refers similarly to Augustine's "psychology of delight" (Brown, *Augustine of Hippo*, pp. 148–9).

[26] James Wetzel, "Prodigal Heart: Augustine's Theology of the Emotions," in *Parting Knowledge: Essays after Augustine* (Eugene, OR: Wipf and Stock, 2013), p. 88. For Augustine's classic articulation of this vision, see *civ.* 14.6–7, 14.9. Both Wetzel and Trettel point out that Augustine's affirmation of a basic Ciceronian schema masks significant differences. See Adam Trettel, *Desires in Paradise: An Interpretive Study of Augustine's City of God 14* (Paderborn: Ferdinand Schöringh, 2019), pp. 52–5, and Wetzel, "Augustine's Theology of the Emotions," pp. 88–90. On the chronological relationship between *civ.* 14 and the different phases of the Pelagian controversy, see Trettel, *Desires in Paradise*, pp. 9–12.

[27] Brown, *Augustine of Hippo*, p. 148. Brown is overstating somewhat: see e.g., *serm.* 159.7 (*PL* 38:871; *WSA* III/5:125), where Augustine discusses the would-be adulterer who "loves pleasure alright, but he's more afraid of pain."

Augustine tells us, it is because we are "lured into it by delight"; when we love God, it is because the Spirit has caused us to "'take delight in the Lord' (Ps. 37:4)."[28]

It is in this context that Augustine refers again and again to the work of the Spirit described in Romans 5:5. When the Spirit pours "love" into the heart of the Christian, for Augustine this refers less to a formal ontological and spiritual capacity than to an experienced affection of delight—a motivating transmission of pleasure through which we are attracted to God.[29] Here Augustine is talking about real rhetorical persuasion undergone by a given person ("God brings it about by the enticements of our perceptions [*visorum suasionibus*] that we will and that we believe"[30]) and about practically recognizable, affectively charged generation of "an ineffable sweetness [*ineffabile suavitate*] in the depths and interior of the soul."[31] Augustine summarizes the connection between delight and love: "one only loves, after all, what delights one." [32] It is in this experienced delight in righteousness that we participate most clearly in the being of the God who is love.

Although it is not wrong to describe the love poured out by the Spirit in ontological terms, it is crucial to recognize that this outpouring always at the same time refers to an activity of God that takes place in bodies and whose energy is delight. In other words, although it is true that the love of God in Christians does not simply reduce to its "affective aspect,"[33] that it has a content and orientation that not only shapes but also significantly exceeds its felt dimension, it remains the case that insofar as we want to talk about the process by which real human desires are sanctified by the Spirit in bodies and in time, the affective dimension is irreducible, and indeed primary.[34]

The affective character of the Spirit's outpouring of sanctifying love comes out particularly clearly in Augustine's repeated discussions of the problem of right motivation in doing good.[35] Over the course of the Pelagian controversy, Augustine came to believe ever more deeply that the Christian gospel is bound up with the problem of moral motivation. The radicality and utter incongruity

---

[28] *Serm.* 159.6 and 159.3 (*PL* 38:870, 869; *WSA* III/5:124, 122). Sermon 159 is one of Augustine's classic reflections on the primacy of delight in human motivation.

[29] Clavier characterizes delight in Augustine as "the transmission of pleasure to the soul" (Clavier, *Eloquent Wisdom*, p. 18).

[30] *Spir. et litt.* 34.60 (*PL* 44:240; *WSA* I/23:184).

[31] *Gr. et pecc. or.* 1.13.14 (*PL* 44:367; *WSA* I/23:398). Likewise, "the gift of the Spirit" causes us to be "delighted by the sweetness of righteousness" (*spir. et litt.* 29.50; (*PL* 44:232/*WSA* I/23:153)) and no longer to "find delight in sinning" (*spir. et litt.* 16.28 (*PL* 44:218/*WSA* I/23:161)). See also *c. ep. Pel.* 2.21: "the good begins to be desired when it begins to be sweet... Therefore the blessing of sweetness is the grace of God, whereby we are made to delight in and to desire, that is, to love, what He commands us" (quoted and translated in Burnaby, *Amor Dei*, p. 222).

[32] *Serm.* 159.3 (*PL* 38:869; *WSA* III/5:122).   [33] Burnaby, *Amor Dei*, p. 222.

[34] See Burnaby, *Amor Dei*, pp. 220–6, as well as Trettel, *Desires in Paradise*, pp. 50–64.

[35] On these dynamics in Augustine's anti-Pelagian writings, see Carol Harrison, *Augustine: Christian Truth and Fractured Humanity* (Oxford: Oxford University Press, 2000), pp. 101–14.

of divine grace for sinners is brought into full relief once they realize that God wants them not just to do His will, but to love and desire to do it as well:

> But we want the Pelagians at some point to admit... not merely the grace by which wisdom is revealed, but that by which we love it as well; not merely the grace by which we are urged on toward everything good, but that which moves us to action... This grace not only makes us know what we should do, but also makes us do what we know; it not only makes us believe what we should love, but makes us love what we believe.[36]

This means that the good must be done out of love and delight rather than fear. Lurking at the heart of Pelagianism, as Augustine understands it, is a vision of religious life as a landscape of fear where the good is done only to avoid punishment from a terrifying God:

> [T]hose who did what the law commanded without the help of the Spirit of grace did so out of a fear of punishment, not a love of righteousness. And for this reason God did not see in their will what human beings saw in their action; rather they were held guilty as a result of what God knew that they preferred to do, if only they could have done so with impunity.[37]

For Augustine this is not a Christian vision. The affective landscape of life under the aspect of grace is one of love and freedom and delight, not of fear. Reflecting on Galatians 5:18 ("If you are led by the Spirit, you are no longer under the law"), he writes:

> For "the love of God is poured out in our hearts", not by the letter of the law, but "by the Holy Spirit who has been given to us" (Rom. 5:5). This is the law of freedom, not of servitude, because it is the law of love, not of fear... Insofar as one is led by the Spirit, one is not under the law, because insofar as one finds delight in the law of God [*condelectatur legi dei*], one is not under fear of the law, because fear produces torment, not delight [*quia timor tormentum habet, non delectationenem*].[38]

The result is that, in Augustine's vision, doing the right thing for the wrong reasons is not Christian holiness. The crucial point is the motivation: one must do the right thing out of the right motivations. And these motivations have a specific affective character: the law is to be followed "gladly,"[39] joyously, out of

---

[36] *Gr. et pecc. or.* 1.10.11, 1.12.13 (*PL* 44:366, 367; *WSA* I/23:397–8). Augustine is reflecting here particularly on Phil. 2:13, "It is God, after all, who produces in you the willing and the accomplishment [*to thelein kai to energein*]." See also *gr. et pecc. or.* 1.5.6 (*PL* 44:363; *WSA* I/23:393–4).

[37] *Spir. et litt.* 8.13 (*PL* 44:208; *WSA* I/23:151). Augustine makes the same point again in *spir. et litt.* 32.56 (*PL* 44:236; *WSA* I/23:180).

[38] *Nat. et gr.* 57.67 (*PL* 44:280; *WSA* I/23:250). See also *spir. et litt.* 32.56 (*PL* 44:237; *WSA* I/23:181), as well as *gr. et pecc. or.* 1.13.14 (*PL* 44:367–8; *WSA* I/23:398).

[39] "That person, of course, who gladly carries out the commandment does so in freedom" (*gr. et pecc. or.* 13.14; *PL* 44:368/*WSA* I/23:399).

"delight." Only so are such behaviors actually "free," and only so are they authentically fruit of the Spirit. Christian holiness thus comes into being in a realm where the "exterior law" is no longer operative as a motivating factor, but the spirit of the law is written into our desires, such that we quite literally cannot desire anything else: "when the life-giving Spirit is present, he makes us love the very same thing, now written within, which the law made us fear, when it was written exteriorly."[40]

The Soteriological Pattern of Sanctification

With the help of Augustine, we have now made some headway towards developing a "practically recognizable" account of the Spirit's sanctifying work by drawing attention to the importance of the motivation of delight in Christian sanctification. But the work is not complete unless we can give a plausible account of how the Spirit actually causes such delight to arise in bodies. How more precisely does the Spirit foster this delight in God, and correspondingly diminish delight in sin? Is the Spirit's gift of delight in holiness ultimately a miraculous irruption into the world, or can we give a more precise, emotionally plausible account of such experience?

In the anti-Pelagian writings, the primary answer Augustine gives to the question of how delight in God comes to be fostered in Christians is very similar to what we have already seen in the soteriologies of Luther and Melanchthon. Delight is generated through a psychological sequence of affective predicates like fear of divine judgment or longing for rescue from some plight being transformed through encounter with the grace of God through the forgiveness of sins secured in Jesus Christ.

In discussing the contours of this transformation, Augustine, like Luther, draws extensively upon Paul's statements about the inefficacy of the law to produce righteousness or salvation, and about the way the "exterior" law tends to exacerbate sin and the sinner's sense of plight rather than provide a path out of it. As he writes in *On the Grace of Christ and Original Sin*, "[the law] commands, after all, rather than helps; it teaches us that there is a disease without healing it. In fact, it increases what it does not heal so that we seek the medicine of grace with greater attention and care."[41] Augustine makes the same point in *On the Spirit in the Letter*: "though the law is good, it increases the evil desire by the prohibition ... Somehow or other, the very object of desire grows more attractive when it is forbidden ... And this is what it means

---

[40] *Spir. et litt.* 19.32 (PL 44:220–1; WSA I/23:164).
[41] *Gr. et pecc. or.* 1.8.9 (PL 44: 364–5; WSA I/23:395).

that sin misleads by the commandment and by it brings death, when transgression is added, which does not exist, where there is no law."[42]

In the case of any given attachment to sinful desire, sanctification thus begins with heartfelt experience of plight. This in turn often comes about through encounter with God's law. It is through God's law that critical light is shone upon the problematic realities of life in the world, at both individual and social levels. It is encounter with the diagnostic judgment of God's law that brings about the revelation of sin and critical awareness of the fallenness of the world in which we participate. This encounter exposes and brings to awareness the many symptoms of sin: particular forms of fearfulness and faithlessness; the disorder and egoism of the heart's desires; the powerlessness that people often experience to solve their problems or to relieve their sufferings; the idolatrous veneration of created things at the expense of the God from whom all created goodness derives; the destructive consequences of the sinner's actions upon others, and the sinner's rationalizations of the same; the exploitative systems of power in which human beings are always embedded, to which they are always subject, and in which they are so often complicit. It is thus the ongoing encounter of the "Old Adam" with God's law that secures the critical dimension of sanctification and gives it content that goes beyond the mere fact of the feelings associated with critical encounter with the law.

As I established in the previous chapter, the agent of this critique is the Holy Spirit, whose work it is to "convict the world of sin and righteousness and judgment" (John 16:8). It is through ongoing encounter with the law, in the Spirit, that "the sinner is discovered to himself"[43] and the nature of the "disease"[44] is diagnosed in its countless instantiations. Often this means divine law as we encounter it explicitly in preaching and Scripture—do not commit idolatry, take care of the poor, love God with all your heart, love your neighbor as yourself. But, as we saw in Chapter 4, experiential encounter with the law that is written on our hearts very often begins with the "horizontal" laws, standards, and expectations which are constantly generated in human relations, and under which we labor whether or not we have encountered God's law in its explicit, "vertical" capacity. And sometimes it is less a matter of conviction as such than of simply becoming more aware of some plight we are in, and of our need for rescue from it.

In the Augustinian picture this critical and diagnostic function of the law remains in place for Christians, and therefore plays a crucial role in sanctification. Insofar as Christians remain embedded in sin and subject to "the

---

[42] *Spir. et litt.* 4.6 (*PL* 44:204; *WSA* I/23:146–7). See also *spir. et litt.* 5.8 (*PL:* 44:204–205; *WSA* I/23:147–8). In these passages Augustine is commenting on 2 Cor. 3:6, Rom. 7:7, and Ex. 20:17.

[43] Wesley, "The Nature and Use of the Law," p. 263.

[44] *Gr. et pecc. or.* 1.8.9 (*PL* 44:365; *WSA* I/23:395).

desires of the flesh" (Gal. 5:16), the mechanism by which the Spirit extricates them from this sin continues to follow the pattern established in justification. As in salvation, it is in the revelation of sin through critical encounter with the law that the "affective predicates" of effective encounter with divine grace are generated, intensified, and made salient. In turn, it is primarily in the context of these affective predicates that desiderative attachments to sin have a chance of beginning to change. That is, it is through specific instantiations of this soteriological pattern in bodies and in time that sin can plausibly come to be experienced as debilitating and a "torment"[45] rather than delightful, and repentance as "sweet,"[46] liberating, and joyous rather than as repressive and stultifying.

Augustine describes the experiential sequence generated via the law-gospel pattern:

> [W]hen the disease of concupiscence that has taken root in [human beings] begins to grow because of the stimulus of the commandment and the increase of transgression, they may take flight through faith to justifying grace. There, delighted by the sweetness of righteousness through the gift of the Spirit, they may escape the punishment which the letter threatens.[47]

Likewise, the purpose of "the commandments of the law" is to "remind human beings of their weakness so that by believing they take refuge in justifying grace."[48] It is in this particular way that encounter with divine grace is generative of delight in the God of grace, and we are "drawn to Christ."[49]

It is worth pausing to reflect briefly on the differences between Augustine, on the one hand, and Luther and Melanchthon, on the other, in their desiderative accounts of the soteriological pattern of sanctification. For all the overriding harmony between the accounts, the two visions are not identical. One significant difference is that Augustine's concept of delight in God is tied more explicitly to an ontology of creation. To delight in God is to delight in "that highest and immutable good that is God." The reason that the

---

[45] *Nat. et gr.* 57.67 (*PL* 44:280; *WSA* I/23:250).

[46] *Gr. et pecc. or.* 1.13.14 (*PL* 44:367; *WSA* I/23:398); *spir. et litt.* 10.16 (*PL* 44:210; *WSA* I/23:153).

[47] *Spir. et litt.* 10.16 (*PL* 44:210; *WSA* I/23:153).

[48] *Spir. et litt.* 34.60 (*PL* 44:240; *WSA* I/23:184). Melanchthon gives a more psychologically precise gloss on Augustine's position: "[H]ow can the human heart love God as long as it believes that he is terribly angry . . . ? However, the law always accuses us; it shows that God is angry. Therefore God is not loved until after we grasp his mercy by faith. Not until then does he become someone who can be loved" (*Ap* 4.128–129; *BSLK*, pp. 185–6/*BC*, pp. 140–1).

[49] *Io. eu. tr.* 26.4. Augustine reflects further on the ultimately christological shape of delight in God: "those whose delight is in the truth, whose delight is in happiness, whose delight is in justice, whose delight is in eternal life, are drawn to Christ, because each of those is Christ" (Augustine, *Io. eu. tr.* 26.4–5; *PL* 35:1608–9/*WSA* I/12:452–4).

"well-being" of the sinner is found in God rather than in the objects of their sinful attachments is not just God's love or power as such but specifically the fact that God is the one "from whom they have their being."[50] The reason objects in the world do not satisfy but become idols when treated as ends in themselves is a function not just of God's prohibition against idolatry, but of the very nature of creation, whereby God made all things for Himself, including the human heart.[51] There is thus a kind of metaphysical substructure and content to Augustine's account of delight that prevents it from being nothing more than a psychology, despite the great importance, and indeed the irreducibility, of the psychological dimension for him.

Although Melanchthon would not deny any of these points, like Luther his tendency is to focus attention on relational realities between God and the sinner, and the pastoral implications of that relation for consolation, rather than on the ontological context in which the relation is situated.[52] The result is a notable difference of emphasis, despite fundamental similarities. In comparison to Augustine, both Melanchthon and Luther make more extensive use of the theology of the atonement in grounding their deeply relational account of Christian consolation. There is also a degree of psychological acuity regarding the nature of the law in early Lutheran theology that in my view is unmatched in Christian thought, including in Augustine. But it is Augustine's elegant and searching identification of love, delight, God, and knowledge of the good, against the backdrop of the doctrine of creation from nothing, that provides one of the most profound syntheses of ontology and experience Christian thought has achieved. As we will see later in the chapter, this synthesis also has implications for Augustine's theology of delight that render it less subject to a charge of oversimplification than the similarly directed work of Melanchthon or Luther.

---

[50] *Spir. et litt.* 3.5 (*PL* 44:203; *WSA* I/23:145).   [51] *Doctr. chr.* 3.3–5.5; *conf.* 1.1.1.

[52] That Luther, in particular, subscribes to a broadly Augustinian ontology of creation is evident in his development of the distinction between the "use" and the "substance" of a thing, in which "use" is theologically prioritized over "substance" without denying the importance as well as the inherent goodness of "substance." Thus, Luther explains, a statue of a god is ontologically "good" in that it is made of substances like wood or stone that are inherently good by virtue of their creation by God; what makes it into an idol is how it is perceived or "used" by the person, i.e., as an object or worship or otherwise (*WA* 40.1:170; *LW* 26:92). This important distinction in Luther's thought derives to a substantial degree from Augustine's similar distinction in *On Christian Teaching* between "use" and "enjoyment," and depends upon an Augustinian account of creation and its ordering to God. On the use/substance distinction in Luther, and related metaphysical issues, see Zahl, "Tradition and its 'Use'." On the use/enjoyment distinction in Augustine, see *doctr. chr.* 1.3.3–1.5.5 (*PL* 34:201; *WSA* I/11:107–8), as well Williams, "Language, Reality, and Desire," pp. 138–45, and Susannah Ticciati, *A New Apophaticism: Augustine and the Redemption of Signs* (Leiden: Brill, 2015), Chapters 5 and 6.

SANCTIFICATION IN AFFECTIVE AUGUSTINIAN PERSPECTIVE

Augustine's desiderative pneumatology of Christian transformation succeeds, in principle, in providing an experiential account of the Spirit's sanctifying work that takes place in bodies in time. It therefore meets the pneumatological requirement of practical recognizability for descriptions of the work of the Spirit for which I argued in Chapter 2. In this it improves substantially on the primarily ontological accounts of sanctification in the Spirit that we saw at the start of the present chapter.

In the remainder of this chapter I will draw out some key features of a model of sanctification that builds upon the basic Augustinian framework described above. In retrieving Augustine in this way, I am not claiming that the desiderative pneumatology we have found in the early anti-Pelagian writings represents all that Augustine has to say about sanctification, and I will also go beyond Augustine in certain ways. In this, what follows can be classified as a theological "retrieval" of Augustine.

My approach to sanctification can be described as an exercise in "affective Augustinianism." As I have argued elsewhere,[53] it is possible to identify a stream in Western theology that has been influenced especially by the anti-Pelagian Augustine, which brings together a particular kind of pessimism about human moral powers (including in the state of regeneration) with convictions about the relatively greater power of affects over rational deliberation and decision-making in determining human behavior. In the early modern era, classic "affective Augustinians" include Luther and Melanchthon as well as Thomas Cranmer.[54] This theological approach reaches a kind of culmination in the 1662 *Book of Common Prayer*, with its Collect for the Fourth Sunday after Easter:

> O Almighty God, who alone canst order the unruly wills and affections of sinful men; Grant unto thy people, that they may love the thing which thou commandest, and desire that which thou dost promise; that so among the sundry and

---

[53] Simeon Zahl, "The Drama of Agency: Affective Augustinianism and Galatians," in *Galatians and Christian Theology: Justification, the Gospel, and Ethics in Paul's Letter*, eds. Mark Elliott, Scott Hafemann, N.T. Wright, and John Frederick, (Grand Rapids, MI: Baker Academic, 2014). The term "affective Augustinianism" is in part a gloss on Ashley Null's reflections on what he dubs "Cranmer's Reformed Augustinianism" (Null, *Thomas Cranmer's Doctrine of Repentance*, p. 130), and describes a theological trajectory that Null has been examining for many years.

[54] See Zahl, "Drama of Agency," pp. 336–40. For an extended exposition of the mature Cranmer's affective Augustinianism, which has influenced my own analysis and account, see Null, *Thomas Cranmer's Doctrine of Repentance*, pp. 98–102, 127–33, 178–84, 211–12, and 251–3.

manifold changes of the world, our hearts may surely there be fixed, where true joys are to be found, through Jesus Christ our Lord. Amen.[55]

It is within this affective Augustinian tradition that both the present chapter and the discussion of Melanchthon and Luther's soteriologies in the previous two chapters can be located.

As an approach to sanctification, the affective Augustinian model has a number of advantages in addition to its success in articulating a practically recognizable pneumatology of sanctification. One is that it can take seriously the variability of experience and the mystery of the self, such that, even as it provides powerful resources for thinking about a particular set of affective energies in Christian transformation, it also avoids reductionism and affective oversimplification. Another is that the affective Augustinian model provides space for a qualified affirmation of the role of practice and habituation in Christian transformation without attributing an efficacy to these dynamics that they do not in fact possess. A third is that in taking account of the relationship between sanctification and the body, including the material conditions to which bodies are subject, the model avoids a problematic individualism or solipsism and directs theologians' attention to the role of social and structural forces in the generation of sinful as well as righteous desire. Finally, and crucially, the affective Augustinian model is able to give a clear-eyed account of the experience of "non-transformation" in Christians, avoiding the tendency in many theologies of sanctification to project onto Christians a transformation that they do not necessarily experience, without excluding the possibility of real transformation in the Spirit. In the remainder of the chapter, I will expand on each of these advantages in turn.

The Enigma of the Heart

An important challenge that an affective Augustinian pneumatology of Christian experience must address is the concern that the affective sequence described here and in previous chapters, by which the terrified heart is consoled and desires transformed, might be too simplistic. Surely, we might ask, the experiential dynamics of salvation and sanctification are more complex and more textured than this? Surely there is a rich variety of affective "patterns" the Spirit can follow to generate transformation in a given instance, and surely the work of the Spirit that "blows where it wills" (John 3:8) resists attempts at schematization in any case?

---

[55] *Book of Common Prayer* (1662), Collect for the Fourth Sunday After Easter (*Book of Common Prayer*, p. 330).

I have already given a partial answer to this question in the previous chapter, where I showed how the affective predicates in question are substantially more capacious, and less plastic across cultural contexts, than some critiques of these dynamics have assumed. There I drew on affect theory's insight that it is far easier to change how we label and interpret affects, and the objects to which they attach, than it is to change the affects themselves. The implication is that a more fruitful way of making sense of perceived differences between the sorts of experiences described by Augustine or Melanchthon and experiences we have today would be to look for alternative manifestations of similar affective structures and patterns under different labels and attached to different objects, rather than assuming, in a naïve cultural-linguistic mode, that affective experiences are simply incommensurate across contexts.

Nevertheless, there remains a kind of phenomenological case for the complexity of Christian experience of regeneration that needs to be addressed. For all its Pauline, Augustinian, and Lutheran pedigree, and even if we accept my argument that its sequence is substantially more textured, underdetermined, and experientially wide-ranging than critics tend to assume, it remains the case that the account of salvation and sanctification I have been building to this point does seem to identify the core of Christian experience of grace in terms of a particular set of emotional responses.

Schleiermacher gives a classic articulation of some of the potential problems here. In his discussion of what he calls the experience of conversion, Schleiermacher argues against the view, which he associates with certain forms of pietism, that,

> every true Christian must be able to demonstrate the beginning of one's state of blessedness in a penitential struggle—that is, in an upswelling of contrition bordering on hopeless self-loathing followed by a feeling of divine grace that borders on inexpressible bliss[.][56]

Rather, he argues,

> the spectrum of excitability among people is so varied that what is in fact extreme excitement to one less able to be moved seems minor to one more readily stirred. Even in the same person, moreover, a similar variation is to be found at different times. As a result, it is already impossible on these grounds to forge a summary and definitive statement on the subject.[57]

Schleiermacher's first point, about the idea that a Christian "must be able to demonstrate" that they have experienced a particular affective pattern, and at a particular moment in time, is more easily dealt with than the second one, about variability. A fundamental difference between the desiderative

---

[56] Schleiermacher, *The Christian Faith* (2016), pp. 698–9 (§108.3).
[57] Schleiermacher, *The Christian Faith* (2016), p. 699 (§108.3).

pneumatology of Augustine or Melanchthon and that of the sorts of pietism Schleiermacher is talking about lies in their respective understandings of the "use" to which the accounts of consolation and transformation are put. In the practical theology of pietists like August Hermann Francke or John Wesley, the pattern of experience is instrumentalized as a tool for determining who is and is not saved and for deriving assurance of salvation via a kind of syllogism ("I have had X experience; X experience is the reliable mark of the 'new birth'; therefore I can safely conclude that I have been saved").[58] In other words, the pattern of experience is transformed from a descriptive truth (simply an account of a common, scripturally and experientially warranted pattern of experience of the Spirit) into a prescriptive one (the idea that one "must" be able to point precisely to such an experience in one's life in order to prove the authenticity of one's faith).

From an affective Augustinian perspective, the "prescriptive" aspect of this sort of pietist model is excluded on the grounds that it turns the experience of grace into a kind of law. In the pietist approach, the fact that Christians often do experience God's grace according to a certain kind of affective pattern is transmuted into an anxiety-provoking standard under which the sinner labors and which one actively seeks to elicit through the manipulation of affects. For Augustine and Melanchthon, by contrast, the pattern describes an organic outgrowth of encounter with divine grace in the context of affective predicates one did not choose, brought about through the providential activity of God in the Spirit. Insofar as the experience of grace becomes an experiential standard that one "must" meet it is no longer authentically grace.[59] And insofar as there is assurance, it is communicated primarily in the experience of grace itself, rather than in later reflection on the fact of the experience.

Schleiermacher's second point, about the phenomenological fact of the variability of human experience, including in relation to the experience of grace, is more interesting. Given what he calls the "spectrum of excitability" when it comes to how people experience conversion, is the model of Christian transformation described by Augustine and his heirs experientially overdetermined?

In part, such variability is simply to be expected of the work of the Spirit. Biblically speaking, a fundamental feature of the Spirit's work from the perspective of human encounter is its freedom, which is often experienced as dynamism, resistance to comprehensive description, and resistance to

---

[58] For a classic articulation of this approach, see John Wesley, "The Marks of the New Birth. Sermon 18, 1748," in *John Wesley's Sermons: An Anthology*, eds. Albert C. Outler and Richard P. Heitzenrater (Nashville, TN: Abingdon Press, 1991). I will return to this text at the end of the chapter.

[59] Luther's emphasis on the ethical priority of "use" over "substance" provides a metaphysically sophisticated technical account of how the same experience can be valuable or problematic, salutary or idolatrous, depending how it is "used." See Zahl, "Tradition and its 'Use'."

instrumentalization. As Rowan Williams observes, "the freedom of the Spirit is uncircumscribed."[60] The classic text here is John 3:8:

> The wind [*to pneuma*] blows where it chooses, and you hear the sound of it, but you do not know where it comes from or where it goes. So it is with everyone who is born of the Spirit.

Building on texts like this, Yong points out that "wind is characterized by vitality, energy, force, and movement," and that this makes wind imagery highly appropriate for representing the "vital, energetic, and dynamic" nature of the Spirit of God.[61] A key consequence of this dynamism, according to Yong, is the "unpredictability,"[62] from the human side, of God's work through the Spirit. In this sense, it is no surprise that experiences of salvation and sanctification can and will exhibit the sort of variation, and the resistance to being definitively pinned down to a precise moment, that Schleiermacher describes.

However, Augustine gives this basic point about the freedom of the Spirit a crucial further layer of theological depth by relating it to the problem of the inscrutability of the self. Augustine was well aware of the question about affective oversimplification, and he addresses it directly in the early anti-Pelgian writings. Indeed, it is Augustine's response to this question that gives his account a psychological and metaphysical sophistication that exceeds what we find in Melanchthon's *Apology of the Augsburg Confession*.

For all his willingness to speak without apology of the sinner's plight in terms of specific affective predicates like fear of pain and fear of punishment,[63] and of the Christian life in terms of outworkings of joy and love and delight birthed through encounter with God's grace for sinners, Augustine of all theologians cannot be accused of a simplistic or reductive view of affective experience.[64] In Augustine's anthropology, a crucial dimension of the plight of human beings is the fact that we are incapable of ever fully fathoming our own feelings and motivations. As he famously asserts in *Confessions*, reflecting upon his grief over the death of a friend, "I had become to myself a vast problem, and I questioned my soul, demanding why it was sorrowful and why it so disquieted me, but it had no answer."[65] Later in Book 4, faced with the vagaries and contradictions of human love, he again throws up his hands at

---

[60] Rowan Williams, "Word and Spirit," in *On Christian Theology* (Oxford: Blackwell Publishing, 2000), p. 126.

[61] Amos Yong, *Spirit-Word-Community: Theological Hermeneutics in Trinitarian Perspective* (Eugene, OR: Wipf and Stock Publishers, 2002), pp. 46–7.

[62] Yong, *Spirit-Word-Community*.   [63] *Serm.* 159.7 (*PL* 38:871; *WSA* III/5:125).

[64] It is the same Augustine who authored the *Confessions*, one of the most psychologically probing and emotionally subtle literary works ever composed.

[65] *Conf.* 4.4.9 (*PL* 32:697; Augustine, *Confessions*, trans. Henry Chadwick (Oxford: Oxford University Press, 1998), pp. 57–8).

the unfathomability of the human heart: "Man is a vast deep, whose hairs you, Lord, have numbered, and in you none can be lost (Matt. 10:30). Yet it is easier to count his hairs than the affections and motions of his heart" [*affectus eius et motus cordis eius*].[66] And in Book 10 he speaks in similar terms of the complexity of memory: "memory's huge cavern, with its mysterious, secret, and indescribable nooks and crannies."[67]

Here there is a significant affinity between Augustine's thought and that of thinkers interested in the "queerness" of desire. As Tonstad points out, for a number of theorists "queerness is about disturbance, incompletion, and the non-transparency of self to self."[68] On this basis, Tonstad follows Althaus-Reid in seeking to resist presumptions of easy "translatability or legibility" in our assessments of ourselves or others, and in expressing skepticism of theologies that presume that human beings are "self-transparent, rational, autonomous individuals."[69] In a similar key, Edelman and Berlant are especially interested in forces that prevent us from "fully knowing or being in control of ourselves and that prompt . . . our misrecognition of our own motives and desires,"[70] and Sara Ahmed asserts bluntly that "emotions are not transparent."[71]

As a theologian who is deeply concerned with the fact that we are in many ways a mystery to ourselves, and yet insists that it still worthwhile to seek to describe core affective patterns of encounter with the Spirit, Augustine provides a salutary reminder that the reality of the affective complexity of Christian experience does not mean that such experience is *entirely* shapeless and mysterious, or entirely impossible to describe. This remains the case even when we are well aware that descriptions of such patterns are a kind of shorthand for speaking about experiences that in a given case will prove to be as variegated and particular as the people who undergo them. Acknowledgement that there are dimensions of human nature that are and always will remain mysterious short of the eschaton is a starting point for theological inquiry, and an ongoing condition that theology cannot escape or dissolve. But for theology in a pneumatological key, a degree of apophaticism can be complemented by a set of constructive affirmations—affirmations that are public and open to scrutiny, even as they are ultimately provisional.

It is in this spirit that Augustine draws out a more precise implication of the unfathomability of the heart in relation to the work of the Spirit to generate delight in God. Although the method by which "God brings it about by the

---

[66] *Conf.* 4.14.22 (*PL* 32:702; Augustine, *Confessions*, pp. 66).

[67] *Conf.* 10.8.13 (*PL* 32:784–5; Augustine, *Confessions*, p. 186).

[68] Tonstad, *Queer Theology*, p. 130.

[69] Tonstad, *Queer Theology*, pp. 90–1, 71. See also Tonstad, "Everything Queer, Nothing Radical?," p. 126–7.

[70] Berlant and Edelman, *Sex, or the Unbearable*, p. viii.

[71] Sara Ahmed, *The Cultural Politics of Emotion*, 2nd ed. (Edinburgh: Edinburgh University Press, 2014), p. 194.

enticements of our perceptions that we will and that we believe"[72] is very often the law-grace/fear-delight sequence, Augustine points out that God does also transform desires in ways that resist easy causal or narratival explanations of this kind. Sometimes, rather, "[God] does this internally where none have control over what comes into their minds."[73]

Here Augustine brings together two features of his theology: the unfathomability of the human heart to itself and the providence of God. Augustine is deeply impressed by how little conscious control we have not only over our actions and feelings, but also over the whole of what transpires in our life, both internally and externally. In his view, we have to have basic knowledge of a thing in order to desire it, in order to delight in it, but the question of what we know, what we think, even what we remember, is always and entirely in God's hands, not ours. "After all, who is unaware that what human beings know is not in their power?"[74] The implication is that both sincere repentance and transformed delight are always set in motion not by our own efforts but by the providential power of God: "Who has it in his power either that an object be presented which can please him [*delectare*], or that when presented it shall please? . . . But the will can by no means be set in motion unless an object be presented which delights and attracts."[75]

In Augustine's theological vision, God is always providentially at work at every level of our experience in the world. Sometimes we get a glimpse of this providence with the benefit of hindsight, as Augustine believed he had regarding his youthful move from Carthage to Rome: "You were at work persuading me to go to Rome and to do my teaching there rather than at Carthage."[76] With the hindsight of faith, Augustine believes that God had made providential use of his mundane desire for less rowdy students. As usual, God effected his will through powers of desire and attraction: "You applied the pricks which made me tear myself away from Carthage, and you put before me the attractions of Rome to draw me there." But the true purpose was soteriological: in fact, "you . . . wished me to change my earthly home for 'the salvation of my soul' (Ps. 34:3)."[77]

It is this same providential power, Augustine believes, that sometimes fosters delight in God and dismay over sin in ways that are partially or indeed completely inscrutable to us, including in hindsight. If we are honest about our

---

[72] *Spir. et litt.* 34.60 (*PL* 44:240; *WSA* I/23:184).

[73] *Spir. et litt.* 34.60 (*PL* 44:240; *WSA* I/23:184). See also *gr. et pecc. or.* 1.13.14 (*PL* 44:367; *WSA* I/23:398): sometimes he "gives the increase secretly."

[74] *Spir. et litt.* 35.63 (*PL* 44:242; *WSA* I/23:186). For Augustine this point is closely related to a verse that haunts him: "For what do you have that you did not receive?" (1 Cor. 4:7).

[75] *Simpl.* 1.2.21–22 (*PL* 40:127). Quoted and translated in Burnaby, *Amor Dei*, p. 223. According to Peter Brown, by this period Augustine had come to believe that "the processes that prepare a man's heart to take 'delight' in God are not only hidden, but actually unconscious and beyond his control" (Brown, *Augustine of Hippo*, p. 148).

[76] *Conf.* 5.8.14 (*PL* 32:712; Augustine, *Confessions*, p. 80).

[77] *Conf.* 5.8.14 (*PL* 32:712; Augustine, *Confessions*, p. 81).

experience, for Augustine, we admit that such desiderative shifts can also happen "internally, where none has control over what comes into their minds." The providence of God sometimes moves the subtle levers of human willing in ways that resist our ability to interpret or understand, and it is thus possible in a given instance that introspective reflection on our desires will render the heart more rather than less mysterious.

Despite the potential inscrutability of desiderative transformation in any given case, this process need not be construed as a miraculous overriding of existing human capacities. This remains the case even if such transformation sometimes *feels* like a miraculous and mysterious disruption. The fact that what causes delight or dismay or fear is often not subject to interpretation or understanding, even in hindsight, does not mean that God is not using real affections and motivations within us in his providence. It means rather that human beings are "a vast deep,"[78] and that the "affections and emotions of [the] heart" are almost unfathomably complex, such that only God has full understanding of why we feel the things we feel and do the things we do.[79] The result is that although the Spirit's gift of the motive power of sanctification often does follow a practically recognizable sequence involving affective predicates of plight paving the way for delight over divine mercy, sometimes we experience the Spirit's transformation of our desires as something more like a mystery. In such cases it is appropriate to give a primarily theological explanation: all we can usefully say is that it is God the Spirit who works upon us to foster delight in him and his ways and dismay over sin. We can know that we have experienced renewed delight in God, or new regret over some particular sin, without being able to understand and explain the reasons.

The consequence of these psychological provisos in Augustine is that his vision can account for the fact that the affective motions of grace are not always fully legible or explicable to us, and that they exhibit variation, without having to appeal to explanations that circumvent what Tanner calls "the operations of our usual faculties."[80] In this his pneumatology successfully addresses a concern that is often raised about theologies that emphasize sudden and dramatic conversions and transformations. It can account for the fact that, as Tanner observes, Christians often describe experiences of the Spirit as taking place "immediately," "in exceptional events," and in "the interior depths of individual persons," without having to set up the Spirit's work as somehow "bypassing . . . ordinary sorts of human operation."[81]

---

[78] *Conf.* 4.14.22 (*PL* 32:702; Augustine, *Confessions*, pp. 66).

[79] *Conf.* 4.14.22 (*PL* 32:702; Augustine, *Confessions*, p. 66). As Pascal has it, in good Augustinian fashion, "The heart has its reasons, of which reason knows nothing" (*Pensées* 423; Blaise Pascal, *Pensées*, trans. A.J. Krailsheimer (London: Penguin Books, 1995), p. 127).

[80] Tanner, *Christ the Key*, p. 276.

[81] Tanner, *Christ the Key*, p. 274. For examples of pietist appeals to "immediate" experiences of God, see Zahl, *Pneumatology and Theology of the Cross*, pp. 88–93.

Augustine examines these dynamics directly in *On the Grace of Christ and Original Sin*. In an illuminating passage, he analyzes the moment when Simon Peter bursts into tears following his three denials. The text in question is Luke 22:61–62: "The Lord turned and looked at Peter. Then Peter remembered the word of the Lord, how he had said to him, 'Before the cock crows today, you will deny me three times.' And he went out and wept bitterly." In his discussion of this text, Augustine hews closer to the complexity of actual human affective experience than a simple description of a law-grace/fear-delight pattern might imply. He introduces a level of texture and even mystery to our understanding of repentance, even as the law-grace sequence remains the baseline psychological model for making sense of what has happened. The context is an explication of certain statements of Ambrose. Augustine's comment is as follows:

> Ambrose . . . says: . . . "Peter at first denied [the Lord] and did not weep, because the Lord had not looked upon him. He denied him a second time and did not weep, because the Lord had not yet looked upon him. He denied him a third time. Jesus looked upon him, and he wept most bitterly." Let these people read the gospel and see that the Lord Jesus was indoors at that time when he was being questioned by the chief priests, but the apostle Peter was outdoors and down below in the courtyard, at one point seated, at another standing with the servants at the fire . . . And for this reason, the action which scripture reports, "The Lord looked upon him" (Lk 22:61), took place interiorly; it took place in the mind; it took place in the will. *By his mercy the Lord in a hidden manner helped him, touched his heart, awakened his memory, visited the interior human being with his grace, and stirred up and produced an affection in the interior human being even to the point of exterior tears [ad exteriores lacrimas movit et produxit affectum].* See how God is present to help our wills and actions. See how he "produces in us the willing and the action" (Phil. 2:13).[82]

Here Augustine gives a fine-grained analysis of the process by which God worked to produce a felt repentance in Simon Peter through an affectively transformative encounter with divine grace. On the one hand, the "site" of God's working is Peter's internal life. As Augustine reads the passage, Jesus is not actually in the same room as Peter but works in a "hidden manner," "visit [ing] the interior human being with his grace." On the other hand, the process by which he does this is not quite a mystery either. The key moment for Augustine is when "the Lord . . . awakened his memory." The memory in question is Jesus's prediction of Peter's denials earlier in the chapter:

> "Simon, Simon, listen! Satan has demanded to sift all of you like wheat, but I have prayed for you that your own faith may not fail; and you, when once you have turned back, strengthen your brothers . . . I tell you, Peter, the cock will not crow this day, until you have denied three times that you know me."   (Luke 22:31–32, 34)

---

[82] *Gr. et pecc. or.* 1.45.49 (*PL* 44:382; *WSA* I/23:414). Emphasis added.

In suddenly remembering this exchange, Peter, it seems, is undone by the simultaneous realization of his sin and of Jesus's mercy. In the abrupt apprehension that the prophecy has come true, that he has proven just as faithless under pressure as Jesus had predicted, Peter encounters in a visceral way the reality of divine grace. He realizes that when Jesus prayed for him earlier and asked him to be the leader who must "strengthen your brothers," he did so in full knowledge of the denials to come. The result is an immediate, powerful, and practically recognizable experience of repentance: God thus "stirred up and produced an affection in the interior human being even to the point of exterior tears." But at the same time, this moment is the product of God's providential working in Peter's heart and mind to bring the key memory to awareness.

Augustine thus understands God's working in Peter to produce "the willing and the action" not as a miraculous implantation of new feelings and desires, but as a pastorally, psychologically, and affectively plausible event in the context of Peter's personal history, drawing on Peter's actual human emotions and affections. And Peter's experience does appear to follow, in a compressed way, the affective sequence Augustine describes elsewhere: present here is both the fear of Jesus's judgment over his denials and the dawning recognition of Jesus's forgiveness, love, and commitment to relation nevertheless.

But there remains an element of mystery as well, due to the enigmatic mechanisms of memory. Why was Peter not cut to the heart by the memory of Jesus's prediction after the first denial? The exchange between Peter and Jesus took place only a few hours before. Why was it only after the second detail of Jesus's prediction has come to pass to pass, the cock's crow, that the memory is awakened? This detail strikes the reader as immediately plausible, even as it resists immediate explanation. The workings of our minds and hearts, and especially the way we can find ourselves undone by emotional responses we do not understand, are often a mystery to us in just this sort way. The law-grace/fear-delight sequence is thus a useful model or pattern for helping to make sense of an affectively charged experience of repentance. Without it, little sense could be made of Peter's tears. But at the same time, Augustine's interpretive application of the pattern is by no means simplistic or overdetermined. It is subtle, closely tied to the details of Peter's personal history, and experientially plausible, even as it refuses total explanation.

We can now see why proper concerns about affective oversimplification do not undermine the desiderative pneumatology of Christian transformation proposed here. The category of desire allows us to account for the experience of ourselves as mystery without having to appeal to a sheer overriding of human capacities in Christian transformation, and it also corresponds to the important pneumatological theme of the freedom of the Spirit, which "blows where it wills" (John 3:8). But the question of oversimplification is a worthwhile one. It underlines the importance of resisting the temptation to overdetermine the precise affective details involved in consoling and liberating encounter with divine grace, and the related temptation to turn the sequence in question into an easily manipulated prescriptive tool for inferring assurance or for judging whether others are or are not saved. The fact that one can speak usefully about certain affective patterns involved in the experience of divine grace, and indeed that the theologian is bound, on scriptural and pastoral grounds, to attempt to speak wisely about such patterns, must always be held together with the equally scriptural and pastoral insights about the Spirit's freedom and the heart's inscrutability. As the Anglican Collect for Purity has it, it is God the Spirit, "unto whom all hearts are open, all desires known, and from whom no secrets are hid," who mediates dynamically between our unknowability to ourselves and our total knowability to God to generate real change in the heart and real encounter with grace.[83]

Desire, Practice, and Virtue

In Augustine's anti-Pelagian writings, the core engine of Christian sanctification is the divine gift of love, poured into human hearts by the Holy Spirit. It is this gift on which Christian holiness depends and which must ground any concrete practice of love and service in the world. For Augustine, the gift of love is not in the first instance a theoretical substance or capacity implanted in our being, although it is not wrong to describe it in such terms in certain contexts. Rather, insofar as sanctification instantiates in experience it does so as a delight in the things of God, efficaciously generated in bodies by the Spirit through the workings of providence.

At the same time, this delight is not just a generic feeling of pleasure either, though it is of course related to other human feelings of everyday pleasure. It is a pleasure with a particular shape and range of content. It is delight in the goodness of God and his ways as they are experienced in concrete lives in the world and a dismay over the reality of sin in the context of its particular instantiations that we experience. It is a delight that manifests as love for particular people and particular features of creation that we encounter, and which is most clearly visible in God's "incongruous" love for sinners, "without regard to worth," in Jesus Christ.[84] And it is an experience of "well-being" that is matched to the creature's deepest purpose and vocation, deriving as it does from "the one in whom they have their being."[85]

---

[83] *The Book of Common Prayer* (1662), The Collect for Purity (*Book of Common Prayer*, p. 390).

[84] Language about the "incongruity" of grace is taken from John Barclay. See the discussion of Barclay's account of grace in Chapter 4.

[85] *Spir. et litt.* 3.5 (PL 44:203; WSA I/23:145).

In the context of a theology of sanctification, a further question now needs to be asked: what space does this vision make for Christian practice and moral exhortation in the generating and fostering of virtue?

This question is especially salient against the background of early twenty-first-century theology, which has witnessed a vigorous ecumenical revival of virtue ethics as the primary model for understanding Christian transformation.[86] Jennifer Herdt's position is representative. In *Putting on Virtue*, Herdt draws on virtue ethics to fund skepticism about the sort of Augustinian model I am describing. According to Herdt, "hyper-Augustinian" models of Christian transformation that emphasize the powerlessness of the individual to follow the law, and which focus instead on the organic, spontaneous character of sanctification as a response to the experience of divine grace, are "denaturalized" and "deracinated" and unable to make theological sense of a positive role for practice and habituation in Christian life.[87] In Herdt's view, only a virtue-based model of Christian transformation can do justice to the idea that God sanctifies *through* natural human processes rather than separately from them. As she sees it, any model of transformation not based around the mechanism of habituation will render sanctification a "miraculous surd," the consequence of "an instantaneous evangelical rebirth, a lightning bolt from heaven."[88]

The question about practice and moral exhortation can arise from another direction as well. Critics of theologies of transformation like the one being proposed here, which foregrounds what I have called the "soteriological pattern" of sanctification, often worry that such visions will leave the Christian life too indeterminate and undefined to sustain a serious Christian ethic. They argue that life in the Spirit and under grace in such models will be nothing more than a kind of empty set, devoid of moral content other than vague feelings of love and gratitude. Oliver O'Donovan makes a classic version of this case:

> It has proved possible to mount [an account of Christian life in the Spirit] which, sheltering behind the Lutheran *simul iustus et peccator* formula, takes only its second half seriously. Sanctification was mentioned only to be bound and gagged, reduced to a disillusioned consciousness of moral possibilities unrealized, speculation on a gracious work of God that was never to be performed. The barrenness of the outcome can be seen in the withering away of vital moral categories, leaving only the reference to "good works", which . . . must be ignored if ever they thrust themselves on the attention. This was the high-road to deism, . . . premised upon

---

[86] The literature here is now very large. For representative works see especially Stanley Hauerwas, *Character and the Christian Life: A Study in Theological Ethics* (Notre Dame: University of Notre Dame Press, 1994), Joseph J. Kotva, *The Christian Case for Virtue Ethics* (Washington, D.C.: Georgetown University Press, 1996), and Herdt, *Putting on Virtue*.
[87] Herdt, *Putting on Virtue*, p. 350.   [88] Herdt, *Putting on Virtue*, p. 350.

a God who worked only through man's inactivity, leaving "sanctification" as a doctrine entrenched in the curriculum with precisely nothing to talk about.[89]

In my view, O'Donovan's critique fails to get traction on the "affective Augustinian" approach to sanctification that I have been describing. A thick account of the affective dynamics involved in the work of the Spirit to save and to sanctify provides a strong counterpoint to his argument in two major respects. The first has to do with the embeddedness of affective experience in the social and material world. As I will argue later, in my discussion of "economies of desire," affective transformations of the kind described by Augustine as well as Luther and Melanchthon include, and direct attention to, the social and political dimensions of Christian life in all their particularity and complexity in a way that hardly reduces to "disillusioned consciousness of moral possibilities unrealized." The second counterpoint is that, properly understood, the affective Augustinian approach does not in fact exclude a role for spiritual practice or moral exhortation in Christian transformation, although it does relativize and reinterpret them in a particular way. The burden of the remainder of the present section is to show how this is the case.

Against the background of the sorts of critiques we see in Herdt and O'Donovan, the initial point to make is that the affective Augustinian model of sanctification that I am advocating actually shares the concerns of virtue ethicists like Herdt to take bodies seriously and to emphasize the importance of social and psychological plausibility in theological accounts of Christian transformation. As should now be clear, I very much concur with Herdt's conviction that the Spirit's work to transform Christians takes place "in time, [through] forces that are embodied and open to view."[90]

What I do not share is Herdt's assumption that the category of virtue and the mechanism of habituation provide the only compelling conceptual scheme for making sense of such transformation. Much of the power of the appeal to "practice" in theology is its perceived ability to mediate between discourse and affective change. As I have shown, however, affect and desire constitute middle terms which do not reduce to questions of "practice," but which can nevertheless mediate very effectively between theological description of the work of the Spirit and a plausible account of how such work plays out in bodies and in time.

Related to Herdt's assumption about the primacy of the mechanism of habituation in moral transformation is a set of presuppositions she holds about the relationship between agency and embodiment. Herdt's account takes for granted the assumption that any socially and psychologically

---

[89] Oliver O'Donovan, *Entering into Rest: Ethics as Theology 3* (Grand Rapids, MI: William B. Eerdmans Publishing Company, 2017), p. 76.

[90] Herdt, *Putting on Virtue*, p. 350. See similarly McKenny's concern that the operation of grace not be seen as "circumvent[ing] the exercise of the capacities of our created nature" (McKenny, "Karl Barth and the Plight of Protestant Ethics," p. 19).

plausible vision of Christian transformation will require a robust affirmation of human agency, and that "hyper-Augustinian" models like that of Luther are necessarily "discontinuous . . . with ordinary moral psychology."[91] Having established that grace and human agency are not in principle opposed,[92] Herdt then presents a false alternative. In her view, the "engine" of transformation is either a process of habituation driven by the noncompetitive operations of human and divine agency, or else it must be a "lightning bolt from heaven" that changes people instantaneously and miraculously.[93]

This characterization is built upon a straw man picture of the alternative to the virtue-ethical model. As I have shown already, attention to affect and desire shows how human encounter with divine grace can have real effects in bodies while also being experienced disjunctively and "passively," in watershed moments of particular affective intensity. A sophisticated theology of emotion shows that virtue ethics is not the only way to integrate the body into a theology of sanctification, and that "ordinary moral psychology" does not by any means reduce to the mechanisms involved in processes of habituation. It is in fact perfectly possible to affirm that transformative grace often acts over and against the opposition of the sinful human agent while still having real embodied and affective effects.[94]

However, the affective Augustinian model does not just provide an additional or alternative way of talking about Christian transformation to that of virtue ethics. In several important respects, it provides a *better* way of talking about such change. One major advantage is its superior ability to illuminate the phenomenon of "non-transformation" in Christians. This is a significant topic, which will be discussed at the end of the chapter in its own subsection. A second advantage is that it can account for the insights of affect theory that were discussed in Chapter 4, especially the ways that affects are often experienced as highly intransigent, resisting the effects of even intensive and sustained attempts to alter them through practice.

But there is third advantage to the affective model that can be discussed now. It is that an account of sanctification that emphasizes the centrality of affective and desiderative change makes substantially better sense than habituation-based models do of how relatively *rapid* transformations are possible, like those that often appear to be taking place in New Testament accounts of Christian conversion. In Herdt's account, "Christians are made such . . . through hearing the scriptures that proclaim the story of God with us and participating in the practices of the church . . . Christian identity is thus formed gradually, in time."[95] From a scriptural and soteriological perspective,

---

[91] Herdt, *Putting on Virtue*, p. 3.   [92] Herdt, *Putting on Virtue*, pp. 343–4.
[93] Herdt, *Putting on Virtue*, p. 350.   [94] See Zahl, "Non-Competitive Agency."
[95] Herdt, *Putting on Virtue*, p. 350. For a similarly practice-focused account of Christian identity, see Jones, *Transformed Judgment*.

however, this gradualistic vision of Christian life is not at all adequate to make sense of what makes a person a Christian. A theory of Christian identity also needs to do justice to New Testament descriptions of the punctiliarity of baptism in the Spirit and of the powerful affective immediacy often involved in Christian conversion. It needs to be able to account for the converts at Pentecost who are "cut to the heart" by Peter's sermon and resolve to get baptized on the spot (Acts 22:37–38, 41), for the eunuch who decides in the middle of a journey to get baptized and then "went on his way rejoicing" (Acts 8:34–39), for Lydia, whose "heart" is suddenly "opened" to "listen eagerly to what was said by Paul," leading directly to her baptism (Acts 16:14–15), and for the conversion of Paul himself on the road to Damascus (Acts 22:6–11). In cases like these, what is happening is much more sudden and dramatic than can be accounted for through the transformative power of habituation, which requires significant durations of time to do its work. In the same way, an account of Christian life primarily in terms of a process of living into an identity-shaping religio-cultural narrative simply cannot do justice to the existential and religious urgency of problems like guilt over sin, the desire for forgiveness, or the terror of death, let alone the radicality of Christian experience of encounter with God.

I have raised a similar point elsewhere in critical appreciation of John Barclay's work on Paul's theology of grace.[96] For all its power and importance, Barclay's focus on Christian transformation in terms of *habitus*-formation in communities over time misses the equally if not more important ways that the transformative impact of divine grace is described in the New Testament in disruptive and temporally sudden terms as well.[97] A major weakness of accounts of Christian transformation that depend primarily or exclusively on processes of habituation is thus their one-sided notion of the chronology of salvation. A compelling account must also be able to make sense of the more rapid and disjunctive dimensions of Christian experience of the Spirit, not just of the long-term changes wrought by the slow inscription of habit upon bodies and hearts. From a theological perspective, Herdt's explicit rejection of such factors as part of her advocacy of a virtue-ethical model substantially limits the descriptive power of her account, and Barclay's relative indifference to the question is a significant problem in an otherwise persuasive book.

Importantly, however, an affective Augustinian approach does not in fact deny a role to practice or habituation in the shaping of patterns of holy desire. As a phenomenon of experience that takes place in bodies, genuinely transformed desire will instantiate concretely, including in changes of practice. And there is no reason to think that practices and habits cannot in principle further inscribe the desiderative changes in question, at least up to a point.

---

[96] See Zahl, "Incongruous Grace."
[97] For Barclay on *habitus*, see especially Barclay, *Paul and the Gift*, pp. 504–8.

But there remains a crucial difference between the two approaches. The difference is in their respective "theories of change." In the Aristotelian model, on which both Herdt's virtue ethical approach and Barclay's appeal to *habitus* depend, the theory of change is built around the mechanism of habituation through action. In the *Nicomachean Ethics*, action is necessary for the acquisition of virtue. Because "like states arise from like activities," it follows that "becoming just requires doing just actions first, and becoming temperate, temperate actions."[98] Aristotle uses the analogy of strength training: "strength . . . is produced by eating a great deal and going through a great deal of strenuous exercise . . . The same applies to the virtues."[99]

In this model, it is not that virtue itself consists merely in right actions. Aristotle himself is clear that the purpose of ethics is to form a virtuous person, not just to generate virtuous action.[100] It is rather that virtue can be formed only through actions. For Aristotle, you begin becoming virtuous by performing virtuous deeds poorly, and then you gradually become more virtuous by performing these deeds incrementally better, and thus through a process of habituation over time.[101] In this picture, it is not a problem if you begin by doing the right thing for the wrong reasons. You are still building towards virtue, because you will eventually be shaped into someone who does the right thing for the right reasons, at least so long as you have virtuous examples to imitate.

By contrast, in Augustine's theory of Christian transformation, which is primarily desiderative and soteriological, sanctification is not driven by the mechanism of habituation in the first instance. In the anti-Pelagian writings, it is clear that insofar as we ever do come to participate sincerely and effectively in virtue-inscribing practices of holiness and discipleship, we do so only because such practices have already been made fundamentally pleasing to us through transformative experiential encounter with grace. The issue of motivation is crucial here. In the Augustinian picture, we engage in such practices only when they have already been made pleasing enough to us that our desire to take part in them is stronger than our desire not to take part in them. The primary engine is the grace of God experienced, in the workings of providence, according to a love- and delight-generating soteriological pattern. The upshot is that virtue-inscribing practices "work" only insofar as they have already been made attractive and delightful through the Spirit. Otherwise for a given hearer they are just demands of the law that kill instead of make alive.

---

[98] *Nichomachean Ethics* 1103b and 1105a. English translations of Aristotle are taken from Aristotle, *Nicomachean Ethics*, trans. Roger Crisp (Cambridge: Cambridge University Press, 2000).

[99] Aristotle, *Nichomachean Ethics*, 1104a–1104b.

[100] "[T]he just and temperate person is not the one who does [just and temperate actions] merely, but the one who does them as just and temperate people do." *Nichomachean Ethics* 1105b.

[101] See Pakaluk, *Aristotle's* Nicomachean Ethics, pp. 102–3.

Augustine is quite clear on this point:

> Whoever then have turned to the Lord their God . . . with their whole heart and their whole soul will not find God's commandment heavy. After all, how can it be heavy when it commands love? For either one does not love, and then it is heavy, or one loves, and it cannot be heavy.[102]

For Augustine, the heaviness or otherwise of the commandment to love depends on a prior affective transformation—the generation by the Holy Spirit of divine delight in the hearts of Christians. In this way, the Augustinian approach is able to take substantially better account than the Aristotelian one of the intransigence of sinful affects that was discussed in Chapter 4.

The difference is especially clear when viewed pastorally. It means that when efforts over time to engage in practices intended to generate virtue are experienced by Christians as abidingly joyless, frustrating, or impossible, then it is a mistake to interpret them as instruments of the Spirit's liberating work of grace. By contrast, if a given exhortation, behavioral ideal, or norm of community life is encountered as attractive, energizing, and liberating, then it is indeed likely to be an instrument of the Spirit's transformative work directly. Of course, the difference can be quite subtle. To have enough desire to continue engaging in a practice successfully over time does not mean that there will never be moments of frustration and challenge. It means, rather, that the difficulties will not ultimately be strong enough to counter a stronger desire to engage in the practice nevertheless.

However, if a given practice or habitual behavior fails to become attractive enough that we persist with it over time, then no matter how wise or good the principle, for the hearer it remains the letter that kills (2 Cor. 3:6). In such cases it is still potentially an instrument of transformation, in the Spirit, but only indirectly, via the law-gospel pattern. In such cases, it is not that exhortation to spiritual disciplines and the like plays no role in the process of Christian transformation. It is that the role they play in the soteriological pattern of sanctification becomes that of law rather than gospel. Their function, in the Spirit, is not the further inscription of "delight in righteousness" through the mechanism of habituation, but the catalyzing of an honest despair over our inability to overcome intransigent desiderative attachments to sin, even when we are engaged in the "correct" Christian practices.

A major advantage of the affective Augustinian approach is thus that it can in principle acknowledge a role for exhortation and habituation in Christian transformation, while at the same time giving a clear-eyed account of the fact that moral exhortations are very often experienced by Christians as joyless, discouraging, or impossible. In these cases, the intransigence of sinful affects and desires is such that mere exhortation does not possess the power to effect

---

[102] *Nat. et gr.* 69.83 (*PL* 44:289; *WSA* I/23:260).

meaningful change. The result is that the question of whether a given practice or exhortation will be transformative, in the Spirit, is something that must be tested experientially in a given case, rather than assuming in advance that it "should" be effective of transformation. The outcome cannot be determined through an application of *a priori* principles; as Luther writes, "Only the Holy Spirit knows this art."[103] An important upshot of this understanding of Christian practice, as I will show in the final section of this chapter, is that it allows more room for making compassionate sense of Christian failure, mediocrity, and non-transformation than is the case when the primary mechanism of change is understood to be the process of habituation.

Economies of Desire

A third and crucial advantage of an affective Augustinian approach to sanctification follows from the fact that the dynamics of desire always occur in the context of real experiences of bodies in time. In this section, I will show that analysis of affects directs attention to the ways that desiring and willing are always substantially shaped by the material and social environments in which bodies are embedded, and that this requires movement beyond the experiences of the isolated individual if the law and the gospel are to accomplish the full range of their work. Ultimately, it means that the transforming work of the Spirit extends to the social, political, and cultural structures that shape how affects and desires play out in the world.

One implication of the tethering of sanctification to embodied experience is that, under the aspect of providence, the entire spectrum of human experience is implicated in the processes by which God frees Christians from bondage to sin and fosters the desires of the Spirit. Although there are important affective patterns that can be described and that can usefully inform how we go about the work of ministry and mission, it is also the case that the transformation of desire will never take place in exactly the same way twice. For example, the fact that the apostle Peter's experience in the courtyard does seem to match, in broad terms, the affective pattern described above, does not make it any less specific to Peter or any less dependent upon his unique history with Jesus or his own particular calling in God's providential purposes.

This is one of the key advantages of a theology of Christian experience that is focused on practically recognizable transformations. Attentive to the experiences of physical bodies, which are never static and whose workings often resist efforts at understanding, such a theology can never rest in idealized pictures of Christian life that are at odds with living experience. Although it is

---

[103] *WA Tischreden* 2:1; *LW* 54:127.

important to describe as best we can the patterns by which Scripture understands sanctification to take place, the theological task also requires that our
accounts of such patterns undergo regular testing in light of experience. As
I argued at the outset of the book, to emphasize such testing is not a matter of
taking sides in a putative contest between "experience" and "Scripture." It is
simply one implication of a major strand of biblical pneumatology.

Experiential testing also helps us to avoid the trap whereby even theologies
that are formally interested in "the body" can end up evacuating the body of
practically recognizable significance. As Althaus-Reid rightly warns, there are
modes of theology in which the "body [remains] at a symbolic level of
exchange, but the real body, that is the body which speaks of the concreteness
of hunger and pleasure, gets displaced."[104] The criterion of practical recognizability means that sanctification in the Spirit does not engage a theological
abstraction that we call "the body," but the "real" body—the body that sweats
and gets flushed, that registers fear through the release of adrenaline, that
laughs and shakes with emotion.[105]

Among the most significant implications of the connection between the
work of the Spirit and embodied affects is that this work is never simply
private or individual, but is always entangled with the structural, material, and
social worlds in which bodies move. As both psychologists and affect theorists
emphasize, emotions are never simply a matter of the "internal life" of
individuals, but function within economies of desire that precede, shape,
and exceed individual experience.[106]

There is a great deal that could be said about the locatedness of affective
experience in such economies. For present purposes I will limit myself to two
main points: first, that the emotions associated with Christian sanctification
tend to be *social* emotions, and second, that these emotions have *histories*.
Here I can provide only an initial sketch of some of these dynamics, in order to
illustrate why the affective Augustinian approach, properly understood, has
both social and political dimensions.

One useful way of articulating the inherent sociality of religious affects is by
borrowing from empirical research on social cognition. For psychologists, one

---

[104] Althaus-Reid, "Queer I Stand," pp. 99–100.

[105] It is important to remember that although a focus on affect does tether theology to
embodiment in important ways, this does not mean that the theological significance of the
body reduces to its affects or that affective analysis is the only angle for getting theological
traction on embodiment. For example, the extended account of the relationship between
displacement and racialization that Willie Jennings gives in *The Christian Imagination* examines
geography and space as crucial features of embodiment that can be analyzed effectively without
focusing on affects (see Jennings, *The Christian Imagination*). What attention to affect does do
very effectively, I would argue, is to shine light on the powerful theological link between the body
and the dogmatic loci of soteriology and pneumatology.

[106] This phrasing is indebted to Sara Ahmed's concept of "affective economies," which is
discussed below.

of the most obvious questions to ask about emotions is about their function. What purpose do they serve in enhancing human survival and flourishing? From a psychological perspective, the data are clear: "humans are social creatures who need social bonds in order to thrive," and emotions help them to do this.[107] As Fischer and Manstead explain, "emotions are experienced and expressed in social contexts, and they help us to deal with the challenges posed by the social environment." For example, some emotions serve an "affiliation function": they help to "establish or maintain cooperative and harmonious relations with other individuals or social groups." Examples of this type include happiness, love, gratitude, admiration, guilt, shame, and regret. Other social emotions, by contrast, serve a "distancing function." Such emotions help to "differentiate the self or group from others" and enable us to "compete with these others for social status or power."[108] Examples of distancing emotions include anger, contempt, disgust, and social fear. What both "affiliating" and "distancing" emotions have in common, according to Fischer and Manstead, is that they tie us to other people and help us to thrive in the social contexts in which we all live and move as complex social animals.

Carrying insights from social cognition over to theology, we can see that the affects involved in practically recognizable experiences of salvation and sanctification fall squarely within the category of "social emotions." Fear of divine judgment, guilt as a result of wrongdoing, gratitude toward God, love and delight in God and neighbor: each serves in a different way to "establish or maintain cooperative and harmonious relations" with other agents, including God.[109] Guilt, for example, functions as an impetus to repair broken relationships, especially with those to whom we are particularly close.[110] Gratitude, likewise, is an affective connection that fosters and rewards mutual support between social creatures.[111] From this perspective, it is no surprise that the emotions and affective patterns associated with the Spirit's transformative

---

[107] Agneta H. Fischer and Antony S.R. Manstead, "Social Functions of Emotion and Emotion Regulation," in *Handbook of Emotions*, 4th ed, eds. Lisa Feldman Barrett, Michael Lewis, and Jeannette M. Haviland-Jones (New York: The Guilford Press, 2016),), pp. 424. For references to the "large body of work" demonstrating that "people are strongly motivated to establish close relationships and that their success affects both physical and psychological health and well-being," see Gráinne M. Fitzsimons and Joanna Anderson, "Interpersonal Cognition: Seeking, Understanding, and Maintaining Relationships," in *The Oxford Handbook of Social Cognition*, ed. Donal Carlston (Oxford: Oxford University Press, 2013), p. 591.

[108] Fischer and Manstead, "Social Functions of Emotion," pp. 424, 434, 425. How this works out in specific instances—what Fischer and Manstead call the social "effects" of emotion, as opposed to its social "function"—is situationally as well as culturally variegated and depends on highly complex interactions between emotional appraisal, social contexts and norms, and practices of emotion regulation.

[109] Even fear of death is difficult to imagine apart from social fears of isolation and loss of relation.

[110] Fischer and Manstead, "Social Functions of Emotion," p. 428.

[111] Fischer and Manstead, "Social Functions of Emotion," p. 427.

work are often generated in contexts that are very directly or obviously social (becoming salient, for example, during communal worship, or while engaging in practices of confession, or while participating in particular liturgies, or while being prayed for by someone, or during a sermon).

Social psychologists hypothesize, with significant empirical support, that social emotions tend to be mediated through complex "mental representations" of people and the world that we develop over the course of our lives.[112] An interesting consequence of the role of mental representations in the generation of social emotion is that it is possible for a schema or model to do its work even if the person represented is not actually physically present.[113] For example, the anxieties a person might feel while reflecting on a job interview after it is over, or the surge of love they might experience while looking at a photograph of an absent child, are no less "social" for the fact that they might occur while the person is physically alone. In the same way, to feel guilt or gratitude toward God is always a "social" experience, cognitively speaking, in that such feelings depend upon a mental representation of God as an "other" to whom the subject stands in a social relation.[114] Attention to the social psychology of emotion thus problematizes simplistic theological dichotomies between "individualistic" and "communal" Christian pieties. It helps us to see that the emotional territories associated with salvation and sanctification are irreducibly social, even when they are experienced in the absence of other people, even as these social emotions are always being mediated through individual bodies and brains.

This dimension of emotion also helps us to understand how the sort of affective transformations I have been describing in this chapter help make sense of the New Testament understanding of the Holy Spirit as being ordered in a fundamental sense to Jesus Christ. As we saw in Chapter 2, one of the most decisive pneumatological developments in Scripture is the specification in the New Testament of the Spirit of God as the Spirit of Christ. This is a process that can be traced especially clearly in Paul's thought, but can be found

---

[112] Most relevant for social emotions are the mental representations of other people that we develop. These are sometimes called "relational schemas" and sometimes "internal working models," depending on which framework is being used. On relational schemas, see Mark W. Baldwin, "Relational Schemas and the Processing of Social Information," *Psychological Bulletin* 112, no. 3 (1992). On internal working models, see Nancy L. Collins, AnaMarie C. Guichard, Maire B. Ford, and Brooke C. Feeney, "Working Models of Attachment: New Developments and Emerging Themes," in *Adult Attachment: Theory, Research, and Clinical Implications*, eds. Steven W. Rholes and Jeffry A. Simpson (New York: The Guilford Press, 2004).

[113] See Fitzsimons and Anderson, "Interpersonal Cognition," pp. 601–2.

[114] On God representations from a psychological perspective, see Bonnie Poon Zahl, Carissa A. Sharp, and Nicholas J.S. Gibson, "Empirical Measures of the Religious Heart," in *Head and Heart: Perspectives from Religion and Psychology* (West Conshohocken, PA: John Templeton Press, 2013), and C.A. Sharp, E.B. Davis, K. George, A.D. Cuthbert, B.P. Zahl, D.E. Davis, J.N. Hook, and J.D. Aten, "Measures of God Representations: Theoretical Framework and Overview," *Psychology of Religion and Spirituality* (2019).

at many other points in the New Testament as well, reaching perhaps its fullest articulation in the Gospel of John.[115] The fact that the emotions involved in practically recognizable experiences of the Spirit in salvation and sanctification are social emotions helps lay important groundwork for understanding how the Spirit establishes a relationship between Christians and Jesus. To feel gratitude, love, and joy in response to experience of the grace of God secured and communicated in Christ is to experience the sorts of affects that make up a core part of what actually constitutes social relationships. In talking about the generation of these social emotions, we are at the same time talking about the forging of thick, personally specific affective ties to the person of Jesus as the source and mediator of such grace. Attention to the social character of these Christian affects thus helps explain how the experience of divine grace is a social experience that establishes a relationship between Jesus and believers that is psychologically and emotionally real, and which is experienced concretely in bodies.[116]

It is not just psychological scientists who have foregrounded the social dimensions of emotion. In a justly famous article, Sara Ahmed uses tools from phenomenology and affect theory to provide a comprehensive challenge to the assumption that "emotions are a private matter, that they simply belong to individuals, or even that they come from within and *then* move outward toward others."[117] Ahmed is particularly interested in the ways that affects develop and "circulate" culturally in ways that are independent of the individuals and groups out of which they might initially emerge. Analyzing the example of "hate," she shows how affects have a kind of emergent life of their own, moving across and within bodily and social spaces via "affective economies."[118] Rather than simply "resid[ing] in a subject or figure," "emotions *do things*." They "align individuals with communities," working in "concrete and particular" ways "to mediate the relationship between the psychic and the social, and between the individual and the collective."[119]

Attention to these sorts of dynamics leads Ahmed to the second point I want to make here: the fact that affects are carriers of cultural, psychological, and biological *histories*. As she writes in *The Cultural Politics of Emotion*,

---

[115] The connection between the Holy Spirit and Jesus is evident in many texts, including Rom. 8:8–9, 1 Pet. 1:10, Acts 16:6–7, and Gal. 4:6; in the Gospel of John, the Spirit takes up, continues, and expands the ministry of Jesus, flowing from him (John 7:37–39; 20:22), standing in for him (14:25–26; 16:7), testifying on his behalf (15:26), glorifying him (16:14) and mediating between him and believers (16:15).

[116] For helpful analysis along similar lines, see T.M Luhrmann, *When God Talks Back: Understanding the American Evangelical Relationship with God* (New York: Alfred A. Knopf, 2012).

[117] Sara Ahmed, "Affective Economies," *Social Text* 79, no. 22 (2004), p. 117. Emphasis original.

[118] Ahmed, "Affective Economies," pp. 117, 119.

[119] Ahmed, "Affective Economies," p. 119.

"through emotions, the past persists on the surface of bodies. Emotions show us how histories stay alive, even when they are not consciously remembered."[120]

Ahmed's observation about emotional histories can be interpreted as functioning at several levels. One level is personal and psychological. Emotional dynamics involve a highly complex traffic between individuals and the world, including other human beings. This traffic is mediated through ongoing psychological processes that psychologists and cognitive scientists theorize in terms of categories like mental representation, perspective-taking, appraisal, attribution, working models and schemas, memory, and the tuning of representations through new sources of cognitive information like perceptual feedback. Because our mental representations vary based on our developmental history, and continue to be updated and tuned throughout our lives, it follows that our emotional experience is shaped by and in a sense "carries" our history.

An example of such traffic that is particularly important from the perspective of affect is the phenomenon that psychologists refer to as "attachment relationships." As Chris Fraley explains, "attachment theory has emerged as one of the leading theoretical frameworks for broadly understanding interpersonal functioning, relationships, and personality development in social and personality psychology."[121] Attachment theory posits, with strong empirical support, that affective and behavioral patterns in close relationships are significantly mediated by "attachment patterns" that are initially constructed by children "as a function of their caregiving experiences."[122] Although the effects of attachment patterns are strongest in relation to parents and other caregivers, there is evidence that they often play a significant role in other close relationships as well, including friendships and romantic partnerships.[123]

Importantly, attachment relationships have significant effects on emotional experience. According to Fraley, many of "the most emotionally powerful experiences that people have in their lives derive from the development, maintenance, and disruption of attachment patterns."[124] Bowlby, the founder of attachment theory, describes these affective effects:

> The formation of [an attachment] bond is described as falling in love, maintaining a bond as loving someone, and losing a partner as grieving over someone. Similarly, threat of loss [of an attachment bond] arouses anxiety, and actual loss gives rise to sorrow; while each of these situations is likely to arouse anger.

---

[120] Ahmed, *The Cultural Politics of Emotion*, p. 202.

[121] R. Chris Fraley, "Attachment in Adulthood: Recent Developments, Emerging Debates, and Future Directions," *Annual Review of Psychology* 70 (2019), p. 403.

[122] Fraley, "Attachment in Adulthood," p. 403.

[123] For an overview of this literature, see Ross A. Thompson, "Early Attachment and Later Development," in *The Handbook of Attachment*, 3rd ed., eds. Jude Cassidy and Phillip R. Shaver (New York: The Guilford Press, 2018).

[124] Fraley, "Attachment in Adulthood," p. 416.

The unchallenged maintenance of a bond is experienced as a source of security, and the renewal of a bond as a source of joy.[125]

For present purposes, the phenomenon of attachment relationships provides a particularly clear illustration of the fact that emotions have histories. It shows how patterns of anxiety, anger, or joy in close adult relationships are shaped in substantial ways by childhood experiences that occurred years or even decades earlier. Here then is a very direct way that Ahmed is right to say that "histories stay alive" through emotions.[126]

But mental representations like those at work in attachment patterns also have histories that exceed the life experience of any particular individual or group. As Ahmed argues, affects are shaped by large-scale social and cultural developments, not just personal ones. For example, children learn emotional patterns and schemas from parents and other attachment figures, who in turn learned from their own attachment figures, who in turn learned from their own attachment figures. In this way, pieces of our cognitive-emotional furniture can persist across generations, even as they are constantly being updated and reconfigured. For example, to be raised in a family with a history of alcoholism, or as a child of immigrants, or as a descendant of slaves, or as a product of a wealthy society with a strong social safety net, is to have one's attachments and other mental representations shaped by a complex and multigenerational cultural past. In practice, that past is mediated most directly at a local level, as children are shaped by what makes their attachment figures feel stressed, or whom they trust, or how they navigate experiences of difficulties like illness or financial hardship. But that does not mean that more distant pasts are not still "alive" in such mediations, however indirectly. It is on this sort of basis that Ahmed can argue that "histories of colonialism, slavery, and violence shape lives and worlds in the present," "even when [such histories] are not consciously remembered."[127]

Indeed, affective experiences are also shaped by histories beyond the social, including material, intellectual, and political histories. For example, psychologically formative experiences like war or migration are often closely interwoven with competition over resources and are thus influenced by distant political, ecological, and even geological pasts. Likewise, to have one's day-to-day desires and aspirations shaped by the values, practices, and structures of late-modern capitalism is to be the product of an intricate tissue of intellectual and political developments—from Adam Smith's economic theories, to the mathematics behind financial derivatives, to previous generations' decisions

---

[125] John Bowlby, *Attachment and Loss,* iii: *Sadness and Depression* (New York: Basic Books, 1980), p. 40; quoted in Fraley, "Attachment in Adulthood," p. 416.
[126] Ahmed, *The Cultural Politics of Emotion,* p. 202.
[127] Ahmed, *The Cultural Politics of Emotion,* p. 202.

regarding market regulation or trade.[128] And beyond all of this, of course, lies the *evolutionary* history of the feeling animal, which is powerfully embedded in the physiological and neurological structures through which emotions and desires are always experienced in human bodies. Indeed, it is this deep biological history that has the most profound shaping effect of all. Without it, we would not be able to feel anything in the first place.

It is clear that emotions have histories. It follows from this that if Christian sanctification subsists to a substantial degree in the critique and transformation of affects, then it is also an intervention in these histories, at the level of both individuals and communities. Critical analysis of any given set of affective experiences thus encompasses, at least in principle, the whole weave of social, cultural, intellectual, material, and political life that stands behind them and informs them. Ultimately, it not possible to attend well to embodied emotional experience without attending to the social and material environments in which such experience is always embedded, including the history of that environment. An account of Christian transformation that attends to embodied experience must therefore be open in principle to a very wide— almost endlessly wide—range of avenues and tools for critical investigation.[129]

The implications for the theology of sanctification are significant. In the affective Augustinian picture, as we have seen, the Holy Spirit transforms Christians by "substituting good desire for evil desire, that is, pouring out love in our hearts."[130] From this perspective, sin is primarily a matter of disordered affective attachments to created goods (including people), and holiness is primarily a matter of right desiderative attachment to God, mediated through the right "use" of created things. In this context, as we saw earlier in the chapter, the function of the law is to expose the truth of sin and to render the negative affects associated with sin acute, in order to bring us to the point where we are willing to flee from even very powerful sinful attachments.

Basic to this vision is the view that the primary site where sin manifests in our lives is in affective structures and attachments that we experience in and through our bodies. As emotional and bodily realities, it is now clear that such attachments do not come from nowhere, but have complex histories. It follows that the critical focus of the law can in principle encompass the full structure of a given sinful attachment, including its embeddedness within a given social and material environment and history. If "the truth will set you free" (John 8:32), then the truth about a given sinful desire comprehends not just the

---

[128] For analysis of how the subjectivities of late-modern people are shaped by finance-dominated capitalism, including at affective and desiderative levels, see Tanner, *Christianity and the New Spirit of Capitalism*.

[129] Here my argument is similar to Rogers' claim that "any theology that rejects the social sciences is anti-incarnational" and therefore anti-pneumatological (Rogers, *After the Spirit*, pp. 55–61).

[130] *Spir. et litt.* 4.6 (*PL* 44:204; *WSA* I/23:146).

surface-level feelings most immediately associated with it, nor even the deeper affects that permeate the individual's experience of it, but the whole set of biological, cultural, and psychological systems that lie behind and around those feelings. The result is that the law exposes cultural and structural sins, not just "individual" ones.

From an affective Augustinian perspective, critical analysis of sin therefore encourages attention to factors that precede and inform sinful desire in a given instance. As Serene Jones argues, in the context of an extended analysis of patriarchy and misogyny in terms of Christian sin-language, "the notion of sin" speaks to the fact that "we are shaped by oppressive dynamics that predate us," that "cannot be escaped by force of will," and that "are so endemic to our language and culture that even when we know they are oppressive, we nonetheless remain determined by them."[131] The sorts of disordered desiderative attachments that produce and sustain the patterns of sin against women that Jones is describing—for example, the market economy's exploitation of women's unpaid domestic labor "to maximize profits,"[132] sexual harassment in the workplace,[133] or the marginalizing of "women who are old, disabled, or unemployed"[134]—are themselves products of multilayered histories (personal, social, cultural, and material) which in turn are operative at multiple levels and diverse timescales. This means that in order for such sins to be fully exposed and rendered acute—in order for what Augustine calls the "disease" to be properly diagnosed—critical attention is required not only to specific instances of suffering and transgression, but also to the whole range of complex forces that stand behind each particular act of transgression, giving such acts their power. Merely exposing one particular instance of sinful pathology will do little to bring about longer term and larger scale transformation. But addressing large-scale structural issues alone is not satisfactory either, since such analysis will have difficulty accounting adequately for the role of specific human affects and desires, as intransigent material realities located in particular bodies, in the generation of concrete sins and sufferings.

The thick account of affects I am presenting here, which takes inspiration from affect theory as well as social cognition research, brings these many dimensions together. In this account, the pneumatological function of the law to reveal sin expands outward from a given experience of "affective predicates" of salvation to expose a multilayered and still living "past" that, as Ahmed suggests, "persists on the surface of bodies" through emotions. Because the Spirit works through bodies, the transformation of desire is implicitly a political event, not just a psychological one.

---

[131] Jones, *Feminist Theory and Christian Theology*, p. 118.
[132] Jones, *Feminist Theory and Christian Theology*, p. 114.
[133] Jones, *Feminist Theory and Christian Theology*, p. 114.
[134] Jones, *Feminist Theory and Christian Theology*, p. 121.

Importantly, the same principle applies to righteousness as well as sin. Sanctified attachment to God similarly includes, depends upon, and has consequences for the full range of systems that underpin affective attachments. For example, to participate in divine love by loving our neighbor can never be simply a vague feeling shorn of practical implications. Such love will have all the concreteness of any real relation of love: it will draw us to see the world through the eyes of those around us, feeling their joy and as well as their pain, and compelling and inspiring us to action to restore relationships, to seek forgiveness, to foster flourishing, and to meet others in the context of their particular needs and desires. As something that always takes place in bodies and in time, a relationship of love is just as embedded in the world, including in the sorts of personal, social, cultural, and material structures and histories described above, as any sinful desire.

The transformative power of grace has broader implications for communal and societal realities as well. For example, John Barclay has described the radical and disruptive social implications in the early church of the "incongruous" character of "the gift of Christ" which "dissolves former criteria of worth."[135] Then as now, reigning cultural values such as "ancestry, education, and social power," as well as "taken-for-granted criteria of ethnicity, status, knowledge, virtue, or gender," are subverted in ways that result in "the formation of communities whose distinct patterns of life bear witness to an event that has broken with normal criteria of worth."[136] This is just one example of how, once again, attention to the affective dimensions of Christian transformation shows us why experience of divine grace, while never less than personal, is never simply "private" or individual. Sanctified affects, no less than the ones which underpin idolatry and sin, are always embedded in multilayered contexts and histories, such that full-orbed attention to such affects directs us towards the world in all its particularity rather than away from it.

Before concluding this section, it is important to remember that attention to affects requires once again the caveat about affective intransigence. As we saw in the previous chapter, affects often exhibit a powerful resistance to transformation, even under very strong cultural and discursive pressures. As products of material and biological processes in bodies, they are also shaped by "long evolutionary timescapes."[137] Although the effects of social emotions are always filtered through personal and cultural histories and contexts, which in turn help determine when and how they occur and which objects they get attached to, their core functions and operating energies are also products of

---

[135] Barclay, *Paul and the Gift*, pp. 566–7.
[136] Barclay, *Paul and the Gift*, pp. 567, 569. See also pp. 573–4.
[137] Schaefer, *Religious Affects*, p. 56.

ancient biological histories that have substantial power to resist transformation through discursive means.[138]

To return to the categories of the previous chapter, discursive processes like
those at work in the cultural, intellectual, political, and social history of affects
help to shape the sorts of objects to which affects get attached, what form the
resultant affects take, where they get channeled, and what effects they end up
having in the world in a given case. But recognition of affective intransigence,
especially when it comes to the powerful social emotions and desiderative
attachments with which salvation and sanctification are concerned, encourages several important qualifications in respect of the shaping power of
discursive factors. First, it reminds us that you cannot "solve" affective pathologies through discursive analysis alone, no matter how accurate or comprehensive the analysis. Second, it predicts that powerful affects will tend to
transgress boundaries of difference that are merely discursive, such that
attention to discursive difference will not suffice for mapping a given affective
economy. Third, it cautions that affects bear a complexity, and a resistance to
intelligibility, that chastens easy assumptions about their discursive legibility.
As Schaefer observes, "affective economies are expansive . . . economies, operating in registers of complexity that often exceed human intelligence."[139]
The result is that attempts to understand either the function or the history
of a given affective experience must be undertaken from a perspective of
substantial humility.

These qualifications allow us to articulate more precisely why it is important
to understand the material and historical embeddedness of any given affective
experience. Such efforts are important not because mere analytical knowledge
has power to produce affective transformation. Rather, they are important
because of the ways that they are caught up in the soteriological pattern of
transformation that we have found in Augustine, as dimensions of the law and
the gospel as they play out in the world through the Spirit.

These reflections on affective intransigence lead us to the theme of the final
section of this chapter: the phenomenon of moral "non-transformation" in
Christians.

Non-Transformation

Robert Markus has argued that Augustine's soteriology in the period from *Ad
Simplicianum* is the product of honest reflection on the stubborn fact of

---

[138] For an extended meditation on these complexities through the category of "accident," see
Schaefer, *Religious Affects*, pp. 164–77.

[139] Schaefer, *Religious Affects*, p. 170.

"Christian mediocrity."[140] Peter Brown, likewise, describes how "hard thought and bitter experience" had led Augustine "to appreciate the sheer difficulty of achieving an ideal life," and to realize that the state of holiness "he wished for most ardently would never be more than a hope, postponed . . . far beyond this life."[141] Give this experiential trajectory in Augustine's intellectual development, it is no surprise that an affective Augustinian theology of sanctification is particularly well-suited to making constructive sense of the problem of "non-transformation" in Christians. This is the final advantage of the affective Augustinian model that will be discussed here.

As we saw at the start of the chapter, models of Christian sanctification often have at their foundation belief in a punctiliar and effective transformation of Christian moral powers that is coterminous with the receipt of the Spirit. For some theologians, this change is understood to take place in baptism, while for others it occurs with the acquisition of the gift of faith. Although such models do make room for the persistence of sin in Christian life in various ways, they also assume a fundamental difference in moral capacities between Christians and non-Christians. For Webster, for example, this difference is the "gift of powers and habits[,] infused by the Spirit, laid into the mind, will and affections, and preserved by God,"[142] while for neo-Thomists like Cessario it is the gift of supernatural virtue, which functions as an operative habit throughout the life of the baptized Christian.

In accounts of sanctification like these, the commitment to the idea of an irreducible and effective change in the moral powers of the Christian will determine how to interpret cases where little or no transformation seems to be taking place. Because the operative theology holds that the gift of the Spirit should be resulting in some sort of transformation that will be evident over time, the phenomenon of non-transformation will tend to be interpreted as indicating either (a) an individual failing on the part of the person in question, such that they are in some sense a problematic Christian who can be distinguished from other Christians who do exhibit transformation, or (b) that the person is not in fact a Christian, in the sense that they either never did receive the Spirit through Christian initiation or (in some theologies) that they did receive it but have since lost it. In such cases, it is difficult fully to exclude the possibility that evaluation of the relative moral progress of a given Christian will come to be deployed as a way of determining whether a person is truly "saved." Evidence of "Christian mediocrity," especially where such mediocrity is both deep and lasting, becomes a troubling phenomenon.

A stark example of these dynamics can be found in John Wesley's influential sermon "The Marks of the New Birth." According to Wesley, one of the

---

[140] Markus, "A defence of Christian mediocrity."
[141] Brown, *Augustine of Hippo*, pp. 140–1, 150.
[142] Webster, "Mortification and Vivification," p. 107.

most important marks of having been born of the Spirit is power over sin: "An immediate and constant fruit of this faith whereby we are born of God . . . is power over sin: power over outward sin of every kind." The result is that a Christian who still seems to be entangled in obvious outward sin either never had, or has now lost, the Spirit: "Say not in your heart, I *was once* baptized; therefore I am *now* a child of God. Alas, that consequence will by no means hold. How many are the baptized drunkards and gluttons, the baptized liars and swearers . . . the baptized whoremongers, thieves, extortioners!"[143] For Wesley, the transformative work of the Spirit is not only real, it is externally evident and demonstrable to others. Egregious "drunkards," "liars," and "thieves" almost certainly do not have the Spirit, and must be born again, even if they have been baptized or have formerly professed Christian faith in some other way.

For Augustine, the problem with this kind of commitment to a relative optimism about Christian moral transformation is that it does not hold true to Christian experience. The phenomenon of "Christian mediocrity" that Augustine learned about through "bitter experience"[144] may not be the whole story, but it is too extensive and too widespread an experiential reality in the church to sustain a theology of sanctification that cannot take clear-eyed account of non-transformation in Christians. Luther's experience was similar: despite years of prayer and ascetic practice in the monastery, Luther observed little fundamental change in his moral character. As he relates in his *Lectures on Galatians*, no matter how hard he tried, "the desires of the flesh kept coming back."[145]

An affective Augustinian approach offers a constructive alternative to models of sanctification that view the phenomenon of non-transformation as indicative either that a person is a particularly bad Christian or that they are not a Christian at all. The crucial difference is that by understanding Christian transformation as something that cannot be fully detached from things that happen in bodies and in time, the affective Augustinian approach is attentive to the empirical experience of Christians in the domain of sanctification. Although it looks and hopes for Christian transformation, especially as an outworking of soteriological patterns, it is not committed to assuming such transformation in advance the way that more punctiliar, ontological models are obliged to do. The freedom of the Spirit means that the manner and extent and progress of sanctification in a given case are ultimately determined by

---

[143] Wesley, "The Marks of the New Birth," pp. 175, 181. Emphasis original.

[144] Brown, *Augustine of Hippo*, p. 141.

[145] *WA* 40.2:91–2; *LW* 27:73. See also *WA Tischreden* 4:260/*LW* 54:334 and *WA* 18:783/*LW* 33:288–9, and the discussion in Zahl, "Non-Competitive Agency," pp. 212–14.

God, who alone generates truly effective conditions for fostering delight in righteousness and fleeing sin.[146]

The positive side of this is that the experienced reality of non-transformation is not nearly as threatening from an affective Augustinian perspective as it is for other approaches. It is simply a new opportunity for prayer, and for the power and extent of divine grace to be revealed ever anew in and to the Christian sinner. Rather than being evidence of an absence of the Spirit, it is evidence that the Spirit is likely to be present in the diagnostic and revelatory mode that is proper to the law, recognizing and condemning sin, and preparing the ground once again for consolation and delight in the grace of God.

In this connection the model I am presenting affirms the Lutheran account of the Christian as *simul iustus et peccator* (simultaneously justified and a sinner), though it does so in a particular way. In his early writings, Luther takes the logic of the Augustinian acknowledgement of Christian mediocrity and non-transformation and draws out its most radical implications. In the *Lectures on Romans*, he glosses the *simul* in a particularly pessimistic way, to mean that Christians "are sinners in fact but righteous in hope" [*peccatores in re, iusti autem in spe*].[147] In *Against Latomus*, Luther extends this idea to issue what must be one of the most pessimistic claims about Christian sanctification of the Reformation period: "the motion of anger and evil is exactly the same in the godly and the godless, the same before grace and after grace."[148] In other words, Luther appears to be saying, there is an intransigence to sinful affects that significantly qualifies and conditions any strong account of the transformative power of the gospel. For Luther, the possibility must not be excluded, either pastorally or theologically, that no change in the deepest affects associated with sin will be observable in the justified Christian.

Yet that is not the end of the story. For Luther, what *is* reliably different, even in these most pessimistic moments, or in those most intransigent cases, is the perception of the consequences of our sin. He continues in *Against Latomus*: "Sin is indeed present, but having lost its tyrannic power, it can do nothing; death indeed impends, but having lost its sting, it can neither harm nor terrify."[149] In other words, just as the baptized still die, but the "sting" of that death is removed, so sinful desire still persists in Christians the same as before, only there is a recognition now that it neither damns nor condemns. The result is that the fear of God's judgment, and the correlative fear of being unloved by God, really are altered in the perceptions of the Christian, and this

---

[146] It is for this reason that Augustine is obliged at the end of *On the Spirit and the Letter* to address the question of why God does not generate such transformation as often or as completely as he presumably could. See *spir. et litt.* 36:66 (*PL* 44:245–6; *WSA* I/23:189), as well as *spir. et litt.* 34.60 (*PL* 44:240–1; *WSA* I/23:185).

[147] *WA* 56:269; *LW* 25:258.   [148] *WA* 8:91; *LW* 32:207.   [149] *WA* 8:92; *LW* 32:207.

feels like liberation—even if the core affective energies of sin ("the motion of anger and evil") do not appear to have been transformed.[150]

What is Luther doing in making these deeply pessimistic claims about Christian sanctification? Partly, he is making an empirical claim, based on his own experience and his knowledge of the experiences of others. Here his observations are similar to those of the pietist theologian Christoph F. Blumhardt, who once observed, after decades of ministry, that "I have never yet experienced someone really being born again. You are still the same old person you were ten and twenty and thirty years ago."[151] Partly, Luther is also making an exegetical claim, based especially on his reading of Romans 7 as well as on Augustine's exegesis of the same text in the treatise *Against Julian*.[152] On these bases, Luther really does have a very pessimistic vision of the extent of transformation that Christians should expect to experience.

At the same time, Luther is not saying that such pessimistic claims are all that can ever be said or that theological assertions about the reality of deeper Christian transformations in the Spirit are necessarily false. As we saw in Chapter 4, Luther also believes in the transformative power of the Christian gospel to generate real consolation, joy, and gratitude in the heart of the Christian believer, which in turn result in concrete works of love in the world. Likewise, his account of the "theological" use of the law takes for granted that in any given case sin really can be exposed, and really can lose its power, by means of this process.

What are we to make of the tension between these affirmations in Luther? We can start by pointing out that Augustine comes up against the same issues. Reflecting on the persistence of sin in the lives of Christians, Augustine starts by pointing to the apostle Paul's experience of the "thorn in the flesh" (2 Cor. 12:7–9). He then appeals to the freedom of God, who alone can create the conditions for effective transformation in Christians. Although it is true that "with God there is no injustice," nevertheless "there always remains something in the hidden depths of God's judgments" to which we do not have access. He concludes once again with Paul: "Who has known the mind of the Lord? Or who has been his counselor?" (Rom. 11:34).[153]

Luther's answer goes one step further. As is often the case with Luther, the point he is making needs to be understood in relation to preaching rather than theodicy. In claiming that the Christian is a "sinner in fact, but righteous in hope," and that "the motion of anger and evil is exactly the same in the godly

---

[150] For further analysis of these claims in *Against Latomus*, see Zahl, "Non-Competitive Agency," p. 215, n. 95.

[151] Christoph Friedrich Blumhardt, *Jesus ist Sieger! Predigten und Andachten aus den Jahren 1880 bis 1888* (Erlenbach-Zürich: Rotapfel-Verlag, 1937), p. 340.

[152] See Zahl, "Non-Competitive Agency," pp. 207–9, 211.

[153] See *spir. et litt.* 36:66 (*PL* 44:245–6; *WSA* I/23:189).

and the godless, the same before grace and after grace," Luther is ultimately less concerned with developing a theoretical account of precisely how far sanctification should extend for most Christians than he is with ensuring, from the perspective of ministry, that there is no degree of sin, no degree of non-transformation, that could exclude the Christian from the circle of the justified. In other words, the function of the *simul* and other pessimistic claims about Christian sanctification is to show in the starkest possible way that even the most untransformed Christian sinner can and must still be treated, and addressed in preaching, as a justified Christian, and that even the most transformed Christian must still be treated, and addressed in preaching, as a sinner in need of overwhelming divine grace. In this they underscore just how capacious, and just how radical, the Christian doctrine of grace is for Luther. There is no experience that it cannot encompass. Wesley's "drunkards," "liars," and "thieves" can be addressed as Christians who are already within the circle of divine grace, in the Spirit. Luther's position is thus designed as a kind of firewall against the devolution of Christian theologies of sanctification into forms of moralism, hypocrisy, and *de facto* Pelagianism.

This "pragmatic" pessimism in Luther, where the vital point is that non-transformation always has to be accounted for as a phenomenon that can and does take place among Christians, makes particular sense if we follow Augustine in recognizing the enigma of the heart. If the heart is as ultimately unfathomable as Augustine believes, and is also the primary site of the Spirit's work of sanctification, how could we ever have reliable knowledge of the extent of our sanctification? Who are we to say that what looks and feels like troubling "non-transformation" does not also entail a deep and sanctified humility in the eyes of the God "unto whom . . . all desires [are] known and from whom no secrets are hid"?[154] Who are we to say that what looks and feels like saintliness does not hide deep subtleties of pride and ambivalence? Under such circumstances, it is better to develop a theology of sanctification that sees grace as indexed to the very "worst" Christians than to try to establish who has and has not been transformed by the Spirit and how far. The process by which God generates the desires of the Spirit in Christians is not a science. It is a living "drama," shaped by the freedom of the Spirit.[155]

In this chapter, I have built on Augustine's pneumatology of desire in the early anti-Pelagian writings to sketch an account of the work of the Spirit to sanctify Christians that satisfies the pneumatological criterion of practical recognizability advocated in this book. I have shown how such an account can describe a major pattern through which desires are transformed, in the Spirit, without denying either the mystery and inscrutability of the heart or the freedom of the

---

[154] *Book of Common Prayer*, p. 390.
[155] For the category of "drama" in this sense, see David F. Ford, *The Future of Christian Theology* (Oxford: Wiley-Blackwell, 2011), pp. 23–30.

Spirit, and how it can affirm the disjunctive character of the action of grace, and the limitations of Christian practice and moral effort in generating virtue, without denying transformative power to Christian practices. I have also shown that attention to affects in sanctification helps us to understand the irreducibly social dimensions of Christian transformation, and the ways in which the work of the law to reveal sin can and must extend into analysis of cultural and structural sins, with the result that the transformation of desire has social and political as well as personal implications. Finally, I have shown that this model can account for empirical experiences of "Christian mediocrity" without transmuting the apparent phenomenon of moral non-transformation into a device for excluding sinners from the circle of the church.

Altogether, this account of sanctification represents an updating and repristination of an "affective Augustinian" theological tradition that can affirm Christian transformation as an embodied reality without falling into a false optimism about Christian moral powers and Christian transformation that does not bear up in experience. It is a vision of Christian life in the Spirit as a movement of desire and delight, taking place in the concrete experiences of real people in the world, under the aspect of grace.

Conclusion

In this book, I have sought to present a fresh theological vision that foregrounds the relationship between theological ideas and the affective experiences of Christians. I have sought to show how theology is always operating in a dynamic landscape of feeling and desiring, and that attending to these affective currents can be both critically and constructively illuminating. I have argued that good pneumatology not only authorizes but requires attention to concrete experiences that take place in bodies and in time, including especially affective experiences. And I have sought to model how constructive theology might be done that is attentive to these insights, through a focus on the work of the Spirit in salvation and sanctification, describing key parameters of an affective and Augustinian soteriology that integrates theology and experience and showing how this approach can help to resolve a number of issues in contemporary soteriology.

The argument I have been making has two distinct dimensions. The first is methodological, about the irreducibility of experience in theology and the theological power of attending to experience and emotion in Christian discourse. The second is constructive and soteriological, drawing on Melanchthon, Luther, and Augustine to describe and propose a particular approach to the theology of grace in an affective and pneumatological key. In this Conclusion, I reflect on some of the further implications of these arguments and draw attention to pathways for future theological work that emerge out of this methodological and soteriological horizon.

THE METHODOLOGICAL ARGUMENT

In principle, it is appropriate to describe the "actualization" of divine activity in relation to creation, including in relation to human creatures, as the work of the Holy Spirit.[1] But modern theology has often resisted pursuing the

---

[1] Anatolios, *Retrieving Nicaea*, p. 142; see Chapter 2.

The Holy Spirit and Christian Experience. Simeon Zahl, Oxford University Press (2020). © Simeon Zahl.
DOI: 10.1093/oso/9780198827788.001.0001

implications of this point into the realm of concrete experience. This tendency, I have argued, can be understood to a substantial degree as a legacy of long-standing Protestant anxieties about subjective experience. The result has been a certain complacency with abstraction in much modern theology, including a preference for describing key dimensions of the work of God in relation to human beings in primarily or exclusively metaphysical terms. In my view, good pneumatology cannot be content with this kind of abstraction. The Spirit of God does not operate merely in what Rahner calls the realm of "purely ontological reality,"[2] but moves in the real world, in real bodies, liberating people from concrete fears, circumstances, and sufferings.

On this basis, I have argued that we should expect activities that Scripture describes as operations of the Spirit to have effects that are "practically recognizable" in bodies and in time. A particularly useful index of such effects is affective impact. Theologically as well as biblically, as we have seen, there is a strong association between the Holy Spirit, affect, and desire. Affect also serves as an unusually powerful bridge-category for mediating between embodied experiences and ontological realities. In this life, to feel and to desire is always to feel and desire in the context of a physical body. And yet, in theology desire is also often understood ontologically, as a category that helps to articulate the creature's core orientation to its Creator.

Together, I have argued, these observations have significant implications for theological methodology. They point us towards procedures of argument and patterns of attention that shed new light on a wide range of issues and debates in Christian discourse. As a way of doing theology, this approach has two primary features. The first is to give explicit methodological attention to arguments in the history of theology about the affective impact of theological positions, viewing these as material theological arguments in their own right rather than seeing them as secondary side effects or mere rhetorical ornaments to more primary dogmatic claims. A classic example in this book has been to show, contrary to what many interpreters have assumed, that the trope of "the consolation of the terrified heart" plays a primary rather than secondary role in Philip Melanchthon's soteriology, such that his account of justification by faith cannot be abstracted from this trope without becoming disengaged from the inner logic and basic persuasiveness of his position.

The second feature of a theological methodology built on these pneumato-logical observations is to suggest that any divine activity that scriptural witness associates with the Holy Spirit as well as with impact on creatures should be expected to have concrete embodied effects of some kind. This claim has both critical and constructive implications. Critically, it means that accounts of the work of the Spirit in salvation and sanctification and in the mission of the

---

[2] Rahner, "Religious Enthusiasm and the Experience of Grace," p. 37.

church that are unable to give an account of such work at the level of affect and experience are likely to be deficient. For example, applying this principle has allowed us to see significant limitations of the soteriology of T.F. Torrance, who describes salvation in terms of changes that occur at the level of ontology without being able to give any account of how such changes relate to embodied experience. Constructively, it means that theologians should seek where possible to give a plausible account of the affective and experiential dimensions of the work of the Spirit, as I have sought to do in relation to soteriology in the later chapters of this book.

The power of this affectively attuned theological method becomes clear as it is put into practice. Although many different topics in theology and many features of traditional theological texts can be illuminated by this approach, in the present book I have focused on its soteriological implications. First, it helps us to understand and critique certain problems that have arisen in the widespread recent turn to "participation" and *theosis* as core soteriological categories. It allows us to give a robust account of why overly vague or else purely ontological accounts of soteriological participation do not in fact succeed as well as has been hoped at reintegrating salvation with embodied experience. It also undermines much of the force of the influential argument that soteriologies based around the mechanism of forensic justification are "cold" and abstract, revealing that it is fact entirely plausible to expect such theologies to generate powerful affective effects in the ways that they claim.

This methodological approach also has implications for the contemporary view that the Christian doctrine of sin is no longer relevant to modern people because they no longer seem to fear divine judgment. Attention to affective dynamics in the history of this doctrine suggests that sin needs to be understood as much more than just a label for helping to determine culpability; it has also served as a way of interpreting certain kinds of *feelings* and *experiences*. While the labels can and do change as cultures and contexts change and develop, such affects and experiences are likely to be more stable across contexts and time periods than has recently been supposed, indicating that early and pre-modern Christian views are less implausible today than has been assumed.

Methodological attention to affects and related experiences also has critical implications for some of the methodological approaches that have been most influential in theology in recent decades. In attending to affects, the door is opened for theologians to make use of a wide range of insights and theoretical tools for investigating emotion that have been developed in fields outside of theology such as critical theory, anthropology, and the psychological and cognitive sciences.

Of particular value, I have argued, is the development in critical theory and queer theory known as "affect theory." As deployed by Eve Sedgwick and her heirs, affect theory attends to the material and biological dimensions of affects, and to their strangeness, intransigence, and tendency towards inscrutability. In doing so, it provides a sophisticated theoretical vocabulary for understanding the highly complex relationship between discourse and the things that actually "make bodies move,"[3] and for articulating a middle path between social constructivism and essentialism. Bringing these insights to bear on issues in theology, I have shown that affect theory helps to reveal key limits of "cultural-linguistic" accounts of what theological ideas are and how they work, and encourages substantial qualifications to widespread assumptions in theology about the effectiveness of mechanisms of religious practice and habituation to generate changes in Christian experience, virtue, and behavior.

A further advantage of affect theory, which parallels insights that have emerged in psychological and cognitive scientific work on affects, is that it gives us tools for understanding just how "thick" affects in fact are as sites of critical and theological investigation. Recent work on emotion from these fields and beyond has put to rest two arguments that have been used in the past to justify ignoring emotional dynamics: the idea that emotions are epistemically thin ephemeralities of feeling that can be ignored in favor of ostensibly more reliable sources of knowledge; and narratives about emotion as a problematically "individualistic" dimension of Christian religious life that draws our attention away from important communal and social dynamics. In relation to the first argument, recent analyses have shown that affects are in fact complex and often highly durable, tying inquiry to bodies and other more stable material realities while still leaving room for examination of the shaping effects of discourse on emotional experience. In relation to the second, it has become clear that the most important emotions in Christian religious life are irreducibly social, even when they are experienced while people are physically alone or when God is the primary "other" in the social relation. Finally, in relation to both arguments, it is now recognized that emotions are neither ephemeral nor limited to the individual due to the way that they function as powerful carriers of histories. Affects and emotions are shaped by early life experience, by larger scale cultural, intellectual, and political "economies" of affects, and by ancient biological and evolutionary processes. Altogether, affects are powerful motivating realities that saturate all dimensions of human thinking and acting and are laden with value and information. The result is that analysis of affects and related phenomena has substantial explanatory power for making sense of what human beings actually do in the world and why they do it, including in religious spheres.

---

[3] Schaefer, "You Don't Know What Pain Is," p. 19.

For all of these reasons, my methodological proposal of attending to both explicit and implicit dimensions of emotion and experience in theological discourse provides a kind of toolkit for reading texts and assessing theological arguments from an illuminating new perspective. Although I have focused in much of this book on themes and questions that have arisen most sharply in Protestant theological contexts, is important to underline that as a method it is ecumenical. It can be used to shed new light on any text or debate that references emotion or has emotional implications, demonstrating unexpected points of contact across eras and confessions, and providing tools for identifying and interpreting the present relevance and experiential power of a wide range of Christian doctrines and practices.

From the perspective of Christian theology, there is a particular affinity between attending to the "affective salience" of theological concepts, texts, and practices, and the doctrine of the Holy Spirit. Although in this book I have focused on the work of the Spirit in salvation and sanctification, there are many further topics in pneumatology that would benefit from this method of analysis. Particularly fruitful here would be the set of activities associated with the Spirit's work of supporting and guiding the mission of the church, including vocation and calling, miracles and healing, day-to-day communication between God and Christians, and gifts of the Spirit like speaking in tongues. Further worthwhile areas for such investigation would be the nature of the Spirit's work in and through Scripture, the work of the Spirit in sacraments, the affective dimensions of prayer and liturgical practice, and the nature and effects of baptism in the Spirit. If my argument about the Holy Spirit and Christian experience is correct, then there will be practically recognizable dimensions of the work of the Spirit that can be usefully analyzed and explored in each case.

Importantly, the methodological approach described and modeled in this book needs to be understood as complementary to other methodological paradigms rather than as a replacement for them. For example, although the present book's way of focusing on affective dynamics in theology does gives excellent justification for attending to the themes of embodiment and contextual embeddedness in theology, bodies do not reduce to their affects, and the material and cultural contexts in which Christian lives unfold are more than just affective economies (although, as I have argued, they are never really less than such economies either). Furthermore, there are areas of theological inquiry where an affective and experiential approach will be less useful than other methods, or will help us to see only one set of factors among many. What this method is particularly effective for, however, is in helping to test whether and to what degree a given theological claim or system bears any relation to concrete human experience in the world. In this it can provide a much-needed ballast against tendencies towards idealization and abstraction in Christian discourse, wherever such tendencies have arisen in the past, and wherever they may arise in the future.

THE SOTERIOLOGICAL ARGUMENT

The second major dimension of this book's argument has been constructive and soteriological. The value of the constructive argument emerges in light of problems that I have identified in a number of influential contemporary accounts of salvation. Attending to affective and experiential factors has revealed that the turn away from the theme of justification by faith and towards soteriologies centered around the themes of participation in God and *theosis* has significant limitations. The fundamental problem that any properly pneumatological soteriology must resolve is of how to describe a plausible connection between ontological and experiential realities that does not ultimately reduce to the one or the other, and this problem has not yet been satisfactorily resolved in contemporary Protestant theologies of participation.

Accounts of participation from a broadly Thomist perspective have also proven to have difficulties, in both Roman Catholic and Protestant forms. The primary advantage of such approaches from the perspective of this book is that they are generally more successful at integrating ontological and experiential discourses than other Protestant approaches to participation have been. Recent Dominican versions of Thomism describe a sophisticated system whereby natural human faculties are caught up in and opened up to supernatural ends following the infusion of supernatural virtue. Protestant versions are not always as interested in these ontological dynamics, but they are effective at drawing out the power of virtue ethics, in particular, to describe a vision of Christian growth in holiness that respects the integrity of the creature, and which takes place in a realm that is "embodied and open to view."[4]

Despite these advantages, such accounts have a number of important problems. One is that they do not in fact fully resolve the problem of the relationship between ontology and experience. The Dominican accounts, for example, do not solve the problem so much as isolate it to a particular point: the irruption of the supernatural into the world in the infusion of supernatural virtue in baptism. The other major problem, which occurs in both Catholic and Protestant versions, is their commitment to a degree of optimism about Christian transformation, and especially about the power of practice and habit to generate significant change in Christian desires and behaviors, that I am not convinced is borne out in Christian experience. As I have argued throughout this book, virtue-based approaches have difficulty giving an adequate account either of the reality and extent of the phenomenon of "Christian mediocrity" that was experienced paradigmatically by Augustine and Luther, or of the closely related insights about affective intransigence and compulsion identified by affect theorists, and are vulnerable to overestimating the power of moral

---

[4] Herdt, *Putting on Virtue*, p. 350.

and spiritual practices to overcome affective resistance and to "make bodies move."

Against this background, I have argued that what is needed today is a soteriology that has four characteristics. First, it must be able to provide a strong affirmation, grounded in the reality of the work of the Spirit, that salvation is not simply a propositionalist abstraction but affects real bodies in time. Second, it needs to be able to acknowledge the continuing pastoral and theological power of core Protestant concerns about the unconditional character of saving grace, the limitations of graced habituation as a mechanism for effecting Christian moral transformation, and the ongoing reality of sin in Christian life. Third, it needs to be able to give a theologically serious account of the participatory language we find in New Testament soteriology. Fourth, it must be able to inform and resource Christian ministry that is experientially powerful and emotionally compelling, doing creative justice to both the dramatic and the more "ordinary" dimensions of the Spirit's work in salvation and in Christian life, in cultural contexts where the plausibility of Christian ideas about salvation is less obvious than in the past.

Over the final three chapters of the book, I have argued that a soteriology that succeeds on all four counts can be developed through a retrieval of key features of an affective and Augustinian soteriological tradition that can be found in various forms in Philip Melanchthon, Martin Luther, and Augustine himself. When this theology is elaborated in light of current resources for understanding affect and emotion, it proves to have substantial theological power.

In the context of the twenty-first-century Protestant theological landscape, this approach has a great deal to offer. In an essay occasioned by the 500th anniversary of the Protestant Reformation, Gerald McKenny has summarized the state of the field by observing that "the standard Lutheran and Reformed doctrine of the justification of sinners" has proven to have a number of problems that have undermined its contemporary plausibility.[5] Perhaps the most important of these, he argues, is the problem of how such an account can respect the integrity of "creaturely capacities."[6] Herdt identifies the same problem as McKenny, criticizing traditional Protestant approaches for giving an account of the operation of grace that is "denaturalized" and "deracinated," rather than "embodied and open to view."[7] Tanner shares this concern, emphasizing that we need to understand the Holy Spirit as always working "in and under the human" and through "the operations of our usual faculties."[8] Here we see a late and salutary triumph for Friedrich Schleiermacher,

---

[5] McKenny is writing specifically about Protestant Christian ethics, but his account applies equally to the field of Protestant theology more broadly.

[6] McKenny, "Karl Barth and the Plight of Protestant Ethics," p. 20.

[7] Herdt, *Putting on Virtue*, p. 350.   [8] Tanner, *Christ the Key*, pp. 298, 276.

who argued in the *Glaubenslehre* against "magical" theories of redemption, whereby the redemptive influence of Christ is "mediated by nothing that is natural."[9]

McKenny then argues that this problem more than any other has led an increasing number of Protestant theologians to seek a new foundation for Protestant theology that is based primarily in the theology of Thomas Aquinas.[10] For theologians who want to preserve the integrity of creaturely nature in the operations of grace, Aquinas' conviction that "grace does not destroy nature, but perfects and elevates it," seems to provide a better solution than can be found in Luther or Calvin. McKenny then spends the rest of the essay arguing in light of these problems that the only serious alternative to this kind of "Protestant Thomism" must come not from the Reformers but from the theological vision of Karl Barth.[11] Protestants who wish to remain Protestant seem to have only two theologically serious options: they must choose between Aquinas and Barth.

In the light of the choice McKenny presents, one of the most important outcomes of this book has been to show that there is in fact a *third* alternative available to Protestants. The affective soteriology of the mature Augustine, as interpreted and extended by Luther and Melanchthon, provides a sophisticated and compelling account of the relationship between salvation and experiences that take place in real Christian bodies, using natural faculties and capacities. This account fully respects the integrity of creatures, understanding the work of the Spirit to take place in and through bodies embedded the world, under the aspect of providence. It can make persuasive psychological and social sense of how grace actually comes to be experienced, including in ways that are sudden and affectively powerful. It directs theological attention to the material and cultural contexts in which such experience is always embedded, and is able to view insights from disciplines outside of theology as a creative asset for helping understand how grace operates rather than as a problem or a threat. It also entails a more persuasive account of the role of human agency than is generally found in "Protestant Thomism," because while it can acknowledge real space for the role of Christian practice in sanctification, at the same time it can account much more effectively for the reality of affective intransigence, and for the significant limitations of habit-based models of transformation for effecting affective and behavioral change.[12] It thus maintains a robust and typically Protestant affirmation of the disjunctive character of the operation of divine grace, without having to

---

[9] Schleiermacher, *The Christian Faith* (2016), pp. 627–8 (§100.3).

[10] On this phenomenon, see also Bowlin, "Contemporary Protestant Thomism."

[11] McKenny, "Karl Barth and the Plight of Protestant Ethics," pp. 20, 21–33.

[12] For more on questions about agency in contemporary Protestant theology, see especially Zahl, "Non-Competitive Agency."

turn such operation into an abstraction that is disconnected from bodies. And it achieves all of this without having to sign on either to Barth's deep ambivalence about subjectivity or to his tendency to uncouple theology from the insights of other modes of intellectual inquiry.

Going forward, the constructive argument of this book points to several areas for further reflection. The first is the doctrine of sin. In drawing attention to the affective and experiential dynamics of sin, a cluster of new and important questions arises. If sin is to be more than just a discursive label, then it is also something that is caught up in bodily and material realities. But if this is the case, how are we to understand the relationship between sin as a moral reality before God and sin as something that manifests in, and cannot be fully disentangled from, innate features of our biology and psychology? For example, are cognitive biases that skew our attention away from the needs of others and towards our own needs sinful? Or, insofar as they are unchosen and unavoidable, is it wrong to describe them in that way? Either way, how are we to make moral sense of the sufferings that seem to occur as a consequence of cognitive biases and other unavoidable conditions that we cannot escape or get behind? Asking these questions, we see that attention to the affective and embodied dimensions of sin opens up an important set of issues to do with the nature of moral responsibility that have become especially acute in light of the medicalization of human pathologies in late modernity.[13]

A second area for further reflection is christological. In the New Testament and in Christian tradition, the Holy Spirit is never less than the Spirit of Jesus Christ. This specification has a number of implications for understanding the shape of Christian experience of the Spirit. Above all, the christological ordering of the work of the Spirit means that experience of the Spirit is always ultimately in some sense experience of Christ. As discussed in Chapter 2, when Jesus says "I am with you always, to the end of the age" (Matt. 28:20), this statement can be specified pneumatologically: Jesus is present to us and dwells within us in and through the Holy Spirit. We have already seen how the soteriology presented in this book can help make sense of what this means. In Chapter 4 we saw that, for Luther, to encounter the saving word of the Gospel is always simultaneously to receive affective consolation *and* to come into a new relationship with Jesus, in whom and through whom that consolation is secured and rendered meaningful. Related to this, we saw in Chapter 5 that the affects involved in the law-gospel/fear-delight sequence are social in nature, such that the gratitude, love, and joy generated by the gospel are not generic

---

[13] Such attention also suggests that phenomena like biotechnological enhancement of human beings are of substantial theological interest and significance. If both sin and righteousness are tethered to the body, does it follow that we might be able to enhance our way to holiness in the future? See Simeon Zahl, "Engineering Desire: Biotechnological Enhancement as Theological Problem," *Studies in Christian Ethics* 32, no. 2 (2019).

but are ordered to a person: gratitude *towards Jesus*, love *for God and his creation*, joy *over a restored relationship*. In this way we can see how the affective sequence associated with experience of grace can be simultaneously generative of a relationship to God in Christ that is psychologically salient to a person. But there is more to be explored here. Above all, the ordering of the Spirit to Jesus Christ naturally draws our attention beyond psychological and affective questions to issues of historical particularity. The Spirit generates a relationship not to a generic divine figure but to *this* Jesus, who was incarnate and lived in Nazareth, who communicated particular teachings and read particular scriptural texts, and who was a Jew who lived under the Roman Empire. In this movement from the affective dimensions of Christian religious life in the Spirit to the historical particularity of Jesus of Nazareth, we see the foundations for another book.

Finally, the pneumatology put forward here opens the door to further engagement with Pentecostal and charismatic theologies. It is no accident that the form of Christianity that seems to speak with the most immediate and transformative power across the world today is one that appeals to the theology of the Holy Spirit to foreground the emotional and experiential force of the Christian gospel. By likewise foregrounding the Spirit and emotion, the present study has, I hope, drawn attention to material points of contact between Pentecostal theologies and non-Pentecostal academic and theological discourse. Indeed, it may even help to create conditions for some of the creativity and pneumatological dynamism of such theologies to make their way into more "sober," less affectively dynamic theological traditions. One example of a topic in Pentecostal theology that would be of particular interest from the perspective of the present study is the recent deployment of the category of "play" to help articulate the freedom, joy, and dynamism of life in the Spirit. Nimi Wariboko, for example, has suggested a connection between grace and play from a Pentecostal perspective: "Grace is the negation of work. But play is its style of negation."[14] In dialogue with Wariboko and others, it would be possible to extend the pneumatology of grace I have been describing in directions that draw out new dimensions of the dynamism and creativity of life in the Spirit in ways that are still consistent with its disjunctive and unconditioned character.

The present book has sought to lay the foundations for a new Augustinian vision of divine grace for a world in which the emotional and intellectual plausibility of the Christian faith can no longer be taken for granted. My account has drawn from Augustine and his Reformation-era interpreters to show that theologians do not have to choose between the disjunctive power of the gospel, operating in mercy over and against the intransigent opposition of

---

[14] Nimi Wariboko, *The Pentecostal Principle: Ethical Methodology in New Spirit* (Grand Rapids, MI: William B. Eerdmans Publishing Company, 2012), p. 183.

the sinful human heart, and an emphatic account of the operation of the Holy Spirit to save and to sanctify in the world of bodies and time. At its best, such an account has abiding critical and diagnostic power, and is safeguarded from a number of errors that can stem from theological visions of Christian life that are at odds with Christian experience. Reflecting on the Pentecostal witness, however, we are reminded that the critical story must never be the final story. The ultimate orientation of any pneumatology worthy of the name must always be to the living Spirit of God, who moves in power, and whose method is delight.

Bibliography

Ahmed, Sara. "Affective Economies." Social Text 79, no. 22 (2004): 118–39.

Ahmed, Sara. *The Cultural Politics of Emotion*, 2nd ed. Edinburgh: Edinburgh University Press, 2014.

Allchin, A.M. *Participation in God: A Forgotten Strand in Anglican Tradition*. London: Darton, Longman and Todd, 1988.

Alsted, J.H. *Theologia scholastica didactica*. Hanover: 1618.

Althaus-Reid, Marcella. "Queer I Stand: Lifting the Skirts of God." In *The Sexual Theologian: Essays on Sex, God and Politics*, edited by Marcella Althaus-Reid and Lisa Isherwood, 99–109. London: T&T Clark International, 2004.

Anatolios, Khaled. *Retrieving Nicaea: The Development and Meaning of Trinitarian Doctrine*. Grand Rapids, MI: Baker Academic, 2011.

Anderson, Clifford B. "A Theology of Experience? Karl Barth and the Transcendental Argument." In *Karl Barth and American Evangelicalism*, edited by Bruce L. McCormack and Clifford B. Anderson, 91–111. Grand Rapids, MI: William B. Eerdmans Publishing Company, 2011.

Aquinas, Thomas. *The Commentary on the Gospel of St John. Part 1*. Translated by J.A. Weisheipl and F.R. Larcher. Albany, NY: Magi Books, 1980.

Aquino, Frederick D. "Maximus the Confessor." In *The Spiritual Senses*. Cambridge: Cambridge University Press, 2011.

Aristotle. *Nicomachean Ethics*. Translated by Roger Crisp. Cambridge: Cambridge University Press, 2000.

Asad, Talal. "On Discipline and Humility in Medieval Christian Monasticism." In *Genealogies of Religion: Discipline and Reasons of Power in Christianity and Islam*, 125–67. Baltimore: Johns Hopkins University Press, 1993.

Asendorf, Ulrich. *Die Theologie Martin Luthers nach seinen Predigten*. Göttingen: Vandenhoeck & Ruprecht, 1988.

Asendorf, Ulrich. *Heiliger Geist und Rechtfertigung*. Göttingen: V&R unipress, 2004.

Athanasius. "On the Incarnation of the Word." In *Christology of the Later Fathers*, edited by Edward Rochie Hardy, 55–110. London: SCM Press, 1954.

Augustine. *Confessions*. Translated by Henry Chadwick. Oxford: Oxford University Press, 1998.

Aumann, Jordan. *Spiritual Theology*. London: Continuum, 2006.

Ayres, Lewis. *Nicaea and its Legacy: An Approach to Fourth-Century Trinitarian Theology*. Oxford: Oxford University Press, 2004.

Baldwin, Mark W. "Relational Schemas and the Processing of Social Information." Psychological Bulletin 112, no. 3 (1992): 461–84.

Barclay, John M.G. *Paul and the Gift*. Grand Rapids, MI: William B. Eerdmans Publishing Company, 2015.

Barth, Karl. "Das Wort in der Theologie von Schleiermacher bis Ritschl." In *Die Theologie und die Kirche. Gesammelte Vorträge*, ii, 190–211. Zollikon-Zürich: Evangelischer Verlag, 1928.

Barth, Karl. *The Epistle to the Romans,* 2nd ed. Translated by Edwyn C. Hoskyns. Oxford: Oxford University Press, 1968.

Barth, Karl. *Karl Barth—Eduard Thurneysen Briefwechsel, i: 1913–1921.* Zürich: Theologischer Verlag Zürich, 1973.

Barth, Karl. *Ethics.* Translated by Geoffrey W. Bromiley. Edinburgh: T&T Clark, 1981.

Barth, Karl. *Die Christliche Dogmatik im Entwurf.* Zürich: Theologischer Verlag Zürich, 1982.

Barth, Karl. *The Theology of Schleiermacher: Lectures at Göttingen, Winter Semester of 1923/24.* Translated by Geoffrey W. Bromiley. Edinburgh: T & T Clark, 1982.

Barth, Karl. *Church Dogmatics I: The Doctrine of the Word of God, Part 1.* Translated by G.W. Bromiley. London: T & T Clark International, 2004.

Barth, Karl. *Church Dogmatics I: The Doctrine of the Word of God, Part 2.* Translated by G.W. Bromiley. London: T & T Clark International, 2004.

Barth, Karl and Martin Rade. *Karl Barth–Martin Rade: Ein Briefwechsel.* Gütersloh: Gütersloher Verlagshaus, 1981.

Bathrellos, Demetrios. "Passions, Ascesis, and the Virtues." In *The Oxford Handbook of Maximus the Confessor,* edited by Pauline Allen and Bronwen Neil, 287–306. Oxford: Oxford University Press, 2015.

Batka, L'ubomír. "Sin." In *The Oxford Encyclopedia of Martin Luther,* iii, edited by Derek R. Nelson and Paul R. Hinlicky, Oxford: Oxford University Press, 2017.

Bayer, Oswald. *Martin Luther's Theology: A Contemporary Interpretation.* Translated by Thomas H. Trapp. Grand Rapids, MI: William B. Eerdmans Publishing Company, 2008.

Berkowitz, L., S. Jaffee, E. Jo, and B.T. Troccoli. "On the correction of feeling-induced judgmental biases." In *Feeling and Thinking: The Role of Affect in Social Cognition,* edited by J.P. Forgas, 131–52. Cambridge: Cambridge University Press, 2000.

Berlant, Lauren. *Cruel Optimism.* Durham, NC: Duke University Press, 2011.

Berlant, Lauren and Lee Edelman. *Sex, or the Unbearable.* Durham, NC: Duke University Press, 2014.

Beutel, Albrecht. "Luther." In *Augustin Handbuch,* edited by Volker Henning Drecoll, 615–22. Tübingen: Mohr Siebeck, 2007.

Billings, Todd. *Calvin, Participation, and the Gift: The Activity of Believers in Union with Christ.* Oxford: Oxford University Press, 2007.

Blowers, Paul M. "The Dialectics and Therapeutics of Desire in Maximus the Confessor." Vigiliae Christianae 65, no. 4 (2011): 425–51.

Blumhardt, Christoph Friedrich. *Jesus ist Sieger! Predigten und Andachten aus den Jahren 1880 bis 1888.* Erlenbach-Zürich: Rotapfel-Verlag, 1937.

Boersma, Hans. *Heavenly Participation: The Weaving of a Sacramental Tapestry.* Grand Rapids, MI: William B. Eerdmans Publishing Company, 2011.

The Book of Common Prayer: The Texts of 1549, 1559, and 1662. Edited by Brian Cummings. Oxford: Oxford University Press, 2011.

Bouyer, Louis. *The Spirit and Forms of Protestantism.* Translated by A.V Littledale. London: Collins, 1956.

Bower, G.H. and J.P. Forgas. "Affect, memory, and social cognition." In *Cognition and Emotion,* edited by E. Eich, J.F. Kihlstrom, G.H. Bower, J.P. Forgas, and P.M. Niedenthal,87–168. New York: Oxford University Press, 2000.

Bowlby, John. *Attachment and Loss, iii: Sadness and Depression*. New York: Basic Books, 1980.

Bowlin, John. "Contemporary Protestant Thomism." In *Aquinas as Authority*, edited by Paul Van Geest, Harm Goris, and Carlo Leget, 235–51. Leuven: Peeters, 2002.

Brecht, Martin. *Martin Luther: His Road to Reformation 1483–1521*. Translated by James L. Schaaf. Minneapolis: Fortress, 1985.

Brown, Joanne Carlson and Rebecca Parker. "For God So Loved the World?" In *Christianity, Patriarchy, and Abuse: A Feminist Critique*, edited by Carole R. Bohn and Joanne Carlson Brown, 1–30. Cleveland: Pilgrim, 1989.

Brown, Peter. *Augustine of Hippo: A Biography*, 2nd ed. Berkeley: University of California Press, 2000.

Bunyan, John. *Grace Abounding to the Chief of Sinners and The Pilgrim's Progress from this World to that which is to come*. Oxford: Oxford University Press, 1966.

Burke, M. and A.M. Matthews. "Autobiographical memory and clinical anxiety." Cognition and Emotion 6 (1992): 23–35.

Burnaby, John. *Amor Dei: A Study of the Religion of St. Augustine*. Eugene, OR: Wipf and Stock Publishers, 2007.

Busch, Eberhard. *Karl Barth & the Pietists: The Young Karl Barth's Critique of Pietism and Its Response*. Translated by Daniel W. Bloesch. Downers Grove, IL: InterVarsity Press, 2004.

Bushnell, Horace. "Preliminary Discourse on Language." In *God in Christ: Three Discourses*, 7–117. New York: Charles Scribner's Sons, 1876.

Calvin, John. *Institutes of the Christian Religion*. Translated by Ford Lewis Battles. London: Westminster John Knox Press, 2006.

Campbell, Douglas A. *The Deliverance of God: An Apocalyptic Rereading of Justification in Paul*. Grand Rapids, MI: William B. Eerdmans Publishing Company, 2009.

Castelo, Daniel. *Pentecostalism as a Christian Mystical Tradition*. Grand Rapids, MI: William B. Eerdmans Publishing Company, 2017.

Cessario, Romanus. *Christian Faith and the Theological Life*. Washington, D.C.: The Catholic University of America Press, 1996.

Chauncy, Charles. "The Heat and Fervour of Their Passions." In *Religious Enthusiasm and the Great Awakening*, edited by David S. Lovejoy, 71–80. Englewood Cliffs, NJ: Prentice-Hall, 1969.

Chester, Stephen J. *Reading Paul with the Reformers: Reconciling Old and New Perspectives*. Grand Rapids, MI: William B. Eerdmans Publishing Company, 2017.

Ciarrochi, J.V. and J.P. Forgas. "On being tense yet tolerant: The paradoxical effect of trait anxiety and aversive mood on intergroup judgments." Group Dynamics: Theory, Research, and Practice 3 (1999): 227–38.

Clark, R. Scott. "*Iustitia Imputata Christi*: Alien or Proper to Luther's Doctrine of Justification?" Concordia Theological Quarterly 70, no. 3–4 (2006): 269–310.

Clavier, Mark F.M. *Eloquent Wisdom: Rhetoric, Cosmology and Delight in the Theology of Augustine of Hippo*. Turnhout: Brepols Publishers, 2014.

Clore, Gerald L. and A. Ortony. "Appraisal theories: how cognition shapes affect into emotion." In *Handbook of Emotions*, 3rd ed., edited by Michael Lewis, Jeannette M. Haviland-Jones, and Lisa Feldman Barrett, 628–42. New York: The Guilford Press, 2008.

Clore, Gerald L. and Alexander J. Schiller. "New Light on the Affect-Cognition Connection." In *Handbook of Emotions*, 4th ed., edited by Lisa Feldman Barrett, Michael Lewis, and Jeannette M. Haviland-Jones, 532–46. New York: The Guilford Press, 2016.

Coakley, Sarah. "Introduction: Faith, Rationality and the Passions." Modern Theology 27, no. 2 (2011): 217–25.

Coakley, Sarah. *God, Sexuality, and the Self: An Essay "On the Trinity."* Cambridge: Cambridge University Press, 2013.

Coates, Thomas. "Calvin's Doctrine of Justification." Concordia Theological Monthly 34, no. 6 (1963): 325–34.

Cocksworth, Ashley. "Theorizing the (Anglican) *lex orandi*: A Theological Account." Modern Theology (2019), doi:10.1111/moth.12524.

Collins, Nancy L., AnaMarie C. Guichard, Maire B. Ford, and Brooke C. Feeney. "Working Models of Attachment: New Developments and Emerging Themes." In *Adult Attachment: Theory, Research, and Clinical Implications*, edited by Steven W. Rholes and Jeffry A. Simpson, 196–239. New York: The Guilford Press, 2004.

"Confutatio Pontificia." 1530. Accessed 21 June 2019, http://www.gutenberg.org/files/853/853-h/853-h.htm.

Congar, Yves. *I Believe in the Holy Spirit*, i: *The Holy Spirit in the 'Economy'*. New York: The Crossroad Publishing Company, 1983.

Congar, Yves. *I Believe in the Holy Spirit*, ii: *'He Is Lord and Giver of Life'*. New York: The Crossroad Publishing Company, 1983.

Constas, Nicholas. "Introduction." In *On Difficulties in the Church Fathers: The Ambigua, i: Maximos the Confessor*, edited by Nicholas Constas. Cambridge, MA: Harvard University Press, 2014.

del Colle, Ralph. *Christ and the Spirit: Spirit-Christology in Trinitarian Perspective*. Oxford: Oxford University Press, 1994.

DelCogliano, Mark, Andrew Radde-Gallwitz, and Lewis Ayres. "General Introduction." In *Works on the Spirit: Athanasius and Didymus*, 11–50. Yonkers, NY: St. Vladimir's Seminary Press, 2011.

DelCogliano, Mark, Andrew Radde-Gallwitz, and Lewis Ayres, eds. *Works on the Spirit: Athanasius and Didymus*. Yonkers, NY: St. Vladimir's Seminary Press, 2011.

Deonna, Julien A. and Fabrice Teroni. *The Emotions: A Philosophical Introduction*. London: Routledge, 2012.

Dodaro, Robert. "'Omnes haeretici negant Christum in carne uenisse' (Aug., *serm*. 183.9.13): Augustine on the Incarnation as Criterion for Orthodoxy." Augustinian Studies 38, no. 1 (2007): 163–74.

Drecoll, Volker Henning. *Die Enstehung der Gnadenlehre Augustins*. Tübingen: Mohr Siebeck, 1999.

Dunn, James D.G. *The Theology of Paul the Apostle*. London: T&T Clark, 1998.

Dunn, James D.G.. *The New Perspective on Paul*. William B. Eerdmans Publishing Company: 2008.

Eastman, Susan. "Participation in Christ." In *The Oxford Handbook of Pauline Studies*, edited by Matthew V. Novenson and R. Barry Matlock. Oxford: Oxford University Press, 2014. doi:10.1093/oxfordhb/9780199600489.013.005.

Ebeling, Gerhard. *Luther: An Introduction to his Thought.* Translated by R.A. Wilson. London: Collins, 1972.

Edwards, Jonathan. *Religious Affections.* New Haven, CT: Yale University Press, 1959.

Ekkekasis, Panteleimon. *The Measurement of Affect, Mood, and Emotion: A Guide for Health-Behavioral Research.* Cambridge: Cambridge University Press, 2013.

Eliot, George. *Janet's Repentance.* In *Scenes from Clerical Life.* ii, 39–317. Edinburgh: William Blackwood and Sons, 1878.

Fee, Gordon D. *God's Empowering Presence: The Holy Spirit in the Letters of Paul.* Grand Rapids, MI: Baker Academic, 1994.

Fiddes, Paul. "Salvation." In *The Oxford Handbook of Systematic Theology,* edited by Kathryn Tanner, Iain Torrance, and John Webster, 176–96. Oxford: Oxford University Press, 2007.

Fischer, Agneta H. and Antony S.R. Manstead. "Social Functions of Emotion and Emotion Regulation." In *Handbook of Emotions,* 4th ed, edited by Lisa Feldman Barrett, Michael Lewis, and Jeannette M. Haviland-Jones, 424–39. New York: The Guilford Press, 2016.

Fitzsimons, Gráinne M. and Joanna Anderson. "Interpersonal Cognition: Seeking, Understanding, and Maintaining Relationships." In *The Oxford Handbook of Social Cognition,* edited by Donal Carlston, 590–615. Oxford: Oxford University Press, 2013.

Flogaus, Reinhard. "Luther versus Melanchthon? Zur Frage der Einheit der Wittenberger Reformation in der Rechtfertigungslehre." *Archiv für Reformationsgeschichte* 91 (2000): 6–46.

Ford, David F. "Review of *The Trinitarian Faith.*" Scottish Journal of Theology 43, no. 2 (1990): 263–7.

Ford, David F. *The Future of Christian Theology.* Oxford: Wiley-Blackwell, 2011.

Forde, Gerhard. *Theology is for Proclamation.* Minneapolis: Augsburg Fortress, 1990.

Forgas, J.P. and E. Eich. "Affective Influences on Cognition: Mood Congruence, Mood Dependence, and Mood Effects on Processing Strategies." In *Handbook of Psychology, 2nd ed., iv,* edited by Irving B. Weiner, Alice F. Healy, and Robert W. Proctor, 61–82. Wiley, 2012.

Fox, Elaine. *Emotion Science: Cognitive and Neuroscientific Approaches to Understanding Human Emotions.* New York: Palgrave Macmillan, 2008.

Fraley, R. Chris. "Attachment in Adulthood: Recent Developments, Emerging Debates, and Future Directions." Annual Review of Psychology 70 (2019): 401–22.

Frei, Hans. *The Identity of Jesus Christ.* Eugene, OR: Wipf and Stock, 1997.

Frey, Jörg. "How did the Spirit become a Person?" In *The Holy Spirit, Inspiration, and the Cultures of Antiquity: Multidisciplinary Perspectives,* edited by Jörg Frey and John R. Levison, 343–71. Berlin: De Gruyter, 2014.

Fridja, N.H. and K.R. Scherer. "Emotion definitions (psychological perspectives)." In *The Oxford Companion to Emotion and the Affective Sciences,* edited by D. Sander and K.R. Scherer,142–4. Oxford: Oxford University Press, 2009.

Gathercole, Simon. *Defending Substitution: An Essay on Atonement in Paul.* Grand Rapids, MI: Baker Academic, 2015.

Gavrilyuk, Paul L. "The Retrieval of Deification: How a Once-Despised Archaism Became an Ecumenical Desideratum." Modern Theology 25, no. 4 (2009): 647–59.

Gilson, Etienne. *History of Christian Philosophy in the Middle Ages*. New York: Random House, 1955.

Gorman, Michael J. *Inhabiting the Cruciform God: Kenosis, Justification, and Theosis in Paul's Narrative Soteriology*. Grand Rapids, MI: William B. Eerdmans Publishing Company, 2009.

Gregory, Brad. *The Unintended Reformation: How a Religious Revolution Secularized Society*. Cambridge, MA: Harvard University Press, 2012.

Gregory of Nazianzus. *On God and Christ: The Five Theological Orations and Two Letters to Cledonius*. Translated by Lionel Wickham and Frederick Williams. Yonkers, NY: St. Vladimir's Seminary Press, 2002.

Hallonsten, Gösta. "*Theosis* in Recent Research: A Renewal of Interest and a Need for Clarity." In *Partakers of the Divine Nature: The History and Development of Deification in the Christian Traditions*, edited by Michael J. Christensen and Jeffery A. Wittung, 281–93. Grand Rapids, MI: Baker Academic, 2007.

Harnack, Adolf von. "Christus praesens - Vicarius Christi." In *Kleine Schriften zur Alten Kirche: Berliner Akademieschriften 1908-1930*, 771–803. Leipzig: Zentralantiquariat der Deutschen Demokratischen Republik, 1980.

Harrison, Carol. *Beauty and Revelation in the Thought of Saint Augustine*. Oxford: Clarendon Press, 1992.

Harrison, Carol. *Augustine: Christian Truth and Fractured Humanity*. Oxford: Oxford University Press, 2000.

Hart, Trevor. "Humankind in Christ and Christ in Humankind: Salvation as Participation in Our Substitute in the Theology of John Calvin." *Scottish Journal of Theology* 42, no. 1 (1989): 67–84.

Hart, Trevor. "Revelation." In *The Cambridge Companion to Karl Barth*, edited by John Webster, 37–56. Cambridge: Cambridge University Press, 2000.

Hauerwas, Stanley. *Character and the Christian Life: A Study in Theological Ethics*. Notre Dame: University of Notre Dame Press, 1994.

Hendry, George S. *The Holy Spirit in Christian Theology*. London: SCM Press, 1957.

Herdt, Jennifer A. *Putting on Virtue: The Legacy of the Splendid Vices*. Chicago: University of Chicago Press, 2008.

Hermann, Wilhelm. *The Communion of the Christian with God: Described on the Basis of Luther's Statements*. Philadelphia: Fortress Press, 1971.

Heyd, Michael. "*Be Sober and Reasonable*": *The Critique of Enthusiasm in the Seventeenth and Eighteenth Centuries*. New York: Brill, 1995.

Höfner, Markus. "The Affects of the Soul and the Effects of Grace: On Melanchthon's Understanding of Faith and Christian Emotions." In *The Depth of the Human Person*, edited by Michael Welker, 218–35. Grand Rapids, MI: William B. Eerdmans Publishing Company, 2014.

Hurtado, Larry W. *Lord Jesus Christ: Devotion to Jesus in Earliest Christianity*. Grand Rapids, MI: William B. Eerdmans Publishing Company, 2003.

Hütter, Reinhard. "'Thomas the Augustinian'—Recovering a Surpassing Synthesis of Grace and Free Will." In *Dust Bound for Heaven: Explorations in the Theology of Thomas Aquinas*, 249–82. Grand Rapids, MI: William B. Eerdmans Publishing Company, 2012.

James, Susan. *Passion and Action: The Emotions in Seventeenth-Century Philosophy.* Oxford: Oxford University Press, 1997.

James, William. *The Varieties of Religious Experience.* New York: The Library of America, 1987.

Jay, Martin. *Songs of Experience: Modern American and European Variations on a Universal Theme.* Berkeley: University of California Press, 2005.

Jennings, Willie James. *The Christian Imagination: Theology and the Origins of Race.* New Haven: Yale University Press, 2010.

Jones, L. Gregory. *Transformed Judgment: Toward a Trinitarian Account of the Moral Life.* Eugene, OR: Wipf and Stock, 1990.

Jones, Serene. *Feminist Theory and Christian Theology: Cartographies of Grace.* Minneapolis: Fortress Press, 2000.

Jong, Jonathan and Jamin Halberstadt. *Death Anxiety and Religious Belief.* London: Bloomsbury, 2016.

Jüngel, Eberhard. "Zur Lehre vom heiligen Geist: Thesen." In *Die Mitte des Neuen Testaments: Einheit und Vielfalt neutestamentlicher Theologie,* edited by Ulrich Luz and Hans Weder, 97–118. Göttingen: Vandenhoeck & Ruprecht, 1983.

Käsemann, Ernst. "Geist und Geistesgaben im NT." In *Religion in Geschichte und Gegenwart,* 3. auflage, *ii,* edited by Kurt Galling, 1272–9. Tübingen: J.C.B. Mohr, 1958.

Keating, Daniel A. *Deification and Grace.* Naples, FL: Sapientia Press, 2007.

Keating, Daniel A. "Typologies of Deification." International Journal of Systematic Theology 17, no. 3 (2015): 267–83.

Kilby, Karen. "Perichoresis and Projection: Problems with Social Doctrines of the Trinity." New Blackfriars 81, no. 957 (2000): 432–45.

Kilby, Karen. "Is an Apophatic Trinitarianism Possible?" International Journal of Systematic Theology 12, no. 1 (2010): 65–77.

Koch, John D. *The Distinction Between Law and Gospel as the Basis and Boundary of Theological Reflection.* Tübingen: Mohr Siebeck, 2016.

Kotva, Joseph J. *The Christian Case for Virtue Ethics.* Washington, D.C.: Georgetown University Press, 1996.

Kraus, Hans-Joachim. *Systematische Theologie im Kontext biblischer Geschichte und Eschatologie.* Neukirchen-Vluyn: Neukirchener Verlag, 1983.

LaMothe, Kimerer L. "What Bodies Know about Religion and the Study of It." Journal of the American Academy of Religion 76, no. 3 (2008): 573–601.

Lampe, Geoffrey. *God as Spirit: The Bampton Lectures 1976.* Oxford: Oxford University Press, 1977.

Lazarus, R.S. "Cognition and motivation in emotion." American Psychologist 46 (1991): 352–67.

Lessing, Gotthold Ephraim. "On the proof of the spirit and of power (1777)." In *Philosophical and Theological Writings,* edited by H.B. Nisbet, 83–8. Cambridge: Cambridge University Press, 2005.

Levison, John R. *Filled with the Spirit.* Grand Rapids, MI: William B. Eerdmans Publishing Company, 2009.

Lindbeck, George A. *The Nature of Doctrine: Religion and Theology in a Postliberal Age.* London: Westminster John Knox Press, 1984.

Linman, Jonathan. "Martin Luther: 'Little Christs for the World': Faith and Sacraments as a Means of *Theosis*." In *Partakers of the Divine Nature: The History and Development of Deification in the Christian Traditions*, edited by Michael J. Christensen and Jeffery A. Wittung,189–99. Grand Rapids, MI: Baker Academic, 2007.

Lovejoy, David S.*Religious Enthusiasm in the New World: Heresy to Revolution* Cambridge, MA: Harvard University Press, 1985.

Luhrmann, T.M.,*When God Talks Back: Understanding the American Evangelical Relationship with God*. New York: Alfred A. Knopf, 2012.

Luther, Martin. *The Bondage of the Will*. Translated by J.I. Packer and O.R. Johnston. Grand Rapids, MI: Fleming H. Revell, 1957.

Luther, Martin. *Luther: Early Theological Works*. Translated by James Atkinson. Philadelphia: Westminster Press, 1962.

Luther, Martin. *Solus Decalogus est Aeternus: Martin Luther's Complete Antinomian Theses and Disputations*. Translated by Holger Sonntag. Minneapolis: Lutheran Press, 2008.

Macaskill, Grant. *Union with Christ in the New Testament*. Oxford: Oxford University Press, 2013.

Macchia, Frank D. *Justified in the Spirit: Creation, Redemption, and the Triune God*. Grand Rapids, MI: William B. Eerdmans Publishing Company, 2010.

Mack, Phyllis.*Heart Religion in the British Enlightenment*, Cambridge: Cambridge University Press, 2008.

Mannermaa, Tuomo. *Christ Present in Faith: Luther's View of Justification*. Minneapolis: Fortress Press, 2005.

Markus, R.A. "Augustine: a defence of Christian mediocrity." In *The End of Christianity*, 45–62. Cambridge: Cambridge University Press, 1991.

Maurer, Wilhelm. *Der junge Melanchthon zwischen Humanismus und Reformation. ii: Der Theologe*. Göttingen: Vandenhoeck & Ruprecht, 1969.

Maximos. *On Difficulties in the Church Fathers: The Ambigua, i: Maximos the Confessor*. Translated by Nicholas Constas. Cambridge, MA: Harvard University Press, 2014.

McCormack, Bruce L. *Karl Barth's Critically Realistic Dialectical Theology: Its Genesis and Development, 1909–1936*. New York: Oxford University Press, 1997.

McCutcheon, Russell T. "Introduction." In *Religious Experience: A Reader*, edited by Leslie Dorrough Smith, Craig Martin, and Russell T. McCutcheon, 1–16. Bristol, CT: Equinox, 2012.

McFadyen, Alistair. *Bound to Sin: Abuse, Holocaust and the Christian Doctrine of Sin*. Cambridge: Cambridge University Press, 2000.

McGrath, Alister E. *Christian Theology: An Introduction*, 3rd ed. Oxford: Blackwell Publishing, 2001.

McGrath, Alister E. *Iustitia Dei: A History of the Christian Doctrine of Justification*. Cambridge: Cambridge University Press, 2005.

McKenny, Gerald. "Karl Barth and the Plight of Protestant Ethics." In *The Freedom of a Christian Ethicist: the Future of a Reformation Legacy*, 17–38. London: Bloomsbury T&T Clark, 2016.

Melanchthon, Philip. *Loci communes 1543*. St. Louis: Concordia Publishing House, 1992.

Melanchthon, Philip. *Commonplaces: Loci communes 1521*. Translated by Christian Preus. Saint Louis: Concordia Publishing House, 2014.

Milbank, John. "Knowledge: The theological critique of philosophy in Hamann and Jacobi." In *Radical Orthodoxy: A New Theology*, edited by John Milbank, Catherine Pickstock, and Graham Ward, 21–37. London: Routledge, 1999.

Milbank, John. *Being Reconciled: Ontology and Pardon*. London: Routledge, 2003.

Milbank, John. "Alternative Protestantism: Radical Orthodoxy and the Reformed Tradition." In *Radical Orthodoxy and the Reformed Tradition*, edited by James K.A. Smith and James H. Olthuis, 25–41. Grand Rapids, MI: Baker Academic, 2005.

Milbank, John. *Beyond Secular Order: The Representation of Being and the Representation of the People*. Oxford: Wiley Blackwell, 2013.

Moltmann, Jürgen. *The Spirit of Life: A Universal Affirmation*. Translated by Margaret Kohl. London: SMC Press, 1992.

Moule, C.F.D. *The Holy Spirit*. London: Continuum, 2000.

Mühlen, Karl-Heinz zur. "Melanchthons Auffassung vom Affekt in den Loci communes von 1521." In *Humanismus und Reformation*, edited by Michael Beyer, Günther Wartenberg, and Hans-Peter Hasse, 327–36. Leipzig: Evangelische Verlagsanstalt, 1996.

Nakashima Brock, Rita. *Journeys by Heart: A Christology of Erotic Power*. New York: Crossroad, 1988.

Neder, Adam. *Participation in Christ: An Entry into Karl Barth's Church Dogmatics*. Louisville, KY: Westminster John Knox Press, 2009.

Ngong, David. *Theology as Construction of Piety: An African Perspective*. Eugene, OR: RESOURCE Publications, 2013.

Niebuhr, Richard R. "Williams James on Religious Experience." In *The Cambridge Companion to William James*, edited by Ruth Anna Putnam, 214–36. Cambridge: Cambridge University Press, 1997.

Null, Ashley. *Thomas Cranmer's Doctrine of Repentance: Renewing the Power to Love*. Oxford: Oxford University Press, 2000.

O'Donovan, Oliver. *Entering into Rest: Ethics as Theology 3*. Grand Rapids, MI: William B. Eerdmans Publishing Company, 2017.

Oakes, Kenneth. *Karl Barth on Theology and Philosophy*. Oxford: Oxford University Press, 2012.

Otto, Rudolf. *The Idea of the Holy: An Inquiry into the Non-Rational Factor in the Idea of the Divine and Its Relation to the Rational*. Translated by John W. Harvey. Oxford: Oxford University Press, 1950.

Paloutzian, Raymond F. and Crystal L. Park, eds. *Handbook of the Psychology of Religion and Spirituality*, 2nd ed. London: The Guilford Press, 2013.

Pannenberg, Wolfhart. "Protestant Piety and Guilt Consciousness." In *Christian Spirituality and Sacramental Community*, 13–30. London: Darton, Longman, and Todd, 1983.

Pannenberg, Wolfhart. *Systematic Theology*, iii. Translated by Geoffrey W. Bromiley. London: T&T Clark International, 2004.

Pascal, Blaise. *Pensées*. Translated by A.J. Krailsheimer. London: Penguin Books, 1995.

Peura, Simo. *Mehr als ein Mensch? Die Vergöttlichung als Thema der Theologie Martin Luthers von 1513 bis 1519*. Mainz: Verlag Philipp von Zabern, 1994.

Phan, Peter C. "A Common Journey, Different Paths, the Same Destination: Method in Liberation Theologies." In *A Dream Unfinished: Theological Reflections on America from the Margins*, edited by Eleazar S. Fernandez and Fernando F. Segovia, 129–51. Eugene, OR: Wipf and Stock Publishers, 2006.

Pickstock, Catherine. "Duns Scotus: His Historical and Contemporary Significance." Modern Theology 21, no. 4 (2005): 543–74.

Pinckaers, Servais. *The Sources of Christian Ethics*. Translated by Sr. Mary Thomas Noble. Washington, D.C.: The Catholic University of America Press, 1995.

Pinnock, Clark H. *Flame of Love: A Theology of the Holy Spirit*. Downers Grove, IL: IVP Academic, 1996.

Prevot, Andrew. *Thinking Prayer: Theology and Spirituality amid the Crises of Modernity*. Notre Dame: University of Notre Dame Press, 2015.

Proudfoot, Wayne. *Religious Experience*. Berkeley: University of California Press, 1985.

Rahner, Karl. "Religious Enthusiasm and the Experience of Grace." In *Theological Investigations, xvi: Experience of the Spirit: Source of Theology*, 35–51. London: Darton, Longman, and Todd, 1979.

Rahner, Karl. "Reflections on the Experience of Grace." In *Theological Investigations, iii: The Theology of the Spiritual Life*, 86–90. New York: Crossroad Publishing Company, 1982.

Riis, Ole and Linda Woodhead. *A Sociology of Religious Emotion*. Oxford: Oxford University Press, 2012.

Ritschl, Albrecht. "Über die beiden Principien des Protestantismus." In *Gesammelte Aufsätze*, 234–47. Freiburg & Leipzig: J.C.B. Mohr, 1893.

Rogers, Eugene F. *After the Spirit: A Constructive Pneumatology from Resources outside the Modern West*. Grand Rapids, MI: William B. Eerdmans Publishing Company, 2005.

Russell, J.A. and L. Feldman Barrett. "Core affect, prototypical emotional episodes, and other things called emotion: dissecting the elephant." Journal of Personality and Social Psychology 76 (1999): 805–19.

Russell, Norman. *The Doctrine of Deification in the Greek Patristic Tradition*. Oxford: Oxford University Press, 2004.

Sanders, E.P. *Paul and Palestinian Judaism: A Comparison of Patterns of Religion*. Minneapolis: Fortress Press, 1977.

Sauter, Gerhard. "Geist und Freiheit. Geistvorstellungen und die Erwartung des Geistes." Evangelische Theologie 41 (1981): 212–23.

Schaefer, Donovan O. *Religious Affects: Animality, Evolution, and Power*. Durham, NC: Duke University Press, 2015.

Schaefer, Donovan O. "You Don't Know What Pain Is: Affect, the Lifeworld, and Animal Ethics." Studies in Christian Ethics 30, no. 1 (2016): 15–29.

Schaefer, Donovan O. "Beautiful Facts: Science, Secularism, and Affect." In *Feeling Religion*, 69–92. Durham, NC: Duke University Press, 2018.

Schaefer, Donovan O. *The Evolution of Affect Theory: The Humanities, the Sciences, and the Study of Power*. Cambridge: Cambridge University Press, 2019.

Scharf, Robert H. "Experience." In *Critical Terms for Religious Studies*, edited by Mark C. Taylor, 94–116. Chicago: The University of Chicago Press, 1998.

Schleiermacher, Friedrich. *On the Glaubenslehre: Two Letters to Dr. Lücke*. Translated by James Duke and Francis Fiorenza. Oxford: Oxford University Press, 1981.

Schleiermacher, Friedrich. *The Christian Faith*. Translated by H. R. Mackintosh. Edinburgh: T&T Clark, 1999.

Schleiermacher, Friedrich. *The Christian Faith: A New Translation and Critical Edition*. Translated by Terrence N. Tice, Catherine L. Kelsey, and Edwina Lawler. Louisville, KY: Westminster John Knox Press, 2016.

Schroeder, H.J., ed. *Canons and Decrees of the Council of Trent: Original Text with English Translation*. St. Louis: B. Herder Book Co., 1941.

Schweitzer, Albert. *The Mysticism of Paul the Apostle*. Translated by William Montgomery. Baltimore: Johns Hopkins University Press, 1998.

Schweizer, Eduard. "*pneuma, pneumatikos*." In *Theological Dictionary of the New Testament*, vi, edited by Gerhard Kittel and Gerhard Friedrich, 332–455. Grand Rapids, MI: Eerdmans, 1964.

Sedgwick, Eve Kosofsky and Adam Frank. "Shame in the Cybernetic Fold: Reading Silvan Tomkins." In *Touching Feeling: Affect, Pedagogy, Performativity*, 93–121. Durham, NC: Duke University Press, 2003.

Sharp, C.A., E.B. Davis, K. George, A.D. Cuthbert, B.P. Zahl, D.E. Davis, J.N. Hook, and J.D. Aten. "Measures of God Representations: Theoretical Framework and Overview." Psychology of Religion and Spirituality (2019): doi.org/10.1037/rel0000257.

Soulen, R. Kendall. *The Divine Names(s) and the Holy Trinity: Distinguishing the Voices*. Louisville, KY: Westminster John Knox Press, 2011.

Stendahl, Krister. "The Apostle Paul and the Introspective Conscience of the Modern West." Harvard Theological Review 56, no. 3 (1963): 199–215.

Tanner, Kathryn. *Jesus, Humanity and the Trinity: A Brief Systematic Theology*. Minneapolis: Fortress Press, 2001.

Tanner, Kathryn. *Christ the Key*. Cambridge: Cambridge University Press, 2010.

Tanner, Kathryn. *Christianity and the New Spirit of Capitalism*. New Haven: Yale University Press, 2019.

Taves, Ann. *Fits, Trances, and Visions: Experiencing Religion and Explaining Experience from Wesley to James*. Princeton, NJ: Princeton University Press, 1999.

Taves, Ann. *Religious Experience Reconsidered: A Building-Block Approach to the Study of Religion and Other Special Things*. Princeton, NJ: Princeton University Press, 2009.

Thompson, Ross A. "Early Attachment and Later Development." In *The Handbook of Attachment*, 3rd ed., edited by Jude Cassidy and Phillip R. Shaver, 330–48. New York: The Guilford Press, 2018.

Ticciati, Susannah. *A New Apophaticism: Augustine and the Redemption of Signs*. Leiden: Brill, 2015.

Tonstad, Linn Marie. "Everything Queer, Nothing Radical?" Svensk Teologisk Kvartalskrift. Årg. 92 (2016): 118–29.

Tonstad, Linn Marie. *Queer Theology: Beyond Apologetics*. Eugene, OR: Cascade Books, 2018.

Torrance, Thomas F. "Come, Creator Spirit, for the Renewal of Worship and Witness." In *Theology in Reconstruction*, 240–58. Eugene, OR: Wipf and Stock, 1996.

Torrance, Thomas F. "Justification: Its Radical Nature and Place in Reformed Doctrine and Life." In *Theology in Reconstruction*, 150–68. Eugene, OR: Wipf and Stock, 1996.

Torrance, Thomas F. "A New Reformation?" In *Theology in Reconstruction*, 259–83. Eugene, OR: Wipf and Stock, 1996.

Torrance, Thomas F. "The One Baptism Common to Christ and His Church." In *Theology in Reconciliation*, 82–105. Eugene, OR: Wipf and Stock, 1996.

Torrance, Thomas F. "The Relevance of the Doctrine of the Spirit for Ecumenical Theology." In *Theology in Reconstruction*, 229–39. Eugene, OR: Wipf and Stock, 1996.

Torrance, Thomas F. "*Spiritus Creator*: A Consideration of the Teaching of St Athanasius and St Basil." In *Theology in Reconstruction*, 209–28. Eugene, OR: Wipf and Stock, 1996.

Torrance, Thomas F. *The Trinitarian Faith: The Evangelical Theology of the Ancient Catholic Church*. London: T&T Clark, 1997.

Torrance, Thomas F. *Atonement: The Person and Work of Christ*. Downers Grove, IL: IVP Academic, 2009.

Trettel, Adam. *Desires in Paradise: An Interpretive Study of Augustine's City of God 14*. Paderborn: Ferdinand Schöringh, 2019.

Troeltsch, Ernst. *Protestantism and Progress: A Historical Study of the Relation of Protestantism to the Modern World*. Translated by W. Montgomery. New York: G.P. Putnam's Sons, 1912.

Vainio, Olli-Pekka. *Justification and Participation in Christ: The Development of the Lutheran Doctrine of Justification from Luther to the Formula of Concord*. Leiden: Brill Academic, 2008.

Vásquez, Manuel. *More Than Belief: A Materialist Theory of Religion*. Oxford: Oxford University Press, 2011.

Ward, Graham. *How the Light Gets In: Ethical Life I*. Oxford: Oxford University Press, 2016.

Ward, W.R. *The Protestant Evangelical Awakening*. Cambridge: Cambridge University Press, 1992.

Ware, Kallistos. "Salvation and Theosis in Orthodox Theology." In *Luther et la réforme allemande dans une perspective oecuménique*, edited by W. Schneemelcher, 167–84. Geneva: Éditions du Centre Orthodoxe, 1983.

Wariboko, Nimi. *The Pentecostal Principle: Ethical Methodology in New Spirit*. Grand Rapids, MI: William B. Eerdmans Publishing Company, 2012.

Weber, Otto. *Foundations of Dogmatics*, ii. Translated by Darrell L. Guder. Grand Rapids, MI: William B. Eerdmans Publishing Company, 1983.

Webster, John. *Holiness*. Grand Rapids, MI: William B. Eerdmans Publishing Company, 2003.

Webster, John. *Barth*. New York: Continuum, 2004.

Webster, John. "Mortification and Vivification." In *God Without Measure: Working Papers in Christian Theology, ii: Virtue and Intellect*, 103–21. London: Bloomsbury, 2016.

Wengert, Timothy J. *Defending Faith: Lutheran Responses to Andreas Osiander's Doctrine of Justification, 1551–1559*. Tübingen: Mohr Siebeck, 2012.

Wenz, Gunther. *Theologie der Bekenntnisschriften der evangelisch-lutherischen Kirche.* Berlin: Walter de Gruyter, 1996.

Wesley, John. "'Awake, Thou That Sleepest'. Sermon 3, 1742." In *John Wesley's Sermons: An Anthology*, edited by Albert C. Outler and Richard P. Heitzenrater, 86–95. Nashville, TN: Abingdon Press, 1991.

Wesley, John. "Free Grace. Sermon 110, 1739." In *John Wesley's Sermons: An Anthology*, edited by Albert C. Outler and Richard P. Heitzenrater, 49–60. Nashville, TN: Abingdon Press, 1991.

Wesley, John. "The Marks of the New Birth. Sermon 18, 1748." In *John Wesley's Sermons: An Anthology*, edited by Albert C. Outler and Richard P. Heitzenrater, 174–82. Nashville, TN: Abingdon Press, 1991.

Wesley, John. "The Original, Nature, Properties, and Use of the Law. Sermon 34, 1750." In *John Wesley's Sermons: An Anthology*, edited by Albert C. Outler and Richard P. Heitzenrater, 256–66. Nashville, TN: Abingdon Press, 1991.

Wetzel, James. *Augustine and the Limits of Virtue.* Cambridge: Cambridge University Press, 1992.

Wetzel, James. "Prodigal Heart: Augustine's Theology of the Emotions." In *Parting Knowledge: Essays after Augustine*, 81–96. Eugene, OR: Wipf and Stock, 2013.

Whitefield, George. "Is It a Crime for a Believer to Speak of His Having Communications Directly from the Spirit of God?" In *Religious Enthusiasm and the Great Awakening*, edited by David S. Lovejoy, 104–6. Englewood Cliffs, NJ: Prentice-Hall, 1969.

Wiles, Maurice. *Faith and the Mystery of God.* Philadelphia: Fortress Press, 1982.

Williams, A.N. *The Ground of Union: Deification in Aquinas and Palamas.* Oxford: Oxford University Press, 1999.

Williams, Delores S. "Black Women's Surrogacy Experience and the Christian Notion of Redemption." In *After Patriarchy: Feminist Transformations of the World Religions*, edited by Paula M. Cooey, William R. Eakin, and Jay B. McDaniel, 1–14. Maryknoll, NY: Orbis Books, 1991.

Williams, Rowan. "Language, Reality, and Desire in Augustine's *De Doctrina*." Journal of Literature and Theology 3, no. 2 (1989): 138–50.

Williams, Rowan. "Word and Spirit." In *On Christian Theology*, 107–27. Oxford: Blackwell Publishing, 2000.

Wolter, Michael. "Der heilige Geist bei Paulus." Jahrbuch für Biblische Theologie 24 (2009): 93–119.

Wright, N.T. *Paul and the Faithfulness of God.* London: SPCK, 2013.

Yeago, David. "Martin Luther on Grace, Law, and Moral Life: Prolegomena to an Ecumenical Discussion of *Veritatis Splendor*." The Thomist 62 (1998): 163–91.

Yong, Amos. *Spirit-Word-Community: Theological Hermeneutics in Trinitarian Perspective.* Eugene, OR: Wipf and Stock Publishers, 2002.

Zachhuber, Johannes. *Theology as Science in Nineteenth-Century Germany: From F.C. Baur to Ernst Troeltsch.* Oxford: Oxford University Press, 2013.

Zahl, Bonnie Poon, Carissa A. Sharp, and Nicholas J.S. Gibson. "Empirical Measures of the Religious Heart." In *Head and Heart: Perspectives from Religion and Psychology*, 97–124. West Conshohocken, PA: John Templeton Press, 2013.

Zahl, Paul F. M. *Grace in Practice: A Theology of Everyday Life.* Grand Rapids, MI: William B. Eerdmans Publishing Company, 2007.

Zahl, Simeon. *Pneumatology and Theology of the Cross in the Preaching of Christoph Friedrich Blumhardt: The Holy Spirit Between Wittenberg and Azusa Street.* London: T&T Clark/Continuum, 2010.

Zahl, Simeon. "Rethinking 'Enthusiasm': Christoph Blumhardt on the Discernment of the Spirit." International Journal of Systematic Theology 12, no. 3 (2010): 341–63.

Zahl, Simeon. "The Drama of Agency: Affective Augustinianism and Galatians." In *Galatians and Christian Theology: Justification, the Gospel, and Ethics in Paul's Letter,* edited by Mark Elliott, Scott Hafemann, N.T. Wright, and John Frederick, 335–52. Grand Rapids, MI: Baker Academic, 2014.

Zahl, Simeon. "On the Affective Salience of Doctrines." Modern Theology 31, no. 3 (2015): 428–44.

Zahl, Simeon. "The Bondage of the Affections: Willing, Feeling, and Desiring in Luther's Theology, 1513–25." In *The Spirit, the Affections, and the Christian Tradition,* edited by Dale M. Coulter and Amos Yong, 181–205. South Bend, IN: University of Notre Dame Press, 2017.

Zahl, Simeon. "Experience." In *The Oxford Handbook of Nineteenth Century Christian Thought,* edited by Joel Rasmussen, Judith Wolfe, and Johannes Zachhuber, 177–95. Oxford: Oxford University Press, 2017.

Zahl, Simeon. "Tradition and its 'Use': the Ethics of Theological Retrieval." Scottish Journal of Theology 71, no. 3 (2018): 308–23.

Zahl, Simeon. "Engineering Desire: Biotechnological Enhancement as Theological Problem." Studies in Christian Ethics 32, no. 2 (2019): 216–28.

Zahl, Simeon. "Non-Competitive Agency and Luther's Experiential Argument against Virtue." Modern Theology 35, no. 2 (2019): 199–222.

Zahl, Simeon. "Incongruous Grace as Pattern of Experience." International Journal of Systematic Theology 22, no. 1 (2020).

Ziegler, Geordie W. *Trinitarian Grace and Participation: An Entry into the Theology of T.F. Torrance.* Minneapolis: Fortress Press, 2017.

Zwingli, Huldrych. "Of Baptism." In *Zwingli and Bullinger,* edited by G.W. Bromiley, 129–75. London: Westminster John Knox Press, 1953.

Zwingli, Huldrych. "An Exposition of the Faith." In *Zwingli and Bullinger,* edited by G.W. Bromiley, 129–75. London: Westminster John Knox Press, 1953.

Index

For the benefit of digital users, indexed terms that span two pages (e.g., 52–53) may, on occasion, appear on only one of those pages.